Be   ahchinmas

9
A S
wSH

BORDER DILEMMAS

Racial and National Uncertainties

in New Mexico, 1848–1912

Anthony Mora

Duke University Press
Durham and London
2011

© 2011 Duke University Press
All rights reserved
Printed in the United States of America on acid-free paper ∞
Designed by C. H. Westmoreland
Typeset in Warnock Pro with Gill Sans display by Keystone Typesetting, Inc.
Library of Congress Cataloging-in-Publication Data appear on the
last printed page of this book.

An earlier version of Chapter 3 appeared as "Resistance and Accommodation in a
Border Parish," *Western Historical Quarterly* 36 (autumn 2005): 301–26.

Duke University Press gratefully acknowledges the support of
the University of Michigan, Program in American Culture, which
provided funds toward the production of this book.

To my sister, Marie

CONTENTS

ACKNOWLEDGMENTS

Writing *Border Dilemmas* has led me to believe that the single-authored history monograph is a myth. Far from being a solitary venture, this book has grown from the scholarship, guidance, suggestions, and encouragement of numerous individuals. I ultimately had the authority and responsibility to reconcile all the feedback, but I hope that the many others who contributed to the book's completion see their imprint on it as well.

Gail Bederman could not have been a better adviser while I was in graduate school and since. She always manages to strike the perfect balance between providing critical assessments of a piece of scholarship and encouraging its continuation. I feel remarkably fortunate to have been her student. Walter T. K. Nugent never ceases to amaze me with his exacting attention to detail, encyclopedic knowledge, and kind support. R. Scott Appleby encouraged one of the earliest pieces from this project and saw it through several incarnations. MaryAnn Mahony kept the project grounded by insisting that I never lose track of the day-to-day life of La Mesilla and Las Cruces in favor of lofty ideological questions. Good fortune has allowed me to know Gregory Dowd as both a cheerful mentor while I was a graduate student at Notre Dame and as a cherished colleague while I was a junior professor at the University of Michigan. In particular, he pushed me to think more deeply about my own assumptions about race and citizenship in the early republic. My daily conversations with Estelle McNair about race, gender, and sexuality continue to inform my thinking all these many years later. Many of my undergraduate professors at the University of New Mexico, especially Melissa Bokovoy, Margaret Connell-Szasz, John L. Kessell, Ann Ramenofsky, Howard Rabinowitz, Jake Spidle, and Ferenc Szasz, inspired me in ways that they might not even know.

Some of my colleagues at Texas A&M University went out of their way to nurture this project. As a brand-new junior professor I depended on the generosity, guidance, and patience of Walter Buenger. Armando Alonzo, Troy Bickham, Julia Kirk Blackwelder, Carlos Blanton, Cynthia Bouton, Benjamin Brower, Jonathan Coopersmith, Leah DeVun, Thomas Dunlap, Katherine Engel, Joseph Jewell, Gregor Kalas, Walter Kamp-

hoefner, Lora Wildenthal, and Harold Livesay all read significant por-
tions of the manuscript or provided critical insights as I worked on
revisions. I particularly benefited from the reading that April Hatfield did
of the entire manuscript. James Rosenheim, likewise, read the manuscript, acted as a mentor, and was one of the best colleagues I have yet
found. It was also delightful working with R. Jovita Baber, who generously
provided me a place to stay when I needed one. The unwavering friendship of Olga Dror and Jennifer Mercieca made the project, and life in
general, seem a bit easier in College Station.

Two of my friends and colleagues, Rebecca Hartkopf Schloss and
Micah Auerbach, made such significant contributions to this book that
they should be listed as editors in their own right. Despite my pursuing a
subject far outside both of their fields, they selflessly read (and reread)
multiple versions of this book. Rebecca always offered a cheerful and
thoughtful sounding board to any new ideas. Micah provided many
insights, unexpected references, and thoughtful critiques. While on fel-
lowship at the American Academy for Arts and Sciences for another
project, the other junior fellows and faculty graciously helped with this
project, too. I appreciate the year of conversation with Victoria Cain,
Ajay Mehrotra, M. Taylor Fravel, Bethany Moreton, Laura Scales, and
Anne Stiles.

I could not be intellectually rewarded more than I am at the University
of Michigan. All of my colleagues in the Program in American Culture,
Department of History, and Latina/o Studies Program push me to be a
better historian through their own example. Thanks go to Evelyn Al-
sutany, Lori Brooks, James W. Cook, María Cotera, Vincente Díaz, Mary
C. Kelley, Lawrence La Fountain-Stokes, Damon Salesa, Kathleen Can-
ning, John Carson, Rita Chin, Geoff Eley, Kali Israel, Scott Kurashige,
Matthew D. Lassiter, Regina Morantz-Sánchez, Rachel Neis, and Silvia
Pedraza.

The Michigan program of manuscript workshops for junior faculty is
something that I hope will be emulated everywhere. In my case the
extensive benefits of that program would not have been possible without
the hard work of Jesse Hoffnung-Garskof, Alexandra Minna Stern, Philip
Deloria, Gregory Dowd, and Mary Freiman. My appreciation also goes to
Catherine Benamou, Magda Zaborowska, Amy Sara Carroll, Micah
Auerback, and Michael Witgen, all of whom found time in their already
overextended schedules to read the manuscript and participate in a full
afternoon of workshopping. George J. Sánchez's kind advice, attentive
reading, and probing questions helped me connect each chapter to a

much wider discussion about race and imperialism in the United States. He helped make this a much better book than it would have been otherwise. I also benefited from having Ramón Gutiérrez as a consistent booster and ally. He has generously read multiple drafts of the book and, at times, offered much needed caution when my ideas did not quite fit together in the ways that I intended. I appreciate his remarkable knowledge of New Mexico almost as much as I do his friendship.

Numerous institutions and reading groups have supported this book. I appreciate that I could work out some early ideas at the Third Annual Mexican American History Workshop at the University of Houston in 2004. My thanks to Raúl Ramos for encouraging me to take advantage of that opportunity. Likewise, the Queer Studies Reading Group at Texas A&M offered a new venue to explore some of my ideas in chapter 4. Funding through Texas A&M's Program to Enhance Scholarly and Creative Activities along with the Melbern G. Glasscock Center for Humanities Research kept the book's momentum going. My translations feel much more crisp thanks to Carlos Marín's careful proofreading and suggestions. Adrian Kitzinger created the excellent map and helped enhance the state seal. I have also greatly appreciated the interest, understanding, and commitment provided by the powerhouse editor Ken Wissoker and the entire staff at Duke University Press. Mandy Earley guided this book through the early process at Duke. Likewise, Tim Elfenbein and Joe Abbott both brought tremendous energy and attention to detail in the last stages of copyediting and production.

Since moving to Ann Arbor, I have found Dario Gaggio to be a solid friend (along with Chester). Dario's easygoing approach to life and academia made me feel instantly welcome in a new town. I have likewise benefited from the cross-linked friendships of Helmut Puff, Scott Spector, Eric Firstenberg, Frederick Wherry, Anthony Dupuis, Terry Theisen, Steve Gutterman, Laura Wernick, Wally Gullett, and Jamie Thick.

In all of my various appointments I depended heavily on excellent staff, especially Mary Johnson and Barbara Dawson at Texas A&M and Judith Grey, Tabitha Rohn, Marlene Moore, Brooklyn Posler, Veronica Garcia, and Mary Freiman at Michigan. Likewise, I owe tremendous debts to the many librarians and archivists who assisted me, especially at the Rio Grande Historical Collections at New Mexico State University in Las Cruces, the Center for Southwest Research at the University of New Mexico in Albuquerque, the Diocese of Las Cruces, the Library of Congress, and the New Mexico State Records and Archives in Santa Fe.

My family inspired this project in many ways. My parents, Ann Kelly and Gerald L. Mora, planted my earliest interest in the unexpected histories of New Mexico. My mother frequently surprised me after she unearthed a remarkably rare copy of a classic text on New Mexico. My parents also provided many needed trips home when I was the one feeling "remote beyond compare." My grandmother and grandfather Mora and my grandmother and "Papa" Kelly were all inspirational through their hard work, love for their families, and commitment to education. Elizabeth Allan and her son, Gabriel, offered a tireless optimism that the book would soon appear in print even when I had doubts. My brother-in-law, Alberto Dávila, continues to offer much appreciated advice for navigating the academic world. Finally, my sister, Marie, has been the most consistent source of support throughout my life. My debt to her is tremendous. Above all others, I hope she enjoys this history of her cherished New Mexico.

INTRODUCTION

Local Borders: Mexicans'
Uncertain Role in the
United States

Martin Amador took full advantage of the economic opportunities on the nineteenth-century U.S.-Mexican border.[1] Based in southern New Mexico's Mesilla Valley, Amador operated a number of lucrative businesses, including a freight-hauling enterprise from Chihuahua to Santa Fe and a major hotel located on Water Street in the center of the American town of Las Cruces, New Mexico. By the time of his death, in 1903, he was a well-known businessman with important cross-border commercial connections, including his daughter's marriage into the powerful Terrazas family in Chihuahua.[2]

At the height of his economic success Amador unexpectedly found himself defending his claims to being American and his status in the region. In 1898 the merchant came to the U.S. Federal Court in New Mexico with a fairly banal request for compensation for horses and other supplies he had lost to Mescalero-Apache raiders in the Mesilla Valley. At the time, federal troops had the duty of protecting American property from "Indian raids."[3] When the army failed in its task, U.S. citizens could request compensation from the federal treasury. Government agents who contested such claims conventionally attempted to prove that the claimant had exaggerated the actual cost or the circumstances of the loss.

The U.S. attorney John Stansbury took a different approach in Amador's case, however, arguing that the merchant was not an American citizen and therefore lacked the right to file a claim for governmental recompense. Although Amador had a long-standing reputation in the region as a loyal American, including service as probate judge and county treasurer, Stansbury asserted that Amador could not be a legal citizen of the United States because he was "Mexican."[4] In the U.S. attorney's framing, Mexican identity was an issue of race; as a Mexican, Amador would have, at best, a limited capacity to claim U.S. citizenship. Indeed, most of the federal attorney's questions focused not on the horses and other materials for which Amador sought compensation but on whether Amador could prove his U.S. citizenship.

In theory Amador should have found it easy to establish his citizenship. He was born in El Paso (today's Juárez, Chihuahua) in 1840 but moved to Doña Ana, New Mexico, with his widowed mother, María Gregoria Rodela de Amador, shortly before the U.S.-Mexican War erupted in 1846. Like many nineteenth-century Mexicans in New Mexico, Amador did not migrate to a new nation: the United States came to him. Four years later, when a tentative peace had been restored to the region, Amador's savvy mother opened a general store in the recently founded town of Las Cruces on the U.S. side of the new border.[5] The Treaty of Guadalupe Hidalgo (1848), which formally ended the war, had explicitly guaranteed that any Mexican citizen who resided in New Mexico in 1848, and who did not formally assert his or her loyalty to Mexico by 1849, automatically became a U.S. citizen.[6] Therefore, all the Amadors were nationally Americans, not Mexicans, by the time they set up shop in Las Cruces in 1850. In practice, however, and as Amador was no doubt aware, U.S. authorities did not consistently respect that provision of the treaty and often imagined that Mexicans were not just citizens of another republic but were racially incompatible with the (white) American nation.

Even as late as 1898, the year that Martin Amador petitioned the federal government, New Mexico territorial authorities had still not established clear procedures by which a Mexican American could prove his or her U.S. citizenship. Thus, in order to pursue his own case, Amador had an additional burden beyond documenting his lost property: he had to show that Mexican and American identities were not mutually exclusive categories. Amador thus found individuals who testified to his residency in the southern New Mexico town of Doña Ana at the time of the Treaty of Guadalupe Hidalgo.

As his first witness Amador called one Pedro Melenudo, an elderly resident of Las Cruces. Melenudo's testimony exemplified one means by which Mexicans could reconcile their conflicting status in the United States. Like Amador, Melenudo argued that he might have been a Mexican by birth but that this did not preclude him from becoming American in 1849. Stansbury, in blatant disregard of the Treaty of Guadalupe Hidalgo, rejected this assertion and sought instead to discredit the two men's claims to U.S. citizenship. He started by asking if Amador's family were Mexican citizens.[7] Of course, he would have known that before the

U.S. invasion of New Mexico in 1846, all residents of the territory were Mexican citizens because that territory had been part of the Mexican nation. This line of questioning, though, attempted to establish Amador's status as Mexican by "blood." Because Euro-American discourse configured Mexican identity as invested in one's body, the status of one's family as Mexican would have had significance in determining an individual's immutable racial status.[8] By this logic, if Amador's family ever *had been* Mexican, then throughout his life Amador could only ever *be* Mexican.

Melenudo understood this logic and kept ahead of Stansbury by demarcating a distinct change in the status of Amador's father. "He was a citizen of Mexico [before 1846]," Melenudo answered reasonably, "because Doña Ana was then part of Mexico, but in 1846 the American forces came in and all of us who lived there took the oath of allegiance to the United States."[9] Melenudo, for good measure, testified to Amador's own precocious performance of American nationalism at that same time. "[Martin Amador] was about seven years old," Melenudo recounted, "but he was right in there in the crowd at the place where the [U.S.] Major had all of the people of the town of Doña Ana to congregate in a placita or court."[10]

This florid testimony did not satisfy Stansbury. He questioned whether Amador had ever obtained naturalization papers to authenticate his U.S. citizenship. Many Mexican Americans had feared that the U.S. government might not honor the Treaty of Guadalupe Hidalgo; in preparation for this possibility some of them requested that local judges issue naturalization papers or other documents as proof of citizenship. Amador later testified that he had petitioned the Doña Ana court in the 1860s to secure such papers. At that time the judge informed Amador that he did not need documents as he was already a citizen under the Treaty of Guadalupe Hidalgo.[11] Stansbury's questioning, though, created a double bind: if a lack of naturalization papers indicated foreignness, then a request for naturalization papers constituted a de facto admission of one's foreignness.

Refuting the double bind, Melenudo steadfastly answered Stansbury by asserting his own right to U.S. citizenship without documentation. "I haven't got any papers," Melenudo responded, "and I am a citizen of the United States."[12] Without hesitation the federal attorney snapped, "Don't you know that you are not a citizen of the United States?"[13] Stansbury did not accept that Melenudo, as a Mexican, could actually be American.

If Stansbury proved hard to convince, not all of Amador's Mexican witnesses applauded his efforts at claiming U.S. citizenship, either. Clemente Montoya, an elderly farmer in the Mesilla Valley, did endorse Amador's monetary claim against the United States government, stating, "It is just."[14] Yet, unlike Melenudo (who resided in Las Cruces), Montoya proved openly hostile to Amador and other Mexicans who claimed to be Americans. Amador, from Montoya's vantage point, had sacrificed his Mexican identity in pursuit of U.S. citizenship. This animosity might have been heightened by the disparity in economic class between the farmer and the merchant. Asked to comment on Amador's honesty, Montoya distinguished between the past, when Montoya considered him Mexican, and the present, when Montoya considered him American. "He used to be a very good man," Montoya stated. "He is not so good now because he is Americanized; I don't like Americans."[15]

Indeed, Montoya performed linguistic acrobatics to avoid having to claim an American identity for himself. Stansbury posed his usual questions about the witness's own claims to U.S. citizenship, but unlike Melenudo or Amador, Montoya avoided answering them explicitly. Rather, when asked directly about his own citizenship, Montoya chose his words carefully: "I was born and raised here [in southern New Mexico]," he responded. "I have sons who are 53 years old; I have four sons; they are all citizens."[16] This meticulous answer implied that, like Melenudo, Montoya understood that he technically *could* claim U.S. citizenship.[17] Unlike Melenudo, he steadfastly refused to do so.

Montoya's indirect response to the citizenship questions stands out in his testimony as the only time when he resorted to vagueness. For the rest of his testimony Montoya answered in short, clear answers. When asked if Martin Amador was a U.S. citizen, for instance, Montoya responded simply, "Yes sir."[18] Montoya could answer easily about Amador's citizenship status because he believed that the hotelier had relinquished his claims to Mexicanness. For himself, though, Montoya refused to accept an American national identity. In the face of ambiguity about the relationship between Mexicans and Americans, Montoya chose a language of calculated prevarication, asserting his U.S. citizenship without being forced to claim the concomitant national identity.

Testimony by Montoya and Melenudo reveals the complexity of claiming or being assigned a Mexican identity along the nineteenth-century Mexican-U.S. border. This case holds special relevance because it suggests that the Euro-American representatives of the U.S. nation-state never secured absolute control over the contours of racial and national identification, despite their having erected and policed those borders themselves.[19] Far from being overwhelmed by hegemonic assumptions about the meaning of either a Mexican or an American identity, all the witnesses and the federal attorney attempted to exploit the slippages and gaps among competing notions for their own purposes. To trace the differences found in these depositions, *Border Dilemmas* considers the ideological processes that ultimately motivated individuals like Amador, Stansbury, Melenudo, and Montoya in 1898. Looking at the depositions from this case leaves us with the historical question of how there could be so many different ideas about Mexican and American national identity in such a small community?

Mexican Identity: Racial or National?

New Mexico's population in 1840 included a diverse mixture of people who identified themselves racially and culturally as Pueblo Indians, Diné Indians, Apache Indians, mestizos, españoles, Euro-Americans, and various other combinations. The people in New Mexico were all Mexican.

For some these two statements might appear contradictory. That contradiction, however, only developed out of a process of racial formation on the U.S. side of the border that labeled *Mexican* as a distinct racial group. With the end of the U.S.-Mexican War in 1848, the signing of the Treaty of Guadalupe Hidalgo redrew the international boundary between the United States and Mexico, cutting Mexico's territorial size by half. For the tens of thousands of Mexican citizens whose homes were ceded to the authority of the United States, questions about their adoption or assignation of a particular national identity could not but emerge as an urgent concern. When Euro-Americans and Mexicans first encountered each other in these frontier regions, they often held contrasting and seemingly irreconcilable ideas about Mexican identity, as either a strictly racial or national identity. In Mexico the national Mexican identity had encompassed multiple racial groups, including "Indians," "whites," "mestizos," and other configurations. Within the United States, however, *Mexican* could connote only one racial group: "mestizos," or individuals of mixed European and Native American ancestry.[20] For most Euro-Americans the United States was a "white" nation. Mexico was not.

Because these modes of imagining identity stood on irreconcilable premises, to claim either (or both) a Mexican or an American identity necessarily connected individuals to distinct, if overlapping, debates about race, nation, and even economics along the border. In this context it is particularly important to note that even among the Spanish-speaking people of the region, contradictory impulses and allegiances divided the settlers and their ideas about which nation was theirs. In the Mesilla Valley an accident of geography allows us to follow this complicated process across two different towns of Spanish-speaking residents in the United States—one that considered itself nationally Mexican and one that considered itself American.

Most Mexican citizens living in the newly acquired U.S. territory decided to take their chances with the occupying government. In retrospect this choice has been depicted as inevitable, but at the time it was not a foregone conclusion, nor was it unanimously embraced. Even today, most U.S. historians are unaware of divided sentiments among Mexican nationals shortly after the war. Thousands of Mexicans in New Mexico even fled the United States to form new towns south of the 1848 border. Whether for practical, sentimental, or nationalistic reasons, these thousands explicitly rejected U.S. citizenship. Less than a decade after the war's end, their effort to evade U.S. political and cultural control was undermined when the Mesilla/Gadsden Treaty took effect in 1854. In that year new negotiations between Washington and Mexico City redrew the borderline yet again, this time incorporating these communities into the United States. This historical development left a legacy of geographically adjacent, but ideologically opposed, population centers—sites on which this study seeks to uncover multiple ideas about "being Mexican" —that coexisted within U.S. border communities between 1848 and 1912.

Although not well known today, some of the most compelling nineteenth-century discussions about U.S. imperialism and national identity played out over a cultural fault line that shot through southern New Mexico's Mesilla Valley. Mexican settlers founded both Las Cruces and La Mesilla on the newly drawn boundary line in 1850. Those who decided to take a gamble with the United States, like the Amadors, built the town of Las Cruces on the American side of the border. Others, unwilling to live under a government that had just waged war against the Mexican republic, established the town of La Mesilla just south of the border. Fewer than five miles separated Las Cruces and La Mesilla, but a wide gap in ideas about their relationship to Mexican identity divided the settlers.

Ideological differences between these modest agricultural communities might have been ignored more readily had the political boundary line stayed constant. Even after ratification of the Mesilla/Gadsden Treaty, many Mexicans refused to allow the new political boundary to disrupt their vision of their communities. As recently as 1978, 125 years after the treaty incorporated New Mexico into the United States, Mesilleros and Cruceños remained at odds over whether they were Mexican or American. Residents of these neighboring towns reimagined the national boundary line to explain divergent Mexican identities in ways that bypassed or obviated the construction of international borders. In an oral history interview from 1974 one longtime Las Cruces resident recalled

> that the town of La Mesilla, about four miles to the west of Las Cruces, was considered to be part of Mexico, and that Las Cruces was in the United States. The two towns were separated by the river, the Rio Grande, and this was also the boundary between the two countries. The rivalry between the two towns was fierce, and no one from either side dared enter into the other country. Those who did in order to visit relations or close friends were beaten. . . . The people of Mesilla were called "Mesillaros" [sic] by the people of Las Cruces. The people of Las Cruces were referred to as "The Gringo Mexicans" by the people of Mesilla.[21]

Technically, the woman's memory might seem questionable because both towns were inside the boundaries of the United States and were administered by U.S. authority. In daily life, though, townspeople in both locations considered La Mesilla "Mexican" and Las Cruces "American." Disregarding the official boundary line between the United States and Mexico, Mesilleros and Cruceños invented their own "local border" to explain their relationship.

The division between the towns concerned not merely the choice of identity to be adopted—American vs. Mexican—but, more fundamentally, the idiom in which that identity was to be articulated. In founding their town as nationally Mexican, Mesilleros consciously rejected Euro-American constructions of Mexican identity as a monolithic racial category. Instead, they envisioned being Mexican as requiring an assertion of nationalism and performance of certain cultural markers, such as speaking Spanish or attending Catholic Mass. They also imagined their town and identity in opposition to U.S. imperialism. Mesilleros consequently believed that individuals would forfeit their Mexican identity if they became U.S. citizens or did not actively assert their allegiance to Mexico. In other words, one could cease to be Mexican.

Euro-Americans quickly dominated Las Cruces, unlike Mesilla. As a result of their presence most Cruceños began by the end of the nineteenth century to imagine Mexican identity much as Euro-Americans did, meaning that to call oneself "Mexican" implied a distinctive and immutable racial identity. Under this thinking Mexican identity was presumed to be part of one's bodily attributes, and one's status as Mexican became a state of being that depended in part on parentage. Actions could no longer identify. This vision, which pivoted on the acceptance of dominant nineteenth-century Euro-American articulations of race, permitted one to be racially Mexican and nationally American at the same time, unlike the vision in La Mesilla.

This division within the Mesilla Valley continued for more than a century, its echoes sounding long after the memory of why the towns were divided had faded. Writing about his own experiences growing up in southern New Mexico, one Mesillero remembered a distinct difference in his experiences attending school in La Mesilla and in Las Cruces. It was, he recounted, only when he started junior high in a Las Cruces school that he heard racist slurs about "dumb Mexicans" or "los mojados" (the wetbacks), deprecations that he had not encountered in Mesilla's schools. In his memory Mesilla represented a safe haven for the Mexican population, whereas Las Cruces was a place of racist exclusion.[22]

Border Dilemmas compares the trajectory of one southern New Mexico town, Las Cruces, against the trajectory of its neighboring community, La Mesilla, as a starting point for rethinking Mexicans' historic role in the United States. Examining the first generation of Mexicans who lived in these sites opens new historical perspectives. It exposes the early limits on racial and national identities created by U.S. imperialism in the latter half of the nineteenth century.[23] Decisions about accommodation and resistance made during that period influenced subsequent generations of Mexicans in the United States. To tell this story, I proceed along two axes. First, I chart broad discussions about race, nation, and place that occurred during New Mexico's territorial period (1848–1912); second, I consider how those discussions influenced the founding, rise, and decline of these two Mexican border towns.

This dual focus intervenes in a historical narrative of the Mexican-U.S. border still haunted by notions of "Americanization." Modern historians in the United States have all too often projected anachronistic assumptions about the meaning of race, nation, and region into their historical studies. One sign of such projections appears in the widely circulating premise that northern Mexico and the southwestern United States developed in cultural and political isolation from other areas in Mexico.[24] As this study will show in some detail, to claim that individuals in New Mexico never adopted identities informed by the Mexican nation-state because of the territory's "isolation" confuses historical *explanans* with *expanandum*.[25] Even more recent scholarship that seeks to trace the origins of racial identities has failed to link ideologies of race to other metadiscourses about nation and region, both in Mexico and the United States. In the absence of such critical consideration conventional narratives continue to highlight New Mexico's colonial era, to discount or skip the brief Mexican national period, and to culminate in an eventual "tricultural" coexistence of Mexicans, Native Americans, and Euro-Americans under the United States.[26] *Border Dilemmas* seeks to confound such tidy periodization by examining southern New Mexico, an area that for more than one hundred years defied incorporation into regional "New Mexican" identity because of its proximity to Mexico.

Spanish vs. Mexican: Whose Racial Fantasy?

Border Dilemmas takes to task a monolithic understanding of Mexican identity that continues to pervade U.S. assumptions about its neighboring republic. It points to the historical creation of *Mexican* as becoming synonymous with only *mestizo* in the nineteenth-century United States that still guides popular and scholarly representations of Mexico north of the border. It is a racial category that remains under contention but nonetheless is assumed to be true.

Like other historians within Chicano/a studies, I focus on the intricacies of local contexts to explore wider issues in the history of racial formation in the United States.[27] Accordingly, this study is not intended as a broad political or social history of southern New Mexico. Key events and people in that history, like Albert Fountain, "Billy the Kid," Miguel Otero, Pat Garrett, and other mythologized figures, have already received ample attention elsewhere, and this study does not retrace these steps.[28] Nor is it necessarily a comparative (binational or transnational) history between Mexico and the United States. Instead, *Border Dilemmas* considers how conflicting notions of race and nation that divided nineteenth-century Mexico and the United States found an uneasy reconciliation after New Mexico transferred to U.S. political authority.

Many historians have written about nineteenth-century New Mexico, but few have specifically considered the meaning of Mexican identity in the territory.[29] With the powerful foregrounding of race as an analytic category, Mexican identity is most often represented in these studies primarily as a lacuna. This established narrative has no place for the many individuals in New Mexico who actively claimed a Mexican national identity, including the founders of La Mesilla.[30] It also leaves unquestioned a regionally specific discourse that was developed, as I will show, expressly to obscure and dilute racial tensions created by the Mexican/American dichotomy along the late-nineteenth-century border. By taking the narrative of "New Mexico's uniqueness" as a problem itself in need of historicization, instead of regarding it as an established historical fact, I intend to avoid the trap of reifying the racial and national categories on which the narrative itself depends.

Border Dilemmas uses the geographer Laura Pulido's notion of "differential racialization" to understand the historical divorcing of indigenous, black, and other racial categories from Mexican identity.[31] Pulido argues that multiple racial groups are created through relational processes. Each group is racialized in unique ways and experiences racism distinctly. Complex racial hierarchies are thereby formed as multiple racially subordinate populations occupy a range of social positions that are contingent upon the positions of other groups. "Hence the idea of Asian Americans as 'model minorities,'" Pulido writes, "exists only in relation to 'less than model' Black, Latina/o, and American Indian movements."[32] I take up that argument to show how the criteria and definition of being Mexican shifted based on local circumstances, national interests, and historical happenstance. The historic decision by Spanish-speaking individuals in New Mexico (which included, among others, Pueblo Indians in the nineteenth century) to either claim or reject a Mexican identity needs to be revaluated as an integral part of the history of U.S. imperialism. I also consider how new understandings of region that emerged in the late nineteenth century accompanied another, though incomplete, process that differentiated between Mexicans in New Mexico with Mexicans in other parts of the border region.

Previous scholarship on New Mexico has been particularly invested in charting how notions of a supposedly nonsensical "pure Spanish ancestry" developed as an alternative to an allegedly racially legitimate Mexican/ mestizo identity in the territory.[33] Since the 1990s, these studies have drawn from pioneering works on the meaning of "whiteness" and American identity by historians including David Roediger, Matthew Frye Jacobson, and Neil Foley.[34] Like their counterparts elsewhere in the nineteenth-century United States, settlers in New Mexico had an imperative to name (and claim) whiteness, "its definition, its internal hierarchies, its proper boundaries, and its rightful claimants."[35] Logically, scholars write about claims to "pure Spanish heritage" as a means through which some Mexicans tried to "whiten" themselves.

The meaning of being Spanish, however, has come to dominate almost all scholarly and political discussions of Mexicans in territorial New Mexico. This trajectory has been at the expense of more nuanced understandings of race, region, and national ideologies. Even as early as 1948, the activist and journalist Carey McWilliams dismissed Spanish identity as the creation of a "fantasy heritage."[36] McWilliams pointed directly to the issue of race in this phenomenon:

> The native-born Spanish-speaking elements resent any attempt to designate them in a manner that implies a "non-white" racial origin. Being called "Mexican" is resented, not on the basis of nationality, but on the assumption of racial difference. Because of the Anglo-American's attitude toward race, the first reaction of the New Mexican . . . "is to disassociate himself from anything that carries a Mexican implication. . . ." Carried to its logical conclusion, this line of reasoning results in the deductions (a) that the New Mexican is not "Mexican"; and (b) that he has no Indian blood.[37]

This early assessment set the tone for subsequent historical discussions about the development of Spanish American identity. The focus on authenticating racial categories has therefore obscured other intersecting identities at play in the territory.

Studies following McWilliams have largely ignored the creation of the much more dominant "New Mexican" regional identity. Although McWilliams put much effort into discrediting the idea of a Mexican being Spanish American, he unquestioningly acknowledged *New Mexicans* as possessing their own "natural" association, seemingly built through a timeless geography. This mode of critique, which rejected any claim to Spanishness, neglected the greater ambivalence that many Mexicans demonstrated when claiming a racial or regional Spanish identity. Evidence of this ambivalence predates the writing of McWilliams, appearing even in the linguist and folklorist Helen Zunser's discussion of her trip to New Mexico in 1935:

> Our friends called themselves Spanish Americans, but called their language Mexican. There was deep antagonism in their attitude towards the people and country of "Old Mexico," and they resented being called Mexicans. "Bad country, old Mexico. Too many bandits. Kill all the time, have long knives. Like to fight." We thought that this feeling was partly due to the fact that in the southwest Mexicans are treated the way Negroes are in the southeast. . . . When our friends left their town they had this experience over and over again, and it was natural to resent the stigma attached to them. But in addition, they always spoke of temperamental differences, as if the Mexi-

can[s] were much more violent than they were. Yet we knew of individual cases where Old and New Mexicans had been friends, and we were told that the language differences were slight.[38]

Zunser's observations suggest a considerable complexity in linking New Mexican identity to Spanishness. Her informants identified themselves as racially Spanish, but they also seemed to acknowledge a cultural tie to Mexico through language. Still, they tried to name New Mexicans as different "temperamentally" from Mexicans; but then they highlighted personal friendships between the two groups. Had Zunser dug deeper, she might have also observed that even language played a key role in naming identities. Many Mexican Americans in New Mexico, as I will show, would use "Spanish American" when writing in English, but continue to use "mexicano" while writing in Spanish. Despite such contradictions and uncertainties, scholars who have discussed Spanish identity in New Mexico have seen claims to "pure Spanish blood" as only a disavowal of Mexicanness in pursuit of whiteness. This interpretation misses the sorts of nuanced meanings and cross-national connections made possible by accounts such as Zunser's.

To couch the discussion of Spanishness solely in terms of the "fallacy" of "obviously nonwhite" Mexicans' claims to "white" identity is to allow contemporary assumptions about racial and national identities to function unchecked. Like their nineteenth-century counterparts, later Euro-American observers too often grounded Mexican identity in the body, diagnosing Mexicans as always already a product of "mixed race." Even scholars engaged in critical race theory implicitly assert that Mexican identity really does mean "mestizo" and nothing else. To the scholars who hold such attitudes, efforts by Spanish-speaking Americans to "lose" their Mexican racial identity seem nonsensical. As progressive figures in their day, Zunser and McWilliams might have intended to demonstrate their solidarity with the peoples of New Mexico when they lamented that Anglo racism motivated the claim of Spanish identity within the Southwest and when they described the adoption of this identity as a form of internalized racism. It is indisputable, though, that in judging the possession of Spanish identity as tantamount to claims to the "white race," these writers acted on their own assumptions that expert Euro-American activists and folklorists retained the exclusive ability and privilege to name authentic racial identities for the Other.

This study rejects those assumptions.[39] It reveals, instead, more ambiguity and uncertainty about Mexican identity in the United States. Coming to terms with the complexity of seeing *Mexican* as a racial category requires an acknowledgment that the ideological processes that defined it encompassed more than the binary of white versus Other. Mexican identity in the United States, for instance, has historically been understood in intricately cross-relational ways as "not white" but also as "not black," "not Native American," "not Asian," and as "mestizo." Historically, too, "whiteness" has hardly been the only identity to shape Mexicans' self-understanding of their role in the nation. Shortly after the 1846 conquest, settlers in the newly occupied territories apparently thought it more urgent to define and limit the racial meaning of Mexicanness and other identities of color than naming whiteness. Once the border moved, in 1848 (and again in 1854), settlers in New Mexico found that prevailing American assumptions about race and nation left them with a narrowed understanding of Mexican identity. The almost immediate exclusion of Native Americans from being Mexicans was one segment of a larger process that came to racially define Mexicans' place within the U.S. racial hierarchy. While certainly not preordained, this ultimate divorcing of American Indians from Mexican identity suggests a shifting and reordering of national and racial categories in New Mexico that did not center only on claims to white Americanness.[40] *Border Dilemmas* explains how U.S. imperialism informed Spanish-speaking individuals' understandings of their own racial and national identities in the region. Many Mexican Americans intervened in debates about race, nation, and region in an effort to alter New Mexico's colonial status. I focus on Mexican identity, in particular, but lay the groundwork for future scholars to consider how Pueblo, Apache, Diné, and other Native American groups came to understand these changes in national, regional, and racial identities themselves.

Following previous Chicano/a scholars, I regard "Mexican" and "Mexican American" identity as contingent on ideological processes. This strand of scholarship challenges historians to consider the historical fluidity of Mexican identity and Mexican American identity. *Border Dilemmas* takes up their challenge in innovative ways. I have deliberately avoided any discussion of the creation of these identities as linear and rooted in a particular period or generation. In fact, the more I examined documents from nineteenth-century southern New Mexico, the more ambivalence I found in ideas about race and nation along the border. The first generation of Mexicans in New Mexico, after all, did not leave Mexico for a "new land," nor did subsequent generations necessarily have a greater tendency to accept the "possibilities of a future" in their communities.[41] Rather, they were forced to reconsider the meaning of their racial and national identities because the meaning of their location had itself changed. The new border suddenly transformed them into racially inferior insiders in the United States.

The new border did not just confound Mexicans, either. Many Euro-Americans in New Mexico eventually came to see the territory's colonial status under U.S. hegemony as unacceptable for their own reasons. Objections to that status certainly did not arise from any abstract commitment to the universal extension of full citizenship rights to all residents of the territory. Rather, Euro-Americans who migrated to the region during the nineteenth century found to their displeasure that their own rights were curtailed by New Mexico's lack of full integration into the United States. Voters in the territory had extremely limited self-government and a nonvoting congressional delegate, amounting to almost no say in national elections (despite their reliance on federal aid for economic development). Moreover, the president of the United States and Congress appointed most of New Mexico's political offices, ensuring dominance by outsiders, many of whom had never even visited the territory before being appointed. The interests of these political patronage appointments did not necessarily conform to those of the established Euro-American colonizers. Furthermore, less tangible, but still very real, prejudices dogged the Euro-Americans of territorial New Mexico. As in other colonial contexts, eastern and metropolitan Euro-Americans often viewed New Mexico's white settler populations with wariness, sometimes suspecting them of having become "racially degraded" through their association with the territory's Mexican majority.

In place of the analytic valorization of race alone, *Border Dilemmas* draws from a wider repertoire of cultural-studies methodologies to consider the ideological processes that informed nineteenth-century U.S. colonialism and border making and to demonstrate the importance of attention to place as a theoretical tool in discussions of race and nation.[42] Actually dwelling in a particular location affected the ways historical actors understood, articulated, and challenged social and cultural relationships.[43] Michel Foucault has noted that "it is somewhat arbitrary to try to dissociate the effective practice of freedom by people, the practice of social relations, and the spatial distributions in which they find themselves. If they are separated, they become impossible to understand."[44] I am therefore interested not in the abstract imposition of U.S. or Mexican ideas onto "blank" territories but in the interplay between Mexican and

U.S. notions of race and nation that accompanied the reorganizing of the border region.

Transforming space can include bringing new biology, new names, new social and political structures, and a new imagining of that place's relation to a wider sense of the globe and cartography.[45] Space has importance both in a materialist sense and in terms of social processes that structure relations of inequality.[46] Materially, space affects the lives of historical actors in concrete ways, shaping the quantity, types, and quality of material resources available. Imaginings of place also shaped these actors' assumptions about themselves in countless and sometimes imperceptible ways. Space is important to this study because historical figures placed tremendous importance on naming the racial and national meaning of being in the place known as the border. As this working definition implies, space cannot be value-neutral. Individuals organize, name, and contest the meaning of space within broader ideological processes that inform their sense of identity. If space is socially constituted, then so, too, is the social spatially constituted.[47]

From this perspective I want to consider how creating or remaking location (that is, actually being in a particular place like La Mesilla, Las Cruces, or New Mexico) affected the ways historical actors understood, articulated, and challenged social and cultural relationships. The complicated relationship between La Mesilla and Las Cruces suggests the ways that competing ideologies about race and nation tangibly influenced the organization of local space, practices, and social relationships. The two towns took shape under competing notions about the relationship between racial and national identities. The Mexicans and Euro-Americans who founded the towns attempted to configure each one to match their own expectations about their nation. This, in turn, influenced issues like land tenure, the types and styles of buildings constructed, and even the distribution of racialized bodies across the landscape. Thus, the imagining of place became a critical component in creating "local borders," ones not coterminous with the official national border, that distinguished Mexican understandings and articulations of their sense of race, nation, and region.[48] Creating local borders required that individuals grapple with the meaning of abstractions like citizenship or national belonging repeatedly.[49]

Meta-ideologies like race or nation circulate widely, but it is only in their immediate, local settings that individuals access and interact with knowledge and power.[50] Naming an expanse of land either "Mexico" or

"United States" was (is) an act of power with profound implications for the ways that individuals in that place understood (understand) their identities and relationships to others. Creating a geography, building permanent structures, and establishing governance influenced how nineteenth-century Mexicans and Mexican Americans made sense of the racially charged international border. Likewise, individuals made sense of and organized their local communities based on their ideas about race and nation. As we will see, by the end of the nineteenth century many individuals presumed that being in New Mexico imparted particular meanings about race and nation. New-Mexican space became "unique," with a specific racial and national meaning.

By scrutinizing the first generations of Mexican residents in the United States, this study identifies and historicizes many of the early anxieties about Mexican racial and national identities, anxieties that influenced subsequent generations' assumptions right up until today. Of course, individuals in the twentieth century and in the twenty-first also contributed, challenged, and constructed unique meanings for *Mexican* and *Mexican American* in ever-changing historical circumstances. As this study shows, though, the long-term processes that created the racial and national meanings of these complex identities in the United States did not originate in the twentieth century. Rather, this study lays the foundations for future work, which will link the ways in which nineteenth-century individuals made sense of their racial and national identities with later, twentieth-century understandings of "being Mexican" in the United States. As the region in the nineteenth-century United States with the largest Mexican population, New Mexico is the best place to begin to consider these issues.

The Mesilla Valley and a History of Colonization

This study examines a host of varied sources and themes that shed light on the ways individuals articulated ideas about race, nation, and region during New Mexico's territorial period. Limited sources exist for this period, especially from individuals who were not part of the elite. Therefore, I have tapped diverse records—newspapers, personal papers, diocese records, printed memoirs, court documents, and other sources that might seem unrelated at first. In some cases I revisited sources and arguments that will already be familiar to those who study the nineteenth-century border—like the Treaty of Guadalupe Hidalgo, or writings by prominent figures such as Charles Lummis and Miguel A. Otero, or the invention of the region's triculturalism—to consider how they shed light on the meaning of space in discussions of race and nation. Most of the sources employed here, however, have been understudied by previous historians. For complicated reasons northern New Mexico has disproportionately attracted historians' attention. This is unfortunate because there are materials unique to southern New Mexico that raise new questions about the region and the meaning of the nineteenth-century border.

Before I outline the chapters, allow me to provide basic information about the Mesilla Valley and its history. The Mesilla Valley is a seventy-five-mile stretch along the Rio Grande from the modern Caballo Dam to the boundary between New Mexico and Texas.[51] One of the richest farming areas in New Mexico, the Mesilla Valley is located at the center of Doña Ana County (created in 1852) and includes the major towns of Hatch, Doña Ana, Las Cruces, and La Mesilla. During the nineteenth century Las Cruces and La Mesilla, located about five miles apart, overshadowed their neighboring towns in population (see Map 1).[52] By the early twenty-first century, most Americans outside of New Mexico first thought of Santa Fe, Taos, and Albuquerque when asked to name the state's major cities. Yet, despite its relatively low visibility, Las Cruces is actually the second-largest city in New Mexico, after Albuquerque. The city occupies an important place as a center for education and trade: New Mexico State University, founded as New Mexico A&M in 1888, is located there, and the major cities of El Paso, Texas, and Juárez, Chihuahua, lie about thirty-eight miles south of it.

Unlike northern New Mexico, the Mesilla Valley lacked nonindigenous settlements until the nineteenth century. Groups of Apaches controlled most of the area's habitable land, easily thwarting occasional attempts by Spain to colonize beyond the Camino Real in southern New Mexico.[53] Two failed efforts to establish colonies occurred during the first decades of the nineteenth century. Antonio García of El Paso filed a claim in 1805 for a silver mine in the Organ Mountains (east of Las Cruces).[54] The governor of New Mexico, however, delayed García's request until he could guarantee the establishment of a colony.[55] García eventually created a small mining operation with about eleven colonists in 1819, known as the Brazito Grant. He and his followers abandoned the site the following year after an Apache group forced them to retreat to El Paso (today's Juárez).[56] Another colonization plan launched in 1822 but failed before the settlers reached the Mesilla Valley. The Mexican emperor Agustín de Iturbide granted the Missouri trader John Heath a

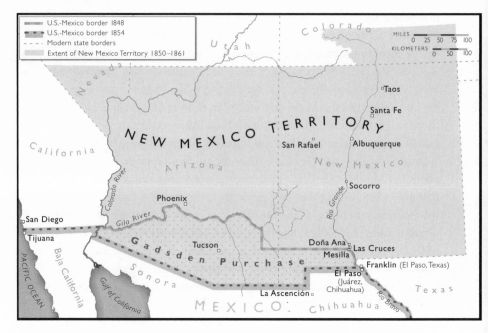

Map 1. New Mexico Territory and its changing boundaries.
Map created by Adrian Kitzinger.

sizeable portion of land in the valley. Heath made arrangements to take possession of the territory and enlisted settlers, but Iturbide's downfall in 1823 ruined Heath's plans even as his colonists arrived at El Paso. Heath relinquished his claim to southern New Mexico when he received word that the governor of New Mexico had declared the grant illegitimate because Iturbide no longer ruled Mexico.[57]

In 1839 Don José María Costales established the first permanent non-indigenous settlement in the Mesilla Valley when the governor of Chihuahua granted Costales twelve miles of land along the Rio Grande. After a few years Costales founded the town of Doña Ana with a mere 107 men, 59 women, and more than a hundred children.[58] The Doña Ana colonists barely survived the first years, and many returned to El Paso rather than trying to eke out a meager existence in the harsh landscape. After several brutal years Pablo Melendres and 241 colonists eventually completed the colony's acequia in April 1843. Once this vital artery provided irrigation for farming, the colony's fortunes began to change. By 1846 Alcalde Melendres reported to the governor that Doña Ana was growing robustly.[59] These Mexican settlers, though, pitted themselves against indigenous groups in bloody confrontations. At the same time, mounting hostilities between the United States and Mexico were developing into war. This point is where the main narrative of *Border Dilemmas* begins.

Use of Terms and Translations

Any scholar who wades into discussions about border populations quickly finds that settling on terms is one of the biggest challenges. The historical term *Mexican*, as I have noted, often obscures a great deal of diversity within that population. Though Mexicans often shared certain cultural practices, like attending Catholic rituals or speaking Spanish, they could individually claim diverse racial and ethnic backgrounds.[60] As others have documented, the progenitors of New Mexico's nineteenth-century Mexicans had intermarried across many cultural and racial boundaries during Spain's colonial era.[61] No standard physiognomy or phenotype could readily group together this population. Even individuals from the same family could appear lighter or darker than the arriving Euro-Americans. Confusion over who was "really Mexican" caused by this diversity only increased Euro-Americans' desire to enforce "Mexican" as a distinctive racial category through the nineteenth century.

For *Border Dilemmas* I have chosen mostly an emic vocabulary, using the terms *Mexican*, *native*, and *New Mexican* as they would have been most widely understood during the nineteenth century. Some terms employed in the following pages are, however, intentionally anachronistic: I use *Mexican American*, for instance, for individuals who purposefully wanted to reconcile these two identities. I also use *Mesilleros* to refer to the Mexican population of La Mesilla and *Cruceños* for the Mexican population of Las Cruces. Historical residents of these towns would have understood and recognized these terms, but they were neither widely used nor necessarily the primary means of identifying an individual. Nonetheless, I hope they will draw attention to the complexity and importance that the local context had in determining the ways that individuals accessed larger imagined associations that were racial and national.

Although most people used the terms *Anglo* or *American* in New Mexico during the nineteenth century, I have opted to use the more recent (and therefore ahistorical) inclusive term *Euro-American*.[62] Many of the "Americans" who arrived in New Mexico during the nineteenth century did not claim Anglo-Saxon parentage. *Euro-American* more aptly captures the variety of settlers who were either recent European immigrants or claimed ancestry in Europe. Not exclusively Anglo or Anglo-Saxon, many of these settlers identified themselves as Irish, French, German, and so forth. *Euro-American*, therefore, acknowledges a greater diversity in this segment of the territorial population.

I have included Spanish-language transcriptions of original sources whenever practical. One personal story that could be told as an outcome of this narrative is that the Moras relinquished their fluency in Spanish in the generation preceding me in an effort (later regretted) to integrate more fully into the United States. As a result I was not raised in a bilingual household and had to learn Spanish more or less from scratch. I therefore feel acutely the personal and political implications of language choices made on the border. Because Spanish proficiency was (and often still is) considered a key marker in claims to Mexican identity, it would have seemed peculiar to me to override historical actors' decisions to write in Spanish by exclusively substituting English translations. As a result I have included both Spanish and English in the text if available. With the help of Carlos Marín I have made some minor changes (such as punctuation and accents) to see that both conform to modern standards of readability. Unless otherwise noted, all the translations are my own. With the methodology and terminology defined, we can turn to the structure of the book.

Chapter Summaries

In six chapters this study explores the complicated meanings of race, nation, and region during New Mexico's territorial period. Chapter 1 considers how differing ideologies about race and nation developed in the United States and Mexico from 1821 to 1850. Part of the ongoing tension between Las Cruces and Mesilla resulted from conflicting visions of Mexican and American national and racial identities that predated the towns' founding. Both Mexico and the United States intermixed notions of a performative national identity with ideas about a racial identity to define their sense of nationalism. The two countries differed, though, in the importance and meaning each assigned to performance and to race.

The second chapter narrows the focus to the founding of La Mesilla and Las Cruces. By using these towns as touchstones, I consider how competing racial and national ideologies in Mexico and the United States translated on the local level. Regulating space in the Mesilla Valley became a primary concern in disputes between Euro-Americans and Mexicans after 1850. Each town developed through a conscious effort to imbue the border cartography with a particular vision of national identity.

One of the most challenging elements of studying the nineteenth-century border is the scarcity of sources, especially from Mexicans. The historical record is too ambiguous and complex to make clear claims about their diverse experiences. As analytic categories I consider two central aspects of daily life in the Mesilla Valley: religion and gender. While the first and last two chapters chart the development of abstract ideologies, chapter 3 considers the specific ways that the Las Cruces Catholic parish, St. Genevieve's, figured in local contests. During the late nineteenth century the arrival of European and Euro-American clergy challenged Mexicans' control over their parish. The chapter considers those instances when religion became visible and salient in discussions about race, nation, and local borders. In so doing, it considers the day-to-day impact of such discussions on Mexican Americans.

Chapter 4 similarly analyzes narratives of gender and sexuality in southern New Mexico from 1850 to 1912. Examining court records, newspapers, and personal narratives, this chapter discusses how different individuals incorporated or rejected ideas about gender and sexuality into their discussions about place. Not only did Mexicans and Euro-Americans have competing ideas about the meaning of the region as Mexican or American, but they also differed in the ways that they imagined the space through gender lines. Debates about Mexican identity frequently focused on what it meant to be, specifically, a Mexican man or a Mexican woman living in a U.S. territory.

Differing ideas about race and nation continued to divide New Mexico through the end of the nineteenth century; however, by 1880 many Euro-American and Mexican American elites wanted to avoid debates over the racial and national meaning of the territory. Prominent individuals became proponents of a racially and nationally unified "New Mexican" regional identity that obscured the local conflicts. The final two chapters consider how certain historical actors wrote about the region in efforts to make New Mexico *knowable* as a distinct geographic entity with its own unique qualities.[63] In other words, I argue that those who wrote about the territory participated in a discourse that configured New Mexico as a subject or object with new meanings intrinsic to that space and, therefore, identifiable and open to study. Euro-American authors that I discuss in chapter 5 composed their understanding about New Mexico partly in conversation with each other and partly in response to "Easterners," whom they imagined had the power to invest in the territory, vacation there, or grant New Mexico statehood.

The final chapter considers how enterprising Mexicans adapted similar ideas and language about New Mexico for their own purposes. Certain members of the Mexican elite willingly accepted the American national identity as they participated in the regional New Mexican discourse. After 1880, for instance, the Spanish-speaking population founded a bevy of newspapers throughout the territory.[64] These editors often endorsed American nationalism, deliberately suppressing an association with a national Mexican identity. At the same time, however, these same editors claimed that being "native New Mexican" distinguished them from Euro-Americans as well.

It is worth remembering that the racial division discussed in chapters 5 and 6 is entirely artificial and structural to allow convenient analysis in this book. The Mexicans and Euro-Americans discussed in those chapters wrote simultaneously and, in fact, often engaged with each other. Neither side articulated a sense of the region unilaterally while the other merely reacted. As we will see, Euro-Americans and Mexican Americans shared, borrowed, and contested their ideas about New Mexico's significance in the United States.

Thinking again about Martin Amador, John Stansbury, and the deposition witnesses, we know that they all disagreed about what it meant to be Mexican or American in an American territory. Such incidents suggest why the Mesilla Valley is particularly important for historians interested in race and nation. It was, after all, one of the first sites in which the nineteenth-century United States grappled explicitly with the implications of its new border with Mexico. Southern New Mexico's history shows that claiming Mexican identity in the United States was a more complex and ambivalent process than historians have previously assumed. Mexicans were forced to reconsider the meaning of their racial and national identities because the meaning of their location had itself changed. Differing strategies developed as individuals attempted to make sense of the shifting local circumstances and their position in meta-ideologies. The strained and complicated relationship between La Mesilla and Las Cruces, in particular, suggests the ways in which competing ideologies about race and nation tangibly influenced the organization of local space, practices, and social relationships.

CHAPTER I

Preoccupied America: Competing Ideas
about Race and Nation in the United States
and Mexico, 1821–1851

La Mesilla and Las Cruces, two towns whose founding and subsequent histories illuminate nineteenth-century struggles over race and nation, emerged in the aftermath of the U.S. invasion of Mexico. In the summer of 1846 Colonel Stephen Watts Kearny, commanding the "Army of the West," entered New Mexico without encountering any military opposition. Rumors that New Mexico's Mexican governor, Manuel Armijo, accepted a bribe and abandoned the territory persist as legends.[1] Whatever the case, he did make a hasty departure that left the people of New Mexico without an organized defense and few options as the United States Army appeared on the horizon. Kearny claimed Santa Fe on behalf of the United States on August 18, 1846, and officially declared the military occupation of the territory. New Mexico, for all intents and purposes, was a colony of the United States in everything but name.[2]

Pointing out that "New Mexico fell without a single shot," U.S. histories of this conflict tended to present the invasion in triumphal terms. This version of events ignores the real anxiety, confusion, and animosity that existed among Mexicans. Even reports by U.S. soldiers in Santa Fe, who presumably had no motivation to exaggerate the nationalist sentiments of the Mexican population, noted that the local women covered their faces and sobbed aloud as the U.S. flag replaced the Mexican flag above the plaza.[3] Wild rumors circulated that, among other things, Euro-Americans planned to brand *US* on Mexicans' cheeks.[4]

Colonel Alexander Doniphan continued Kearny's campaign and solidified the military's control of the territory shortly thereafter. He marched a portion of the United States Army south, through a brutal trek across New Mexico's Jornada del Muerto, capturing the town of Doña Ana. Doniphan garrisoned 850 troops in the small farm town, commandeer-

ing food and supplies from the Mexican settlers.[5] This military occupation in southern New Mexico quickly overtaxed the meager resources of
Doña Ana residents. As a result two groups of Mexican settlers migrated
from Doña Ana, establishing the competing towns of La Mesilla and Las
Cruces.[6] These two towns became local manifestations of the uncertainties underlying the newly drawn U.S.-Mexican border. Out of this flux
Cruceños and Mesilleros came to conceive of the relationship between
race and nation in opposing ways. Cruceños eventually adopted a U.S.
model, configuring Mexicanness as a distinctive and immutable racial
identity. Mesilleros, in contrast, defined *mexicanidad* (Mexican identity)
as more transient. For them it did not necessarily imply any particular
racial category but did require enactments of certain cultural markers.[7]

This chapter charts the development of Mexican and American nationalisms as imagined associations that were unremittingly redefined
and reshaped during the nineteenth century.[8] The same eighteenth-
century and nineteenth-century liberal philosophies underpinned republican ideals in both Mexico and the United States.[9] The two nations
each claimed that a good government must recognize full citizens as
equal before the law and must rest on the consent of the people. Who
qualified as full citizens or even "the people," however, was hotly contested. Notions of innate inequalities proved consistent stumbling blocks
in securing either nation as an idealized republican state. The status of
"Indians," in particular, became crucial to determining Mexican and
American notions of full citizenship.[10] Mexico and the United States, as
we will see, ultimately diverged in their solutions to these questions.

The chapter then turns to the ways those divergent nationalisms col-
lided at midcentury as the United States invaded Mexico. The brokering
of a treaty to end the war left both an uneasy peace and unanswered
questions about the relationship between race and nation in New Mexico. Mesilla and Las Cruces, born from military occupation and dispossession, were implicated in ongoing struggles in both Mexico and the
United States to reconcile liberal theories of nation with exclusionary
practices based on race, gender, and other factors.[11]

Nineteenth-Century Euro-American Understandings
of Race and National Identity

Traditional discussions about U.S. imperialism tended to disconnect
later nineteenth-century U.S. ventures into the Caribbean and Asia from

histories of westward expansion into places like New Mexico. Under that interpretation the 1901 Supreme Court case *Downes v. Bidwell* was a key moment when U.S. imperialism emerged or, at least, changed significantly.[12] Ostensibly about tariffs, this case was thought to represent a major shift in U.S. imperialism from "absorbing new territories into the domestic space of the nation to acquiring foreign colonies and protectorates abroad."[13] Indeed, the Supreme Court ruled that the Constitution did not extend to Puerto Rico or its inhabitants because Puerto Rico was merely a "possession" of the United States.[14] Yet this ruling only codified existing notions that *places* could be part of the United States in terms of international and national boundaries, even as the *residents* of those places remained "foreign" to the U.S. national community (usually imagined as Euro-American).[15] Euro-Americans had long taken advantage of these possessions' resources, cheap labor, and land while excluding the colonized people in those places from the national community.

Rather than seeing *Downes* as a sudden rupture in U.S. policy, more recent scholarship has reoriented our view to see it as one step in an ongoing process of U.S. imperialism that had been at play since the invention of the nation. We should not forget that the United States had not at all "absorbed" all the territories and people within its continental borders at the time of the *Downes* case. Nor did certain colonies' location on the North American continent make them a natural or obvious part of the United States. Native Americans had an uncertain role in the nation as their lands became ever smaller. In the 1831 case *Cherokee Nation v. Georgia*, Chief Justice John Marshall foreshadowed the notion that some groups could be "foreign to the United States in a domestic sense" seventy years prior to *Downes*. He argued that Indian tribes were "domestic dependent nations" that "occupy a territory to which we assert a title independent of their will. . . . They are in a state of pupilage. Their relation to the United States resembles that of a ward to his guardian."[16]

Likewise, New Mexico and Arizona (which had been carved out of New Mexico) were still territories without full congressional representation at the time of *Downes*. It would be another eleven years before either became a state (if statehood is to be considered the marker of absorption or the end of colonialism, a condition about which I have some doubts based on New Mexico's twentieth-century history). Indeed, as I will discuss later, Puerto Rico and New Mexico became mutually reinforcing examples of the necessity of keeping the U.S. community "pure" by restricting either's full incorporation into the nation owing to their "mixed" populations.[17]

The dilemmas Euro-Americans confronted in 1831, 1846, 1854, and 1898 were the same as dilemmas faced by Dutch, French, and British imperial authorities everywhere in the nineteenth century. Asserting colonial authority over a place simultaneously incorporated that space into the metropolitan community even as it distanced that space from the metropolitan center.[18] Colonial governments often claimed that the existing inhabitants' racial inadequacies (whether Native American, Mexican, African, or Asian) resulted in an alleged "misuse" of local resources that demanded their intervention.[19] Those people and places needed the European and Euro-American intercession to "advance" to the next stage of civilization and capitalist production. Nineteenth-century colonial governments therefore wrestled with the same philosophical and legal questions in terms of race and citizenship. What role and rights did colonized people have? If European and Euro-American colonizers were caretakers of "lesser" races, just when would certain groups be ready for full citizenship? What were the appropriate mechanisms to allow their full incorporation into the national community?

Enlightenment discussions of republicanism always stipulated that certain individuals lacked sufficient "reason" and therefore were incapable of expressing their consent. Children or the insane, for instance, could be governed without their consent because they did not have the ability to govern themselves.[20] That same logic permitted race, gender, and cultural markers to serve as evidence of a lack of reason, which excluded certain individuals from equal participation in either Mexico or the United States.[21]

Other scholars working on nation and empire have found the notion of "interior frontiers" useful in discussing this complexity.[22] National frontiers mark sites of enclosure, exclusion, contact, exchange, passage, and difference. The concept of interior frontiers pays attention to the dilemmas and compromises created when imaginings of a "pure" national community face internal ruptures.[23] New Mexico became a site of such ruptures because most Euro-Americans presumed that race was a key marker that defined the national difference between Mexico and the United States in 1846.[24]

My temptation at the start of this project was to assume that most nineteenth-century Euro-Americans believed that American citizenship connoted whiteness exclusively. This seemed self-evident for a society that condoned race-based slavery and the genocide of indigenous people. It turns out, though, that the trajectory of U.S. national and racial ideologies was more complicated and contradictory than one might expect.

American nationalism developed as a set of everyday practices used at the local level. Public performance was a crucial component of those practices. The historian David Waldstreicher argues that such performances "empowered Americans to fight over the legacy of their national revolution and to protest their exclusion from that Revolution's fruits."[25] Groups of Americans used public events and occasions that forged a sense of national identity and eased divisions created by unavoidable regional, class, or political differences. Community celebrations, parades, and various other cultural events became a means for individuals to imagine themselves as defining and partaking in American nationalism during the early years of the republic.[26] Yet questions persisted about the consequences of such participation by nonwhite bodies, whose mere presence sparked contentious debates about the meaning of race and citizenship.

The 1787 Constitution provided few answers. Drafters of that cherished document did not give a great deal of consideration to citizenship and intentionally evaded discussions of race in the republic.[27] Only a few mentions of racial identities appear in the document, such as the exclusion of "Indians not taxed" from full citizenship and representation. Aside from that, even the infamous "three-fifths" clause lacked any explicit mention of race.[28] Although the Constitution had been unclear about the necessity of one's being white to claim full citizenship, the first federal legislation on naturalization, drafted in 1790, restricted the process to "free white persons." Such restrictions kept African American men from full citizenship until 1870 and excluded people of East and South Asian birth until 1952.[29] Nonetheless, such legislation provided no criteria for deciding who would count as "white."[30]

Given that the federal guidelines on citizenship were often ambiguous, it fell to individual states to determine the qualities one needed to claim full citizenship until the ratification of the Fourteenth Amendment in 1868.[31] Race, gender, property ownership, religious affiliation, and place of birth all became important qualifications for full citizenship in various state laws and common practices.[32] Creating common cultural acts might have eased regional or political differences, but racial distinctions proved too deeply rooted in most Euro-Americans' vision of their national identity.[33]

By 1848 many believed that numerous interior frontiers defined the limits of *full* American citizenship and national identity (that also signaled the right to vote, own land, participate in the military, carry a gun, and so forth).[34] Creating such interior frontiers, however, did not mean that Euro-Americans could not also claim other groups as "American."[35] Women, children, and free nontribal racial minorities would all have been construed as American citizens, but not full citizens. Rather than figuring that these groups could not be "American," the government stipulated that they were particular *types* of Americans (who did not have equal status and needed the rational oversight of white American men).

Defining a stylized repetition of acts specific to each type of American helped institute these categories in daily practice.[36] All identities—racial, national, and gender—have elements of cultural performance that solidify their legitimacy and uphold the illusion of their stability.[37] Racial and gender performances depend on a presumption of an interior and organizing core that is thought to be natural to particular types of bodies.[38] Racial and gender categories are imagined to exist transnationally and transhistorically. National identities, therefore, depend more heavily on the presumed stability of race and gender than vice versa. They frequently become the constitutive building blocks for imagining the nation and distinctions between nations. European, Euro-American, and Latin American notions of national identity were fragile because these nations (and empires) necessarily comprised heterogeneous racial and gender groups.

In the United States racial restrictions precipitously narrowed access to full citizenship over the course of the nineteenth century.[39] By 1857 the Supreme Court ruled in *Dred Scott v. Sandford* that the progeny of African slaves did not derive from "the people" who founded the United States and, therefore, could be excluded from the rights of full citizenship.[40] The growing difficulty faced by Native Americans who tried to claim full citizenship from 1789 to 1820 is instructive in understanding how thinking about race, cultural performance, and nation changed in the United States. That story is actually critical to understanding what would happen to Mexicans and other nonwhite groups who also became enmeshed in this nationalist discourse.

Because the Constitution excluded only "Indians not taxed," it implicitly left open the possibility that tax-paying Indians could be construed as equal citizens. Indeed, some Euro-Americans imagined that erasing the social and civic gap between Native Americans and whites could be achieved if the former simply reconciled themselves to "American" customs, behaviors, and "civilization." In 1789 George Washington initiated such a civilization program, which promised the full integration of Indians east of the Mississippi within fifty years.[41] To do so required that Native Americans disavow their identity within a tribe or nation and adopt the stylized repetition of acts and cultural markers that Euro-Americans deemed "civilized." Native Americans had to construe themselves exclusively as individuals, eliminate tribal titles to lands, learn English, and denationalize their communities. Comparable federal versions of these plans would continue to reappear through the nineteenth century, including the Dawes Act of 1887, which provided tracts of land and the promise of equal citizenship for individual Indians who willingly disavowed tribal membership.[42] These actions almost always accompanied the sale of millions of acres of tribal lands to white settlers. Such civilizing efforts attempted to reconcile Enlightenment ideals of egalitarian republican citizenship with the status of colonized peoples within U.S. boundaries. These federal initiatives, however, frequently fell apart in local contexts, where racial status increasingly trumped cultural performances.[43]

Native Americans' local circumstances and experiences varied widely across the nation. Some states did make the disavowal of indigenous customs and affiliations as grounds for granting full citizenship. Michigan's Constitution of 1850, for example, guaranteed "every civilized male inhabitant of Indian descent, a native of the United States and not a member of any tribe," the right to "be an elector and entitled to vote."[44] Thus, the notion of Native Americans' potential for civilization was common enough to be incorporated into certain states' definitions of full citizenship, although it was certainly not consistently respected throughout the United States.

Discrepancies could even appear within the same state. The Massachusetts legislature conducted three investigations into the status of Indians in 1849, 1859, and 1869. It found that treatment, social position, and presumed citizenship status of Native Americans varied based as much on economic status as race.[45] Civic leaders in the town of Carver definitively excluded "Indians not taxed" (including mixed-race families) from citizenship based on their reading of the U.S. Constitution. Yet the nearby town of Pembroke, which had no tax-paying Indians, reported that Native Americans still "enjoy political rights as citizens." Others implicitly argued that all Native Americans were citizens but only in the same sense that children were citizens.[46] For their part many Native American leaders disavowed those who participated in civilization programs or ceded land to Euro-Americans. As Gregory Dowd shows, leaders of Shawnee, Delaware, Creek, and many other tribes drew on shared religious language and traditions in joint efforts to thwart the federal government.[47]

Confusion and inconsistencies in Native Americans' status was not limited to the Northeast. A minority of nineteenth-century Native Americans tested the limits of performing a national American identity in the South. One such experiment occurred under an 1817 treaty signed between 311 Tennessee Cherokee families and the U.S. government. As reward for disavowing their association with former tribes and communities, these Cherokee settlers received 640 acres of land under private ownership and full U.S. citizenship.[48] Federal officials, however, underestimated southern whites' opposition to granting Native Americans equal citizenship. Many southern whites imagined race as an impassable frontier that kept Native Americans from being truly American, no matter what their cultural affiliations may have been.[49] Georgia's governor, George M. Troup, warned that "civilized" Cherokees who participated in the federal programs would, at best, be treated analogously to free blacks in the state, forbidden from voting or otherwise participating in the government.[50] A Georgia congressional delegation echoed these sentiments in 1824 when it condemned the federal government for trying to "fix permanently upon them [the people of Georgia] any persons who are not, and whom she will never suffer to *become*, her citizens."[51]

Setting race as the final criterion for full citizenship had real economic and social consequences. White settlers in Georgia, Tennessee, North Carolina, and Alabama employed legal trickery or outright force to dispossess many Cherokee settlers. Most of the Cherokee participants eventually abandoned any effort to claim U.S. citizenship and reintegrated with their former tribes by 1828.[52] At about the same time, Andrew Jackson's administration shunned previous policies that favored "transforming" Native Americans into full citizens. Although Jacksonian policy makers stopped short of declaring that Native Americans' race would forever preclude them from full citizenship, they did insist that the indigenous population would be insufficiently civilized to exercise such a right for at least another fifty years.[53] This notion of "civilizational infantilism" recalls similar rhetoric used by contemporary imperial powers to justify the exclusion of colonized groups.[54] Much as children were imagined to need time to learn their proper role as citizens, entire societies could be dismissed as "immature" and incapable of rational participation in self-governance. Congress would not grant all Native Americans, regardless of tribal status, full U.S. citizenship until 1924.[55]

Many Euro-Americans thus arrived in northern Mexico in 1821 thinking that racially incompatible Mexicans could only corrupt the American body politic. As much as their own national imaginary constituted the

United States as a white nation, most Euro-Americans would conclude that Mexican national identity signaled status as a degraded "mixed-race" country. Mexicans did not share this view.

Colonial Roots: Race and *Calidad* before Mexican Independence

Mexican philosophers, government leaders, and even average citizens actively debated the meaning of racial difference within Mexico as much as their northern neighbors did. Too often studies of the U.S.-Mexican border have simplistically opposed Euro-American colonizers to the hapless Mexican colonized. Obviously, that story has some truth as the United States did engage in an imperial project that treated New Mexico and other border regions as colonies. Focusing on that story only, how-ever, ignores the reality that Mexican authorities had been grappling with their own forms of imperialism before Euro-Americans arrived. I pro-pose that we acknowledge a "Mexican imperialism" at play in New Mex-ico before the U.S. invasion.

From the perspectives of many Pueblo, Apache, or Diné (Navajo) groups, the Mexican settlers in New Mexico were themselves unwelcome colonizers (or descendants of colonizers).[56] Indeed, many border histo-rians gloss over the fact that the nation-state of Mexico emerged as a self-described empire that later made a rocky transition to a republic.[57] At the time of the U.S.-Mexican War, officials in Mexico City governed New Mexico as a territory, not as an equal state within the nation (much like the United States would govern it after the invasion). It is critical for our understanding of later conflicts between Mexicans and Euro-Americans to acknowledge that Mexican nationalism was entangled with that na-tion's own colonial project to subdue indigenous communities (as well as those comprising inhabitants of African descent) in places like nineteenth-century New Mexico. New Mexico's shifting geography did not transform "innocent settlers" into "victims of imperialism." Rather it marked a shift from one form of imperialism (Mexican) to another (U.S.). What was somewhat unusual in New Mexico was that the previous colonizers, who were the majority of the population, suddenly became the racially colonized.[58]

Both the United States and Mexico excluded certain groups from full citizenship based on the same Enlightenment-based philosophies. Mexi-cans, however, came to understand the meaning of race and nation in somewhat different ways than Euro-Americans did. Native Americans constituted a significantly larger percentage of the overall population in Mexico than they did in the United States. By some estimates, as much as 60 percent of Mexico's 6.1 million residents were indigenous in 1820.[59] Another 10 percent were of African heritage.[60] Excluding that combined percentage of the nation's population based on race would not have been possible. Mexico, therefore, came to depend much more heavily than did the United States on cultural affiliation, itself modulated by economic class and social status, to determine full citizenship.

Before proceeding, we should be careful to understand that racial categories appeared natural, logical, and immutable to most people in nineteenth-century Mexico (as in the United States). Intellectuals, more-over, worked to erase or minimize the presence of Afro-Mexicans in the national imaginary.[61] Gender ideologies further complicated affiliation and nationalism, informing cultural practices that gave particular mean-ing and power to being either a Mexican man or a Mexican woman, whose access and opportunities were more restricted.[62]

In contrast to patterns evident in the mid-nineteenth-century United States, though, Mexican national discourse distinguished civic and racial identities as separate categories. In Mexico one's ability to claim Mexican identity was, to some extent, coterminous with one's legibility in relation to fluid, yet predetermined, racial categories. What perhaps proved more important for any given individual in the claiming of mexicanidad were practices of the everyday, where economic class and social status dic-tated an individual performer's credibility and cultural capital.[63] Almost regardless of race, an individual could perform the set of cultural prac-tices associated with Mexican identity if he (and, to a lesser extent, she) had access to the material resources. This is not to say, of course, that Mexican and New Mexican society eliminated colonial divisions deter-mined by *casta* (caste or race) and *calidad* (social status). Border histo-rians, however, have frequently ignored nineteenth-century discussions about race and nation entirely. Leaping from colonial ideas about race in New Mexico to the development of a "Spanish" identity in the early twentieth century, they have neglected crucial nineteenth-century dis-cussions about nation that occurred at both the local and federal levels.[64] Only recently did Andrés Reséndez lay the groundwork for challenging previous assumptions about Mexican identity in the northern frontier of the nascent Mexican republic.[65] As Reséndez suggests, areas frequently dismissed as peripheral to Mexico City—like Texas, Chihuahua, or New Mexico—did develop their own sense of Mexican national identity even if they lacked an allegiance to a particular government or political faction.[66] Contrary to many historians' expectations, then, independence from Spain did not pass unnoticed, even in a territory "remote beyond compare."[67]

Of course, inhabitants of these outlying territories did not invent their vision of Mexican nationalism ex nihilo. Mexico City frequently asserted the central government's presence in distant areas and contributed to the building of a national identity. Government officials created tangible reminders of federal authority even during (and maybe especially because of) the instabilities of the nineteenth century.[68] To make sense of Mexican national identity, they reconfigured existing paradigms of race and status.

The earliest ideas about race to appear in modern-day New Mexico came with the arrival of Spaniards in the sixteenth and seventeenth centuries.[69] Spain's byzantine system for categorizing and labeling colonial groups developed during hundreds of years of imperial and religious conquest. Known as the Régimen de Castas, it centered on concerns about *limpieza de sangre* (blood purity).[70] By the seventeenth century Spain's imperial authorities had established a hierarchical system of classification that presumed that certain characteristics were inheritable.[71] The racial position of one's parents determined the child's social status. Based on (often invented) family lineages, the colonial casta created labels derived from three official racial archetypes: *español* (pure-blooded Spanish), *indio* (Indian), and *negro* (black).[72] Social rank derived from the alleged proportion of blood an individual possessed from these three groups, as well as one's place of birth. As intermarriage increased throughout the empire, ever more elaborate schematic systems signified status and parentage in excruciating detail. Government regulations, for instance, labeled a child of an español and an india a *mestizo*. The label *castizo* referred to the offspring of a mestizo and an español. If a mestizo and a castiza had a child, that child carried the label *chamisa* and so on.[73]

Significantly, colonial officials imagined that indio "blood" could eventually be minimized after several generations. An individual who was only one-eighth indigenous (a child, for instance, of a castiza and an español) was considered an español.[74] Racial traits of Spaniards, they believed, prevailed and permitted these "mixed" individuals into the ruling colonial society.[75] This same mathematical formula, however, did not apply to black descendants.[76] Rather than an español, the comparable one-eighth configuration of black-to-Spanish blood produced a supposedly degraded and unhealthy *albino*.[77] Indian blood in Spanish colonial

imagination, therefore, appeared more mutable ("redeemable" by Spaniards' standards) than black blood.[78]

At the same time, the casta system included elements other than race.
Economic class, cultural markers, and stylized acts were critical in naming the social position of individuals or groups.[79] Those indios who
modeled elements of Spanish identity were classified as the *gente de
razón* (people of reason).[80] Refusal to adopt these roles earned groups the
label *gente sin razón* (people without reason). Heirs to Renaissance notions of "civilization" and "savagery," Spanish (and later Mexican) colonial
authorities also grouped together racialized populations based on their
supposed integration into the empire. Of particular interest for New
Mexico was the creation by Spanish authorities of entirely separate judicial and administrative institutions for the indigenous population.[81]
"Pure" Indians were organized as a separate republic within the empire,
requiring spatial segregation and different bureaucratic apparatuses than
other settlers required. In New Mexico at least twenty distinct communities were collapsed into a single category of *Indios de pueblo* (Pueblo
Indians) under Spanish administration.[82]

Individual Pueblo settlements were spread along the Rio Grande and
what would become western New Mexico and eastern Arizona.[83] Four
different language groups—Tewa, Tiwa, Keresan, and Towa—traverse
the mostly sedentary Pueblo communities. Moreover, since all of the
individual Pueblos had been in constant contact and trade, they developed shared religious practices and traditions.[84] Spaniards distinguished
the Pueblos, who were centrally involved with the colonial settlements
and attempts at religious conversion, from groups of Apaches, Comanches, and Diné (Navajos) who kept themselves on the periphery of the
imperial project (and sometimes attacked such settlements).[85]

Spain's colonial officials argued that all Indians needed distinct paternalistic institutions because they were less rational and could not participate in the empire in the same ways as whites.[86] Moreover, Indian Catholics, like Jews who converted, fell into an irregularly permanent category
of "new" Christians regardless of how many generations previously their
ancestors had converted. This status worked in conjunction with the
religious basis of blood purity to keep Indians in a subjugated position
perpetually.[87]

Spanish colonial law labeled a detribalized indio who adopted cultural
markers that matched the *gente de razón* as an *genízaro*, a label signifying
indigenous persons who spoke Spanish, swore allegiance to Spain, traded
within imperial economic networks, wore Spanish clothing, and ob-

served Catholic practices.[88] In New Mexico, though, genízaros lacked the protection that Pueblo villages or nomadic communities provided. They likewise did not have the same civil status as those deemed español and often worked as near-slaves. Spanish law still regarded genízaros as racially indio and therefore "inferior," but it reserved for them a slightly higher status than their less-assimilated counterparts.

Spain's emphasis on stylized *acts* organized the distinctions between the gente de razón and the gente sin razón, an emphasis that opened up exploitable ambiguities within the casta system.[89] Despite the elaborate and exacting racial categories based on lineage that dominated urban life, in rural or remote areas the casta ranking system showed some flexibility based on appearance, economic status, and cultural markers. Individuals were more clearly drawn or pushed to the three racial touchstones of español, indio, and negro or an ill-defined "mixed" group.[90] Calidad and racial status became greatly intertwined in the eighteenth century.[91] Civil officials recorded a person's race based on a mixture of appearance and self-reporting.[92] Therefore, assigning an individual to a particular racialized category went beyond assessing skin color or documenting a family tree. The determination of one's racial status also included clothing, hairstyles, religious participation, occupation, and so forth.[93] Sometimes the historical record reveals individuals' conscious efforts to remake their cultural appearance to match their desired social position. María Francesca, a Cochiti Indian, murdered her husband for failing to give her proper "Spanish" clothing.[94] In this episode María Francesca placed a profound emphasis on *appearing* as a Spaniard when she left Cochiti.

Again in contrast to the trends prevailing in the nineteenth-century United States, chances for the transgression of racial boundaries multiplied during the same period in Mexico. In the more remote areas along the northern frontier, only incompletely governed by imperial authority, an emphasis on *seeming* like a member of the imperial community opened up opportunities for the discreet movement across racial categories. This is not to say that changing one's casta was easy, however. Quite the contrary. Gonzalo Aguirre Beltrán points out that there was considerable social surveillance and policing of passing.[95] Many nonetheless maneuvered to alter their government classification when the chance appeared given the material benefits that accrued to those categorized as closer to white/pure Spaniard. Some who started with the label of "indio" or "mulatto" eventually declared themselves "mestizos." Likewise, those whom Spain labeled "mestizos" reported themselves as "españoles." In other instances, service in the military provided a means for improving one's social and racial position.[96]

By the end of Mexico's War for Independence in 1821, an emphasis on performing calidad had substantially eroded the older complexity of caste classifications across the northern frontier.[97] Eventually the elaborate colonial casta system collapsed into a sharp distinction between españoles and indios.[98] In 1820 an official New Mexican census labeled any settler not clearly living, dressing, or identifying with a Pueblo community as an español (also often referred to as a *vecino*).[99] Paradoxically, the demise of the larger number of caste categories only increased the emphasis on other attributes, like parish membership, religious traditions, languages, and participation in the government.[100]

Postindependence Mexico simultaneously borrowed and refuted various aspects of the surviving colonial racial ideologies in crafting a national identity. Nineteenth-century notions of a liberal state hinged on the supposition that a single people formed and participated in a democratic state.[101] Despite the many regime changes in the central government, officials consistently worked to unite the country across existing racial and geographic lines—even in remote areas like New Mexico.

Making the "Mexican Family": Race, Nation, and Performance in Mexican National Identity, 1821–1846

Government leaders, as Andrés Reséndez notes, produced and circulated countless material representations of Mexico as a nation immediately after independence. They adopted commonly acknowledged symbols of nation-states that reached the far edges of the country: flags, coins, medals, and seals, each symbolically defined Mexico as a distinct entity.[102] In conjunction with these symbols the same leaders also emphasized certain rituals as a demonstration of nationalism. Public celebrations of the birth and death of war heroes and Independence Day festivities were the most obvious that occurred throughout Mexico.[103] When one acquired a land grant, the government required that the grantee shout, "Long live the president and the Mexican nation," before taking title to the land.[104] In these small ways leaders in Mexico City expected citizens far removed from the center to act out Mexican patriotism.

This fragile, new sense of Mexican national identity coexisted uncomfortably with already established racial categories. Independence leaders had opposed the inequity of the casta system to appeal to people of color during the fight to oust Spanish rule.[105] Following the war, some national leaders obligingly claimed the casta system's final collapse. In 1821, when Agustín de Iturbide issued his Plan de Iguala, a document not generally associated with revolutionary changes, he proclaimed, "Todos los habitantes de la Nueva España, sin distinción alguno de europeos, africanos ni indios, son ciudadanos de esta monarquía con opción a todo empleo, según su mérito y virtudes" (All the habitants of New Spain, without distinction of Europeans, Africans, or Indians are citizens of this monarchy with the option to any employment, according to his merit and virtues).[106] Only a year later, the federal government expressly forbade the identification of persons according to race.[107]

Despite its official exorcism, race stubbornly reappeared in public debates over the succeeding decades.[108] Social and economic practices upheld the polar divide between Indians and whites, especially if the former fought against encroachments on their lands (often referred to as "indios errants").[109] Officials in Mexico City and elsewhere recognized they could not eliminate ideas about racial difference by simply outlawing the use of racial categories. To describe the complicated relationship between race and nation, officials defined a racially inclusive "Mexican family" as a popular metaphor for national identity.

The governor of Chihuahua used this metaphor in typical fashion in 1841. In a proclamation to his citizens he wrote, "All the children of this great nation form but one family, and . . . this family has sworn to be free and sovereign."[110] The family metaphor worked particularly well during this transitional and uncertain period. Family suggested a harmonious collection of distinct individuals or groups linked together into the larger identity of the nation. Mestizos, indios, and españoles were therefore all imagined to be separate members of the same family (and sometimes they literally were members of the same family). Claiming Mexicanness did not necessarily imply the preeminence or exclusion of any one of these racial categories.

Eradicating the caste practices that kept racialized subjects in inequitable positions, however, proved much more complicated than revising the laws.[111] Notions of race had been too deeply ingrained to be easily displaced in favor of a universal mexicanidad. Local officials merged the older colonial opposition between gente sin razón and gente de razón with newer nineteenth-century notions of a liberal nation-state, a mixture of ideas that resulted in official distinctions based on one's actions and associations.[112] Mexican identity could include multiple racial groups, but those groups had to exhibit certain cultural markers, typically speaking Spanish and participating in Catholicism.[113]

In the northern frontier Mexican officials distinguished between Pueblos and other indigenous groups, like the Apaches or Diné, based on their cultural and political associations. In short, race never lost its salience in Mexico, but it was displaced from its position as a defining element of Mexican national identity. Pueblo Indians, unlike most Apaches or Navajos, served with their fellow citizens in the militia, paid their taxes, and maintained their own municipal governments, all gestures that enabled them to claim full Mexican citizenship.[114] In 1825 a member of New Mexico's legislature declared to the Pecos Pueblo that they were "equal, one to the other, to all the other citizens who with them form the great Mexican family."[115] Pueblo Indians actively claimed a Mexican identity, as well. During this time members of the Pecos Pueblo defended their landownership based on their "rights as citizens."[116]

Concerned that the Pueblos could unite and violently overthrow the territorial government, many local and federal officials prioritized the incorporation of New Mexico's Pueblos into the nation.[117] As a result Mexican federal authorities created propaganda campaigns geared just to those communities.[118] This is not to say that the Pueblos' inclusion into the "Mexican family" came with total civic equality. The family metaphor that kept racial groups as separate social sectors included patriarchal assumptions. Indians became the "children" within that family.[119] New Mexico's assemblymen distinguished the Pueblos from their "non-Indian" neighbors through labels such as *hijos* or *naturales*, despite the Pueblos' integral role in the local economy and society.[120]

Government authorities were even more uncertain about the citizenship status of Indians who refused to *act* like Mexicans.[121] Unlike most Pueblo communities, most Diné and Apache communities, formerly characterized as the gente sin razón, refused to adopt the nascent national identity.[122] They also refused to accept the authority of the state. New Mexico governor Manuel Armijo attempted to entice Navajos into signing a peace treaty by offering to make them all naturalized Mexican citizens in 1839 (based on similar reasoning as the 1817 Cherokee treaty in the United States).[123] Armijo did not acknowledge or understand that Mexican law already guaranteed citizenship as a birthright of the Navajo tribes. His offer to naturalize Navajos as citizens, however, made sense within the context of Mexican identity. Navajos, in Armijo's mind, would *become* Mexican symbolically and legally by ending their war with federal forces and incorporating themselves into the national community. This

vision of Mexican national identity permitted Armijo to consider Navajos a racialized other and still imagine a process through which they
could gain a civic Mexican identity.

Assimilation to Mexican cultural attributes became a commonly discussed solution for the problem of continuing racial enmity. Antonio
José Martínez, a priest in New Mexico, argued that the "naciones bárbaras" could learn to be Mexican by integrating themselves into existing
communities.[124] Martínez deemed growing crops, producing marketable
goods, and raising livestock the most salient actions for claiming a Mexican national identity. Most significant, he advocated these culturally
defined performances as a means to transcend racial categories. Prioritizing cultural practices over racial lineages meant that "civilized" persons could also secure adoption into the Mexican national family.

Consistent with their own imagining of their national community,
Mexico's high-ranking leaders registered little objection to allowing
Americans to become Mexican. One Euro-American, James Baird, for
instance, arrived in New Mexico in 1812 and eventually became a Mexican citizen in order to advance his fur-trading enterprise. Baird understood and participated in the Mexican discourse on citizenship. By 1826
the trapper fully identified himself as Mexican in local documents and
expressed this identity as a "bounden duty."[125] Baird even appealed to
Mexico City to establish laws excluding Americans from trading in Mexico. He claimed Mexico needed such legislation so that "we Mexicans
may peacefully profit by the good with which the merciful God has been
pleased to enrich our soil."[126] Baird's sense of a unified Mexican identity
did not necessarily imply a claim to a particular racial identity (as Mexican identity would under Euro-American discourse) or threaten his own
sense of self as white. Sometimes Mexican officials even enticed Euro-
Americans to become Mexican.[127]

The Limits and Strengths of Mexican Nationalism:
The 1837 Chimayó Rebellion

As I mentioned in my introduction, some historians dispute that New
Mexico participated in the development of Mexican nationalism at all.[128]
Skeptics about the depth of Mexican nationalism in New Mexico point to
the Chimayó Rebellion (1837) as evidence that the far northern territories lacked integration with the larger nation. This assessment, though,
presumes that rebellion against the ruling government equaled a disen-

gagement from the national imaginary. Scrutinizing the rhetoric of the Chimayó Rebellion actually reveals that northern Mexicans considered themselves entirely vested in the direction of the nation. We can see that territorial actors, both Pueblo Indians and vecinos, adapted circulating notions of Mexican nationalism for their local purposes. Far from "being dimly aware" of power struggles in Mexico City, Mexicans took up arms in New Mexico precisely because of those national conflicts.

Less than a decade after independence, Mexico became bitterly divided between two political factions that traded power during the 1830s: Federalists, who worked to limit the power of the Church and the military, and Centralists, who attempted to concentrate all state power in Mexico City by undermining elected state legislatures and governors' powers.[129] By 1835 the Centralists had taken control of the Congress, and they found President Antonio de Padua María Severino López de Santa Anna sympathetic to their ambitions. On December 29, 1836, Santa Anna abolished the 1824 Constitution, replacing it with the "Siete Leyes" (Seven Laws, also known as the "Departmental Plan"), essentially disbanding elected state governments. Revolt against the Centralists spread across the nation, engulfing Zacatecas, Sonora, Sinaloa, Tamaulipas, Yucatán, Coahuila y Texas, Alta California, and New Mexico.[130]

The latter Chimayó Rebellion was sparked by dissatisfaction with New Mexico's Centralist governor, Albino Pérez. Santa Anna had appointed Pérez in 1835 to increase tax collection and to assert a centralized style of political control over the territory. For their part most Mexicans in New Mexico viewed Pérez's administration as riddled with corruption. The governor's expensive tastes and indulgence in luxuries, like extravagant velvet costumes and hot chocolate, alienated him from the modest citizens around him.[131] Hated as the personification of Centralists' dictatorial attitude toward states and territories, he was executed and his head paraded on a pike through Santa Fe in 1837.[132] About twenty of his officials also lost their lives during the rebellion.

Mexicans across the nation wondered about the meaning and cause of these assassinations in New Mexico. Outside of the territory fevered speculation drew parallels between the Chimayó Rebellion and Texas's simultaneous quest for secession.[133] The language used during the actual Chimayó Rebellion, however, suggests a more complicated understanding of the rebels' relationship to the rest of Mexico.

The revolt represented a protest against the territory's existing relationship to the national government, not a desire for independence or absorption into the United States. Significantly, the revolt united both vecinos and disgruntled Pueblo Indians. Explanations for Pérez's assassination among vecinos centered on his implementation of the Centralist system of direct tax and undermining of local political authority.[134] Wild rumors circulated that families would have to pay amounts equivalent to half their property. According to a witness, many citizens grew angry over the taxes, "which they supposed were used only in sustaining the luxury and waste of a few individuals in Santa Fe."[135] New Mexico's elite also understood that the Department Plan would curtail their own municipal authority. Not only did the plan call for replacing state legislatures and governors, but it also replaced New Mexico's elected officials with prefects who answered directly to the appointed governor. This change would have greatly altered New Mexico's internal political dynamics by bypassing the territory's leading families.[136] The majority of rebels sought to rid the nation of Centralists, starting in New Mexico.

Pueblo Indians resented the militia system that the Mexican government had long imposed on them. Pérez increased this resentment when he conscripted Pueblos for four major campaigns against Diné raiders.[137] Centralists had also curtailed Pueblo self-government and permitted settlers to increasingly encroach on their traditional lands. The rebellion showed more than a little animus to the central government by the people in New Mexico, including the native populations.

The rebel rallying cry, however, was "Cantón" (translated as territory or district of the nation). This checked the revolutionary imagination within the movement by upholding the geography of New Mexico as a subsection of Mexico.[138] The Chimayó rebels were more reactionary than revolutionary. In their opening declaration they employed the language of national unity, rather than division or independence, objecting to direct taxes and the Departmental Plan. The document reiterated their commitment to Mexico several times, emphasizing that they were fighting for "God and Nation and the Faith of Jesus Christ." As this implies, most of the rebels saw themselves as reformers of Mexico, not as the founders of a new nation or as Americans.[139] From their perspective the Centralists had illegitimately subverted Mexican law. Rebelling against Pérez, they argued, was an action that defined them as patriotic Mexican citizens, not revolutionaries.

We can think of both vecino and indigenous rebels embarking on a "strategic nationalism" (playing off Gayatri Spivak's notion of "strategic essentialism").[140] Mexican nationalism permitted an expediency to rebels as they mobilized vecinos and Pueblos in the fight against Centralists. Because Mexican nationalism had racial flexibility, it did not need to

t the rebels imagined themselves as racially one people or as
nared consciousness. Nationalism could encompass disparate
uses unique to New Mexico. Pueblo Indians could use slightly
...erent language or associations than vecinos and still fall under the
umbrella of Mexican nationalism. Locally vested interests used their
notions of nationalism to restore their own authority. We will see a
similar strategic nationalism employed in the Taos 1847 revolt against
the United States.

As it turned out, the Chimayó Rebellion lasted only a few weeks. The
rebels created a temporary government and appointed their own governor, the hapless José Gonzales.[141] Almost immediately, the usurper governor made serious miscalculations.[142] He extended feelers to various
non-Mexican citizens to join him in offering New Mexico to the United
States but found only rebuff. Such an idea did not please most Mexicans,
for whom the plan to annex New Mexico to the United States could only
register as a betrayal of their ideals.[143] Gonzales arranged instead to send
a message to Mexico City to "express the entire obedience of the Department to the Supreme Government."[144]

Having rejected independence and U.S. annexation, New Mexico's
population became divided on how to resolve the crisis. In Taos and
other parts of northern New Mexico the rebels repudiated Gonzales's
authority and began a reign of terror. Pablo Montoya, who once served as
alcalde of Taos, emerged as the primary leader in Río Arriba, imprisoning
anybody who he believed had been sympathetic to Pérez.[145] Counter-
forces, meanwhile, began to coalesce in the center of the territory. The
rebellion exacerbated non-Indian Mexicans' anxieties about the possibility of permanent Pueblo revolt.[146] Quashing the Pueblo dissenters unified
a number of competing factions, still under the rubric of Mexican nationalism. They drafted their own resolution, known as the Plan of Tomé,
on September 8, 1837. In it they claimed to "love their country and favor
the constitution and the laws, and . . . fear the anarchy and abuse of
property threatened by the Cantón of La Cañada."[147] Manuel Armijo, a
lieutenant in the Albuquerque militia, took command of this new army
and began acquiring supplies and building forces to combat the rebels.
Narrowly avoiding prolonged bloodshed, the rebels agreed to a treaty.
On September 21, 1837, Armijo became the political and military leader
of the territory until Mexico City appointed an official governor. Montoya and the others also agreed to turn four of the rebel leaders over to
the authorities so that they could face trial. In exchange Montoya received a pardon and returned to Taos.[148]

As individuals came to terms with being Mexican citizens, they adapted elements of the larger national discourse to their local circumstances. Even remote areas, like New Mexico, actively debated the meaning of the new nation. Sometimes these disputes turned bloody, as in the case of the Chimayó Rebellion. This, though, did not mean that they stopped imagining themselves as "Mexicans."

In Mexico the ability to claim a Mexican identity was based on practices and status more than on racial categories. As I have already noted, this is not to say that Mexican society eliminated colonial divisions determined by *casta* and *calidad*; however, proponents hoped that the development of a postcolonial national Mexican identity would transcend these categories. Indeed, even in the bloody Chimayó Rebellion, Pueblo Indians and other citizens made tenuous allegiances under the claim of being patriotic Mexican citizens. Most of Mexico's citizens imagined that Mexican identity neither excluded nor implied a particular racial identity. Mexicans had probably not anticipated that Euro-Americans would ignore the racial complexity of Mexico in favor of their own assumptions.

Euro-American Imaginings
of the Mexican Racial Other, 1821–1850

Euro-Americans started arriving in New Mexico in 1821. Overwhelmingly, Euro-Americans rejected any distinction between Mexicans as citizens of another nation and Mexicans as a distinct racial group. Unlike most Mexicans, who defined Mexican identity by one's actions, associations, and location, most Euro-Americans imagined Mexicanness as an immutable ontological state, a distinctive category of mixed ancestry. They scrutinized individual Mexican bodies for telltale physical characteristics and cultural mannerisms. The term *Mexican* automatically signaled a "mestizo" or an individual whose parentage reflected both European and Indian elements.[149] One veteran of the U.S.-Mexico War, W. W. H. Davis, catalogued the perceived intermixture that he thought produced the Mexican people. "Here was a second blending of blood and a new union of races," he wrote; "the Spaniard, the Moor, and the aboriginal were united and made a new race, the Mexicans."[150] He further informed his readers that the intermixing continued to occur and that "there is no present hope of the people improving in color."[151] Their "color" meant Mexicans were necessarily morally and physically weak compared with the supposedly superior Euro-American traders.

Even before the Treaty of Guadalupe Hidalgo, Euro-Americans circulated a literature that made the frontier between the United States and Mexico a racially charged divide.[152] Distinguishing Mexicans as a racial group afforded Euro-Americans an inverted mirror in which they could assert their own sense of national and racial identity as superior. If Euro-Americans were "pure whites," then Mexicans must be "mongrels"; if Euro-Americans were industrious, then Mexicans must be lazy; if Euro-Americans were rational Protestants, then Mexicans must be superstitious Catholics.[153]

The period of the Santa Fe Trail (1821–46) produced sensational tales encapsulating such images. These rapidly produced texts, often serialized in newspapers, offered the most readily available information on Mexicans in the United States to eager American readers. Collectively, they created an image of the "Mexican" as a distinct form of being that was both interchangeable (one Mexican was indistinguishable from any others) and immutable (Mexicans could never stop being Mexican). It was an unconscious reversal of the Mexican discourse that identified deliberate cultural practice as the cornerstone of Mexican nationalism. Euro-Americans imagined that the performance of cultural markers resulted from an innate Mexican identity created by racial "amalgamation."

In 1844 Josiah Gregg released *Commerce of the Prairies*, which became one of the most prominent Euro-American narratives of northern Mexico. Recounting his experiences in New Mexico, Gregg explicitly defined Mexicans' racial origins as the "intermixing blood."[154] Even as he acknowledged that a wide range of skin complexions existed among the Mexicans in northern Mexico, he concluded that those deemed "fair" still had the visible "darkness" of the racial Other. Gregg wrote: "Their darkness has resulted partly from their original Moorish blood, but more from intermarriages with the aborigines. . . . The present race of New Mexicans has thus become an amalgam, averaging about equal parts of the European and aboriginal blood . . . [and] the tawny complexion pervades all classes—the rich as the poor."[155] Gregg emphasized that a racial difference between Mexicans and Euro-Americans pervaded all social and economic classes. In colonial contexts, as Stuart Hall reminds us, skin color functioned as "the most visible, the most manifest and hence the handiest way of identifying the different social groups."[156] Imagining Mexicanness as visible in skin pigmentation highlighted the immutability that Euro-Americans like Gregg assigned to that identity.

A common narrative pattern emerged to persuade American readers of the validity of their claims. Typically, a Euro-American author started his story by proclaiming his own "shock" on realizing the racial difference between Euro-Americans and Mexicans.[157] This literary tactic blurred the boundaries between the author and reader by creating a common emotional response to Mexicans. The author would reflect on his own (and the implied readers') initial naive belief that he would find no distinction between Euro-Americans and Mexicans. After the narrative established that the difference was "real," the author would list a long litany of dissimilarities he observed between Euro-Americans and Mexicans. Far from construing these as cultural, Euro-Americans portrayed the supposed differences as natural elements of Mexicans' racial character. The authors even attributed Mexicans' cultural expressions, like Catholic religious rituals or agricultural practices, to predispositions created by racial intermixing. Being Mexican, in all aspects, derived from one's body and therefore was unchangeable.[158]

In one such account a Kentucky traveler, James O. Pattie, dissuaded Euro-Americans from assuming any commonality with Mexicans in New Mexico. Telling his narrative in the first-person, Pattie recounted his own supposed shock in 1831 when he first observed "proof" of racial difference between Euro-Americans and Mexicans in New Mexico. The author recalled his first stop in New Mexico: "On the evening of the 26th, we arrived at a small town in Tous, called St. Ferdinando [San Fernando de Taos]. . . . The alcaide [*sic*] . . . was a man of a swarthy complexion having the appearance of pride and haughtiness. The door-way of the room . . . was crowded with men, women and children, who stared at us, as though they had never seen white men before. . . . I had expected to find no difference between these people and our own, but their language. I was never so mistaken."[159] Pattie's shock at encountering Mexicans for the first time served to emphasize their status as "not white." Readers might have been in danger of also expecting "to find no difference" between themselves and Mexicans. Pattie corrected any such ideas by highlighting his own mistakenness. He created signifiers of difference between whites and Mexicans, like the latter's "swarthy" complexion and "haughtiness."[160]

Many Euro-American writers took the additional step of arguing that the racial disparity demanded that whites take control of the newly independent Mexico. If they did so, many argued, then whites would naturally outproduce Mexicans if they controlled Mexican land because of the imagined superiority of white bodies.[161] Thomas J. Farnham printed such a vision of Euro-American superiority in his description of California. "The law of Nature, which curses the mulatto here with a constitution less robust than that of either race from which he sprang," he wrote, "lays a similar penalty upon the mingling of the Indian and white races in California and Mexico. They must fade away."[162]

It is important to remember that this was not just a U.S. discussion about race and Mexico. Far from exclusive to North America, these Euro-American narratives constituted one node within an emerging *global* discourse that configured all of Latin America's racial, social, and economic relationships to Europe and the United States. British, French, and (Euro-)American travelers published contemporaneous accounts (often in dialogue with each other) of their visits to Mexico, Peru, Argentina, and other fledgling nations emerging from Spanish colonialism. These tales depicted Latin American societies and people as backward, indolent, and unproductive because of their race.[163] They therefore needed (even demanded) European and Euro-American capitalism and ingenuity to transform those places into truly productive lands.[164]

Fully consistent with this racial essentialism, Euro-Americans did not often propose changing behaviors as a means by which to incorporate Mexicans into the United States. Imagining that as a possibility would have drawn into question the validity of casting Mexicans as a distinct racial type. The U.S. Senate recorded a European medical doctor's observations from his travels through New Mexico and Chihuahua; his observations gave scientific credence to such ideas. Even if the United States "raised [Mexicans] from an ignorant and oppressed condition to the level of republican citizens," the doctor argued, they "could not be as easily assimilated to the republic as a similar number of European immigrants."[165] Like many Euro-Americans, this doctor believed that one's racial status as Mexican would forever prevent him or her from becoming American even if his or her behaviors changed. In another section he noted that even years after local citizens had reconciled themselves to the U.S. government, they would be "Mexican still."[166] To preserve U.S. racial superiority, the doctor recommended that the United States acquire only those territories that had the fewest Mexicans.

Imagining the possibility that Mexicans could become Americans would have undermined Euro-Americans' justification for their imperialism. Most Euro-Americans did not believe that Mexican identity was the performing of (mostly negative) traits. Mexican identity was the embodiment of those negative traits that were expressed through their actions. A Mexican, under this vision, might change location, language, or citizenship but would always *be* Mexican.

New Mexico Invaded: The Impossibility
of Making Mexicans into Americans

Individuals throughout Mexico understood that a disparity existed between Euro-American and Mexican ideas about race and nation. The
first Mexican minister in Washington warned his superiors in Mexico
City as early as 1822 that Americans thought of Mexicans as racially
inferior.[167] Knowledge of this racism prompted ominous warnings about
Euro-American imperialism. An 1839 edition of Chihuahua's *La Luna*,
for instance, predicted that an invasion by the United States would result
in Mexicans' being "sold as beasts" because "their color was not as white
as that of their conquerors."[168] In 1841 the governor of Chihuahua, Pedro
García Condé, received word that Euro-American Texans planned an
invasion of New Mexico and Chihuahua. Issuing a proclamation on July
28, Condé incited his citizens to defend New Mexico and their state. The
invading Euro-Americans, he warned, used their understanding of a
racial hierarchy to justify the enslavement of "those who are not white."
He posed a question: "Do you know who the Texans are? They are
adventurers who despise you as barbarians, weak minded and corrupt
men. They blaspheme your religion and scoff at your pious customs . . .
men who distinguish their fellow men by the color of their faces in order
to impress the stamp of slavery on those who are not white. . . . Their
design is . . . to invade this Department; they approach your frontiers to
despoil and enslave you."[169]

While the governor warned of Euro-American violence and racism, he
also tapped into the circulating ideas about Mexican identity. Condé
believed that he could recruit soldiers by claiming that a distinct difference existed between Mexico and Texas. He contrasted the Mexican
central state's view of citizenship with the Texans' use of color as a
defining characteristic for national identity. Mexico, he argued, depended on men's actions to define their citizenship. Conveniently, he
offered such an opportunity to prove one's Mexicanness by suggesting
that citizens of all races take up arms against the Texans.[170]

Much like Condé, the Durango governor, Marcelino Castañeda, issued
a directive calling for financial and military contributions to the war effort
in 1846. Castañeda called the war a "cuestión de vida ó de muerte" (a
question of life or death) because "no se trata solamente de usurparle su
territorio sino de suplantar en el otra raza, sea exterminando la hispano-
americana, se reduciéndola al estado humillante de extranjera en su pro-

pietaria" (it is not only a question of usurping territory but of supplanting another race, the exterminating of the Hispano-American, and diminishing the state to the humiliation of foreign ownership).[171] He further scorned the idea that the nation would not unite against the United States based on a sense of national duty.[172] Without citizens' active participation in the financing and defense of the nation, the governor predicted that future generations would revile Mexico for having failed to become a nation. In this way he linked citizens' public actions with the creation and continuation of Mexico as a nation-state.

It is not surprising that the U.S. invasion of New Mexico resulted in grief and consternation.[173] Unhappiness among the Mexican population was clearly evident in the first weeks after Kearny's arrival. Many Mexican residents were apparently shedding tears in the streets of occupied Santa Fe.[174] The acting governor, Juan Bautista Vigil y Alarid, addressed the issue in a letter to the U.S. military commander. The nervous governor swore his allegiance to the United States and attempted to discount the obvious resentment directed toward the military. The governor's overeager assurances suggest that more was at play than he was willing to admit.[175] Indeed, Vigil y Alarid, despite pledging loyalty to the invaders, would be among the first Mexicans who migrated south of the new borderline to escape the United States shortly thereafter.[176]

Only a month after the U.S. invasion of New Mexico, 104 Mexicans signed and dispatched a report to Mexico's president detailing the failure of the Mexican governor, Manuel Armijo, to defend the territory. The U.S. victory hinged on Armijo's desertion, they stated, not on New Mexico settlers' desire to join their northern neighbor. These Mexicans testified to the territory's sense of Mexican nationalism and vowed that "without doubt [they] would have fought the invaders, firing at them day and night."[177] They ended by noting that they continued to imagine themselves as part of the larger Mexican nation. "At no time may it be believed," they wrote, "that we have been a disgrace to the Mexican nation, with which we are bound by so many ties."

Kearny, seemingly unaware of such Mexicans' bitterness, believed that he had handily secured New Mexico. On September 27, the day after Mexicans dispatched their report to Mexico City, Kearny appointed Charles Bent the first U.S. territorial governor. Bent had a long-standing reputation as a merchant in New Mexico but had also garnered some prominent enemies, such as the Taos priest Antonio Martínez.[178] In addition to Bent the U.S. military commander also installed prominent

Mexicans in government positions, such as Donaciano Vigil as secretary and Manuel Otero as judge, to ease the transition.[179] Kearny informed his commanding officer that he had "made the necessary Military arrangements for maintaining the perfect order, peace & quiet, now so happily existing."[180] He confidently rode off to Alta California, leaving little more than two companies of dragoons to keep New Mexico pacified.

Kearny and Bent woefully underestimated Mexican hostility to the U.S. invasion. With trade routes disrupted, New Mexico's key source of income and supplies had been cut off. The occupation left food and other necessities in short supply. Moreover, many Mexicans in the territory felt aligned to the Mexican republic, not the United States. "It seems a general mistake has been made by all that were acquainted with the *gente* of this Territory," a Euro-American trapper wrote nervously in January 1847; "in regard to their willingness to be subject to the rule of the United States . . . not one in ten is *a gusto.*"[181] Less than a month after Kearny departed, the threat of insurrection prompted the U.S. Army to place Santa Fe under martial law. The first tangible evidence of such a conspiracy started on December 12, the Feast Day of the Virgin of Guadalupe, Mexico's key religious and national icon.[182] Rebel leaders asked Santa Fe residents to pledge their fidelity to Mexico before a cross. In doing so, these Mexicans committed themselves to rising up against the invaders on December 19.[183] At the end of December Bent reported to Washington that he had foiled the anti-U.S. plan.[184]

The initial invasion, which had seemed like a simple triumph to the Euro-American invaders, suddenly appeared less settled. At the end of 1846 Bent closed his letter uneasily, noting that the United States needed to maintain "here, for several years to come, an efficient military force" to prevent Mexican rebellion.[185] Despite this warning, Bent believed himself personally immune from attack. Having spent almost twenty years in the territory, he fantasized that both Pueblo Indians and Mexicans would see him as their ally. Bent, who had built a home in Taos, traveled there without a military escort on a winter weekend in 1847. The supplanted governor seriously misjudged the situation.

Before he even reached his home, Taos Pueblo Indians stopped the governor in the middle of the trail and requested the release of tribesmen who were being held in the territory's jail. Bent refused, pushed through the crowd, and went on with his journey, seemingly unconcerned about the growing animosity that surrounded him.[186] He did not know that the Mexican nationals Pablo Montoya (who had led Cantón forces in the

Chimayó Rebellion) and Manuel Cortés had joined with the Taos Pueblo leader "Tomasito" (also known as Tomás Romero) in a plan to crush U.S. authority.[187]

On January 18, 1847, two thousand Mexicans and Pueblo Indians formed an alliance with a common goal: to restore the territory to the Mexican republic.[188] Early in the morning of January 19 these self-proclaimed Mexican nationalists broke down the door to the governor's private residence and murdered him. To assure the populace that the governor was truly dead, the cadre of Mexicans and Pueblo Indians severed his head and paraded it through the Taos plaza.[189]

The rebellion quickly spread to neighboring Mora (Cortés's home), La Cañada, and Arroyo Hondo, where Mexicans destroyed a Euro-American mill and distillery.[190] Assassins violently attacked dozens of Europeans, Euro-Americans, and their Mexican allies. Any person whom the rebels perceived as faithful to the United States faced gruesome recompense for New Mexico's invasion. One American soldier reported seeing a victim "stripped naked, scalped alive, and his eyes punched out: he was groping his way through the streets, beseeching someone to shoot him out of his misery, while his inhuman Mexican tormentors were deriving the greatest amusement from the exhibition."[191] Such reports might have been exaggerated to satisfy Euro-American expectations of Mexican and Indian "savagery,"[192] yet the level of deadly violence clearly suggests that these Mexicans and Pueblo Indians were not by any means reconciled to the U.S. invasion.

The U.S. military, en route to Taos, battled insurgents between January 20 and February 3, when the troops finally arrived at the scene of the revolt. Mexican and Pueblo rebels had fortified themselves within the community church as a place of last retreat. The U.S. Army laid siege to Taos throughout the evening. By morning, 150 Mexicans and Pueblos were killed, and Taos was occupied by the U.S. military.[193]

Once the occupying forces quashed the rebellion, territorial officials charged a number of Mexicans with treason and executed them. The attorney general of the United States, however, sent an opinion on the case the following summer. He noted that it had not been proper to charge Mexicans with treason since he did not acknowledge them as full U.S. citizens. "The territory conquered by our arms does not become, by the mere act of conquest," he wrote, "a permanent part of the United States, and the inhabitants of such territory are not, to the full extent of the term, citizens of the United States."[194] Consequently, the attorney general advised that "it is not the proper use of legal terms to say that their offences was [sic] treason committed against the United States." This is not to say that he disputed the end result. He fully endorsed the Mexicans' execution, explaining they would have been easily convicted for murder or conspiracy. Through such legal theorizing, many Euro-Americans expressed uncertainty about Mexicans' inclusion in the national community, even posthumously.

Despite the bloody resolution at Taos, fighting continued for months in northern New Mexico. Colonel Sterling Price, the territory's military commander, was forced to acknowledge that the "opinion that the New Mexicans are favorably inclined to the United States Government is entirely erroneous."[195] Cortés, along with several hundred followers from the Taos uprising, again surprised Euro-Americans by making more cross-racial alliances with Comanche and Kiowa Apache Indians.[196] Caravans along the Santa Fe Trail fell to dozens of attacks by these elusive forces. In June and July 1847 survivors testified that Comanches and "renegade Mexicans" had ambushed them.[197] Rumors circulated that Governor Angel Trías of Chihuahua had commissioned Cortés as a captain in the Mexican Army to restore the territory to Mexico. Whether true or not, Cortés's cross-racial guerrilla campaign lasted until a decisive battle forced him to retreat to Chihuahua in March 1848.[198] Agents sent to clean up Cortés's camp after his withdrawal reportedly found a stash of propaganda that celebrated the Taos rebels as "true patriots of the Mexican nation."[199]

Histories of the U.S.-Mexican War have most often glossed over these gruesome encounters following the territory's conquest. The Taos rebellion has been seen as an anomaly that did not fit the story of New Mexico's eager and "bloodless" transition to the United States.[200] It has also been disconnected from the later battles involving Comanches and Apaches. We need to stop and consider, though, what the Taos rebellion suggests about race and nation as the border changed. Significantly, these rebellions drew Pueblo Indians, Plains Indians, and Mexican settlers into a defense of the territory as a Mexican place.[201] Historians have speculated about why Native Americans would willingly join a battle that was so clearly framed around Mexican nationalism. As one historian points out, Pueblo Indians were the "least Mexicanized portion of New Mexico's population."[202] This would be even more true for Apache and Comanche groups.

Pueblo Indians, Mexican nationals, Comanches, and Apaches undoubtedly fought the United States for their own reasons, but the language of Mexican nationalism, as was the case during the Chimayó Rebellion a decade earlier, was flexible enough to encompass their disparate interests. Indeed, Native Americans had suffered under the weight of Spanish and Mexican imperialism. Their participation, therefore, should not be construed as an indication that they blindly accepted the authority of the Mexican state in their lives. More plausibly, Pueblo Indians, Comanches, and Apaches adopted a strategic nationalism based on which nation represented the most immediate threat. Euro-Americans were rapidly encroaching on traditional Pueblo hunting and agricultural grounds. Charles Bent and other Euro-Americans had already announced plans to infringe on these lands by creating new settlements along the Poñil and Cimmarrón rivers.[203]

Members of the Taos Pueblo likely saw aligning with Mexican nationalists as their best chance to prevent any further Euro-American encroachment into their territory.[204] Likewise, Apaches and Comanches joined in raids in order to ensure their access to much needed supplies.[205] Such efforts spoke to various groups' desires to retain their own social and economic control of the territory.[206] Still, we should not dismiss the role that Mexican national identity played in these strategies. Pueblo, Comanche, and Apache participation in revolts on behalf of Mexico makes sense because, in its nascent form, Mexican identity did not make race the primary marker for national identity. Mexican nationalism was a convenient way of imagining cross-racial unity while evading the deeper problems that divided these populations.

Euro-Americans, for their part, found such unity perplexing. Mexican identity, they believed, could not include the Pueblos because, as "pure Indians," they were racially distinct from "mestizo Mexicans." Instead, most Euro-Americans filtered their understanding of the rebellion through their own assumptions about racial hierarchies rather than viewing it as part of the international conflict. Because they imagined Pueblo Indians at the bottom of such hierarchies, they often discounted them from any type of leadership role, ignoring the obvious centrality of Taos leaders. Instead, actions taken by the Pueblos resulted from "instinct" in many Euro-Americans' minds. The Pueblo Indians appeared simultaneously as Mexicans' hapless pawns and as "bloodthirsty savages."[207]

Because of their own emphasis on race, Euro-Americans believed that racial division between Mexicans and Euro-Americans had to be the operative element in the rebellion. One Euro-American claimed that "the Mexicans had massacred all the white inhabitants" of Taos.[208] Another said that the Pueblo Indians and Mexicans intended to "kill every white man, woman and child."[209] Moreover, he said that "half breed children were . . . marked for slaughter . . . [and] the color of the hair and eyes was made the test of blood."

Despite the presumption that the revolt had to be racially driven, Euro-Americans' own recollections of the attack show slippages that suggest otherwise. Discussing the death of one Narcisso Beaubien, an individual of mixed heritage, one Euro-American pointed to Beaubien's Euro-American father as the explanation for his murder. Later in his testimony, the same Euro-American noted that Beaubien's "sympathies . . . were with the Americans, and he was not allowed to escape the fate of all those who were supposed to lean that way."[210] The initial claim that Beaubien died simply because of his mixed ancestry gave way to the acknowledgment that his national allegiance to the United States made him a target. Indeed, almost all of those who fell to attack had direct links to the U.S. government or its business ventures.

Euro-American witnesses nonetheless had difficulty distinguishing nationalist from racial motives for the violence. Under Euro-American thinking, all Mexicans should have been united based on their common race against the Pueblo Indians and vice versa. One soldier reported an incident in which Euro-Americans even administered a deadly rebuff to an indigenous man for failing to behave based on racial unity. In this story a Pueblo Indian appeared among the U.S. Army and professed his allegiance to the United States. One Euro-American man asked the Pueblo man to prove his devoutness by murdering other Pueblo Indians who hid nearby. The Pueblo returned with evidence that he had completed the deed. The U.S. soldier stated, "Then you ought to die for killing your own people," and he shot the Pueblo man.[211] If the veracity of this account is dubious (and I think that it is), even the telling of such a story suggests the importance that Euro-Americans placed on race.

Only the intervention of a local Mexican official slowed the spread of the deadly conflict. The well-known Mexican political figure Donaciano Vigil became provisional governor after Bent's death. Unlike his Euro-American counterparts Vigil understood the patriotic rhetoric that bound the revolt and diverse interests in New Mexico. Indeed, the newly appointed governor had been one of the Mexican citizens who had sent a letter to the Mexican president pledging his patriotism and desire to resist the U.S. occupation.[212] Apparently, though, Vigil did not have the stomach for the violence.

In his address to New Mexico's population, penned shortly after the start of the uprising, Vigil focused on issues of nationalism, not race. The governor's proclamation shrewdly avoided linking the reigning territorial government directly to U.S. military occupation. Rather, he suggested that New Mexico's ultimate status remained unsettled at that moment. His language even suggested some sympathy with Mexican nationalists as he called Mexico the territory's "native" country. He cautioned against using deadly force: "Whether this country has to belong to the Government of the United States or return to its native Mexico, is it not a gross absurdity to foment rancorous feelings toward people with whom we are either to compose one family, or to continue our commercial relations?"[213]

If calls for prudence alone could not quell the violence, Vigil also looked to undermine the rebellion's leaders using their own strategies. Vigil questioned Pablo Montoya's sincerity and dissociated him from Mexican nationalism.[214] He reminded the population of Montoya's role in the previous decade's Chimayó Rebellion and pointed out that Montoya did not fight the U.S. troops when they first arrived in New Mexico. "Why, if he is so full of patriotism," Vigil asked, "did he not exert himself and lead troops to prevent the entry of American forces in the month of August?" The leader's tainted relationship to the Mexican nation made the Taos rebellion an illegitimate showing of Mexican nationalism to Vigil.

Calling for peace as the representative of the United States after the rebellion, Vigil's word choices showed some interesting calculations. Vigil noted his uncertainty of "whether this country has to belong to the government of the United States or return to its native Mexico." Claiming the local space as "native Mexico" implied that Vigil had not yet accepted U.S. authority as natural. Rather, he resurrected the familial idiom that had dominated discussions of Mexican citizenship as he called for an end to rebellion, promising that the people in the territory would "compose one family." Though racial differences would exist, as they had under Mexico, those differences would be understood as part of a national "family."

The Taos rebellion revealed the conflicting assumptions about race and nation that existed along the nineteenth-century border. Mexicans and Euro-Americans would be forced to reconcile these conflicts to preserve the peace in the territory. Some Mexicans, though, saw little value in working with the invading Americans. Southern New Mexico quickly became a haven for those disenchanted by the war.

Making Borders: An Uneasy Peace
between the United States and Mexico

By the time of the U.S.-Mexican War in 1846, Euro-Americans and Mexicans who lived at the boundaries between the two nations understood that they had conflicting views about national and racial identities. While the armies waged war, leaders from each side grew increasingly interested in establishing what separated Americans from Mexicans.

In 1848 Senator John C. Calhoun argued against annexing lands with a substantial Mexican population. Deploying a typical rhetoric of white superiority, his words typified many Euro-American ideas about Mexican identity. The senator warned that incorporating Mexicans into the United States "would be the first instance of the kind of incorporation of an Indian race; for more than half the Mexicans are Indians, and the other is composed chiefly of mixed tribes. I protest against such a union as that!"[215] Calhoun then linked "Spanish America's" military failure to Mexicans' racial inferiority: "Ours is the government of the white man. The great misfortune of what was formerly Spanish America, is to be traced to the fatal error of placing the colored race on an equality with white.... Are we to associate ourselves as equals, companions, and fellow citizens, the Indians and mixed races of Mexico? I would consider such an association as degrading to ourselves and fatal to our institutions."[216] For Calhoun, whether Mexicans were "mixed" or "Indian," they certainly were not "white."

Such views were not just the exclusive province of proslavery southerners, either. Senator Lewis Cass of Michigan responded to a similar 1846 speech delivered by Calhoun. "I fully agree," Lewis stated. "It would be a deplorable amalgamation. No such evil will happen to us in our day. *We do not want the people of Mexico, either as citizens or subjects.* All we want is a portion of territory."[217] The Vermont-born abolitionist Thaddeus Stevens delivered an almost identical sentiment when he addressed Congress.[218] Describing New Mexico's population, Stevens stated, "The mass of the people are Mexicans, a hybrid race of Spanish and Indian origin, ignorant, degraded, demoralized and priest-ridden."[219]

Given the prominence of such rhetoric on the U.S. side, the drafting of a peace treaty that would settle Mexicans' role in the United States proved a daunting task for negotiators. Though too often neglected by historians, the product of their work, the Treaty of Guadalupe Hidalgo, offers new insights into how Euro-Americans and Mexicans first at-

tempted to reconcile their competing notions of race and national community.[220] As much as the negotiators redefined the boundaries between
nations, they also attempted to define the meaning of Mexican and
American identities. On one hand the Mexican negotiators sought to
reduce Euro-American racism and to ensure that their compatriots had
the option of U.S. citizenship. Negotiators for the United States, on the
other hand, understood that many of their countrymen would refuse to
accept Mexicans as their racial or civic equals. The final document necessarily deployed an ambiguous language that shakily bridged the two
conflicting visions of race and nation.

In contrast to the circulating Euro-American discourse that configured Mexican identity as racial, Article VIII of the Treaty of Guadalupe
Hidalgo framed Mexican identity as strictly national. This decision reflected a compromise between Mexican and American negotiators. In
the first draft Mexico's negotiators seemingly prevailed as the treaty
framed Mexican identity as a mutable national identity. Article VIII
never explicitly addresses issues of race, however:

> Those [Mexicans] who shall prefer to remain in the said territories, may
> either retain the title and rights of Mexican citizens, or acquire those of
> citizens of the United States. But, they shall be under the obligation to make
> their election within one year from the date of the exchange of ratifications
> of this treaty: and those who shall remain in the said territories, after the
> expiration of that year, without having declared their intention to retain the
> character of Mexicans, shall be considered to have elected to become cit-
> izens of the United States.[221]

Under the logic of this provision individuals could opt to change their
"Mexican character" to American citizenship simply by residing in
United States territory for one year.

Elsewhere within the treaty the framers explicitly attenuated Euro-
Americans' ability to racialize Mexicans in the United States. As we have
seen in Governor Condé's remarks, Mexicans understood how Euro-
Americans used race to justify the enslavement of "those who were not
white."[222] Fearing Mexican citizens could face a similar fate, drafters of
the treaty added elements that explicitly forbade Mexican enslavement.[223] Article XI made illegal, "under any pretext whatever, for any
inhabitant of the United States, to purchase, or acquire any Mexican or
foreigner residing in Mexico" from slave-trading Native Americans.[224]
The decision to use the treaty to prohibit outright enslavement of Mexicans also revealed the framers' uncertainty about their racial status in the

United States.[225] Had there been a shared understanding of Mexican identity, there would have been no need to outlaw the purchasing of Mexicans explicitly.[226] Because Euro-Americans' discourse configured Mexican identity as racial, located in specific bodies, it also created the potential for Euro-Americans to purchase those bodies. Acknowledging this potential (even by outlawing it) reified the notion that Mexicans occupied a particular racial category. The framers might have tried to deploy a sense of Mexican identity as a mutable national identity, but they could not ignore the potential implications of the Euro-Americans' view of them as nonwhite.

In spite of the care put into the drafting of the treaty, the U.S. Congress thwarted many of the draft's protections for Mexicans. Most members of Congress refused to reconsider their assumption that Mexican identity was a separate racial category. Like John C. Calhoun, they believed that Mexicanness was not merely citizenship; rather, for them, it was racial. Undermining the design of the original draft, congressional leaders altered the language of key sections of the treaty.

For example, Congress redrafted Article IX in such a way as to institutionalize inequality between Mexicans and other Americans. The article's original language explicitly guaranteed Mexicans in the newly acquired territories "the enjoyment of all the rights of citizens of the United States." This original version further specified, "With respect to political rights, their condition shall be on an equality with that of the inhabitants of the other territories of the United States."[227] While avoiding a direct discussion of race, the initial amendment implicitly guaranteed Mexicans the same privileges that Euro-Americans associated with whiteness.

Congress's revised version reveals much through its conspicuous deletions.[228] The greatly truncated Article IX approved by the Senate provided only vague assurances that Mexicans living in the acquired territories would gain the rights attached to full U.S. citizenship. Replacing the original language of civic equality, the new article created a paternalistic relationship between Euro-Americans and Mexicans:

> The Mexicans . . . shall be incorporated into the Union of the United States and be admitted, at the proper time (to be judged of by the Congress of the United States) to the enjoyment of all the rights of citizens of the United States according to the principles of the Constitution; and in the meantime shall be maintained and protected in the free enjoyment of their liberty and property, and secured in the free exercise of their religion without restriction.[229]

The revised treaty granted Congress the exclusive power to oversee and determine Mexicans' status in the United States. Like the original article, the newer version avoided a direct discussion of race. Congress, though, did not accept the original's implication of racial and civic equality between Mexicans and Euro-Americans. Because Mexicans were racial subalterns, Euro-Americans believed that Congress needed the ability to judge the "proper time" for Mexicans to gain their full rights.

In the years following the treaty, Euro-Americans sought to solidify their authority within the former Mexican territories by further narrowing the scope of the treaty. Before the war Euro-Americans concentrated on establishing Mexicans as "not white." There was no unanimity therefore among Euro-Americans about whether Mexicans could claim U.S. citizenship before the U.S. Army arrived in New Mexico in 1846. In the first decade after the war a few Mexicans even found some means to use that uncertainty to their advantage. The excuse that Mexicans were ineligible to serve as jurors in New Mexico courts because they were "foreigners" became a common legal maneuver to overturn indictments or convictions.[230] Displeased that a number of people had gone free on the "mere technicality" that Mexicans had served on the jury, Governor Abraham Rencher persuaded the territorial legislature to pass an act in 1859 stating that any Mexican who was a U.S. citizen, or who had merely declared his intention of becoming a naturalized citizen, could serve on a jury.[231] Rencher and the legislature intended only to expedite the functioning of the territorial court system, which required the participation of Mexicans, who constituted the majority of the population. The very need for such a measure, however, exposed the precariousness of Mexicans' claims to U.S. citizenship.

Many Euro-Americans aggressively tried to narrow the definition of Mexican identity within the United States in the years immediately following the Treaty of Guadalupe Hidalgo. Cave J. Couts's 1848 military journal records a clash between the Mexican and Euro-American vision of Mexican identity. Couts, an officer in the United States Army, traveled from Nuevo León to Alta California, penning his impressions of the former Mexican territories. Like most Euro-Americans, Couts felt confident in his understanding of Mexican identity as a distinct racial category. The town of Tubac, Arizona, though, challenged the young officer's vision of racially distinctive categories. Couts believed that he could easily discern one group of bodies as either Mexican or Indian. Describing his first impressions of Tubac, Couts confidently called the inhabitants "Indians" rather than "Mexicans." "Tubac itself might be called an

Indian village," he wrote, "for there are two or more Apaches to one Mexican."[232]

Mexicans, though, configured their national identity through actions and associations, not race. The revelation that individuals in Tubac believed that Apaches could be both Indian *and* Mexican astounded Couts. Dumbfounded, he reported that the Apaches "are regarded by the Mexicans as *Mexicans*."[233] To explain this seemingly impossible cross-identity, Couts posited that those Mexicans and Indians were simply confused about the natural racial distinctions between the two groups.

Although Couts could not grasp Tubac's meaning in Mexico, his description of the town is consistent with the Mexican national discourse. This town collectively participated in a cultural performance that marked the space as Mexican. Although racialized as indios, these Apaches were considered "Mexican by Mexicans" because they deployed the necessary cultural markers. Tubac's primary language, clothing, and spatial organization all corresponded with established notions of mexicanidad. Assessing the Apache leader, Couts noted he dressed "just as a slick-shin, broad-brim [sic] straw hat, *Chinese shoes*, leather leggings, and a blanket around the shoulders, a la Mex." He also noted, "All, or nearly all the Apaches, as well as Camanches [sic], talk Mexican."[234] Under the dominant model for national identity, therefore, the Apaches had adopted the necessary markers that cemented them in the national community. Mexican authorities had officially and unofficially established wearing clothing "a la Mex," speaking Spanish, and participating in a municipal government as key indicators of their national identity. For Couts, who imagined Mexican and Apache identities as rooted in one's body (and mutually exclusive), these displays and claims appeared nonsensical.

Euro-Americans even feared that they could be "tricked" into confusing the Mexican and Indian races through the 1870s. An editor of a Las Cruces newspaper intended to strike dread into his English-language readers when he reported that a wanted Apache man had eluded authorities by "passing" for a Mexican. He reported: "Bold, almost reckless; skilled in warfare, looking as much like a Mexican as he did like an Apache, speaking Spanish fluently, he accomplished, by his audacity, what others would have failed to perform. Donning the costume generally worn by the poorer classes in northern Mexico, he would frequently enter houses in Sonora, and claim hospitality for a few days."[235] In this case Euro-Americans turned this trespassing of supposedly immutable racial categories into an exception that proved their rules. They argued that only this unusually audacious Apache man could adopt the clothing, language, and other cultural markers of a Mexican. Less remarkable men, they confidently asserted, would "have failed to perform" this seemingly impossible transformation from Indian to Mexican.

Even the Treaty of Guadalupe Hidalgo threatened to undermine Euro-Americans' racial hierarchy by granting rights to indigenous people who had been Mexican citizens prior to the war. Most Euro-Americans would not be inclined to grant these aboriginal people rights denied to other indigenous groups in the United States. To avoid this challenge, Euro-Americans interpreted the language of the treaty that referred to "Mexican citizens" as excluding "Indians." Euro-Americans refused the Mexican discourse, which emphasized performance over race.

Racial Borders Defined: Mexican Identity and New Mexico's Pueblo Indians

The Treaty of Guadalupe Hidalgo, as I have mentioned, never explicitly discussed the meaning of race and Mexican identity in the territories ceded to the United States. Negotiators noted only Indian groups that already fell outside of Mexican identity because they had been labeled as "indios bárbaros." Article XI, for instance, deployed a language that would have been familiar in both the United States and Mexico when it called particular indigenous groups the "savage tribes." Mexico's officials would have understood this to refer only to Indians who, though Mexican citizens, did not submit to federal authority. Euro-Americans, however, understood all Indian identities, "savage" or "peaceful," as excluding Mexicans and vice versa.

In New Mexico redefining Mexican identity as exclusively "mestizo" resulted in the disfranchisement of thousands of Pueblos. Many Pueblo Native Americans initially considered themselves as much U.S. citizens in 1849 as they had considered themselves Mexican citizens in 1825. The Treaty of Guadalupe Hidalgo, after all, had ostensibly granted rights to all former "Mexican citizens" after one year of residence.[236] Several Pueblo villages actively participated in elections following the war, and their residents surely assumed that the newly ratified treaty protected them as much as other Mexican citizens.

During a particularly tense election for New Mexico's single (nonvoting) congressional delegate in 1853, though, the United States Congress refused to accept ballots cast by local Pueblos.[237] The mass exclusion of these votes culminated efforts started four years earlier when the president had appointed James S. Calhoun (not to be confused with John C. Calhoun, the South Carolina senator who spoke out against incorporating Mexicans into the United States) as Indian agent in New Mexico.[238] Calhoun, whom the president would appoint New Mexico's governor in 1851, arrived with a mission to bring Pueblos under the "protection" of the U.S. federal government.[239] Calhoun approached this task with an understanding of Mexicans and Indians as separate racial groups. While his motive is unclear, Calhoun's influence ultimately resulted in the disenfranchisement of more than eight thousand Pueblo Indians.[240] Pueblos, however, had a long tradition of electing officials in their own community. Understandably, they complained to Calhoun in 1850 when American authorities appointed people to these offices without their vote.[241] Calhoun, however, believed that Mexican elites manipulated Pueblo elections and, therefore, could not be trusted.[242] Until Mexicans could be excluded from Pueblo affairs, Calhoun stated, the Pueblos would not have elections.

By 1851 Calhoun and other Euro-Americans used this situation to convince several tribes to disavow their association with the Treaty of Guadalupe Hidalgo.[243] Calhoun persuaded Pueblos to claim an exclusive identity as Indians and to reject claims as former Mexican citizens. Doing so, Calhoun hinted, would return their authority over their own affairs. Being Indian, not Mexican, meant that the federal government would place the Pueblos under the 1834 Indian Intercourse Acts. Pueblos would receive "federal protection," which limited access to Pueblo communities by non-Indians. If Pueblos disavowed their rights as former Mexican citizens, Calhoun promised, they "could govern the Pueblo in their accustomed manner with no interference from outside authorities."[244] Basically extorted to do so under the prospect of losing their internal authority, several Pueblo tribes disavowed their former Mexican citizenship and rights under the Treaty of Guadalupe Hidalgo. It was an impossible situation. Had they challenged their exclusion from the treaty (and some did), they would have been tied up in court for decades with an uncertain chance for success. Calhoun's suppression of local elections proved the most immediate threat that needed resolution. Most Pueblo communities, as a result, voted to accept ward status.[245]

As the United States assumed greater control over the territory, Euro-Americans hardened the division between Indians and Mexicans. They considered Pueblos "pure Indian," whereas "Mexicans" were "mixed Indian and European blood." By 1854 the New Mexico legislature, composed of Euro-Americans and non-Indian Mexicans, prohibited all

Pueblo tribes from participating in elections (except for electing water officials).[246] John Greiner replaced Calhoun as New Mexico's superintendent of Indian affairs in 1852. He, like Calhoun, blamed Mexicans for all of the Pueblos' problems. He reported: "The Pueblo Indians are planting their grounds—digging their Acequias—herding their stock, and making every effort to support themselves by their own industry. Could they be protected from the depredations of the Mexicans they would not only be examples for their *red* brethren—but for some other people of a light complexion."[247] In this instance Greiner believed that Pueblos demonstrated their superiority over Mexicans.

Lieutenant Colonel E. V. Sumner wrote similar remarks to the *New York Times* in 1853. "The New-Mexicans are thoroughly debased and totally incapable of self-government," he warned. "They have more Indian blood than Spanish, and in some respects are below the Pueblo Indians, for they are not as honest or industrious."[248] Because Greiner, Sumner, and others believed Mexicans were racially mixed, their preference for "pure" Indians resulted from their presumptions about race and "amalgamation." The mongrelization of Mexicans, they believed, made them more suspicious than the Pueblos. These ideas about a racial divide between the two would be institutionalized by the newly formed territorial government. U.S. imperialism informed this process of differential racialization to make sense of New Mexico's heterogeneous population. The demands and expectations that inform differential racialization were therefore linked to regional concerns and circumstances. Whereas national narratives about race circulate widely, racial hierarchies and racial divisions of labor are experienced at the regional and local levels. Euro-Americans, as part of the colonization of nineteenth-century New Mexico, engaged in processes of differential racialization to mark clear distinctions between the Mexican and Pueblo populations. Both of these groups had to be kept as distinct and were given a different place in the emerging colonial order.

Nevertheless, uncertainty about the Pueblos' relationship to the Treaty of Guadalupe Hidalgo resulted in numerous court challenges through the nineteenth century.[249] The New Mexico Supreme Court decided in multiple cases in 1869, 1874, 1876, 1904, and 1907 that Pueblos had the same citizenship rights as other former Mexican citizens.[250] These rulings amounted to little, though, as New Mexico's 1912 Constitution prohibited "Indians not taxed" from voting. The United States Supreme Court also ruled on the issue in 1913. In *United States v. Sandoval* 231 U.S. 28, the justices determined that Pueblos were entitled to "federal protection" but that their citizenship status was not clear. Pueblo Native Americans would not overturn these discriminatory provisions until 1953.[251]

Mexican American members of the territorial legislature, meanwhile, constantly petitioned the U.S. government to honor its treaty obligations by recognizing their own rights as citizens in the decade between the U.S.-Mexican War and the Civil War. To appeal to the U.S. House of Representatives, these Mexican legislatures tried to position themselves as loyal agents of U.S. imperialism. Several memorials drafted in Spanish and translated into English for the U.S. House declared that Mexicans and Euro-Americans shared a common enemy in "Indian savages." If the federal government contained the various Apache, Utes, and Navajo tribes, then Mexican Americans could transform New Mexico into a place of tremendous mineral mining and cattle production that would benefit the United States.[252] One memorial even proposed that New Mexico's Mexican Americans could serve as convenient brokers to facilitate trade between Mexico and the United States.[253]

Even as these memorials asserted Mexican American loyalty as U.S. citizens, they also reminded the U.S. Congress that it had not been their choice to become part of the nation. They tried to shame members of the U.S. House into action by noting that New Mexico had fared much better under the Mexican government than it had as a U.S. possession.[254] "Although we would not be understood as expressing any regret at being transferred as citizens to the model republic of the north," one memorial stated, "yet candor and justice require us to say that the protection of our people against Indian hostilities has not been improved by the transfer of our Territory."[255] In these documents we see Mexican Americans trying to position themselves as full citizens deserving the protection of the U.S. government. They also sought to restore their own role in the region as colonizers worthy of protection by the central government. To do so, they easily excluded nomadic Native Americans from those same rights as citizens. Such strategies, however, fell on deaf ears in Washington, as Congress largely ignored these petitions. Only when New Mexico's status as a U.S. colony was truly threatened did federal authorities begin to reconsider allowing Mexicans to serve as U.S. agents.

Many scholars have written about Mexicans' relationship to "whiteness" after the U.S.-Mexican War.[256] Of equal importance, however, is understanding Mexicans' relationship to "Indianness" in the postwar era. Many Native Americans had considered themselves Mexicans and legally were Mexican citizens at the time of the Treaty of Guadalupe Hidalgo. A mere six years later, the territorial legislature excluded Native

Americans from ever claiming a Mexican identity. Euro-American discourse had an established racial position for Native Americans that could
not conflict with the emerging notion of Mexican racial identity. Disregarding distinctions under the Mexican discourse, Pueblo, Navajo, and
Apache groups all became blurred under the Euro-American blanket
category of "Indian." The disfranchisement of Native Americans signaled
an initial restructuring of Mexican identity in New Mexico at the moment that settlers created the border towns of Las Cruces and La Mesilla.

Conclusion

Mexican and Euro-American understandings of racial and national identities had differed considerably prior to the U.S.-Mexican War. Both
countries had traditions that emphasized public performance and actions as part of nationalism. Voting, speaking a particular language,
publicly celebrating certain holidays, and other such activities all connoted a sense of belonging to either Mexico or the United States. The
meanings ascribed to those performances, though, were tempered by the
ways that race figured into each country's national identity and imperial
ambitions. Each nation created different sets of interior frontiers to help
explain and control their heterogeneous populations.

New Mexico was a place where liberal notions of the nation-state
existed alongside debates about colonial settlements. Native Americans'
relationship to Mexican national identity in this region, as throughout
the nation, was a critical issue. Because Mexico outlawed the use of racial
categories in defining citizenship, the articulation of a national identity
had increased the importance placed on "acting like" a Mexican. Mexican
officials drew from colonial notions about race and status that had defined the divisions between "civilized" and "savage." In this way Mexico
retained preindependence social and economic inequalities despite the
official ban on racial categories. Yet, leaders throughout Mexico also
articulated a nationalist agenda that connoted a unity of purpose and
civic equality regardless of race. Their words glossed over the tangible
ways that race continued to influence social relations. Instead, a common
simile developed that conceptualized Mexico's various racial groups as
different members of the same national family.

Euro-Americans who arrived in northern Mexico asserted a contrasting vision of race and nation as they remade the colonial order in New
Mexico. Mexicans, who had been imperial agents, became a colonized

people. Their strategies for using a Mexican national identity to unite with Pueblos and other indigenous groups was discarded when the border shifted. Instead, the Euro-American traders and, later, soldiers who first arrived from the United States construed their national identity and Mexican national identity as connoting distinct racial categories. For Euro-Americans, being Mexican signified a particular type of "nonwhite" body, one of mixed Indian and Spanish ancestry. Indians, Mexicans, and whites each occupied a particular racial position within the Euro-American imagination. In New Mexico Euro-Americans created and enforced a racial divide between Mexicans and Indians, refusing the notion of Mexican identity as multiracial and dependent on the carrying out of cultural practices.

Conflicting ideologies over space, nation, and race shaped the history of southern New Mexico. Mesilleros would not be willing to forfeit their assumptions about national identity. We turn now to those Mesilleros and consider how both Mexicans and Americans sought to imprint the landscape with their notions of national identity. These broad divisions and disputes over the meaning of Mexican identity would necessarily need to be worked out among Euro-Americans and Mexicans in local contexts. In the Mesilla Valley, conflicting allegiances altered the local geography.

CHAPTER 2

"Yankilandia" and "Prairie-Dog Villages":
Making Sense of Race and Nation at
the Local Level, 1850–1875

In 1853 Guadalupe Miranda sent a terse message to the recently founded Mexican colony of La Mesilla. Miranda, the Mexican consul serving in Franklin, Texas (today's El Paso), was annoyed that a group of Mesilleros had conducted business in Las Cruces, the neighboring town five miles away. "I am informed that two wagon loads of people from Mesilla, a few days ago, went to Las Cruces to get salt," he wrote, "and since this is a territory of the United States you are hereby ordered that this will not be repeated."[1] Miranda, who also owned property in Mesilla, saw the messiness created by the 1848 political boundary that separated Mexico from the United States.[2] By restricting Mesilleros' ability to travel the mere five miles to Las Cruces, Miranda attempted to remedy the situation by giving the border concrete significance in these communities.

Miranda's letter suggests the profound implications for individuals when a new border suddenly divides their communities. Unlike later generations of Mexicans who migrated to the United States, the first generation of Mexicans dealt with a border that changed the meaning of their location beneath them. This chapter examines the myriad interests that sought to organize the geography, practices, and social relationships along that boundary. Prior to the U.S.-Mexican War the town of Doña Ana had been one of only a handful of Mexican settlements in southern New Mexico. After the war ended, the town saw an influx of U.S. war veterans and land speculators claiming farmland. This compounded the problems created by the prolonged military occupation of Doña Ana. Hungry soldiers had already overtaxed its meager resources. As a result, two groups of Mexican settlers migrated from Doña Ana and established the competing towns of La Mesilla and Las Cruces.[3] Euro-Americans and Mexicans each wanted the ultimate authority to name, structure, and police the border between these towns based on their own ideas about race and nation. Competing ideologies influenced the way the two groups physically laid out the towns of La Mesilla and Las Cruces and, in turn, affected the meanings individuals drew from being in those places.

Making the border meaningful was no small task. Most settlers crossed back and forth without much thought. Indeed, even the Rio Grande (Río Bravo), the supposedly "natural" boundary between the United States and Mexico, shifted unpredictability in the first year after the treaty.[4] In 1849 the river altered course southward of the towns of San Elizario, Isleta, and Socorro, abruptly transferring the chihuahuenses in those places to U.S. territory because they were then north of the Rio Grande.[5]

The end of the war also triggered economic and political upheavals across the transnational region, putting into question who would control the borderlands. Some areas, like Alta California and Texas, witnessed massive demographic changes. Following the discovery of gold in Alta California, the Euro-American population increased tenfold between 1848 and 1850. Violence and dispossession of Mexicans became unrelenting companions to that increase.[6] The Alta California indigenous populations suffered even more profoundly. A Euro-American campaign of almost total genocide decimated their communities from 150,000 in 1845 to just 16,000 in 1900.[7] California authorities also disregarded the rights guaranteed to Mexicans under Article VIII of the Treaty of Guadalupe Hidalgo. To keep both Mexicans and Asians out of the mining industry, the state created a "Foreign Miners' Tax." In reality this was a "race tax" designed to exclude Mexicans and Asians from the state's mineral wealth.[8] Texas lawmakers, meanwhile, created the infamous Texas Rangers to brutally enforce a new racial order that placed Euro-Americans at the top. Many Mexicans had fought on the side of the Texas rebellion in 1835, but the postwar period saw some of those same Tejanos expelled from central and east Texas.[9]

Changes also occurred on the Mexican side of the border. Northern Mexican states suddenly became international gateways. The same gold rush that transformed Alta California had a domino effect that expanded Euro-American settlement in Sonora and Baja California. Recurring filibustering expeditions appeared in those states in the nineteenth century. Much to the agitation of Mexican authorities, Euro-Americans pursued their fantasies of untapped mines in northern Mexico comparable to those in Alta California.[10] Conversely, mining in Chihuahua had all but ceased during the war, leaving that newly made border state bankrupt.[11] Likewise, political instability and scarcity of resources fostered armed conflicts and civil rebellion in Nuevo León. Violence between Mexican settlers and Comanche and Lipan Apaches escalated to a 250-year high in the immediate aftermath of the U.S.-Mexican War.[12]

Mexicans dealt with all of these sudden changes and uncertainties in different ways. Some reconciled themselves to the new economic and social order created by their sudden proximity to, or actual residence in, the United States. Mexicans in northern Sonora's Tucson (in what would later become part of the U.S. state of Arizona) enjoyed an economic boom as they eagerly traded with the traveling wealth-seekers heading west.[13] Others withdrew from the region entirely. Still others criss-crossed the new border, availing themselves of the economic benefits of its porosity.[14]

Ambiguity about Mexicans' racial and citizenship status positions on the U.S. side of the border continued through the end of the nineteenth century, even after the incorporation of Mesilla into the United States in 1854. To chronicle the multiple ways that Mexicans made use of that ambiguity, this chapter charts nineteenth-century border conflicts in three distinct periods: (1) the decade surrounding the founding of La Mesilla and Las Cruces from 1848 to 1860; (2) New Mexico during the U.S. Civil War period (1860–65); and (3) the postwar period, when new ideas about Mexican identity started to appear in the local press. Taken together, these sections review prominent moments when debate over the meaning of Mexican and American identity appeared most critical along the nineteenth-century border. In short, I argue in this chapter that the concrete exigencies of locality were always critically intertwined with more abstract notions of racial and national belonging. Physical changes along the border (such as the river's shifting course, the construction of new towns, and the movement of bodies) necessitated constant reassessments from both Mexican and U.S. authorities.

Texans, Africans, and *Indios Bárbaros*: U.S. Imperialism and Mexican Nationalism as Twins

To account for the divisions between Montoya, Amador, and Melenudo revealed in the introduction, we must first understand the divisions that split Mexicans shortly after the U.S.-Mexican War and then scrutinize the role of U.S. and Mexican government representatives in shaping border communities. Both governments engaged in similar strategies to transform the local geography but to opposing ends. These transformations ultimately associated Las Cruces with being "American" and La Mesilla with being "Mexican." Even though the war resulted in Mexico's defeat, agents for the Mexican state and notions of Mexican nationalism persisted on the U.S. side of the border. These same Mexican authorities played instrumental roles in creating several new towns on the Mexican side of the border, including La Mesilla, by drawing settlers from the ceded territories. To attract colonists, they used a mixed rhetoric of Mexican nationalism and anxieties about U.S. imperialism. U.S. agents, for their part, worked to change those same territories based on their own sense of nationalism.

In practice the new border had meant little. People, goods, and capital flowed back and forth across it with little restriction. Governmental authorities attempted to manage the chaos by remaking towns and places, imbuing them with particular cultural markers, language, and architectural styles. Taken collectively, these geographic and visual measures were intended to signal the national and cultural authority of one group or nation over the other. Such marking either incorporated or excluded Mexicans and Euro-Americans by physically enabling or constraining social interactions.[15]

During this early period popular Mexican imagination about life in the United States was dominated by two archetype figures: the "Texan" and the "African slave." Both of these figures appeared continually in discussions about the risks of staying in occupied New Mexico. Images of land-hungry (Euro-American) "Texans" had circulated widely in Mexico since before the U.S.-Mexican War.[16] A failed invasion of New Mexico in 1841 by Texas rebels gave those images particular salience in the territory.[17] Just five years before Kearny arrived, an armed party of three hundred men constituted the "Texan–Santa Fe Expedition." They marched into New Mexico ostensibly to open trade between Austin and Santa Fe. In reality the small band had orders to seize "all public property" and force New Mexico to join Texas by overthrowing the territorial government and coercing the local population. New Mexico's governor, Manuel Armijo, learned of the expedition's plans and easily defeated their efforts.

That expedition fueled a local resentment and hostility toward Texans that lingered for decades. Though Mexicans in New Mexico harbored their own complaints against Mexico City, they had not desired to join Texas in breaking away from the nation. Indeed, they celebrated the Texans' defeat through festivities that centered on Mexican patriotism. Some settlers in New Mexico even developed a stage drama in the mid-nineteenth century depicting the 1841 Texan invasion and a heroic Mexican victory. Characterizing Texans as cruel and greedy, the play culminated in the invaders' capture and highlighted Mexicans' success at keeping New Mexico for Mexico. "You insolent Texans," the Mexican hero of the play chastised, "how dare you profane the territory of the Mexicans?"[18] As we will see, that invasion and dread of Texans (or "diablo Texans") lived on in local memories for more than a century.[19] In Doña Ana immediately after the war, some settlers feared that their rights would never be respected if self-named Texans continued to surge into the area. Their fears were justified. Backed by newly created Texas laws, U.S. settlers blatantly disregarded established Mexican land grants.[20] Most Mexicans who attempted to protect their property rights found only frustration from U.S. authorities in New Mexico and Texas.[21]

If Texans came to represent the worst of Euro-American aggression, then the figure of "African slaves" stood for Mexicans' greatest fears about their own future in a new nation.[22] As we saw in chapter 1, Mexican government agents like Pedro García Condé invoked the specter of race-based slavery in war propaganda.[23] Dire rumors that Texans intended to enslave Mexicans as they did African Americans continued to circulate in the first years after the treaty.[24] One Mexican official, Ramón Ortiz, reported that these fears motivated a number of Mexicans to move south of the new border. "Querían perderlo todo," he wrote, "mas bien que pertenecer a un gobierno en el cual tenían menos garantías y eran tratados con mas desprecio que la raza de África" (They wanted to lose everything rather than to belong to a government in which they had fewer guarantees and were treated with more scorn than the African race).[25] Established residents bristled under the realization that Euro-Americans assumed their status as Mexicans had racial connotations as "not white." Moreover, Ortiz's comparison of Mexicans' treatment as worse than African Americans' suggests Mexicans' uneasiness about their future prospects in the United States.[26]

Antipathy for Texans and fear of race-based slavery accounted for thousands deciding to relocate south of the new borderline. This southward movement did not occur spontaneously but instead developed as part of a larger, if sporadic, Mexican federal project. In the wake of the Mexican defeat influential leaders in Mexico City argued that the nation's military failures against the United States had resulted from the paucity of Mexican settlements in the north. To remedy this situation, President José Joaquín de Herrera issued a colonization plan on August 19, 1848.[27] His program presumed that settlements of devoted Mexicans just along the northern frontier would serve as both physical and military defense of the nation against another U.S. invasion. Regional officials also looked to these settlements as part of their ongoing fight against Native Americans who refused to submit to Mexican authority (which still referred to them as *indios bárbaros*). As envisioned in this plan, the ideal Mexican settler needed to acknowledge the authority of the Mexican federal government, pledge militia service to it, and above all, reject the authority and temptations of the United States.[28]

This colonization program increased the importance of place and location to Mexican identity along the border. Moving south of the new borderline became one of the most important expressions of Mexican patriotism in the first decade after the war. Most Mexicans in New Mexico had been born in the territory, but the Mexican president's decree alienated them from that space. Herrera addressed an official message to "Mexican Families" in the United States who wished to "emigrate to their native country."[29] He asserted that Mexicans born in New Mexico no longer could expect to claim that territory as their "native" land. Nativeness was a question of national belonging, not of birthplace. Whether they had spent a lifetime there or just a few years, New Mexico was now alien territory.

Mexican officials, of course, did not naively rely on a sense of patriotic duty to attract settlers to the border. They explicitly wanted these new colonists to place themselves in danger by serving as a military against the United States and "indios bárbaros" who disrupted trade and settlement along the northern frontier. Mexico's colonization plan therefore offered cash and land-grant incentives to reward those who stayed loyal to Mexico. The federal plan promised twenty-five dollars to Mexican nationals living in the ceded territory who willingly repatriated.[30] Soldiers, vital to this defensive plan, received an additional salary beyond the standard payment. The emphasis on defense also resulted in limits on who could participate in the program. Article 13 of the decree, for instance, excluded those facing a criminal trial and those who had been previously convicted.

Herrera's decree provided for the appointment of commissioners with the authority to grant land to migrants from Alta California, New Mexico, and Texas.[31] Many in Mexico City argued that these colonization efforts were vital to the nation. Juan Nepomuceno Almonte, who had served as the secretary of war, urged the Mexican Congress to invest in these programs even further in 1852. Almonte claimed that "pues es urgente salvar a nuestro hermanos de la frontera y aumentar cuanto antes los recursos de la hacienda federal" (it is urgent to save our brothers of the border and increase as soon as possible the resources of the federal estate).[32] Among other measures, Almonte's recommendations included expanding the amount of land granted to "las familias mexicanas que se trasladen de Téjas o de Nuevo-México a las fronteras del Norte de la República" (Mexican families in Texas and New Mexico who move to the northern borders of the republic).[33] This type of enthusiasm resulted in officials' close attention to organizing the colonies, at least initially.

Repatriates from New Mexico eventually created four substantial Chihuahua towns: Guadalupe in 1849, La Mesilla in 1850, Refugio in 1852, and Santo Tomás de Iturbide in 1853.[34] While repatriation efforts stimulated some settlers to leave Texas and Alta California, New Mexico provided the greatest number of settlers thanks in part to its dynamic commissioner.[35] In 1848 the Mexican government selected the priest Ramón Ortiz to serve in that role "en vista de las buenas cualidades de ilustración, probidad y patriotismo que le adornan" (in view of the good qualities of enlightenment, propriety, and patriotism that surround him).[36] Ortiz had already lived a remarkable life by the time of this appointment in 1848. Born in Santa Fe in 1813, he studied for the priesthood in Durango and was eventually assigned as the main curate in El Paso, Chihuahua (today's Ciudad Juárez) in 1836. Ortiz used his priestly position to criticize the United States and increase nationalist sentiments in the far north, eventually taking his views to the Mexican Congress as a Chihuahua representative. After the war Ortiz gained renown for his outspoken opposition to the terms of the Treaty of Guadalupe Hidalgo, which he saw as having required disproportionate concessions by Mexico.[37]

As we might expect of such a figure, Ramón Ortiz proved a model booster as repatriate commissioner.[38] Within the first weeks of his being in New Mexico in 1849, he reported that an astounding number of Mexicans wished to leave the Euro-American-controlled New Mexico. Sixty miles east of Santa Fe, in San Miguel del Vado County, nine hundred out of a thousand Mexican settlers signed the necessary documents to participate in the resettlement program.[39] The initial enthusiasm for repatriation implies that these Mexicans were experiencing the implications of their transformations from colonizers to colonized and from members of a multiracial "Mexican family" (of which they were the patriarchal head) to racialized Others of the dominant Euro-American settlers.

Officially, the Treaty of Guadalupe Hidalgo guaranteed that Mexicans could keep both their Mexican citizenship and residence in New Mexico. In practice, however, acknowledging numerous claims by community members to foreign nationality would have undermined attempts to make New Mexico "American." At the same time, the labor provided by Mexican bodies would be indispensable to the immediate development of the territory. U.S. officials expected New Mexico's Mexican population to be docile workers with appropriate allegiance to U.S. interests without claiming any of the rights associated with citizenship. Accordingly, Euro-American territorial officials worked to curtail Mexicans' ability to retain Mexican citizenship. Ortiz reported that he interviewed two men who had petitioned to preserve their Mexican citizenship, Don Juan Baca and Don Miguel Jaramillo. "Por única respuesta obtuvieron," Ortiz relayed, "malos tratamientos y un pasaporte para salir del país cuando quisieran" (The only response they received was bad treatment and a passport to leave the country whenever they wanted).[40] The commissioner recounted another instance in which territorial citizens wrote an open letter in the *Santa Fe Republican* (*Republicano de Santa Fe*) requesting information about retaining Mexican citizenship. When hundreds of Mexicans attempted to follow the guidelines printed in response, John M. Washington, the appointed governor of New Mexico, arbitrarily established more difficult measures to make Mexicans' declarations "official."[41]

The *Santa Fe Republican* ran another Spanish-language editorial outright discouraging migration to Chihuahua.[42] Two Euro-Americans had established the *Santa Fe Republican* in 1847 as the territory's first bilingual paper. One of their explicit goals was to link the remote territory to the larger United States. It is not surprising, therefore, that they criticized Ortiz and the repatriation plan. Leaving New Mexico, the editorial argued, would be costly even with federal aid. They accused the Mexican federal government of being stingy with its assistance to these settlers. If Mexican authorities were really sincere, the *Santa Fe Republican* declared, they would have dedicated a third of the $15 million received by the United States for New Mexico, Texas, and California for this resettlement program. The paper concluded that "que claramente no desean [las autoridades mexicanas] que ustedes vuelvan al número de su familia" (clearly the Mexican authorities do not wish you to return to the ranks of their family).[43]

Resistance to Ortiz's mission came from the highest levels of the territorial government as well. While recruiting in Pojoaque, a Pueblo Indian community, Ortiz received word that the governor had forbidden him to travel in the territory.[44] Ortiz, thereafter quartered in Santa Fe, assigned agents to enlist interested migrants on his behalf. After a short time the governor required that Ortiz recall his agents as well, citing "civil unrest" caused by the recruitment of settlers. The governor blamed the priest for a resurgence of Mexican nationalism and resistance to U.S. rule. Ortiz described the situation:

> El señor gobernador me mandó llamar inmediatamente para prohibirme aún el uso de este medio, bajo el pretexto de que los alborotos se hacían ya extensivos hasta en la capital, y el de que había recibido quejas de todos los prefectos, manifestándole que desde mi llegada al territorio todos los pueblos se negaban casi abiertamente a obedecerlos.[45]

> (The governor sent for me immediately to prohibit me from even using this method under the pretext that disturbances were already extensive even in the capital, and he had received complaints from all of the prefects, saying that since my arrival in the territory all villagers had openly refused to obey them.)

Fearing a mass exodus or the eruption of armed resistance, territorial officials permanently expelled Ortiz and his agents from New Mexico.[46] The Mexican federal government issued a formal protest to the U.S. secretary of state on September 18, 1849; however, Ortiz's campaign was permanently stalled.[47]

Some of the highest estimates suggest that three thousand to five thousand individuals followed Ortiz to Chihuahua.[48] This, of course, represented only a tiny minority of the estimated fifty-four thousand Mexicans residing in New Mexico in 1850.[49] Still, even several thousand repatriates cut the territory's already small population between 5 and 10 percent, making the drop significant enough to prompt the intervention of U.S. authorities.

La Mesilla as a Mexican Colony, 1848–1853

Simply relocating settlers would not satisfy the expectations of Mexican leaders for the new colonies. President Herrera charged local governors with regulating the physical settlement of the towns created by the colonization campaign. He wished these towns to instill a distinctive type of patriotism, partly to ensure that they would also provide Mexican soldiers when needed. Chihuahua bureaucrats, as a result, engaged in a nation-building project at the local level. Much more than those in Mexico City, it was the local and state authorities who worked to make colonies like La Mesilla match their own vision of proper Mexican towns.

Nineteenth-century leaders in the Mexican government believed that controlling institutions and constructing government buildings created tangible and visible reminders of national identity in areas far removed from the capital.[50] Peter Guardino has commented on the importance the central government placed on asserting a presence in local communities. Municipalities, Guardino argues, provided the primary link between "the idea and praxis of the nation-state."[51] Likewise, Ana María Alonso notes that authorities in Chihuahua blurred the defense of local territory, or patria chica, with notions of Mexican nationalism.[52] Raymond Carib, moreover, shows that nineteenth-century Mexican state officials, bureaucrats, and military personnel worked to "give space a stable signification, permitting it to be more effectively appropriated, transformed, and regulated."[53] After the U.S.-Mexican War, "Mexican space" was self-consciously created through cultural and semiotic codes.[54] Surveyors and other government agents named, ordered, and divided space to match their expectations for a bounded nation. In doing so, they naturalized the authority of the central state.[55]

Mexico's federal authorities may have set the broad parameters of the nationalization of localities, but the concrete design and implementation fell to local bureaucrats. The governor of the state of Chihuahua created regulations prescribing markers of a legitimate Mexican settlement on May 22, 1851. Angel Trías's "Regulaciones de colonización" laid out the official standards for towns applying to be recognized as Mexican municipalities. From the first article Governor Trías dictated the town's physical contours: its shape and the distribution and administration of land. According to Article II, all new towns, including La Mesilla, needed to be square, with "landmarks and the limits clearly defined" at four corners.[56] Article VI required that new houses or other buildings follow an established pattern for construction. Each street needed to be at least twelve *vara* (thirty-three feet) wide and had to meet other roads at right angles.[57] These towns had to have a community-owned area "for the recreation of the settlers" and "the exit of their stock without committing damage" in proportion to the size of the population.[58] Residential lots ranged in size from nineteen by fifteen varas to fifty by ninety varas. On the north, east, and south of Mesilla agents marked land for agricultural use in blocks that were usually 960 by 320 varas (about twenty acres).[59] Mesilleros built their town around certain buildings in their plaza and distributed land according to these official measures. Its physical layout regulated by government fiat, La Mesilla literally bore the imprint of state authority.

Regulations dictated that Mesilla and its counterpart towns were not only to be planned according to a specific layout but also to include specific structures. Article VII of Chihuahua's guidelines required the commissioner to "see that in the center of the settlement there be a regular and proportioned plaza, in which shall be designated lots for the church and Erota's house and for schools and government buildings, and in convenient places other lots for a jail, barracks, stations and so forth."[60] The expectation that colonies like Mesilla would serve as defense against additional U.S. incursions and *indios bárbaros* increased the importance of allotting spaces for military barracks and similar buildings. The construction of these buildings, in turn, inserted the central state into the frontier community. Explicitly requiring towns to grant the Catholic church a plot of land at the town's center physically manifested the expectation that only one religion connoted *mexicanidad.*[61] Taken together, these requirements for land allocations and public buildings imbued these communities with a particular vision of Mexican national identity. This vision linked the mission of the central state for providing order through barracks and jails with a religious basis traced to the Catholic Church.

Such policies influenced Mesilla well beyond its physical layout.[62] Leaving no element to chance, the Chihuahua ordinances even established standards for naming public places, requiring that a commissioner provide a name for each new settlement and that "such name be in Spanish."[63] The commissioner also required colonists to name streets and municipal property in Spanish only. Mesilleros built their town according to these official measures (see Figure 1). They labeled their streets with a mixture of religious and patriotic names: Calle de Guadalupe, Calle de Guerra (seemingly a reference to the recent war), and Calle de San Albino (the patron saint of the town). By insisting that a town's geography be named in Spanish, officials at all levels emphasized a collective national identity expressed through shared language. The experience of seeing Texas overwhelmed by a Euro-American majority just a decade earlier probably prompted such efforts to keep out English and other American cultural markers. Such policies also foreshadowed the increasing emphasis placed on creating a monolingual nation by the end of the nineteenth century. Key figures in the Mexican federal government wished to foster nation building by excluding not only English but also the multiple indigenous languages.[64]

This is not to say that Mesilla existed as a nationalist utopia or that every Mesillero moved there out of a burning patriotism. The Mexican federal government more often than not failed to deliver promised mon-

TOWN AND VALLEY OF MESILLA
NEW-MEXICO.

1. The earliest known Euro-American representation of La Mesilla,
circa 1854. Courtesy Archives and Special Collections Department,
New Mexico State University Library.

etary, subsistence, or military aid.[65] It is entirely plausible that, had the
border not shifted, Mesilleros would have experienced the same frustra-
tions with the Mexican federal government as the neighboring town of
Ascensión (which, indeed, included many Mesilleros who fled the United
States in 1854 and 1871).[66] Settlers in that town ultimately rioted against
local and federal Mexican authorities in 1892.[67] The circumstances at-
tendant on the founding of Mesilla remind us of the need to conceive of
nationalism in more complicated ways than as mere allegiance to state
authority or as an expression of a unified populace free of strife. On the
contrary, nationalism necessarily involves the obscuring of divisions
within a population to maintain the fiction of community.[68] The language and symbolism that connoted Mexican nationalism in Mesilla far
outlasted the Mexican state's role in that town.

Mexican officials and settlers not only controlled and limited the structures of Mesilla as a Mexican community, but they also positioned its

northern twin, Las Cruces, as entirely "foreign" and "non-Mexican" because it lacked most of those same structures. Founding Mesilla was an explicit act of Mexican nationalism because it was an escape from Euro-American imperialism. Indeed, settlers literally celebrated their move. John Bartlett, the lead Euro-American assigned to set the 1848 official boundary line, noted, "The whole population [in Mesilla] had determined to abandon the place if the boundary line had run south of the village, and thus placed them under the jurisdiction of New Mexico. . . . The event [announcing the Bartlett-Condé line] was celebrated by firing of cannon and a grand ball. . . . After this the population continued to increase."[69] Bartlett had already expressed these same sentiments to leaders in the U.S. government. In letters published as part of the Senate record, Bartlett outlined the history of La Mesilla, noting that "Many Mexicans have in consequence removed from our side [of the border] . . . to avoid the bad treatment from the Americans there."[70] Euro-Americans, Bartlett observed, were not as inclined to move to the seemingly unfriendly Mexican town.[71]

By February 1852 Mesilla had grown so rapidly that the Mexican government divided the colony to create the new town of Santo Tomás de Iturbide.[72] Mexican federal authorities and Chihuahua regional authorities imprinted these colonial towns with structures and symbols of Mexican nationalism. Even as Mesilla swelled with fleeing Mexican nationalists, though, settlers of different political persuasions opted for Las Cruces.

Building Las Cruces in an "American Fashion"

Much as Mexican officials self-consciously developed La Mesilla as a Mexican town, the United States military charged Second Lieutenant Delos Bennett Sackett to develop Las Cruces "in [an] American fashion" in 1848.[73] U.S. officials engaged in the same type of process as did their counterparts in Mexico, bringing settlements into conformity with their vision of national identity. Although Sackett found a small population already living in the intended town site, he reorganized it to match his notion of a proper American place. Sackett divided Las Cruces into eighty-four blocks, which he marked mostly in English. Las Cruces's newly developed street grid included names like "Main," "Church," or "Water." Aside from the lack of any state-sponsored church, the greatest difference between the two town plans lay in their handling of property: In contrast to

2. A Mesilla Valley house constructed of adobe brick. Euro-Americans tended to denigrate all adobe houses as "miserable," but the glass windows suggest that this Mexican family was doing quite well financially. Courtesy Archives and Special Collections Department, New Mexico State University Library.

Mesilla's policy of communal landownership for grazing lands, Sackett redistributed local land as private parcels to 120 individuals.

Race and nation were also more tightly intertwined for Euro-Americans than for Mexicans. Remaking the space as American required not only imposing cultural markers like English street names but also displacing Mexican structures, national symbols, and ultimately Mexican bodies. To Euro-Americans even the adobe structures dotting the New Mexico landscape stood out as uncomfortable reminders that Mexicans inhabited an American place. Disparaging their homes as dirty and uninhabitable, therefore, became a standard element in Euro-Americans' complaints about New Mexico (see Figure 2). In a memoir entered into the U.S. Senate Record, A. Wislizenus described New Mexico's architecture as almost animal-like: "I perceived before me the irregular cluster of low, flat roofed, mud built, dirty houses, called Santa Fe, and resembling

3. Euro-Americans imported their own architectural styles into the Mesilla Valley.
Here a Euro-American woman poses in front of her Las Cruces home. Despite their
aspirations to obliterate all Mexican construction, even this house used adobe brick to
complete the white-picket fence. Courtesy Archives and Special Collections
Department, New Mexico State University Library.

in the distance more a prairie-dog village than a capital."[74] Waterman
Ormsby, a correspondent for the *New York Herald*, expressed a similar
racialized association with Mesilla's adobe buildings on his 1858 visit.
Ormsby disdained Mesilleros and described their adobe homes as "miserable dog kennels."[75] Ormsby, like many Euro-Americans, believed the
arrival of Euro-American bodies would directly transform New Mexico
and eradicate these dwellings and, presumably, the "lazy and indolent"
people inside.[76]

One of the Euro-Americans' first actions in remaking the territory
involved the erasure of Mexican architecture. Following a pattern common throughout New Mexico, a Euro-American judge forbade the construction of adobe structures on Las Cruces's Main Street and ordered
the demolition of those that already existed.[77] Replacing the existing
buildings with Greek Revival or Italianate façades connoted the removal
of Mexicans in favor of "progress" and "[white] culture" (see Figure 3).[78]

Such contests over configuring space as a means of demonstrating national and racial identity was not limited to Mesilla and Las Cruces or even the U.S. side of the border. The Mexican state of Sonora witnessed a similar dispute when the U.S.-owned Atchison, Topeka and Santa Fe Railway began operations there in 1880. Euro-Americans rejected the established Mexican port city of Guaymas as "a city of yesterday in the land of mañana."[79] Instead, they created an entirely new town, which they named "Junction City" over the objections of the local Mexican elite. Junction City, boosters claimed, was a "pretty little American town" that catered to a Euro-American minority. To make the town American, Euro-Americans deployed many of the same markers that guided the remaking of Las Cruces. Junction City's streets had names like Calle Morley or Calle Willard. Euro-Americans imported their own architectural styles for houses, including white picket fences, and opened a store that sold U.S. goods.[80] Mexicans derisively referred to the new town as "Yankilandia."

The tensions between Guaymas and Junction City mirrored the earlier tensions between La Mesilla and Las Cruces. Mexicans and Euro-Americans battled over attempts to remake territory with their own nationalist markers. In this case it appears that guaymenses pushed back against U.S. imperialist policies as the town was eventually renamed *Empalme* (the Spanish term for *Junction*).[81] As will be discussed later, Cruceños also recognized the remaking of their town through these imported designs as U.S. imperialism.

To be sure, certain officials, like Governor Washington, had worked to limit the outflow of Mexicans from New Mexico; however, most Euro-Americans imagined the presence of Mexicans and Native Americans, especially groups like the Mescalero Apaches, as an obstacle to the integration of the territory into the United States. New Mexico would never be more than a wasteland, they argued, as long as it had a Mexican and indigenous majority. As one Euro-American military commander advised in 1852, "There can never be an inducement for any class of our people to come here whose example would improve this people."[82] If the Mexican population could not be replaced, he predicted a grim future for the territory as a "heavy burden" on the United States. His plan called for the United States to cut its losses by placing the territory "under the entire control of the Governor." Without a Euro-American population to remake the territory, this military commander suggested abandoning the Mexican population "to get from the soil the few articles that are necessary for their subsistence."

Other voices, though, were more optimistic that whites could "civilize" and "tame" the newly acquired region. Many predicted that Euro-Americans would pour into New Mexico, eager to transform the land into a lush agricultural paradise. Mexicans would then die off because they would be unable to compete with the presumed racial superiority of whites. In his 1852 inaugural address Governor William Carr Lane admitted that "New Mexico is now a burden to the United States." Only when the territory "team[ed] with a healthy, sturdy, brave, intelligent and virtuous population," the governor told his Santa Fe audience, would that burden be lifted.[83] Racist assumptions in Euro-Americans' approach to Las Cruces threatened Mexicans' autonomy and restricted their ability to claim an equal American identity.

Despite these assumptions, many Mexicans took their chances with the United States. Although his memory was obviously biased, Major Enoch Steen of the U.S. military reported in 1853 that Mesilla Valley settlers' greatest concern had been avoiding life in Texas: "A large number of the people who settled the valley were from what is now New Mexico. . . . They said to me 'We do not want to live in Texas, we are afraid of the Texans, nor do we want to live in Mexico. Where shall we go to be quiet? We wish to live in the United States.' "[84] Steen's recollections favored U.S. authority over the valley. It is certainly plausible, though, that those who founded Las Cruces hoped their fortunes would improve in a new nation (as long as they could avoid the dreaded Texans). Mesilla and Las Cruces might have continued to develop as independent border towns. A conflict over the boundary line in 1853, however, increased the tensions that contrasted Las Cruces with Mesilla.

Remaking the Border: The Conflict over La Mesilla

Violence and unrest marked Mesilla's earliest years, much as they marked the rest of the border. Various Apache groups saw the creation of Mesilla and its sister colonies as a continuation of Mexican imperialism that threatened their autonomy and the fragile supply of resources in the area. Mesilleros created the Guardia Móvil (later Mesilla Guard). Initially commanded by a Pueblo Indian who resided in Mesilla (fully in line with Mexico's notion of race, performance, and nationalism), this unit continued Mexicans' wars against *indios bárbaros*.[85] Bloodshed followed as Mesilleros used "defense" as an excuse to raid Apache settlements.[86] Leaders of the Mescalero Apaches attempted to broker a peace with

Mesilleros on four occasions in 1853, but they found only sharp rebukes.[87] Such actions only returned retribution to Mesilleros. Even after Mesilla transferred to the United States, Apache groups disproportionately attacked Mesilla over neighboring Doña Ana or Las Cruces.[88]

Not surprisingly, the Mesilleros' opposition to U.S. expansion also created animosity among Euro-Americans and Mexican Americans. Mexican policies that closed the newly bustling trade center to U.S. citizens (including Mexican Americans) appeared unfair to them. As early as 1851 a group of "Americans and New Mexican Citizens" complained to Santa Fe about Mexico's enforcement of the new border, including the construction of Mesilla's customshouse. They appealed to the territorial government, complaining that Mexican officials took "away lands from Americans and others who are favorable to American rights and privileges" and gave "them to those who profess to be Citizens of Mexico."[89]

Compounding these pressures was the fact that the Treaty of Guadalupe Hidalgo had imprecisely defined the U.S.-Mexican border using an inaccurate map.[90] In 1851, to remedy the problem, Mexico and the United States established a joint commission that proposed a compromise borderline at 32°22′N, known as the "Bartlett-Condé line." Mesilla, according to the 1851 report, was situated in Mexico.[91] Many Euro-Americans, particularly in Texas and New Mexico, rejected this line. A diplomatic crisis resulted between Mexico City and Washington in 1853. Some Euro-Americans asserted that the entire Mesilla Valley, including the town of La Mesilla, had always been part of New Mexico. Therefore, they argued, the valley should have been annexed into the United States under the terms of the Treaty of Guadalupe Hidalgo.[92] Southerners, in particular, desired Mesilla and additional lands as part of their plan for a transcontinental railroad through the nation's South.[93]

New Mexico's governor, William Carr Lane, became the biggest agitator for claiming the Mesilla Valley. In March 1853 Lane appeared on the border threatening military intervention to settle the boundary dispute.[94] Raising the tension in the area, Lane declared himself the "appointed Governor of all New Mexico, and not a part."[95] He explained his arrival in southern New Mexico as "re-taking possession" of the disputed lands for the United States. The governor then threatened to occupy La Mesilla with troops until Mexico yielded, increasing the possibility of another war.[96] Chihuahua's governor, Angel Trías, responded to Lane's threats by guaranteeing that he would use equal military force to challenge any U.S. soldiers who entered the repatriate's town.[97]

Lane found support from New Mexico's business leaders whose interests hinged on the expansion of the United States. Under the pseudonym Fernandez de Taos, one such supporter printed an English-language pamphlet entitled "A Review of the Boundary Question and a Vindication of Governor Lane's Action in Asserting Jurisdiction over the Mesilla [*sic*] Valley."[98] The pamphlet argued that Mesilla had never fallen under Chihuahua's jurisdiction. The author also dismissed the idea that La Mesilla had been founded in opposition to the United States as a "romantic and marvelous History." Instead, he asserted, "Good land and a high price for its products contributed more to the foundation and rapid growth of Mesilla than either persecution or patriotism." Settlers from Doña Ana, he claimed, created the town of Mesilla to sell "their corn and beans at [$2.50 per bushel] if not higher to the boundary commission and the army."

Mesilleros countered these types of arguments with their own pamphlet, a reprinting of a historic document known as "Exposición sucinta y sencilla de la provincia del Nuevo México, hecha por su deputado en Cortes Don Pedro Baptista Pino, con arregio sus instrucciones: Cádiz, 1812."[99] This pamphlet originally went to the Cortes in Cádiz in 1812. That assembly had gathered representatives from Spain's empire to ponder Joseph Bonaparte's installation as king by Napoleon in 1807. It might have seemed an unlikely source of rebuttal as it was tangential to the contemporary concerns of 1850. Mesilleros nonetheless distributed this historical report as part of an implausible claim that their town had really existed since 1812, the date of the report to Spain. In particular, they highlighted a reference to a military base "en la Mesilla del Pueblo del Paso." Making Mesilla a historical part of El Paso (today's Juárez) was intended to cement the town into Chihuahua. As a Washington surveyor noted, though, this "Mesilla" referred to a flat topographical formation outside of El Paso in 1812, not the town (founded in 1850). By claiming that their town was much older than its documented age, Mesilleros manufactured a historical rationale for keeping it in Mexico.

Reprinting the Cádiz report might have been unconvincing, but some Euro-Americans did have doubts about shifting the borderline further south. Mesilleros' overt hostility to U.S. expansion, they noted, was reason enough not to bring them into the United States. An American military general in New Mexico cautioned his superiors about plans to forcibly take control of the town. He euphemistically warned that there was "not much friendly feeling towards" the United States in Mesilla.[100] Indeed, Colonel Edwin U. Sumner, in charge of the Ninth Military Department, refused to cooperate with Governor Lane. On the contrary, he explicitly ordered U.S. troops to stay clear of the Mexican side of the border and the ambitious governor.[101]

Euro-Americans outside of New Mexico appeared similarly cautious and conflicted about incorporating the remainder of the Mesilla Valley into the United States. The *New York Times* provided its readers with clippings from across the nation about the Mesilla crisis. Initially, the *Times* reported in April 1853 that the Mesilla Valley "had always been under the jurisdiction of New Mexico" and therefore should be claimed for the United States.[102] Less than a month later, however, the paper printed several articles dismissing such claims. The lack of Euro-American settlers in the Mesilla Valley proved a decisive argument in eastern press coverage opposing the annexation of more Mexican land. The *New York Times* informed readers in May that Mexicans who "were greatly annoyed by the encroachments of the Americans" had founded Mesilla within the limits of Mexico. Since that time, Mesilla's population had grown to nineteen hundred, and "very few Americans ever settled there; in fact . . . it is probable that there never were twenty altogether."[103] This large proportion of Mexicans seemingly convinced the authors of the May articles that Mesilla should not be taken by the United States.[104] In June the *Times* reprinted a pointed jab at Lane from the *Providence Journal*. Noting that the governor had retreated from the Mesilla Valley, the paper dismissed the notion that Americans populated Mesilla. "Where are the 2,000 American citizens in the Mesilla Valley which Gov. Lane says . . . are so anxious to be taken under his fatherly protection and made citizens of the United States?" the article blithely asked. "Why did he not call on them to sustain him?"[105] If there were no (Euro-)Americans in the Mesilla Valley, the *New York Times* had serious misgivings about making it a part of the United States. By March 1854, the *Times* reported, "We are among those who have always maintained . . . that the United States has no title to the Mesilla Valley."[106] Articles like these shunned direct discussion of the Mesilleros' hostility toward the United States, but the mere implication of such hostility could imbue the place with an aura of danger.

In spite of cautionary sentiment evident in both governmental communications and media coverage, the United States negotiated a new treaty (known as the Gadsden Treaty in the United States and the Tratado de Mesilla in Mexico) with Antonio López de Santa Anna in 1853 to purchase 29,142,000 acres of land for $10 million. The finalized agreement took effect in 1854, creating a new boundary line at latitude 31°47′N

Grande, running west for one hundred miles before turning
1°20′N, running to the junction of the Colorado and Gila
he treaty incorporated not only the contentious valley but also
at is today southern Arizona, including Tucson.[108] Mexican
officials reminded American officials that Mesilleros had relocated in
Mexican territory because they felt persecuted in the United States.[109]
Nonetheless, the United States insisted that Mesilla be included in the
purchase and thus changed national jurisdiction. This led to Mesilleros
being dubbed "los vendidos de Santa Anna" (those sold out by Santa
Anna) by their Mexican neighbors.[110]

The treaty may have defused the crisis between the two governments,
but it left local tensions unresolved. Even before the treaty Euro-Americans had represented Mesilla as a lawless and dangerous town. The *New
York Times* recounted the arrest of a Mesillero for a sensational murder
and implied in the language of the report that the majority of Mesilleros
were criminals. Mesilla, the *Times* claimed, was "a perfect harbor and
refuge for all the villainous in the country who are continually crossing
the river, committing some depredations, and returning again if pursued."[111] This perception of Mesilla persisted for decades. W. W. H.
Davis's 1857 personal narrative, *El Gringo*, repeated many of the same
accusations that Mesilleros were all "villains." "The glowing accounts that
have been written about the beauty and fertility of La Mesilla," he declared, "are not sustained by the reality."[112] Davis claimed that Mesilla had
been a haven for criminals prior to the Mesilla/Gadsden Treaty: "Before
this territory (La Mesilla) was reacquired under the Gadsden Treaty, it
was a source of constant annoyance to our authorities. The villains who
found a home there would slip across the river, commit offenses, and
return before they could be apprehended; and the rascals from this side
would flee to the other after the commission of a crime—and both were
equally safe, there being no treaty between us and Mexico for the rendition of fugitives from justice."[113] These scathing descriptions stood in
contrast to Davis's notes on Las Cruces, where he stayed during his visit to
southern New Mexico. Las Cruces, Davis noted, was a "modern-built
Mexican village, and in Yankee style."[114] While linking *modern* and *Mexican* would have seemed an oxymoron for many Euro-Americans, it was
the "Yankee style" that placed Las Cruces on the road to progress. Mexicans just lived there.

The continued presence of the military fueled the Mesilla Valley's
economy in the first years after the Mesilla/Gadsden Treaty.[115] The
military established Fort Fillmore (where Kit Carson would be stationed

in 1861) six miles south of Las Cruces in 1851. Starting in 1857, the Butterfield Overland Stage ran passengers and mail from San Antonio to San Diego and from St. Louis to San Francisco. Mesilla became an important center of trade and communication when the Butterfield company named the town a transfer point in its 1858 route network.[116] Negative press aside, Mesilla also continued to attract a greater overall population than Las Cruces until 1870.[117] Because of its size, Mesilla replaced Las Cruces as the county seat in 1855. Moreover, Mesilla's population remained largely Mexican with few Euro-Americans locating within the town.[118] The continuing influx of Mexicans suggests that they understood Mesilla as a place compatible with their aspirations for autonomy. In 1859 a paltry two hundred Euro-Americans lived among four thousand Mesilleros.[119] To the dismay of many Euro-Americans, Mexicans in Mesilla controlled all of the municipal government institutions except the sheriff's office (who was elected through a countywide ballot).[120]

Mesilleros even fulfilled some of Euro-Americans' worst fears in March 1860. Newspapers as far away as Chicago reported the ominous story of armed Mexicans forcibly driving all Americans out of Mesilla.[121] Apparently a brawl between a Mesillero and a Euro-American gambler escalated into a riot that left six Mexicans dead, including a Mesillera.[122] The Mesillero probate court judge responded to the violence by ordering all Americans' houses boarded up.[123] Mesilleros then escorted Euro-Americans out of Mesilla at gunpoint, claiming that they were ridding the town of an "unsavory element."

The eviction of Euro-Americans by Mesilleros revealed the tenuousness of U.S. authority along the border. The *Chicago Tribune* balefully noted that Mexicans "appear determined on revenge, and being largely in the majority, the danger is indeed serious."[124] Reacting to the expulsion of Americans, the U.S. military dispatched troops from nearby Fort Fillmore. Upon their arrival Mesilla's prefect "resigned, by request."[125] With its own resources stretched thin by the continuing war against Apache tribes, however, the U.S. military had no choice but to accede to a power-sharing compromise in Mesilla. Even the *Chicago Tribune* pointed out that the U.S. military could not simultaneously fight both Mexicans and Native Americans in New Mexico.[126] The military, therefore, installed two provisional prefects, one Euro-American and "one of the most popular Mexicans we have."[127] They also agreed to issue arrest warrants for the Euro-Americans who first started the commotion in the town. Though Euro-Americans demonstrated that they would use military force to quash overt resistance to U.S. occupation, this instance also showed that they understood their precarious position along the border, and Mesilla remained a Mexican town.

The organization of local space through differing visions of national and racial identities reflected the divide between Euro-American and Mexican national and racial discourse. Though imperialism forcibly incorporated Mesilleros into the United States in 1854, resolving the differing ideas about racial and national identities would prove more complicated. Las Cruces and La Mesilla became polarized as each side attempted to secure the validity of its own notions of racial or national belonging.

New Mexico's Civil War

La Mesilla had been part of the United States for only six years when South Carolina attempted secession on December 24, 1860. Fought in the Southwest, as well as the East, the U.S. Civil War generated renewed interest in New Mexico on the part of the rival Union and Confederate regimes. Such interest was not necessarily welcome. Mesilleros again suffered under multiple military occupations. The lasting legacy of the Civil War for the rest of New Mexico lay in stimulating a broad transformation in the local imagining of race, nation, and region. The military conflict prompted new ways to integrate the heterogeneous inhabitants of the territory into the United States even if they were unable to defy outright the rigid Euro-American conflation of racial and national identities. Both Euro-American and Mexican American elites began to resort to a language of region *as* identity that would become increasingly dominant throughout the United States in postbellum years. This language bypassed—without directly challenging—the barriers in dominant Euro-American conceptions of racial and national categories.

At the start of the Civil War, Union and Confederate leaders alike claimed that the majority of Mexicans in New Mexico favored their cause.[128] In February 1861 a high-ranking territorial official attempted to exploit existing racial and national tensions to prepare New Mexico for a Confederate invasion.[129] In a report eventually forwarded to Jefferson Davis, New Mexico's secretary of state, Alexander Jackson, stated that he had been working covertly to raise Mexicans' ire toward the United States by reminding them of the nation's anti-Catholic and anti-Mexican sentiments.[130] Even before the war broke out, southern sympathizers specifically advocated breaking the Mesilla Valley into a new territory.[131] Confederate military occupation followed a year later with little resistance from Mesilleros.[132] Lieutenant Colonel John R. Baylor and 350 Confederate soldiers claimed the Mesilla Valley under the direction of Colonel Henry Sibley in August 1861. La Mesilla became the unlikely capital of the newly created "Confederate Territory of Arizona" with the enthusiastic support of a small number of Euro-American Texans (whom Mexicans still called "diablo Texans"), including Sam Jones, the publisher of the pro-Confederate *Mesilla Times*.[133] It is not surprising that Jones overstated the Mesilleros' enthusiasm for the invasion. "Vivas and hurrahs," Jones printed, "rang them welcome from every point."[134]

Colonel Sibley, who had been stationed in Taos as part of the United States Army before the Civil War, understood that the Confederacy's long-term success in the territory hinged on placating the Mexican majority. Accordingly, he issued a bilingual proclamation shortly after the Confederate army occupied Mesilla.[135] He described a benevolent role for the Confederacy in New Mexico by assuring Mexicans that this military invasion would be different from the previous American one. He promised that the arrival of the Confederacy would "liberate" Mexicans "from the yoke of military despotism," end Euro-American dominance of the territorial government, and stop anti-Catholic harassment.[136] Sibley thus attempted to draw on Mexicans' existing resentment toward the United States while sidestepping the actual racist goals of the Confederacy elsewhere.[137]

For their part, Union Euro-Americans contested claims that Mexicans celebrated the Confederacy's arrival. The *New York Times* accused the Confederate Euro-American rebels of forcing Mexicans' consent to the invasion of New Mexico. "The Mexicans . . . are [with] but few exceptions, loyal to the Government," the *Times* asserted, "but . . . they are kept in abject silence and inactivity by the threats and execrations of these dastardly rebels."[138] Likewise, the *Los Angeles Semi-Weekly Southern News* noted that Mesilleros clearly did not support the Confederate invasion if Jones's *Mesilla Times* could not even obtain enough supplies to print regular editions. According to that Union paper, Mesillero merchants "would not sell . . . to a secession newspaper."[139]

Although sources illustrating Mexicans' actual feelings about the invasion and the larger Civil War are scarce, such reactions were probably more diverse and complicated than either Union or Confederate Euro-Americans acknowledged. Mesilleros most likely did not give out "vivas and hurrahs" when another invading army entered their town.[140] With little investment in the survival of either warring government, many Mexicans probably saw minimal difference between them.[141] This might account for the apparent lack of resistance to the Confederate presence at first.

What is clear, though, is that Mexicans did quickly tire of the new Euro-American authorities. Only a few months after the invasion, an outbreak of smallpox claimed the lives of both Mesilleros and soldiers, making for a tense atmosphere in the town.[142] Despite Sibley's willingness to imagine Mexicans' complaints about American imperialism, he did not truly disagree with the management policies of the United States for the territory. As military commander, he declared Martial Law in the Mesilla Valley because of "civil unrest" in December 1861. The official explanation blamed "desperadoes, gamblers, &c.," who, he claimed, "incited innocent citizens of the valley to rebel against the proper authorities."[143] Resorting to such drastic measures, though, suggested that the majority of those "innocent citizens" had come to see the Confederates as unwelcome intruders.[144] Confederate leaders then made matters worse when they seized supplies and other materials from Mexicans who refused to accept Confederate money as payment.[145] Union military leaders played on these stories to increase resentment against the Confederates. They circulated a letter from a Mesillero who compared the occupying "Texans" to locusts who "consumed and destroyed everything, even the growing crops."[146]

More than the occupation, the main turning point for the war in New Mexico came with the mobilization of the Mexican population for Union military service. Both Confederate and Union military officials initially disdained incorporating Mexicans into their "white" regiments. The Confederate military held this position for the duration of the war, with only a few exceptions. Even when a Mexican known as Pablo Alderete raised a local company for the Confederates, military commanders declined to muster it into service.[147] Indeed, Sibley's proclamation conspicuously omitted any call for Mexican participation in the Confederate army. He instead advocated for Mexicans to disengage entirely from the Civil War.[148] The only exception for the Confederacy in New Mexico was if Mexicans could be used to fight against Native Americans.[149]

More significant for our interests is the fact that leaders in the Union army did begrudgingly bring Mexicans into their military to fight Confederate forces. Union military commanders ultimately decided that they could not do without Mexican involvement in the war if they wanted to preserve the territory for the United States. A shift occurred thereafter as Union leaders began to experiment with a different language for explaining Mexicans' role in both New Mexico and the larger United States. This is not to say that Euro-American Union military commanders suddenly subscribed to a different vision of national and racial identities than they had previously. Many had served with Sibley when he was part of the U.S. Army in New Mexico. They were as likely to consider Mexicans as "racially inferior" as he. Early in the war, most Union military leaders stated that Mexicans (as a racial group) lacked the physical ability to serve successfully in the military.[150] Colonel Edward Canby, the commander of the territory's military, discouraged the use of Mexicans in the military because he believed that they had "no affections for institutions of the United States," and they openly expressed their hatred for Americans.[151]

Pragmatism and the need for bodies in uniform, however, took precedence over these dire assessments. Union officials quickly found that motivating Mexicans to join the war posed serious challenges. Some, like the Mesilleros, were even hostile to claiming U.S. citizenship. Union military leaders solved these problems by reinventing the Civil War as particular to the conditions in New Mexico. Rather than making blanket calls for American patriotism, they framed the conflict as a battle between local Mexicans and Texans. Governor Henry Connelly and the New Mexico legislature issued a rousing bilingual proclamation that called on Mexicans to defend the region.[152] Connelly never named the invading army as part of the Confederacy or referred to rebelling states. Rather, he articulated a threat specific to New Mexico. Connelly proclaimed that "this Territory is now invaded by an armed force from the State of Texas." He ominously warned that these Texans were determined to "subject us to the dominion and laws of the Government of Texas."[153] Connelly urged Mexicans to take decisive action based exclusively on their associations with an imagined "New Mexico" territory.

Although his text was lengthy, its formulation merits extended citation:

> Citizens of New Mexico, your Territory has been invaded; the integrity of your soil has been attacked, the property of peaceful and industrious citizens has been destroyed or converted to the use of the invaders, and the enemy is already at your doors. You cannot, you must not, hesitate to take up arms in defense of your homes, firesides and families. Your manhood calls upon you to be on the alert and to be vigilant in the protection of the soil of your birth, where repose the sacred remains of your ancestors and which was left by them as a rich heritage to you, if you have the valor to defend it. I feel that I appeal not in vain to those who love the land of their fathers; a land that has been the scene of heroic acts, and deeds of noble daring in wars no more

patriotic than that for which preparations are now being made. As your ancestors met the emergencies which presented themselves in reclaiming your country from the dominion of the savage and in preparing it for the abode of Christianity and civilization, so must you now prove yourselves equal to the occasion and nerve your arms for the approaching conflict.[154]

Connelly's proclamation epitomizes the means by which Euro-American civil and military leaders attempted to deal with the issue of Mexicans in the Union army. Permitting racial Others to serve in the U.S. military could not but raise questions about their status as full citizens. Connelly and other Euro-Americans deflected some of these concerns by avoiding language that depicted "Americans" fighting "Confederates" or "rebels," for such a formulation would have too closely interlinked Mexicans with full citizenship. Nor did he or other Union leaders cast the war as "Mexicans" versus "whites," which would have created other obvious problems. Instead, the language of the proclamation cast the Civil War strictly as a regional defense of New Mexico against its despised historical foes, Texans.

If the use of region could keep Euro-Americans from grappling with the complexity of racialized Mexicans fighting white Confederates, the language of "fighting Texans" could also appeal to Mexicans who did not wish to claim a national American identity. For these Mexicans, joining the Union army could be a necessary means for defending their communities without the threat of sacrificing a national Mexican identity. Indeed, some could even interpret their actions as those of patriotic Mexicans like their forefathers who repelled the Texas–Santa Fe Expedition in 1841. Clearly aware of the possibility of reading his proclamation in this style, Canby employed influential Mexican elites to carry the message into Mexican towns.[155] These tactics, and a promise of consistent wages, proved successful for the Union army, which recruited several thousand Mexicans.[156] Even newspapers far removed from New Mexico commented on this localized strategy. The *New York Times* reported that "great indignation is felt by the native population. They dread the 'Texans.' "[157]

Of course, some Mexican Americans believed that joining the Union cause promised them a path to full citizenship. One Mexican American reported to his superiors that he joined the Union army because he was "filled with the most sincere patriotism . . . in defense of the just cause of Union and Freedom."[158] The discussion of the "Texas" invasion, however, provided a convenient means for both Euro-Americans and Mexicans to discuss the conflict.

This Euro-American strategy confidently ignored the fact that a Texan identity often implied a racial meaning for Mexicans. People in New Mexico, in many circumstances, referred to *all* Euro-Americans as Texans regardless of their actual geographical origin. One German national, for instance, recorded such a perception in his journey through New Mexico during the U.S.-Mexican War. "Riding through a solitary valley," he stated, "I met with a Mexican soldier, who recognized me at once as a 'Tejano.'"[159] In another section he noted, "A crowd of ragged loafers and vagabonds received us at the entrance as 'Tejanos,' the usual abusive appellation to Americans." Though he migrated from Europe, he was identified as Texan because Mexican soldiers perceived him as a different racial and national identity from themselves. This complicated vision of Texan identity went unexplored by Euro-Americans during the Civil War. It likely would have made their strategy too messy to acknowledge that they were appealing to some Mexicans along racial lines.

Confederate Euro-Americans initially dismissed the Union call for Mexican soldiers. Sam Jones, editor of the *Mesilla Times*, declared the Union's recruitment efforts a ploy that was doomed to failure because of Mexicans' racial inferiority: "The better part of the army officers and men are composed of native New Mexican volunteers, who do not differ, in any essential degree, from the people of Old Mexico, who neither know nor care anything about the principle involved, and are, with a facility proverbial with the Mexican race, ready to espouse the side of the successful."[160] Jones argued that Mexicans, as a race, were fickle and not trustworthy. Even more interesting, the Mesilla editor retained the language of American identity as implying a specific racial identity. He declared that the Confederate military was more racially American than the Union army even without the incorporation of Mexicans. Jones condemned the Union's regular troops as "everything but Americans— an incongruous string of nationalities in which the German and Irish predominate." The Confederate army, according to the *Mesilla Times*, would be victorious because it maintained a racially strict American composition.[161]

Apparently that strictly American army was really not enough for the Confederacy to hold control of New Mexico after all. Learning of the approach of a massive force of Union troops from California, the Confederate army withdrew from Mesilla in early July 1862. Ten companies of the First California Infantry of the California Column arrived in the valley on August 15, 1862. Mesilleros found that Confederates were simply replaced by another occupying army. This one lingered a full year, commandeering local resources and labor that left many hungry and exhausted. Some Mesilleros left the town and moved across the border to Chihuahua.[162] After the Civil War the United States military closed Fort Fillmore and built Fort Selden. Located near modern-day Radium Springs, Fort Selden was critical to the local defense and economy from 1865 until it closed in 1891.[163]

Mesilla's history during the Civil War differed from the other parts of the territory. For the rest of New Mexico the rhetorical strategy of making the region the priority marked a lasting shift. The language of Mexicans fighting Texans persisted long after Confederate forces retreated from New Mexico and the war ended. At the same time, this language could be accepted by Euro-Americans because it did not challenge their notions of race.[164] Although thousands of Mexicans acted as loyal Americans by serving in the military, Euro-Americans continued to limit their possibilities for claiming full citizenship based on assumptions about their racial bodies.[165] Using the intermediate space of the region solved, at least temporarily, some of the questions about Mexicans' status as Americans.

Mesilleros, in contrast, contended with occupying armies, either Confederate or Union, in their own town. This strained their willingness to participate in either form of nationalism. Compounding the challenges of war, the Rio Grande changed course after flooding in 1862 and 1865. These changes swept the river to the west of Mesilla.[166] The economic, political, and environmental instabilities prompted some Apache groups to drive many Mexican and Euro-American settlers from their lands during the 1860s. Moreover, circumstances in Mexico infused Mesilla's population with a new round of Mexican settlers during this same period. Through most of the 1860s, liberal forces under the command of President Benito Juárez fought the army of the French-imposed emperor Maximilian I. During that conflict Juárez took refuge several times in El Paso, Chihuahua, bringing the military conflict to the border region. Many refugees from those battles resettled in La Mesilla—some temporarily, some permanently.[167] They likely brought with them, regardless of their length of residence, a renewed sense of Mexican nationalism for Mesilleros. Even as Euro-Americans and Mexican Americans in other parts of the territory worked to pull the territory into tighter unity with the United States, Mesilla increased its links to Mexico.

Postbellum Adjustments: Differential
Racialization Defines the Region

Dramatic changes punctuated the discussion of race, nation, and region
from the end of the Civil War through the 1880s. Questions over landownership became a dominant issue throughout the United States during the 1870s and 1880s.[168] The U.S. federal government enacted a significant shift in policy with the 1862 Homestead Act. Rather than selling
land to individuals or companies, the government now gave away 160
acres to any settler willing to live on it.[169] Railroad companies also received massive pieces of "public domain" lands as incentives for building
long-range trackage. The arrival of the railroad in New Mexico in 1881
increased the incentives for land speculation. Despite treaty guarantees
that the United States would protect existing land titles, some wealthy
Euro-Americans and Mexican Americans took advantage of instability in
the territory by attempting to purchase, discredit, or misrepresent existing Spanish and Mexican land grants. A few individuals amassed fortunes
in land, mostly through illicit means.[170]

The Mesilla Valley was not exempt from these trends. Confirmation of
most of the original Mexican land grants was delayed for decades. As Euro-
Americans poured into the area, petitioners filed paperwork on June 23,
1874, to confirm both the Doña Ana Colony grant and the Mesilla Civil
Colony grant. During the 1870s and 1880s the Las Cruces–based William
Rynerson amassed a small fortune through his New Mexico Town Company and a sister company, the Rio Grande Land Agency.[171] Mesilleros' suit
against Rynerson's claim, filed in 1875, was not resolved until 1899.[172] Some
few Mexican Americans also prospered through this period, accumulating
wealth and land on their own or as partners with Euro-Americans. The
Amadors in Las Cruces, as I have mentioned, found the new border quite
profitable. Likewise, Nestor Armijo partnered with Rynerson in a number
of ventures. At his death Armijo had an estate estimated at $1.5 million.[173]
Most Mexicans and Mexican Americans, however, found that their land
grants were slowly eroding.

Violence often accompanied these land disputes. The most sensational
instance in southern New Mexico occurred in Doña Ana's neighboring
county, Lincoln, in 1878. Popularly known as the "Lincoln County War,"
this dispute between factions of landholders and merchants lasted from
1878 to 1881. In the end the Lincoln County War gained national attention and exposed the territory's political and economic corruption.[174]

Despite the reality that most Mexicans were losing their lands, the minority of Euro-American and Mexican American elites who were profiting began to expand calls for cross-racial unity. Their way paved by the success of the Union's Civil War campaign, similar appeals based on region would grow increasingly elaborate by the end of the nineteenth century. We will see in chapters 5 and 6 how both Euro-Americans and Mexican Americans seized on this sense of a regional identity to advocate for statehood or economic investment from the eastern United States at the end of the nineteenth century. How these ideas developed in the immediate aftermath of the Civil War, however, remains a bit murky. To solve this puzzle, we can look for hints of change in the process of differential racialization that appeared in newspapers in the 1870s.

Nehemiah V. Bennett created and edited the most stable postbellum newspaper, the *Borderer (Fronterizo)*, in the Mesilla Valley starting in 1870.[175] Like most of the nineteenth-century newspapers printed in New Mexico, the Las Cruces–based *Borderer* and its competitors claimed objectivity while printing highly partisan opinions and articles in both Spanish and English. Bennett dedicated his own paper to the Democratic Party and to the promotion of Euro-American immigration into New Mexico.[176] Bennett certainly imagined a racial divide between Anglos and Mexicans. Mexican bodies were endowed with inescapable negative characteristics in the Las Cruces editor's mind. In a typical English-language editorial Bennett explained that Mexicans' alleged idleness and lack of initiative resulted from the "peculiar conformation of their heads."[177] He tapped into claims that cranial structure indicated both behavioral and racial characteristics that had been circulating since the middle of the nineteenth century.[178] In other instances he warned Anglophone readers that "Mexicans' nature" precluded them from ably participating in a republican-style government. Intending to shock his readers, Bennett reported that a territorial official promised that "any legislature composed of Mexicans could be bought and sold; like sheep and very cheap at that."[179] These types of articles leave little doubt that Bennett considered Euro-Americans racially superior to neighboring Mexicans.

Bennett and his peers, however, were not merely pundits but also political boosters and businessmen with practical concerns. They found that alienating the substantial Mexican population from their readership was costly during the 1870s.[180] As a result, they experimented with multiple ways of discussing racial and national identities in the region, altering their language (literally and figuratively) depending on whether they addressed Euro-Americans or Mexicans. Bennett spoke with a double tongue, printing his articles in both Spanish and English, a necessary move because of the lack of a fully bilingual readership at that point. He also used subtle linguistic dodges to garner support for his political positions, a harbinger of later developments. His writings incorporated both virulent anti-Mexican racism and new efforts to build bridges with Mexicans, sometimes even in the same edition of the paper.[181]

Bennett fostered Cruceños' sense of belonging to New Mexico and the larger United States in his Spanish-language section. Addressing these pages to local "Mexicanos," Bennett purported that the *"Fronterizo les viene como un amigo" (Borderer* will come as a friend).[182] Bennett further promised that the Spanish version provided "a nuestra populación nativa con un órgano peculiarmente suyo y sea un visitador bien venido en cada casa a conde se habla el idioma ESPAÑOL" (our native population with an organ peculiarly its own and is a welcome visitor coming into each house where SPANISH is spoken).[183] Later editions of the paper also showed that Bennett tempered his calls for the total exclusion of Mexican customs from the territory. Bennett, for instance, wrote an impassioned plea in 1872 for all children in New Mexico to learn English. Keeping with a newly emerging effort to assuage Mexican readers, though, he offered, "We would by no means discourage the study of Spanish."[184]

Even as he published English-language editorials that denounced Mexicans as "backward," he could also suggest a sense of unity between Mexicans and Euro-Americans against racial and regional Others. He argued that the two groups shared common enemies, like Native Americans (whom he frequently referred to as "fiendish savages") or a neglectful federal government, which retarded the territory's economic and political progress.[185] The *Borderer* and other Euro-American newspapers held "Easterner ignorance" as partially responsible for the slow economic development in the territory.[186] Geography thus became important to building a sense of political unity in the *Borderer*. Indeed, comparisons to easterners was one of the main ways that Bennett discussed his sense of shared purpose with Mexican Americans. New Mexico's Euro-Americans often bristled when the other states' major newspapers printed racist critiques of the territory, despite the fact that they also published the same types of articles in their own local papers.[187] Bennett, for instance, blamed unfair "Eastern attitudes" for preventing Congress from fully funding the territorial government.[188]

Accompanying these nascent notions of regional identity would be a more subtle discussion of race and Mexican Americans' place in the national hierarchy. Bennett put special effort into distinguishing Mexicans from African Americans in pursuit of his political goals. What made this part of the process of differential racialization diverge from his discussion of Native Americans was that African Americans did not have a major role in the territory's economy or society per se.[189] At its highest number during the end of the territory period, the African American population constituted barely 11 percent of New Mexico's total population.[190] Yet the historian Pablo Mitchell documents how racist stories about African Americans circulated throughout the territory in numbers far higher than their proportion of the population in the late nineteenth century. Antiblack images in New Mexico's late-nineteenth-century newspapers asserted Euro-Americans' racializing discourse without overtly antagonizing members of the Mexican elite.[191] The fear among many Mexicans that they would have the same racial status as African Americans that appeared at the time of the U.S.-Mexican War certainly lingered (and perhaps escalated) after emancipation. In the aftermath of the Civil War the image of African Americans had particular power in New Mexico. Given that Mexicans remained in a territory with only limited self-government, it was not hard to stoke a sense of injustice that African Americans were being given preferential treatment through Reconstruction policies.

Bennett drew on those antipathies when he wished to build political solidarity between Mexicans and Euro-Americans in an 1871 editorial. He used an ambiguous *we* to connote unity without drawing out race specifically: "Denounced as ignorant and degraded, yet while hundreds of thousands of dollars have been appropriated to establish schools in the South for the Negroes, we are left unassisted in the education of our children. Numbering a population of nearly one hundred thousand, among whom are many men of marked ability, and capacity, we are left a prey to swarms of hungry carpet bag politicians, who hold all of the office of trust and honor in the Territory."[192] The editorial's carefully calculated language retained, if implicitly, the author's ideas about race. He did not deny the claim that Mexicans actually were "ignorant." This time, however, he implied a shared injustice in the territory perpetrated by "Negroes" and "carpet bag politicians." Euro-Americans and Mexicans were left without any means to correct the territory's problems. From which race the territory's "many men of marked ability and capacity" came, however, Bennett did not specify.

Bennett again drew on Mexican racism against African Americans when he wanted to erode support for the Republican congressional delegate José Francisco Chaves. Territorial voters could elect a single nonvoting congressional delegate. Chaves, a well-known Republican political figure, had been serving in that role since 1865. As the delegate, Chaves selected one candidate to attend the United States Military Academy at West Point. Bennett attempted to stir up anger and resentment against Chaves by drawing on the developing understanding of race and region. Bennett printed editorials in both English and Spanish that focused attention on Chaves's failure to appoint a "son of New Mexico" to West Point.[193] The topic of a West Point cadet, in particular, had greater urgency as many in the territory began an active campaign to "prove" Mexican American patriotism for the United States.

Bennett first raised the issue by calling attention to a young African American attending West Point. Printed identically in both the English- and Spanish-language sections of the *Borderer*, Bennett wrote:

> Otro cadete negro esta para ser mandado a West Point, llamado se Juan McCree una nominación hecha por el Sr. Turner, miembro negro del congreso del estado de Alabama. ¡Oh Pardon! Hagase Vd. a un lado entonces de lugar algún de vuestros hermanos negros, quien tal vez no se parara al pie de la clase. ¡Infortunado Nuevo Mexico! Que el Sr. Turner, un miembro negro del congreso pudo conseguir el nombramiento de uno de su raza; pero el señor Chaves no pudo hayan un hijo de Nuevo Mexico, digno de ese nombramiento.[194]

> (Another Negro cadet is to be sent to West Point, John McCree by name, a nomination made by Mr. Turner, colored member of the Congress from the state of Alabama. Oh Pardon! Get out of the way then and give a place to some of your colored brothers who perhaps may not stand at the foot of the class. Alas New Mexico! That Mr. Turner, a Negro member of Congress can obtain the nomination of one of his race; but the gentleman Chaves can't find a son of New Mexico worthy of the appointment.)

Euro-Americans reading the English article would likely interpret the admission of an African American as an infringement of their status as white men and the humiliation of being in a colonial context without representation. Yet Mexicans could also find meaning in the identical Spanish-language article. Noting that an African American congressman had secured a position for "one of his race," Bennett's article might have also created a sense of betrayal among Mexicans toward Chaves.

The *Borderer* continued the West Point discussion a week later. In an editorial entitled "Shameful," Bennett tried again to incite a sense of a united outrage that one of "our" sons had not been admitted to the military academy. He complained that Chaves had appointed one Julius Pardee, who, Bennett claimed, had no association with New Mexico at all. To make matters worse, Bennett asserted that Pardee, whose academic performance was lacking, had turned out to be "the booby of the whole school."[195] "Does Mr. Chaves," Bennett asked rhetorically, "mean to say that no young man of this Territory is capable of receiving an education?" Bennett worked carefully to avoid using race-specific language by calling for the nomination of a "young man of New Mexico." Euro-Americans and Mexican Americans both would have been sensitive to the gendered language of the narrative and the implied loss of manhood.

This type of language presumed the existence of a regional unity (through words like *we* and *our sons*) among Euro-Americans and Mexican Americans. That unity, though, came through a process of differential racialization that distinguished Mexicans from Native and African Americans. It did not, however, actually make claims of a shared racial identity between Mexicans and Euro-Americans.

Bennett's *Borderer* preceded the 1880s language of a "bicultural" or "tricultural" New Mexican identity, which I will discuss in chapter 5. Looking at the *Borderer*, therefore, suggests some of the experimentation that Euro-Americans did in that critical postbellum decade. By framing, and thereby limiting, certain debates through the territory, Euro-Americans like Bennett could occasionally discuss cross-racial interests. Neither Euro-American nor Mexican American elites, however, forgot the racial categories or their meaning.

Conclusion

Martin Amador, Pedro Melenudo, and Clemente Montoya discussed Mexicans' relationship to American nationalism in distinct ways. Cruceños, like Amador and Melenudo, responded to Euro-American assumptions that Mexican identity was racially monolithic, a result of "mixed blood." "The simple native population of the present day, the Mexican," one Las Cruces Euro-American wrote, "has lived here for centuries intermarrying with the Indians of which there were great numbers in earlier times."[196] To survive in Las Cruces, Mexicans slowly accepted the Euro-American idea that they occupied a distinct racial position. Their resistance turned to creating a vision of themselves as "ethnic Americans" by creating a type of "Mexican American" identity.

Mesilleros, in contrast, developed their town as a self-conscious Mexican national project. While Mesilleros sometimes recognized bonds with Cruceños after 1854, the split in their vision of Mexican identity created divisions within the valley's communities. Montoya's comments suggest that he recognized a fluidity in the racial and national identities Mexicans claimed. The predominant Euro-American discourse relied on an assumption that Mexican and American identities were fixed and determined along racial lines. Montoya's statements contested these ideas about race and nation. Amador, in Montoya's mind, opted to "become Americanized," implicitly forfeiting his "Mexicanness." For Montoya Mexican identity relied on individual choice.

Mexicans divided over the best strategy to pursue or adapt to Euro-American imperialism. The organization and settlement of the local space were shaped by and shaped competing notions about the relationship between racial and national identities. These ideological divides about race and nation also appeared in the organization of the local geography. Mexican and Euro-American government agents imprinted La Mesilla and Las Cruces with tangible reminders of their own sense of nationalism. Even after Mesilla transferred to the United States, being in one town or the other had important implications for mexicanidad.

Indeed, an emphasis on place became a means to elide lingering uncertainties that accompanied Euro-American imperialism in New Mexico. Although a sustained military rebellion against the United States never emerged, nineteenth-century New Mexico witnessed several violent episodes between Mexicans and Euro-Americans. Towns like Mora, Taos, and Mesilla erupted in bloody battles in 1847, 1860, and 1871. Indeed, Euro-Americans often feared that Mexicans would unite and violently overturn their control, as they did do in Mesilla in 1860. Assassinations of local officials like Governor Charles Bent in 1847, of course, fueled these suspicions.[197] During these moments of stress Euro-Americans feared that a bloody "race" war was imminent. One Euro-American Civil War officer, for example, reported to his superiors on June 7, 1861, that he believed that Albuquerque's Mexican population planned to cut the throats of all "white men."[198] Only a year later another military officer reported that the Mexican residents in Peralta had conspired to murder all "whites" in the area.[199] After a violent episode in Mesilla in 1871, Bennett himself feared that Mexicans from El Paso would enter the valley to engage in a war between "Mexicans and Americans."[200] Euro-Americans' dependence on race framed their perceptions of conflict.

Perhaps the rise of *Las Gorras Blancas* (the White Caps) in San Miguel County created the most fear among Euro-Americans.[201] A secret organization composed of Mexicans, Las Gorras Blancas sought to end the accumulation of land and wealth in the hands of a few Euro-Americans and Mexican Americans through radical means in 1889. During the evening small groups destroyed landowners' wire fences and dispersed their stock. In extreme instances the Gorras Blancas also burned houses and barns. They sometimes assumed a public presence, wearing white caps to conceal their identities, to intimidate those who acquired land from an older Spanish or Mexican grant.[202] While the Gorras Blancas clearly showed dissatisfaction with U.S. imperial authority, they did not necessarily operate along strict racial lines. Indeed, they often targeted Mexican American landholders or law enforcement agents along with Euro-American targets.[203] Despite that fact, many Euro-Americans could only conceive of the group as driven by racial antagonism.

These violent episodes, however, only appeared sporadically. Engaging Mexicans with the Union cause during the Civil War provided an early means to secure the territory and opened the possibility for a new type of cultural hegemony. Union officials found that they could sidestep discussions about race and nation by basing their appeals on a language of region. These appeals would continue to develop in the decades after the Civil War. Conflicting ideologies of race and nation were not mere abstractions. They had consequences and informed the ways that individuals organized their lives. The next two chapters consider how these notions influenced day-to-day life in the Mesilla Valley and New Mexico by looking at religion and gender.

CHAPTER 3

"Enemigos de la *Iglesia Católica* y por consiguiente de los ciudadanos Mexicanos": Race, Nation, and the Meaning of Sacred Place

During the November 1851 term of the Doña Ana County District Court, a typical jury submitted its report with mixed religious and secular legal language.[1] Finding Joaquín Torres guilty of assaulting his neighbor, the jury explained the shooting as resulting from Torres's weak character and supernatural influences. Jurors determined that Torres attacked Refugio Abalos without "having the fear of God before his eyes but being moved and seduced by the instigation of the Devil."[2]

Although it may have been common practice to include God and the Devil in legal proceedings, historians often take such religious language fairly lightly. The Latin American historian Sabine MacCormack has commented on the danger of such easy dismissals.[3] Historians, few of whom believe in the Devil, frequently gloss over his presence or other religious language as less important than discussions framed through secular terms, like nationalism and race. Yet religious language often helped to define those latter categories along the U.S.-Mexican border. Whether Mexicans might have literally imagined the Devil influencing Torres, his inclusion suggests that they structured their understanding of civil relationships through religious tropes. Likewise, many nineteenth-century Euro-Americans imagined Catholicism as irreconcilable with American identity. Catholic faith, to their mind, was both evidence of Mexicans' racial inferiority (Mexicans must be racially inferior because "rational" individuals did not participate in a "superstitious" Church) and a product of that racial inferiority (because Mexicans were inherently irrational, they could not help but choose Catholicism over any other religious doctrine).

Catholicism figured centrally in discussions of Mexican identity on either side of the Mexican-U.S. border.[4] Each section of this chapter shows that religion was important in local discussions of race, nation, and region. My focus here on religion, and in the next chapter on gender, also provides a means to show how ideologies affected daily life along the border. Debates over the meaning of race and nationalism, in other words, were not merely the domain of intellectuals and elites. Rather, the conflicting visions of race and nation had significant consequences for the material and daily practices of each town.

I begin with a discussion of Catholicism's role in Mexican national identity before the war with the United States. After Euro-Americans assumed control of New Mexico, a transition from Mexican to European clergy unfolded gradually in the Mesilla Valley. Two bishops, one Mexican and one French, battled for jurisdiction over southern New Mexico and over the meaning and obligations of being a Catholic in a U.S. territory. In the midst of this ecclesiastical struggle, Mesilla became embroiled in a political riot literally at the front door of the church. Subsequently, the European clergy became more vigilant in solidifying its authority in the valley, particularly Las Cruces, where it found allies among the Euro-American population.

When compared to border communities in Texas and California, New Mexico drew relatively little migration from Mexico in the twentieth century.[5] Unsurprisingly, those Mexicans who did migrate into the Mesilla Valley preferred La Mesilla.[6] Conflicts that influenced the valley's early history, therefore, more readily haunted the ways Mexicans structured their memories and stories about their local parishes. The final portion of this chapter considers the longevity of these conflicts by examining oral histories and memories about the Las Cruces parish, St. Genevieve's. Even when the owners and custodians of those accounts figured centrally in the historical events, the popular memories and oral histories that they relate may at times obscure real racial and religious tensions in the church.[7] Mexicans organized their memories about their religious communities as part of an ongoing process. In exploring this historical process, we may better understand the difficulties Mexicans faced in their religious institutions.[8] Even twentieth-century memories about parish life testify to Mexicans' varied strategies to retain their racial and cultural distinctiveness. In this sense the "accuracy" of these memories is less interesting than understanding the decisions that were made in producing such accounts and the longevity of nineteenth-century conflicts.

José Jesús Baca and the Battling Bishops: Clashes over
Religious and Political Authority, 1854–1872

In 1854, the same tumultuous year that brought Mesilla's transfer to the
United States, José Jesús Baca arrived as the town's new priest. The curate
became a central figure in the Mesilla Valley until 1872, when he moved
with a group of Mesilleros to northern Mexico. His two decades in
Mesilla often found him at the center of numerous political and ideological debates. Before we can understand how those events unfolded,
though, we need to understand why Catholicism itself had such a prominent place on the new border.

Mexico's War for Independence exposed the contradictory relationship between Catholicism, the state, and Mexican national identity. After
all, it was an unconventional priest, Miguel Hidalgo, whom historians
continue to credit with instigating the revolt against Spain in 1810.
Through the decade of fighting, nationalists depended on religious imagery, such as the Virgin of Guadalupe, to mobilize soldiers. Catholicism
figured so centrally in the creation of a national identity that Mexico's
1824 Constitution named it as the nation's only legal religion.[9]

Despite Catholicism's critical role in creating the new nation-state,
however, the institutional Church resisted many of the changes demanded by Mexican nationalist leaders. For remote areas like New Mexico the war for independence compounded an already significant absence of priests in local churches.[10] By 1812 only twenty-two friars and
two secular priests served all of New Mexico.[11] After formal independence in 1821, Mexico City's chilly relationship with the Vatican resulted
in the collapse of the Church's administrative structure across the fledgling nation. When each side demanded final authority over the appointments of priests and bishops, the two found themselves locked in a
stalemate. As a result not a single active bishop served Mexico by 1829.
The total number of priests, both secular and regular, in the nation
declined from 9,439 in 1810 to 4,350 in 1850.[12] New Mexico felt this
ministerial breakdown with the greatest severity. By 1826 only nine friars
and five secular priests tended to New Mexico's tens of thousands of
faithful.[13]

Despite the clergy's shrinking numbers, the stiff nationalist positions
about clerical assignments did not represent full-scale assaults on Catholicism. In fact, for most of the 1820s and 1830s any discussion of
severing Catholicism from Mexican national identity appeared extreme

in the political discourse.[14] Not until Mexico's Reforma period (1854–67) did discussions about distinguishing national from religious identities gain momentum. For most of Mexico's early existence, the question was not whether Catholicism was a part of Mexican nationalism but rather what type of relationship existed between the state and the Catholic Church. This unanswered question haunted New Mexico even after it transferred to the United States.

By 1830 the Mexican central government and the Vatican broke the stalemate. For New Mexico this resulted in the first tour by a bishop in seventy-two years. The newly appointed bishop of Durango, José Antonio Laureano de Zubiría y Escalante, entered New Mexico in 1833 with both a religious and secular mission in mind. Before that tour, the almost total absence of formal clergy had permitted the laity a greater freedom from Catholic dogma and religious fees for services like baptism, marriage, and burial. Pueblo Indians and Mexicans had latitude to select elements from Catholicism that met their immediate needs. That latitude, however, had self-imposed limits as New Mexico's laity did not repudiate Catholicism itself. On the contrary, they continued to consider themselves devote believers, the Penitentes being the most extreme manifestation of that devotion. These lay confraternities assumed spiritual leadership roles within their communities.

Zubiría prioritized the reassertion of the institutional hierarchy of the Church. He condemned the Penitente brotherhoods, demanding that they disband and relinquish authority to the curates who started to filter into the territory.[15] Among the Pueblos the bishop called for all indigenous children to be baptized, and he mandated that couples seek the Catholic Church's sanction for marriage. He also increased the authority of the See of Durango by giving patronage appointments to influential New Mexicans.[16] Because of the links between religion and the state, Zubiría's visit reinforced the connection between religion and Mexican nationalism in New Mexico.[17] Marriages, baptisms, and other religious services carried fundamental meanings for an individual's relation to the Mexican state. The parish priest often represented both divine and earthly power in one body. Likewise, civic expressions of Mexican patriotism included religious elements: A solemn mass and *Te Deum* always accompanied civic commemorations of important national holidays.[18] For most nonelite Mexicans, no firm division separated the state from religious authority when war broke out in 1846. As we will see, Baca, appointed by Zubiría, would continue the work of the bishop even under the U.S. regime.[19]

Conflicts over local parishes erupted almost immediately after the United States annexed New Mexico in 1848. Mexicans and the clergy suddenly grappled with the meaning of being in an American parish. After the U.S.-Mexican War European-born clergy supplanted Mexican priests across the northern border, arrogating all positions in the clerical hierarchy from parish priests in Texas to the post of archbishop of Santa Fe.[20] Catholic scholars have long been aware of the tensions between clergy and laity that resulted from the displacement of Mexican religious leaders along the northern border.[21] They, however, have been slow to integrate the study of these religious challenges into the broader ongoing scholarly conversation about U.S. imperialism.

In defense of their appropriation of Catholic positions in the U.S. Southwest and Texas, the European-born hierarchy argued for the universality of the Catholic community, thus rebutting calls for the retention of Mexican priests. They further promised to integrate Mexicans into the United States by encouraging assimilation. Some historians have also suggested that the newly arrived European priests differed theologically from the Mexican laity. Orlando Espín argues that Latin American Catholic practices developed two generations before the Council of Trent in the mid-sixteenth century. European clergy who arrived in the U.S. Southwest thus placed a greater emphasis on doctrinal orthodoxy than did their parishioners.[22] Indeed, European priests implemented substantial changes in the predominantly Mexican parishes of New Mexico.

To Protestant Euro-Americans, European Catholic priests might have seemed unlikely agents of Americanization. In the middle of the nineteenth century, European clergy found themselves members of an embattled religious minority in a nation virulently hostile to Catholicism. Euro-American Protestants throughout the United States expressed concern about the growing number of Catholics and argued frequently that Catholic loyalty to the Pope in Rome precluded them from being loyal citizens of the U.S. republic. Sometimes these anxieties emerged in anti-Catholic riots or even political mobilization, such as the anti-Catholic "Know-Nothing" party.[23]

Catholic intellectuals carried on a lively debate over the desirability and practicability of Americanizing the Catholic Church in response to this hostility. One such debate emerged in 1854, the same year that Baca arrived in Mesilla. A prominent Catholic editorialist created a firestorm when he proposed that German and Irish Catholics should "lose their own nationality and become assimilated in general character to the Anglo-American race."[24] For some leaders in the Catholic Church, like the French priests who arrived in New Mexico, keeping their parishioners Catholic while "assimilating" them into the United States emerged as a primary goal. Assimilation seemed like an ideal solution to the anti-Catholic environment they faced throughout the nation. This larger experiment with assimilation within U.S. Catholicism had some of its earliest tests among Mexican Catholics. Racial and ethnic tensions first seen on the border played out within the Catholic Church in multiple contexts. The assimilating and hierarchal inclinations of parish priests often created discord within parishes across the United States. Nineteenth-century and early-twentieth-century Italian immigrants in New York, for instance, found that the mostly Irish Catholic hierarchy disparaged their religious traditions and worked to limit their authority.[25] Moreover, Italian communities often expressed anticlerical suspicions and rebuked notions of assimilation. The Mexico-U.S. border was merely one of the first foci of such disjunction between priests and their parishioners.

Northern New Mexico churches transferred to U.S. dioceses after the U.S.-Mexican War. As part of that transition, European clergy, mostly from France, rapidly displaced Mexican clergy in the north. By 1870, thirty-seven European priests had arrived to assume control of churches throughout the territory, including southern New Mexico.[26] The European and Euro-American clergy felt a duty to preserve Mexicans in their Catholic faith but participated in the same discourse that named Mexicans as racially different from white Americans. While Protestant Euro-Americans frequently conflated racial and religious identities when they disparaged local Mexicans, the European clergy grappled with race and religion in different ways. On one hand, the French clergy equally discounted Mexicans based on their European assumptions about race, stating explicitly that they believed Euro-Americans (and white Europeans) to be superior in most respects. However, their shared (and putatively universal) religious identity meant that their relationship with local Mexicans differed from that of the Protestant Euro-American settlers. Such differences are best known through the story of Jean-Baptiste Lamy (1814–88), who almost single-handedly orchestrated the French takeover of New Mexico's churches during his tenure as archbishop of Santa Fe from 1850 to 1885. Willa Cather might have immortalized Lamy in *Death Comes for the Archbishop*, but the reality of his administration was mixed for the majority of New Mexico's Catholics.[27] While not often discussed explicitly, Mexicans must also have had some suspicions of the arriving French clergy given that France invaded Mexico during the "Pastry War" of 1838 and again during the Franco-Mexican War (1861–67).

Lamy made no secret that he distrusted the Mexican clergy, whom he rapidly replaced with his own European candidates.[28] He recorded his vision of the territory: "Our Mexican population has quite a sad future. Very few of them will be able to follow modern progress. They cannot be compared to Americans in the way of intellectual liveliness, ordinary skills, and industry; they will thus be scorned and considered an inferior race."[29] European priests used these racist ideas to undermine Mexicans' authority and justify the shaping of parishes to meet their expectations. In some cases the clergy altered everything from religious practices to remodeling the church buildings themselves. The peculiarity of European clergy, most of whom were recent immigrants themselves, imposing their vision of "American" Catholicism should not be ignored.

European priests arrived in the Mesilla Valley more than a decade after their peers in Santa Fe or other cities in northern New Mexico. Bishop Zubiría tenaciously refused to relinquish the Mesilla Valley from his diocese after the U.S.-Mexican War (or after the Mesilla/Gadsden Treaty). He retained jurisdiction over the towns of Doña Ana, La Mesilla, and Las Cruces, frustrating Lamy's attempts to claim authority over southern New Mexico until 1868.[30] To Zubiría the new international border did not change these parishes from being Mexican. Priests loyal to Zubiría developed a tradition of resisting Euro-American pressures to relinquish their political authority in Mexican communities on the U.S. side of the new border. Shortly after the U.S.-Mexican War, for instance, a group of mostly Euro-American citizens protested the tenure of the cura Antonio Severo Barrajo. They complained to Bishop Zubiría that "él [Severo Barrajo] en todos tiempos en sus platicas a los ciudadanos nativos de este condado les ha hecho entender bajo su poder y autoridad, al los ciudadanos que residen aquí y que son naturales de los Estado Unidos, Francia, Hermanía, y Irlanda so todos herejes y *enemigos* de la *Iglesia Católica* y por consiguiente de los ciudadanos Mexicanos" (at all times in his preachings, he [Severo Barrajo] has let the native people, under his power and authority, know that the citizens residing here who are natives of the United States, France, Germany, and Ireland are all heretics and *enemies* of the *Catholic Church* and, as a consequence, of the Mexican citizens).[31] Given Zubiría's role in building Mexican nationalism before the war, it should not surprise us that these parishioners' complaints went unanswered. Instead, Zubiría appointed a fellow Mexican nationalist, José Jesús Baca, as the senior priest of the Mesilla Valley.

Baca followed the precedents set by curates like Barrajo.[32] Indeed, his assignment to the Mesilla Valley resulted from his falling-out with the incoming French hierarchy. Baca started his career in the northern New Mexico town of Tomé. Shortly after Lamy took control of the Diocese of Santa Fe, however, Baca asked to join the Diocese of Durango. The priest complained in particular about Lamy's obvious hostility to Mexican clergy.[33] In 1854 Zubiría answered his request by charging Baca with supervising all of the major parishes in southern New Mexico, including San Albino's in Mesilla and Santa Genoveva (St. Genevieve's) in Las Cruces.[34] Baca established his main residence in Mesilla, a choice that suggests he felt more at ease with the Mesilleros and their reputation for distrusting the United States.

Although Lamy never realized his ambition for adding Las Cruces and Mesilla to the Archdiocese of Santa Fe, Zubiría ultimately lost control of these towns with the creation of the Diocese of Tucson in 1868.[35] When the new diocese assumed authority over southern New Mexico's churches, Baca's role in the area initially remained unchanged as he rejected the Tucson bishop's authority.[36] A violent episode at the center of Mesilla, however, altered all priests' religious and political authority in the territory for the next century.

In June of 1871 Baca issued a letter to his parishioners directing them to vote for Republican candidates in an upcoming territorial election.[37] The priest distrusted Democrats, whom he associated with southern Euro-American land speculators. He argued that Republicans would better defend Mexicans' land titles. "Que si los ciudadanos votan por el partido demócrata," a local newspaper paraphrased Baca, "perderán su religión, y no solo su religión pero hasta su propiedad, que si los demócratas ganan volverán los Tejanos otra vez" (If the citizens vote for the Democratic Party they will lose their religion, and not only their religion but their property; if the Democrats win the Texans will return again).[38] This partisan letter suggests how he imagined his role in local affairs. Given opportune circumstances, he would not hesitate to use his position as a priest to advocate for a particular political party. The letter further suggests another major concern that Baca imagined common to his parishioners: the ability to keep their land.

Not only did the letter articulate a divide between Euro-American Texans and Mexicans, but it also fueled tensions within the Mexican community. Although Mexicans had a numeric majority in Mesilla, Cruceños and Euro-Americans vied for control of the neighboring town. The greater proportion of Euro-Americans in Las Cruces often forced Mexicans there to take positions that diverged from those in Mesilla. Indeed, even Baca seems to have modulated his stance when he spoke in Las

Cruces only a few weeks before issuing his letter.[39] A local newspaper reported that during his visit to Las Cruces, Baca stated "to one of the most prominent citizens of this county, that his ministerial functions prevented him from having anything to do with politics and that he should take no interest in this election."[40]

In Mesilla, backed by a strong Mexican population, he felt at liberty to take a political position on behalf of the Church. Baca could not be as outspoken in Las Cruces, where Euro-Americans threatened the Mexican Catholic population in that town. When his letter became public knowledge, Euro-American newspaper editors in Las Cruces condemned him for being involved in politics. N. V. Bennett's highly partisan Democratic newspaper, the *Borderer*, attacked Baca for transgressing the supposed boundaries between religion and politics, drawing on a long-established vision of Mexicans as the pawns of manipulative Catholic priests.[41]

Baca's political engagement also drew attention from Mexicans who did not always envision religion and politics in the same fashion as the priest. Most parishioners in the valley sought to retain their parish as "Mexican" and considered Catholicism an integral part of their identity. As the theologian Roberto Goizueta argues, broadly speaking, U.S. Latinos historically used Catholic practices to define their sense of self and to resist full assimilation.[42] Whether Republican or Democrat, then, most Mexicans considered the Catholic Church critical to their identity.[43] They were divided, though, over whether the Church should continue to participate in political affairs. Baca's appeal to loyal Catholics (and therefore loyal Mexicans) to vote for Republicans implied that Democratic Mexicans betrayed their religion. He further insinuated that Mexicans who voted for the Democratic Party were willingly sacrificing Mexicans' futures in the territory by inviting the ever-dreaded Texans to take over their land. Political devotions became emotionally volatile.

The political and religious divides in New Mexico emerged from the specific circumstances surrounding the border. Elsewhere in the nation, such as the urban Northeast, the Democratic Party drew heavily on Catholic voters.[44] Indeed, after the Civil War the party drew on an unexpected and uneasy teaming of inner-city Catholics and former Confederates. To say, though, that the Catholic voter was likely Democratic is to ignore Mexican Catholics in the United States. In New Mexico the association between the Democratic Party and exclusionary white southerners, particularly Euro-American Texans, made that party suspect for many Mexican individuals like Baca.

During those tense summer months, most Euro-Americans who wrote about the rising conflict could only frame it through their understandings of race. So, instead of seeing Baca as exposing fault lines within the Mexican community, they imagined that any tensions could only escalate into a battle between Mexicans and Euro-Americans. The Republican Santa Fe newspaper *New Mexican* printed a nervous warning to N. V. Bennett, the Las Cruces editor of the *Borderer*. The *New Mexican* disparaged Bennett's inflammatory coverage of Baca, which it represented as having "aroused" the Mexican settlers. The concerned *New Mexican* editor hinted that this arousal could lead to Mexican resistance or even the violent overthrow of Euro-Americans. Distancing himself from Bennett, the *New Mexican* editor attempted to calm mounting racial tensions that split local Mexicans and Euro-Americans by calling for calm among the racially ambiguous "our people." A few weeks before Mesilla erupted in violence, the paper warned: "Our people are getting considerably aroused as to politics. . . . The *Borderer* in its onslaught on Padre Baca; its publication of slang Mexican verse reflecting upon many of our best citizens in terms not polite, and its ready use of such words as 'little creature,' 'ass,' 'thing' and such like inelegant terms has done the work."[45] Bennett not only attacked the central religious leader in the valley but also made the issue explicitly about race. The editor of the *New Mexican* feared that such rhetoric would result in a race war.

The fear was not misplaced. Political and religious disagreements spawned in the early summer months of 1871 eventually did escalate into a deadly riot in front of Baca's Mesilla parish, San Albino's. In actuality, though, the fight did not develop along strictly racial lines as the *New Mexican* editor had predicted. Instead, opposing *political* factions clashed violently on August 29, resulting in the deaths of nine men and the wounding of fifty others.

Except for the fact that Mexicans constituted a significant portion of the crowd, it was a scene that could have played out during any election throughout the United States in the nineteenth century.[46] Following the Civil War, U.S. political campaigns frequently involved local community events like rallies, picnics, parades, and public speeches. Brass bands became a key feature of these events, playing party songs to raise the crowds' emotions.[47] So, too, in Mesilla mixed groups of electioneering Mexican and Euro-Americans circled through the streets of Mesilla accompanied by musical bands.[48] Each group, one Democrat and one Republican, sought to build support for its political party as it went through the town. The two bands met in front of San Albino's, where tensions flared and violence erupted.

Mexicans and Euro-Americans fought on both sides, but the riot's location in Mesilla distorted the initial news coverage. As we saw in the previous chapter, Mesilla already represented Mexicans' resistance against Euro-Americans. For Euro-Americans in Las Cruces the riot's location in Mesilla fostered a terror that Mexicans throughout the valley would take up arms to overturn Euro-American dominance. Bennett instantly presumed that the riot resulted in fighting along racial lines. The nervous Las Cruces editor printed rumors that "a large number of men from El Paso, Mexico, are on the way to Mesilla and Cruces, induced by reports that the trouble[s] of last Sunday were the commencement of hostilities between the American and Mexican population. Already a large number of those strangers are about on our streets. One of them made a fiery appeal to his countrymen at the republican meeting on Sunday."[49] Mesilleros' known hostility to the United States threatened Euro-Americans' sense of security, especially during moments of strife. Mesilla's potential for harboring a hidden horde of disgruntled Mexicans waiting to massacre Euro-Americans occupied Bennett's thoughts in the first days after the riot.

What Bennett and other Euro-Americans did not appreciate was that not all the tensions in border churches or politics revolved around race. Baca's intervention had heightened tensions internal to the occupied Mexican community as it grappled with its devotion to the Church and its diverse political and national interests. Lay Mesilleros had previously challenged the authority of their own Mexican priests in 1866. While still under the Diocese of Durango, a group of 144 Mexicans petitioned the local justice of the peace to intervene when the Church required that each citizen contribute a specific payment to the local parish.[50] As this incident suggests, although religion was critical to their sense of Mexican identity, members of the laity could still confront the priests or other parishioners over the Church's role in the community.

Thus, racial unity was not the issue for Mexicans as it might have been for Euro-Americans. Both political parties, after all, ran a Mexican American candidate for the position: the Republican Francisco Chaves challenged the Democrat José M. Gallegos for the position of congressional delegate in the summer of 1871.[51] Some Mexicans had been drawn to the Democratic Party, and they likely had not imagined this choice would challenge their link to Catholicism. Gallegos had himself been ordained a

Catholic priest in 1840. Though politically at odds in 1871, Baca and Gallegos had shared an opposition to French control of New Mexico's parishes, as both men had pledged their support to the Diocese of Durango twenty years earlier. Indeed, Bishop Lamy had suspended Gallegos when he sided with Bishop Zubiría over the jurisdiction dispute in 1853.[52] Gallegos thereafter lost a contested election of 1855, partly because his opponents used that religious position as evidence that he aligned himself with Mexico rather than the United States.[53] Baca supported Gallegos's candidacy when he testified to congressional investigators in that 1855 case.[54]

By 1871, however, Baca had declared Gallegos's participation in the Democratic Party a threat to Mexican Catholics. Padre Baca's demand for a particular political allegiance drew local Mexicans into a new debate. San Albino's parishioners gave their allegiance to the bishopric of Durango, which they saw as a statement of Mexican authority.[55] Baca's call for loyal Catholics (and therefore loyal Mexicans) to vote for Chaves implied that Democratic Mexicans, like Gallegos, did not support their religion or their neighbors. In doing this, he actually pushed these Mexican Americans out of Catholicism. This created an immense discord within the Mexican population; no group of Mexican Americans wished to be dissociated from the Church or to be associated with the reviled Texans. It is not surprising that the riot erupted when the two parading political groups crossed paths outside the doors of San Albino's, Mesilla's Catholic church.

Following the riot and the Democratic victory, some Mesilleros, a few Cruceños, and at least one Euro-American from Mesilla decided to leave the United States.[56] After petitioning the Mexican government for land, these settlers followed Ygnacio Orrantia, the U.S. deputy marshal for Doña Ana County, and Fabian Gonzales, the sheriff of Doña Ana County, to the newly created town of Ascensión, Chihuahua, in early 1872.[57] This move mixed elements of politics, nationalism, and religion.[58] Some took the Republican defeat as a bad omen for their future in the valley, perhaps taking to heart Baca's earlier warnings about the Democratic Party.[59] For some of these settlers the move represented a reclaiming of their Mexican national identity in the same way as the first Mesilleros had done with their move south of the border. They took with them a statue of the Virgin of the Immaculate Conception from San Albino's, signifying their devotion to Catholicism that figured so importantly in their conception of Mexican identity.[60]

It was a short-lived victory for Democrats, though, as Republicans defeated Gallegos's reelection bid in late 1872. That election also announced the emerging power of the "Santa Fe Ring," a Republican political machine that dominated the territory for the rest of the nineteenth century. Members of the Ring would be notorious for using their political power in a series of land grabs.[61] The loss of land Baca had predicted under a Democratic banner occurred under a Republican administration nonetheless.

In the Mesilla Valley the bloody end to the Baca controversy left many questions about Catholicism's role in local affairs unresolved. The newly installed Mexican archbishop of Durango, José Vicente Salinas y Infanzón, conceded authority over Mesilla to the French bishop of Tucson. In the aftermath of this riot Baca had little support from the European bishop of Tucson, who had tried repeatedly to replace Baca with a French-born priest.[62] Early in 1873 the fiery priest followed the other Mesilleros who founded Ascensión, where he remained until his death in 1885.[63] The end of Baca's tenure in Mesilla marked a transition for southern New Mexico. Baca and other Mexican priests had served as leaders in resisting U.S. imperialism both within and outside the Catholic Church. The arrival of European clergy, though, altered priests' role as religious and political authorities in southern New Mexico's communities.

Protestant Euro-Americans, of course, continued to view Catholicism with suspicion. Four years after the riot, Mesilla's only newspaper exposed some lingering tensions. The *Mesilla News* published an anti-Catholic and anti-Mexican article headlined "Mexican Religious Toleration" in 1875. The author of the English-language article intended the title to be ironic. Claiming that Mexicans lacked religious tolerance, he chronicled a rioting Acapulco mob that had leveled a Protestant church.[64] The attitude evident in this editorial was common among Euro-Americans who imagined that Mexicans' religious adherence to Catholicism precluded them from being fully integrated into U.S. society. It also revealed a studied obliviousness to the lack of religious toleration for Catholics or other non-Protestant groups within the United States. Mexicans and Catholics, so the logic went, were intolerant of Protestantism, which meant that Euro-Americans should not tolerate Catholicism within the United States.

For Mesilleros and Cruceños, though, the politically motivated riot brought a dramatic change to the valley. On the U.S. side of the border the riot shifted the administration of the local parishes and made race a more pressing issue. The radical transition in southern parishes from Mexican clergy to European clergy exposed the complexity of being both Mexican by race and Catholic by faith in the border region.

The Pistol-Packing Priest: Pierre Lassaigne in Las Cruces, 1870–1909

Following Baca's departure, the laity and the clergy wrestled over the role that the Church would play in local affairs. Both Cruceños and Mesilleros found themselves in a conflicted relationship with the newly arriving priests two decades after they built their local churches. This is not to say that the arriving clergy imagined themselves as hostile to the Mexican population. In the classic missionary spirit they seem to have had few problems balancing racist assumptions with their roles as spiritual leaders.

Moreover, the U.S. incorporation of the border territories fulfilled the Church hierarchy's desire to increase the Catholic presence in the nation.[65] When the bishop of Tucson, Monsignor Henry Granjon, visited southern New Mexico at the end of the nineteenth century, he noted with satisfaction that almost all Mexicans along the border professed the Catholic faith.[66] Although they sought to remake Mexican parishes, the clergy did not wish to completely alienate this large Catholic constituency. Catholic leaders worried that they might "lose" the Mexican Catholic population to Protestantism at any moment if they did not work diligently.[67]

Las Cruces's Loretto Mother Superior acknowledged this fear in a letter congratulating a former student on his admission to a Catholic college. She wrote, "Now I am not afraid you will be too proud to recognize your old teachers [the Sisters of Loretto] when you return neither do I expect to find you a Protestant but the contrary a staunch Catholic a credit to the Brothers and Sisters."[68] Likewise, Granjon wrote ominously about Protestant missionaries from the "biblical societies of New England" who visited southern New Mexico "loaded with gold and astounding promises."[69] Similar motivations can be seen throughout the border during this period. The Texas bishop Jean Marie Odin, for instance, increased the Church's presence in Brownsville when he learned that a group of New York Protestants had arrived in the area.[70]

Protestant missionaries, especially Presbyterians, did work hard at establishing schools and churches to attract and Americanize the local Mexican population. By 1899 the Presbyterian Women's Executive Committee of Home Missions operated 347 mission schools across the United States,

Puerto Rico, and Cuba, of which New Mexico alone accounted for twenty-five.[71] On the Mexican side of the border liberal officials likewise began to relax restrictions on foreign missionaries as a means to curb the Catholic Church's power in the late nineteenth century. Protestant missionary activity escalated sharply after the death of President Benito Juárez in 1872.[72] Permitting Protestant missionaries into Mexico, however, was not of concern only to anticlerical liberals. The dictatorial government of Porfirio Díaz imagined that the infusion of Protestant beliefs could be a key component for "modernizing" Mexico's economy and further integrating it with the United States.[73] During the Porfiriato (1876–1911) Protestant missionaries focused on border cities like Matamoros and Ciudad Juárez, as well as Mexico City, with the implicit blessing of government officials.

Despite their best efforts, however (and a tendency of some historians to overplay their role), Protestant evangelicals had little success converting Mexicans in either country. In the northern Mexican states less than 1 percent of the population had declared themselves Protestant by 1900.[74] Missionaries had slightly better luck on the U.S. side of the border, but even there less than 10 percent of the Mexican population in New Mexico had converted to Protestantism by 1900.[75] Rather than considering the few who converted, a bigger question is why the majority of Mexicans remained faithful to the Catholic Church when the clergy did not meet their needs.

Even as the clergy worked to redefine New Mexico's parishes as nationally "American," Mexicans recognized that the clergy could not do without their participation in those parishes. Although never realized, fears of a mass conversion to Protestantism nonetheless allowed Mexicans certain opportunities for resistance within their churches. The hierarchy's sense of obligation and religious devotion required them to have Mexican bodies to fill their pews. To combat the lure of Protestant schools, Archbishop Lamy authorized the Sisters of Loretto to develop an academy in Las Cruces in 1870.[76] These religious women would have a profound influence on shaping the intellectual development of an entire generation of middle-class Cruceños. Archbishop Lamy, always looking to assert his presence in the disputed area, also called for clergy to volunteer in southern New Mexico's parishes in 1870. Pierre Lassaigne responded, determining to control St. Genevieve's parish and the other churches in southern New Mexico.[77] Not surprisingly, Lassaigne found himself in the middle of a tense legal conflict three years after he appeared in Las Cruces.[78]

Only a few of the court records survive from this important case, but available details suggest that Lassaigne refused to acknowledge that anyone racially "Mexican" could have authority over him. On December 18, 1873, Justice of the Peace Perfecto Armijo issued an order that the priest pay ninety dollars in damages to a Cruceño and five dollars to the court for costs incurred in a dispute whose particulars are now obscure.[79] Lassaigne refused. On review, a second justice of the peace, Morena Chaves, upheld Armijo's decision and directed Constable José Chaves to collect payment from Lassaigne. When the dutiful constable appeared at the priest's door, Lassaigne shot him.[80]

Mexican American officials were surely tired of Lassaigne's refusal to acknowledge their legal authority, but shooting an agent of the court must have seemed outrageous. As he recovered, Chaves filed charges against Lassaigne for assault and resisting an officer of the court. On August 24, 1874, Sheriff M. Barela arrested the priest. Lassaigne found little sympathy with the grand jury, most likely composed entirely of local Mexicans. Though Protestant Euro-Americans liked to allege that priests enslaved local Mexicans, the grand jury issued a swift indictment against Lassaigne. Moreover, their official report signaled their belief in the priest's guilt.[81]

Lassaigne nonetheless engineered his release and never faced trial in this case. Once the Doña Ana County Grand Jury issued its decision, Lassaigne turned to the Euro-American-controlled district court to quash the indictment. Lassaigne claimed that the indictment lacked validity because of technical errors in the paperwork. He further suggested that he did not know that Chaves was acting as an agent of the court when he shot him.[82] The Euro-American district judge overturned the grand jury's decision, allowing Lassaigne to resume his ministry.

Having failed to remove him forcibly from local affairs, Cruceños appear to have resigned themselves to accept Lassaigne as a permanent figure in their parish. Thereafter, more subtle forms of resistance are evident. Ten years after Lassaigne's scrap with Mexican authorities, his vision of New Mexico's Catholic Church as an American institution had brought serious physical changes to the Las Cruces landscape. Working with the Loretto Mother Superior, Praxedes Carty, Lassaigne changed almost every element of St. Genevieve's.[83] The two successfully solicited funds—mostly from prominent Euro-American members of the business community—for the destruction of the original adobe church and the erection of a new St. Genevieve's in its place. These Catholic figures subscribed to the same assumptions as other Euro-Americans who worked to transform the local landscape. They believed that only certain architectural styles suited an American identity and that the Mexican adobe had to be destroyed in the name of "progress."

4. The second St. Genevieve's, built in 1887, with a French façade. Courtesy Rio Grande
Historical Collections/Hobson-Huntsinger University Archives,
New Mexico State University Library.

In keeping with his own vision of American Catholicism, Lassaigne
replaced the Mexican-built building with an expensive brick structure
that he dedicated on October 15, 1887.[84] The form of the new St. Genevieve's made tangible how much the New Mexico church had changed
by the late nineteenth century. The parish priest preferred a French
architectural façade for the church to the Mexican architecture dominant in the area (see Figure 4). To further his physical reformation,
Lassaigne imported French-made stations of the cross, a French statue of
St. Genevieve, and other French elements, all in the name of making the
church "American."[85]

Beyond the physical changes he wrought, Lassaigne found other
means to downplay Mexican authority in his church. He worked to
increase the Euro-American presence in his parish by creating additional
services for "English-speaking" Catholics. While the mass would always

be in Latin, Lassaigne began offering English homilies. "Language" here could be read as a code for "race." A local newspaper interpreted and applauded these additions as an attempt to add more Euro-Americans to the area (thus diluting the Mexican numeric superiority).

In eastern and midwestern states Euro-American Catholics were largely Irish, German, and Italian immigrants and their descendants—groups whose relationship to "whiteness" was not always certain. However, as Linda Gordon shows in her study of early-twentieth-century Arizona, racial and religious presumptions depended on context and local circumstances. In places like New York or Boston, Irish and Italian Catholics figured as inferior to Anglo-Saxon Protestants in the eastern U.S. racial hierarchy. On the border, though, where the racial divide between Mexicans and Euro-Americans had greater urgency, Irish and Italian Catholics found that their Protestant neighbors could more readily accept them as white or Anglo.[86] In Las Cruces these "white" Catholics were praised in ways that would have been unimaginable in the East. "The second mass," the *Las Cruces Citizen* reported, "will be for the English-speaking people. . . . We are glad to see any movement inaugurated for the upbuilding of our community, that will encourage the best element of the country to become our citizens."[87] For the editor, increasing the number of English-speaking Catholics was an important means for displacing the supposedly less advanced Mexican population.

Cruceños seem to have been dismayed by the new St. Genevieve's, and some clearly resented it. While they still attended mass regularly in the first years after the French-styled building had been erected, Mexicans declined to volunteer their labor to maintain the structure. Cruceños initially refused even to help clear the pile of adobe debris that remained from their first St. Genevieve's.[88] Euro-Americans eventually used prison laborers to care for the grounds of the new church; but Cruceño parishioners' refusal to maintain the new structure irritated the church's priests.[89] In 1909 Lassaigne's replacement at St. Genevieve's complained in the Spanish-language press about having to do most of the upkeep for the physical structure himself. Making his request for assistance, he declared:

> Le importa al cura que espera completar, limpiar adornar el lugar santo de los vivos, de tener cuidado también del camposanto de los muertos. Pero como hay tantas cosas que atender: casa, templo, coro, doctrina, funciones, convento, plaza, sin hablar de la disciplina de la parroquia y de las varias cofradías, pido encarecidamente que se me de un corto plazo, un poco de tiempo.[90]

(It matters to the priest who expects to complete, to clean and adorn the holy place of the living and has also to take care of the cemetery. But since there are so many things to attend to: house, temple, choir, doctrine, functions, convent, plaza, without mentioning the discipline of the parish and the various confraternities, I ask earnestly for a short term, a little time.)

Their faith as Catholics prevented them from leaving the church entirely, but Cruceños rejected Lassaigne's version of St. Genevieve's even years after the French priest's death.

This type of resistance also appeared in south Texas, where priests complained of Mexican parishioners' similar disinterest. As in the Mesilla Valley, the south Texas parishes had increasingly fallen under the authority of French or other European priests in the nineteenth century. Even as they neglected to learn Spanish, this clerical hierarchy expressed surprise that Mexicans, both rich and poor, did not contribute financially to their parishes beyond minimal payments for weddings or baptisms. Ignorant of Spanish and unwilling to speak up in defense of their parishioners' civil rights, these priests had rendered themselves mostly irrelevant to Mexican communities.[91] Similarly, Cruceños certainly did use the new church building, but most were not willing to volunteer time or labor for a structure whose architecture alienated them.

The materiality of the church did not deter Cruceños from pushing against the Church's efforts at Americanization. In one incident parishioners shocked Lassaigne's superior, Bishop Henry Granjon, when he visited their parish in 1902. Granjon noted the important role Catholicism played in the local communities. "Among the Mexicans [in Las Cruces]," Granjon wrote, "the Church is still the uncontested queen of their existence. Its life is their life; its joys are their feast days; its laws, their rules of conduct."[92] Yet when the bishop delivered a sermon in St. Genevieve's, he observed that the parishioners had limited patience with the clergy's importing of English into their church. Granjon noted that Cruceño parishioners became unruly when he switched from Spanish to English: "Since the audience was mixed, it was a matter for my addressing them in two languages, English and Spanish. I began with Spanish. The short speech was given without incident before an attentive audience, but I had scarcely begun my discourse in English, for those who did not understand Spanish, when I perceived among the Mexican ranks some kind of growing agitation. Men and women were rising, leaving their benches, going from here to there passing by each other. Uncooperative babies soon began to scream their heads off and fill the church with a deafening commotion."[93] Granjon interpreted this behavior as restlessness, but we might also read in his tale a conscious form of resistance within St. Genevieve's. His account noted that it was only when he switched to English that the Mexican parishioners began to make a disturbance. Cruceños made it clear that they were not inclined to give the English language a place in their Mexican church.

As these incidents suggest, Mexicans and their non-Mexican religious leaders frequently clashed over language. The Mesilla Valley Mexicans had a numeric superiority, which enabled them to resist the complete erasure of Spanish in favor of English. Religious leaders in New Mexico understood, however, that Mexicans who traveled elsewhere in the United States entered an already secure "English-speaking place." No longer in the contested zones of St. Genevieve's, Cruceños would be unable to counter the Church's efforts to enforce English as the primary language (aside from Latin). A nun who had instructed Martin Amador's son Juan in Las Cruces wrote to him during his attendance at a St. Louis college. "Well, you must speak English very well now," she surmised, "so I shall not write you in Spanish this time."[94] Nor did Sister Vida ever write him in Spanish again.

While the nun could not require Juan to speak English in Las Cruces, she could insist on communicating with him only in English once he left New Mexico. Juan's move to a place that the sister imagined as "English speaking" (a St. Louis Catholic college) changed her attitude toward communicating with him in Spanish. Stories such as Juan's surely circulated among Mexicans in the Mesilla Valley. Wishing to preserve their use of Spanish, they did not want the valley or their parishes to become places where English dominated. To prevent this, they resisted by discouraging the clergy's use of English.

Despite the physical changes to their parish, Mexicans never acknowledged that the new façade might undermine St. Genevieve's existence as a Mexican parish. During his tenure Lassaigne replaced Mexican clergy, destroyed the adobe St. Genevieve's, and established a campaign to bring in more English-speaking ("white") Catholics. In spite of these changes Mexicans found means to preserve St. Genevieve's as theirs by celebrating mass and the major events of their lives there.[95] For instance, Emilia Amador de Garcia, daughter of the Cruceño merchant Martin Amador, grew up in Las Cruces. When she wrote to her mother in 1893 about her experiences in attending mass in Chicago, she noted her preference for New Mexico's churches. "Esta mañana fuimos a Misa en la Iglesia de los Santos Angeles," she wrote, "dies [*sic*] centavos y dán asiento en bonita Iglesia al estilo

americano; pero mucho más me gustan las Iglesias Mexicanas, tan sol-
emnes, tan divinas, tan grandes" (This morning we went to mass at the
Church of the Holy Angels; ten cents and they give you a seat in a pretty
American-style church; but I much prefer the Mexican churches, so solemn, so divine, so great).[96] Attendance at St. Genevieve's would certainly have influenced Amador de Garcia's early impressions of Catholic
churches. She did not, however, seem to consider St. Genevieve's to be in
the "American style" like the Chicago parish, despite its French façade and
cleric. Instead, she identified her childhood church with the "Mexican"
style of New Mexican parishes. Despite Lassaigne's remaking St. Genevieve's in a European architectural style, then, the parish could still remain
Mexican in the imaginations of parishioners like Emilia Amador de Garcia.

Mesilla's San Albino's after 1871

Saint Genevieve's parishioners were not alone in their experiences with
the European clergy. Mesilleros faced almost an identical challenge as the
Catholic Church began a policy to change their New Mexican parish into
a "[Euro-]American" space, although they had been able to delay the
implementation of this policy. In 1872 the Vicariate of Arizona replaced
José de Jesus Baca with Lassaigne in Las Cruces and the French cleric
Augustè Morin in Mesilla. Morin and his French successors, Jean Monfort and Jounne (Jean) Grange, wanted to break the exclusive association
between San Albino's and Mesilleros. Just as Lassaigne remade St. Genevieve's, Morin, Monfort, and Grange also adapted San Albino's. Morin
oversaw the removal of traditional Mexican architectural elements, such
as San Albino's vigas and low set windows.[97] By 1906 Mesilleros lost their
original adobe structure entirely, as Cruceños had lost the original St.
Genevieve's in 1887. Father Grange dedicated a new brick San Albino's
with a Romanesque façade.[98]

While Cruceños and Mesilleros faced such similar challenges from
their parish priests, their response and forms of resistance did not always
assume the same pattern. Mesilleros were better able to prevent their
local priest from implementing many of Lassaigne's policies. While the
Las Cruces cleric pursued a program of encouraging English, his contemporary in Mesilla, Jean Grange, failed to institute a similar platform.
Bishop Granjon even noted Grange's failure to learn English himself.
"Not familiar with English," Granjon wrote, "[Grange] speaks Castillian
as if it were his mother tongue."[99]

Both Lassaigne and Grange arrived in the Mesilla Valley with similar backgrounds. Likewise, they had a common ambition to remake their parishes as Euro-American. Only Lassaigne, though, had the power to push the English language within his parish. Las Cruces, after all, had a greater number of like-minded Euro-Americans, including the Sisters of Loretto, to support him. Mesilleros, in contrast, imagined their identity as more radically Mexican than their Cruceño neighbors and overtly demanded that their parish reflect their own sense of identity. Rather than forcing English on local Mexicans, Grange found the Mesilleros required that he learn to speak Spanish "as if it were his mother tongue." While Cruceños struggled with an immediate threat from the Euro-American population, Mesilleros had an advantage through their larger numbers to preserve more cultural elements in their religious sites.

We should not construe the Mesilleros' ability to keep their space defined as "Mexican" as a complete triumph over Euro-American imperialism, but the differences between Mesilleros and Cruceños do suggest the importance of local context to the expression of resistance. Mesilleros' preservation of their parish as Mexican in the valley's imagination had costs. Mexicans fought for and won a space for their religious practices that acknowledged their national and racial background, but as we saw in chapter 2, Euro-American newspaper editors in the Mesilla Valley frequently cast aspersions on Mesilla by noting its continuation as a Mexican town. A small newspaper article in 1878 recounted the Mexican celebration of the Feast Day of Guadalupe in Mesilla. After reviewing the Mesilleros' activities for the day, the article ended with the statement, "We congratulate the Mexicans, who do not forget their ancient religious and national feasts."[100] The author of the above article constructed Mesilleros' physical presence in Mesilla as foreign. The English-speaking writer, in referring to "Saint Guadalupe," described the religious practices with the assumption that his English-speaking readers would have no existing knowledge about these "Mexican" practices. In doing so, the author naturalized the Euro-American presence in the larger valley by demarcating Mesilla as a place where such "foreign" religious traditions occurred.[101]

San Albino's experienced similar architectural changes to those in St. Genevieve's. The difference between the parishes, though, derived from the same circumstances that affected the relationship between Las Cruces and Mesilla. Cruceños resisted the demands and changes of the European priests, but an increasing number of English-speaking Catholics had started to attend their parish. Because Lassaigne and his successors promoted their involvement in the Church, these Anglo Catholics had a disproportionate influence on parish life and a priority in religious services. Mesilleros, meanwhile, remained the almost exclusive constituency for San Albino's. This gave them substantial authority within the parish when compared to St. Genevieve's. That contrast became a means for Euro-Americans to isolate Mesilla as a supposed exception in the territory because of its "Mexican" majority.

Cuentos, Bells, and the French Priest with a Mexican Name: Catholicism, Memory, and St. Genevieve's

Mesilleros' and Cruceños' decisions during the nineteenth century continued to influence the ways that subsequent generations understood their relationship to the Catholic Church. The tense relationship between Mexicans and European priests becomes obvious on historical investigation; however, public memories and popular histories sometimes obscure these stories despite their continued relevance. Thinking about the ways that later generations described this history allows us to understand how Cruceños and Mesilleros came to understand the history of Catholicism in their towns. Memories about these religious battles persisted, but often became reworked based on twentieth-century assumptions about race and nation. Though it extends beyond the chronology of this project, considerations about how Cruceños and Mesilleros remembered religion, nation, and race are too valuable to omit. By extending the story a bit, we can more fully see how notions of Mexican and American identity developed and redeveloped as part of an ongoing process.

As a young girl, Teresa Garcia witnessed the eruption of the bloody 1871 riot in Mesilla.[102] Discussing the incident with a magazine reporter seventy years later, Garcia framed her memories through her perspective within Mesilla's San Albino Catholic Church:

> I was swinging on the church doors listening to the music of my father's band. . . . Suddenly in front of the church, the republicans and democrats came face to face. How could they pass each other, for nobody wanted to be the first to step aside? . . . Then a shot! Apolonio Barela had fired a pistol. Señor Kelley, a democrat, got excited and hit Señor Lemon, a republican, with a pick handle, killing him. Felicitas Arroyas y Lueras drew his pistol and killed Kelley. There were many, many shots. As I still swung on the church doors I saw men falling down in the dust.[103]

By the time of Garcia's interview in 1944, the riot had become a key component in the telling of southern New Mexico's history. As an eyewitness to the events, Garcia likely retold and reorganized her memory countless times before the reporter from *New Mexico Magazine* filed her story. The elderly Garcia's decisions about describing the riot are intriguing. She did not mention the public debate about the Catholic Church's position a few months before the riot (nor was José Jesús Baca often mentioned in the decades after the riot).[104] Furthermore, she never explicitly named any racial or religious tensions that might have contributed to the violence. Only the emphasis on her location within San Albino's provides the subtlest suggestion about Catholicism's importance in the riot. Garcia opened and closed her recollections by noting her location, "swinging on the church doors." This roundabout allusion only hinted at the centrality of the parish to the events of the riot. Memories such as Garcia's suggest that many Mexicans sought to forget the divisions and trauma that resulted from the reordering of New Mexico's political and social life.

Interconnections among racial, national, and religious ideologies continued to affect the ways that Mexicans imagined their position in the twentieth-century United States. Popular stories about the nineteenth century served as a means to explain and shape different visions of race and nation. Although I used historians' tools to uncover information about St. Genevieve and San Albino's early years, the memories that survived about these parishes did not always reflect the historical record.[105] Instead, Mexicans structured memories about their border parishes based on their need to explain their relationship to the American Catholic Church. This meant that neither social memories nor perceptions about race and religion were static.

By the middle of the twentieth century some residents preferred not to acknowledge the historical tensions that had disrupted their local parishes. Cruceños, for instance, sometimes told *cuentos* (stories) that suggested cooperation between Mexicans and Euro-Americans in St. Genevieve's. Mexicans highlighted their contributions and claims to their parish, but they avoided labeling it as exclusively Mexican. In these memories Mexicans contributed alongside Euro-Americans during critical moments in the parish's history. On a fall day in 1863, a frequently repeated Las Cruces story recounts, an informal group of Mexicans and Americans watched as an elderly European priest cast the first bells for St. Genevieve's in a placita near the center of town. The priest poured a molten mixture into his crude molds that contained every piece of metal that the town's people could find. Women gave their best jewelry, a visiting Mexican circus parted with their coins, and townspeople even placed small quantities of gold into the crucible so that their church could start mass with the sound of ringing bells.[106] It was a magical story of sacrifice that resurfaced throughout the following century.

On first glance nothing could be more effective in making a claim of cross-racial ownership of the parish than this seemingly distinctive story of collective offering, except that we find that this story is not as geographically specific as it might first appear. Mesilleros recount an almost identical cuento about the casting of San Albino's bells. While Cruceños remembered their bells as having been cast with Euro-American cooperation, Mesilleros framed the casting of their bells as part of a uniquely Mexican tradition. Comparing popular memories in the two towns provides an opportunity to consider how differing ideas about Mexican identity influenced the organization of popular stories. Typical of similar versions in Mesilla, an older Mexican named Manuel Valles recalled his childhood memories about the manufacture of San Albino's first two bells:

> There was a big cauldron in the *patio* of the priest's house, and the man was stirring a red hot mass which gave off a great heat. My big sister boosted me up on the *patio* wall, and I saw walking around the cauldron all the fine *señoras* and *señoritas* of Mesilla. My eyes popped out when I saw what they were doing. They were tossing gold coins, gold rings, and bracelets into the big pot. "Are they crazy?" I asked my sister. "You're the crazy one, *muchacho*," she told me, "don't you know that's the custom? They're winning the favor of San Albino by giving their jewelry and money so the bells of Mesilla may ring with a sweet tone."[107]

For Valles the construction of the bells gave Mexicans (and Mexican women in particular) claim to San Albino's through their unselfish contributions. Unlike in Las Cruces, Valles framed the construction of the bells as steeped in Mexican tradition: "that's the custom," his sister had noted.[108] Indeed, stories about local church bells being cast from precious metals circulated for some time in the Mesilla Valley. A distorted version of this story even caught the imagination of a *Chicago Tribune* editor in 1887. In a column entitled "Out of the Ordinary" the *Tribune* erroneously reported that Mesilla's bells had been cast in 1775, some seventy-five years before the town's founding. It further reported that more than a thousand dollars' worth of Mesilleros' gold and silver jewelry had gone into their casting.[109] In this instance the story received by the

Tribune created an imagined legitimacy to Mesilleros' position in the valley by claiming that their town had been in place for more than a hundred years (and even predated the creation of the United States itself). The bells were the symbol of that (exaggerated) legacy.

Cruceños and Mesilleros deployed remarkably similar stories to assert their claim to each town's church. The stories relate almost identical accounts of the casting of their parish's bells as an act of tremendous sacrifice for local Mexicans. Their differences, therefore, become even more important. While the Las Cruces story never referred to existing customs, Valles made the revelation that the Mesilleras acted under Mexican tradition his story's focal point. Valles thereby replicated the creation of this knowledge to establish San Albino's as a Mexican parish. In Las Cruces, though, the emphasis was on cooperation and joint ownership of the parish between Euro-Americans and Cruceños, perhaps as a way to diffuse lingering tensions. Discussing these types of memories and collective stories about St. Genevieve's and San Albino's suggests the ways that Mexicans organized their past to articulate their position within the community.[110] Mesilleros framed their stories about San Albino's as exclusively Mexican. Cruceños, in contrast, often discussed the history of St. Genevieve's while balancing their ethnic claims to the parish with a wider idea of Catholic and American community.

Reflecting on the past glories of St. Genevieve's, Mexican American residents commonly made statements such as Rita Sosa's: "It was the heart of Las Cruces for me."[111] Another resident recalled that St. Genevieve's "was more than a church to followers, it was a gathering place."[112] Forty years after his arrival from Mexico, one man remembered becoming a parishioner at St. Genevieve's as his first act upon migrating to Las Cruces.[113] Mexicans often conveyed their sense of identity through the parish and measured their lives against the church's daily cycles. One Cruceña resident marked her birth at the time "on June 14, 1891, as the bells of St. Genevieve's summoned people to five o'clock mass."[114] These collective memories and stories developed as Mexicans attempted to balance their devotion to the church with the problems they faced as parishioners.

Although they did not appear in twentieth-century public discussions about the church, tensions that developed in the nineteenth century continued to inform the relationship between Euro-Americans and Mexicans in border parishes. Therefore we must consider more intently how the organization of memories structured, and were structured by, ideas about race. Euro-Americans in the twentieth century, for instance, would often forget the first adobe St. Genevieve's that served as the Catholic center for Las Cruces for thirty years. When discussing the fate of the second St. Genevieve's almost one hundred years later, English-language newspaper reporters rarely mentioned the first structure built by Mexicans and Mexican Americans.[115] Stories that highlighted the second building likely did so because of its appearance as an American structure. Euro-Americans preferred to consider St. Genevieve's a creation of the American Catholic Church that manifested Euro-Americans' colonizing efforts in the area.

In contrast, Cruceños wished to link the existence of any subsequent St. Genevieve's with their ancestors' initial construction of the small adobe parish. Although Euro-Americans might have forgotten about the first adobe structure, its existence remained clear in Mexican collective memory. When asked about her knowledge of St. Genevieve's, María Gonzáles Carriere started her history by citing its construction in 1859, not 1887, the date of the second church.[116] Other Cruceños recited similar stories about devoted Mexicans and Father Manuel Chávez dedicating the first adobe St. Genevieve's on January 3, 1859.[117] Cruceños were not alone in emphasizing the Mexican origin of their parish. Mexicans throughout southern New Mexico had interchangeable stories about their parishes, as well. These traditions asserted Mexicans' central role in building churches in Doña Ana, Mesilla, and other towns near the border.[118] Mexicans frequently cited (and still cite) these buildings as physical representations of their longtime presence and authority in the Mesilla Valley.[119]

Mexicans even made Lassaigne himself a site for resistance in public memories about the French cleric. Lassaigne's first name became known as "Pedro" instead of Pierre as early as his death in 1909, even in English-language newspapers.[120] A 1949 newspaper article celebrated the centennial of the town and paid special respect to Father Lassaigne. The newspaper writer, confused by the strength of this memory, described the priest as "a Frenchman who oddly had a Spanish first name."[121] Mexicans in the area seemingly felt that Lassaigne needed Mexican markers to enable him to operate in their sacred rituals. Lassaigne might have succeeded in changing the structure of the church, but Mexicans succeeded in changing his name.

Cruceños sometimes asserted their authority more directly to gain concessions from the Church. The most dramatic demonstration of this process may be found in the constant remodeling of St. Genevieve's physical structure in the first fifty years of the twentieth century. Mexi-

5. The second St. Genevieve's after being covered
with stucco in the "mission" style. Courtesy Archives
and Special Collections Department, New Mexico
State University Library.

can American and even Euro-American parish members increasingly
demanded that the Church recognize cultural elements that distinguished St. Genevieve's from other American parishes. By the 1940s,
physical instability required that the two bell towers be lowered. For
many in the area this presented a unique opportunity to renegotiate the
appearance of St. Genevieve's. In place of the French-styled domes, St.
Genevieve's emerged from under the construction scaffolding topped
with Mexican red tiles and stucco to simulate adobe (Figure 5). This
substantial change in appearance brought the church closer to the architectural styles that the community imagined as "Mexican."[122]

To Cruceños the image of St. Genevieve's as a southwestern church
seemed so logical that their collective memory sometimes lost the French
architectural style. Indeed, a sociologist lamented the 1960 urban renewal

program in Las Cruces because it "meant the destruction of adobe buildings to be replaced with cinder block, concrete, and stucco surfaces which
give the appearance of adobe."[123] More specifically, he mourned the loss
of St. Genevieve's, a building "built in the old mission style."[124] This
sociologist apparently did not realize that the St. Genevieve's that he
remembered was really a French design covered with stucco to give the
appearance of adobe. For its part the Mexican community had no reason
to keep St. Genevieve's French façade in the public memory. Even years
after Lassaigne's death, Cruceños resisted his legacy by forgetting his
architectural changes entirely. It seemed obvious to the sociologist that
St. Genevieve's "mission" façade had always represented Mexicans' cultural background.

Such architectural transformations were not unique to the valley. Across
the Southwest, Euro-American and Mexican American boosters increasingly invested in architectural styles like "California Mission" or "Pueblo
Revival," which they believed distinguished their local communities. The St.
Augustine Cathedral in Tucson witnessed a similar twentieth-century re-
invention as St. Genevieve's in Las Cruces. Tucson lost its original Mexican
church when the French bishop Peter Bourgade commissioned a Gothic
brick structure in 1897. In 1928, however, St. Augustine's received a new
Mexican-baroque façade modeled after the cathedral in Querétaro, Mexico, that masked its French origins.[125] These changes in physical structures
resulted from complicated, and sometimes contradictory, visions of the
region by both Mexican and Euro-American elites. Euro-Americans often
saw these architectural moves as part of marking the local geography with
romantic emblems of the "past." Many Mexican Americans, on the other
hand, saw these transformations as acknowledgment of their continued
presence in the area and their cultural contributions.

It was only one way that Mexicans asserted their presence within the
Church and society. Mexicans outside of Las Cruces highlighted memories that controverted the nineteenth-century Church's emphasis on
claiming an American national identity. An elderly man's reminiscences
about Fourth of July celebrations illustrate religion's multiple meanings
along the border that contrasted Las Cruces and Mesilla. Cruz Alvarez
spent his life in Refugio, a town that first developed as part of the same
nineteenth-century federal Mexican project that created Mesilla. Like its
neighboring town, Refugio was added to the United States under the
Mesilla/Gadsden Treaty in 1854. To the Euro-American population the
massive fiestas that Mexicans conducted each July 4 appeared to testify
to their devotion to the United States; however, Alvarez made it clear

that these fiestas did not originate in U.S. nationalism. "One of the largest [fiestas]," Alvarez recollected, "was to celebrate 'Our Lady of Refuge' on July 4 of each year. . . . I can remember when I was a child, many people would come from El Paso to help celebrate. They would say, 'How patriotic you people are! We don't celebrate July 4 in El Paso the way you do here.' We always laughed when we told them we were not celebrating Independence Day—that it was our Patron Saint's day!"[126] Alvarez's recollections reveal that Mexicans understood the national significance of celebrating the Fourth of July; however, his distancing of their celebration away from the American national event to a Catholic religious event diminished their feelings of alienation from the United States. The fact that a reference to their American patriotism resulted in laughter further suggests a subtle attempt to keep their identity from slipping into being "purely American."

Memories and popular stories about the past are inextricably tangled with present concerns and are filtered by age and perspective. Discussion about the memories of southern New Mexico's parishes, therefore, gives much needed clues to the ways that Mexican Americans understood the relationship between their religious and racial identity at the local level. Like Garcia's memories about the Mesilla riot, most of the stories that circulated (and still circulate) about the nineteenth century are often coded.

Open discussion about past difficulties did not appear in local print or even oral traditions about the Catholic Church. Baca's involvement with the riot or Lassaigne's shot at an officer of the law did not remain in the town's collective memory. Instead, individuals and groups attempted to explain the history of their parishes through subtle assertions about authority in the Church. One Mesillero acknowledged that the struggles between the laity and priests continued well into the twentieth century. Mesilla, he explained, was a "closed community," which was "demonstrated by the test that each new Parish Priest is put through before partial acceptance by the community."[127] Religious authority alone did not guarantee a place of honor in Mesilla; a potential priest also had to be "tested" in his willingness to accommodate the Mexican majority. Even in the best of circumstances, the "outsider" priest would only be "partially accepted."

Conclusion

In 1967 the bishop of El Paso, who then oversaw the Mesilla Valley, authorized the demolition of St. Genevieve's second building. Its destruction revived the bitterness in the Mexican community and continues to appear prominently in Cruceños' stories. Once again, the Catholic hierarchy appeared indifferent to parishioners' desires. One newspaper printed an article in 1995 that attempted to capture Cruceños' persisting memories about the parish. Lori Kubinski tied the destruction of the parish to a broader range of racial and social conflicts in southern New Mexico. She noted that many Cruceños refused to discuss St. Genevieve's with her:

> Some of the old-timers from the old church were reluctant to talk to me about the story of St. Genevieve's; even after 27 years, the memory of losing their church home is too painful to bring up, especially to a stranger. Some say the old church should've been torn down and rebuilt on the original spot, and that because Las Cruces was under the direction of the El Paso Catholic Diocese . . . the old church was not as well cared for as it could've been, and that the bishop "sold us down the river" in the name of progress and "urban renewal." Many local customs were lost with the advent of an Anglo population and boundaries were raised, boundaries which are evident today in the demarcation of neighborhoods, the pronunciation of words, the distribution of our schools.[128]

Kubinski expressed the idea that St. Genevieve's had particular relevance in the local struggles between Euro-Americans and Mexicans. Based on her informants' recollections, she conflated the destruction of the parish with the "advent of an Anglo population" that created a "loss of local customs." This loss, Kubinski claimed, occurred simultaneously with the erection of boundaries between Mexicans and Anglos. She did not realize that the organization and narrative of this story predated the 1967 destruction of St. Genevieve's.

Virtually since its founding, St. Genevieve's parish had been a contested space. Its history became intimately tied to the tensions many Mexicans faced in reconciling the demands of their religious leaders with their own sense of identity. Reluctance to talk to a "stranger [i.e., a Euro-American]," not surprisingly, resulted from these same tensions. Cruceños and Mesilleros both grappled with these changes, though their tactics and achievements differed in key ways. Even the modern names associated with the two parishes signal differences between the two towns. Euro-American dominance eventually forced Cruceños to relinquish the Spanish name (Santa Genoveva de Las Cruces) for their parish as they adopted the English "Saint Genevieve's." In contrast Mesilleros preserved the original Spanish name "San Albino" for their parish. At the most fundamental level the ability to name space signifies power. This outcome suggests that Mesilleros were more successful than Cruceños in retaining their parish's Mexican heritage.

Although I have primarily explored the Cruceños' particular parish, certain patterns will prove to apply generally. St. Genevieve's history points to the complex ways that Mexicans along the border navigated conflicting ideas about race and nation. Because their religious participation was both supremely intimate and highly public, sacred spaces often appeared at the center of ideological conflicts. At times Mexicans made decisions about which changes to their space they would accommodate and which changes they would resist.

CHAPTER 4

"Las mujeres Americanas están en todo":

Gender, Race, and Regeneration,

1848–1912

Euro-American traders who arrived in New Mexico between 1821 and 1857 commented forcefully on gender and sexuality as a key sign of racial difference between Euro-Americans and Mexicans. These firsthand accounts created fantastical visions of Mexicans as sexually depraved and immoral. M. M. Marmaduke recorded his 1824 journey into New Mexico using such language about settlers in northern Mexico. "Men and women," Marmaduke noted, "will indiscriminately and freely converse together on the most indecent, gross and vulgar subjects that can possibly be conceived, without the least embarrassment or confusion."[1] James Pattie's 1831 personal narrative contained similarly unfavorable impressions of Mexicans. He claimed that unending violence plagued Mexican communities because the men were slaves to "unmanly" jealousy that led to countless murders. Mexican women, he hinted, fueled these men's passions through their dalliances.[2] Josiah Gregg likewise wrote in 1844 that Mexicans carelessly disregarded the "institution of marriage." Projecting an image of Mexican men and women as equally wanton, Gregg disparaged local sexual practices by contending that in "New Mexico, the institution of marriage changes the legal rights of the parties, but [it] scarcely affects their moral obligations."[3] Such sensational accounts invited Euro-American audiences to take control of lands populated by Mexican women who ran gambling houses, lascivious priests who seduced their parishioners, and fathers who sold their daughters into prostitution.[4] Many Euro-American readers would have felt a libidinal investment in these images, which provided titillation and exoticized Mexican sexual practices while justifying U.S. imperialism.[5]

Stories of "sinful women," "neglectful wives," and "lecherous men," of course, could be found anywhere in the United States at the turn of the century.[6] Along the Mexican-U.S. border, they assumed particular significance and dominated discussions about sexual morality far more than any other issue. Stories about "wanton Mexican women" or "lascivious and jealous Mexican men" explained and justified their exclusion from full citizenship by depicting them as sexual deviants.[7]

Building on the emerging scholarly consensus concerning the relationships between sexism and U.S. imperialism in general, and between sexism and racism along the Mexican-U.S. border in particular, the present chapter highlights some of the ways in which the discourses of race and gender mutually informed one another.[8] Here the focus is less on differences between La Mesilla and Las Cruces than the ways that gender figured in the remaking of towns like Las Cruces into American or New Mexican, which is to say "non-Mexican," sites. As we will see, middle-class Cruceños ultimately used discussions about gendered space as a means by which to describe their town and the larger territory as geographically specific to, and unique within, the United States. These discussions anticipated the emerging regional identity, which distinguished New Mexico within the United States and set it apart from Mexico or other Latin American nations.

Race, Gender, and the "Sinful" Borderlands

As I mentioned in chapter 1, a central trope of early Euro-American personal narratives centered on the "shock" of first encountering the radical difference of the Mexican Other. Often these narratives adduced Mexicans' gender and sexual behavior as the most obvious evidence of racial difference. Accordingly, as Mexicans and Euro-Americans vied for control of New Mexico, the daily interactions of men and women came under close scrutiny and debate.[9] Early personal narratives and calls for "Manifest Destiny" rarely considered the social dynamics that would need to be confronted after annexation. In contrast, they generally imagined that converting Mexican territory into American territory would be simple. George Wilkins Kendall, for instance, wrote in 1847 that Mexicans were "morally, physically and intellectually" inferior to Euro-Americans and would either become "extinct or amalgamated with Anglo-Saxon stock."[10]

Given Mesilla's known opposition to U.S. dominance, it is not surprising that Euro-Americans sometimes mentioned the valley as a particularly egregious area in which vice went unchecked. In 1859 the *Weekly*

Arizonian claimed that the abundance of "dark eyed prostitutes" made Mesilla infamous.[11] Such writings presented Mexican women as "wanton" and as the cause of violence and disorder on the U.S. side of the border. The mere presence of a majority Euro-American population, some believed, would snuff out the existing Mexican population.[12] By such logic, the sexual vices that legitimated Euro-American annexation ought to disappear as soon as the Mexican population disappeared.

In the midst of these discussions about who would ultimately survive in the territory, Euro-Americans sometimes drew divisions between the racial significance of Mexican men and Mexican women. The legal scholar Kimberlé Crenshaw coined the term *intersectional identities* to highlight the ways that race, gender, class, and other notions of difference create particular experiences and knowledges.[13] While racism and sexism intersect in people's daily lives, Crenshaw argues, activists and scholars tend to treat race and gender as exclusive or separable categories.[14] Attention to the nineteenth-century border between the United States and Mexico quickly shows that individuals did not so easily disentangle these identities. In other words, no individual could exist as a gender-neutral "Mexican" or as a racially ambiguous "man." Gender ideologies informed the meaning of an individual's racial identity and vice versa.

A medical doctor who traveled through New Mexico in the middle of the U.S.-Mexican War, for instance, argued that Mexican men reflected their inferior racial status by being physically and morally uglier than Mexican women: "The men are generally taken, ill-featured, while the women are often quite handsome. Another striking singularity is the wide difference in the character of the two sexes. While the men have often been censured for their indolence, mendacity, treachery, and cruelty, the women are active, affectionate, open-hearted, and even faithful when their affections are reciprocated."[15] Given that many Euro-Americans married Mexican women, it is not surprising that some made these complicated racial distinctions along gender lines. In those early estimations Mexican women could be "elevated" to a higher moral standing if they escaped the cruelty and detachment of Mexican men.

These foreign Euro-American men thereby cast themselves as heroes who liberated Mexican women from the oppressive yoke placed on them by a "backward" society. Fantasies about Mexican women as degraded victims even became poignant literary devices in U.S. fiction.[16] As Shelley Streeby documents, Euro-American authors created a recurring imperialist allegory through stories of an "irresistible romance" between U.S. soldiers and (mostly white) Mexican women.[17] These widely circulating fictions presented Mexican women as being forced into unnatural gender roles because the Mexican men who surrounded them were either "savage" or "decadent." Americans believed that their own model of restrained manhood and virtuous womanhood was the only valid civilized and moral gender ideology. Only the influx of white U.S. manhood could ever redeem these poor women and return them to their rightful place in the home.[18]

Fantasies about Euro-American men saving Mexican women, in line with a larger imperialist fantasy that Gayatri Spivak has classically described as "white men saving brown women from brown men," would linger through the nineteenth century.[19] An 1870 article in the *Mesilla News*, for example, expressed such a perspective about race and sexuality in southern New Mexico. The author proposed heterosexual intermarriage as a solution for the imagined problems with uncooperative Mesilleros: "Everywhere in the territory will be found intelligent, educated Americans married to the black-eyed daughters of New Mexico, whose beauty and accomplishments command the admiration of all unprejudiced visitors, and not unfrequently a blue-eyed, accomplished, educated daughter of the North will be found wedded to an educated Mexican."[20] The paper argued that the influx of Euro-Americans who were willing to intermarry would "dilute" the Mexican dominance in the territory: "It should be borne in mind that the Mexican element is at its maximum and the American and European is following in with a constant and increasing certainty, and must soon predominate and the races soon become blended together and all distinctions lost."[21] The editor, who had married a Mexican woman himself, thus evaded questions about racial intermixing. Instead, he believed that Euro-Americans' racial superiority would ultimately triumph in future generations.[22] Conceived in this way, Mexicans' racial distinctiveness could be neutralized by white blood within several generations if brought into white households and families. Such ideas of racial mixing as a potential "solution" to New Mexico's Mexican majority were markedly different from contemporary discussions of "miscegenation" between whites and African Americans in the United States.[23] This sharp difference in these two coetaneous styles of thinking about race reminds us that even under regimes of brutal racial discrimination, "race" never achieves complete hegemony as a homogenous set of laws or assumptions. Rather, it is always already internally fractured and incoherent as a category.

Perhaps the difference in these notions had its roots in colonial assumptions about the differences between Indian and "Negro" blood.

Recall that Spanish colonial law permitted an individual who was "one-eighth" *indio* to be classified as a full *español* but that the same was not true for someone who had one-eighth *Negro* blood.[24] Seemingly some Euro-Americans comparably imagined that, since Mexicans were already a mixture of Indian and European blood, their progeny could be incorporated into the white race in ways that they deemed impossible for African Americans. Nothing was certain, however, nor was there consensus about the meaning of Mexicans intermarrying with whites.

Once the serious work of occupation took hold in New Mexico, many Euro-Americans expressed frustration that Mexicans had not vanished, or become "amalgamated," as they had hoped. Ten years after the Treaty of Guadalupe Hidalgo, W. W. H. Davis produced one of the last antebellum personal narratives about New Mexico, *El Gringo*. Having become a U.S. territory a decade earlier, New Mexico's "problems" could no longer be dismissed as resulting from its status as nationally Mexican. Davis therefore had to explain New Mexico's semicolonial status and its possibilities for future integration into the United States. As a result Davis still used local gender and sexual practices as evidence of Mexicans' inferiority, as had previous Euro-American writers, but he inflected this interest in new ways.

Like previous Euro-American writers, he claimed that Mexicans accepted adultery among both men and women without censure. "The marriage vow," he wrote, "is held sacred by a very few, and the ceremony is more a matter of convenience than anything else."[25] In another section Davis argued that "prostitution is carried [on] to a fearful extent; and it is quite common for parents to sell their own daughters for money to gratify the lust of the purchaser, thus making a profit from their own and their children's shame."[26] What distinguished Davis's narrative from previous works, though, was his new call for Euro-Americans to police Mexicans' gender and sexual behaviors. The previous narratives' predictions that Mexicans, particularly Mexican men, would inevitably "fade away," unable to compete with the superior Euro-Americans, seemed less certain. Ten years after the U.S. conquest, Davis called for Euro-Americans to regenerate the territory's majority population. He argued that Euro-Americans had a duty to rescue Mexicans from vice and immorality so that New Mexico would be worthy of full membership in the larger nation.

Mexicans, in Davis's mind, were not inherently immoral but had become so from a combination of historical and racial pressures that had degraded them. Only Euro-Americans' paternalistic intervention could tame immorality in the territory. But he saw this as a difficult task, call-ing for Euro-Americans to rise to the occasion: "The vices that prevail [among Mexicans] are constitutional and national—more the result of habit, example, and education—or, rather, the want of it—than from natural depravity. We should bear in mind that such have been the habits of the Spanish race from time immemorial, and charity should induce us to make a reasonable allowance for their infirmities. They should be compassionated rather than shunned because of their degraded condi-tion, and efficient effort should be made to raise them to the standard of enlightenment that is found in other sections of our land."[27] He drew on the existing and durable "Black Legend," which presumed that Spain's imperial expansion had been unusually cruel and violent compared with other European powers. Davis believed that these "habits of the Spanish race," which Mexicans inherited, could be partially offset if Euro-Ameri-cans sought to educate them in the ways of (white) civilization.[28]

Davis's writings suggest that Euro-Americans had complicated, and sometimes mutually contradictory, imaginings of Mexicans as "sinful." They saw the cause of vice as resulting partly from Mexicans' "racial nature" and partly from their "culture." Nineteenth-century discussions about racial difference were not neatly divided between biology and culture in the United States; instead, these two were often conflated or imagined as mutually reinforcing.[29] Additionally, Lamarckian notions about environment and location further complicated the divide between culture and race.[30]

During the nineteenth century, U.S. newspapers frequently printed arti-cles that used gender and sexuality to declare Mexicans unfit for full U.S. citizenship.[31] One 1886 *New York Times* article jumbled together such assumptions about race, environment, morality, and even food to account for the supposed sinfulness of Mexicans in New Mexico. Like most Euro-Americans from the period, the author of this *Times* article, "H.G.C.," argued that Mexicans' racial inferiority resulted in their moral laxity. The alleged shortcomings of the "Mexican race" were only worsened by the desert climate and the use of red chile in New Mexico. "Can you inform me," the author asked rhetorically, "how morals will develop in a climate where the rain falls every day for six weeks and the air is as dry as powder the rest of the year, and where the steady diet of the average citizen is red pepper, onions, and blue beans?"[32] It was not just that this author found the regional cuisine and weather disagreeable. Rather, he believed that the New Mexico desert and diet compounded Mexicans' already degenerate nature. Indeed, he claimed that only Mexicans could tolerate such harsh circumstances because of their unique racial characteristics.

Mexicans' use of red peppers literally rotted their bodies and souls from inside out. "Without the red pepper, the greaser's life would be a burden to him," he wrote. "The pods he uses are . . . hotter than a blast furnace, and one of them taken inwardly will smelt all the Christianity out of a white man in three minutes."[33] Because Euro-Americans conflated notions of culture and race, the two categories offered mutually reinforcing evidence that Mexicans were immoral. Whether they believed it was a matter of culture or "blood," most Euro-Americans appeared skeptical that Mexicans could be reformed enough to be full American citizens.[34] Euro-Americans thereby placed an emphasis on certain expressions of gender and sexuality as necessary to being "properly civilized" and as indicative of readiness for equal admission to the United States.

In the midst of these discussions Mexican women became a particular target in assessing the territory's moral fitness. Detailing her travels through New Mexico in 1889, the Protestant missionary Alice Blake wrote openly of her contempt for Mexican women, calling them "so corrupt in their moral nature that they would scorch the soul of an angel."[35] Women who participated in public activities or owned businesses, especially bars and gambling salons, automatically became prostitutes in most Euro-Americans' minds. The struggle to transform New Mexico into an American territory through the nineteenth century could not but include debates about the appropriate location of Mexican women. U.S. colonialism in Las Cruces pivoted on efforts to "domesticate" Mexican women even as many Euro-Americans claimed it a quixotic cause.

Gender and Space

Policing gender and sexuality figured prominently in New Mexico's colonial administration. On July 10, 1889, the *Las Cruces Daily News* published a tantalizing report of a young Cruceño who faced jail time for transgressing gender expectations. The paper reported that the city police apprehended the youth "for masquerading in female clothes."[36] The arrest indicates the seriousness of such actions, as men who flouted traditional masculine behavior faced increasing harassment, arrest, and even physical attacks throughout the United States in the late nineteenth century.[37] Popular and medical discourse linked men who behaved effeminately with "abnormal" same-sex sexual desires that defined (by contrast) the meaning of "heterosexual manhood."[38] Given the arrest for cross-dressing, many Las Cruces civic leaders seemingly took men's gender conformity as seriously as did their counterparts elsewhere in the nation.

Yet this isolated account also hints that such incidents were not the main priority for either Mexican or Euro-American reformers along the nineteenth-century border. Articles about men cross-dressing were extremely rare in New Mexico's newspaper coverage, much less discussions of same-sex sex. Even this incident did not capture much attention in Las Cruces. After the cross-dressing man had spent two nights in jail, the justice of the peace released him with the explanation that "he was only having 'a little fun with the boys.' "[39] We may never know the type of fun that the young man and "the boys" had wearing women's clothes. Not many Cruceños appeared all that interested in finding out, either.

This is not to say that New Mexico's newspapers did not occasionally print sensationalized incidents involving same-sex relationships or gender nonconformity. Nor do I mean that most settlers in New Mexico condoned or ignored same-sex relations. Overall, though, the vast majority of articles and legal cases concerning gender and sexuality involved ideas about heterosexuality and womanhood. A priority on "reforming" sexual behavior, particularly women's behavior, emerged among differing elite groups in New Mexico.

Euro-Americans placed a priority on reform because their own status was at stake. Ann Laura Stoler points out that nineteenth-century European writers frequently viewed white settlers in colonial lands as morally suspect.[40] While notions of racial superiority might have bound together Europeans against the colonized Other, they also remained subject to anxieties that colonial Europeans could become degenerate through their association with the colonies. As a result, imperial authorities and social institutions rigorously enforced the moral prescriptions that separated the "civilized" from the "savage."[41] So, too, in New Mexico could whites like Davis feel threatened that their own place in the United States would be diminished should the territory's immorality remain unchanged.[42] Comparably, many Euro-Americans considered their future in the United States to depend on their ability to reform the territory, including local Mexicans. As long as New Mexico remained a territory, even Euro-American settlers' participation in the larger nation was curtailed.

Euro-American efforts to remake all New Mexico, and the Mesilla

Valley in particular, as American, therefore, included attempts to re late and control sexual expression in the territory. In 1853 the *Roches Frederick Douglass Paper*, an abolitionist periodical, printed an indicti story of the Euro-American military occupation of New Mexico. The paper reported that U.S. commanders had arrested two women, "probably for hanging about the Fort."[43] According to the story the military commanders gave each woman fifteen to twenty-five lashes on her bare back and then cut off all her hair as punishment for her transgressions. In this instance these Euro-Americans enforced their moral standards with violence. Others depended on legal apparatuses.

Shortly after Mesilla was pulled into the United States in 1854, the Doña Ana County district attorney, M. Claude Jones, leveled a number of legal complaints against Mesilleros, starting with a host of charges against Mexicans who ran gaming tables and "indecent" enterprises. In March 1855, only a year after Mesilla had been incorporated into the United States, Jones charged Maria Dolores Morelos with "maintaining a Bawdy House, and disturbing the neighborhood by loud, boisterous and indecent conversations and by quarreling and fighting."[44] In another case that autumn he empaneled a grand jury against Jacinto Ybarri. The grand jury indicted Ybarri because he "unlawfully did erect a public nuisance, which was then and there a vulgar, indiscreet and obscene dancing puppet show, called Títeres [Puppetry], to the great inconvenience and prejudice then and there of the citizens of Mesilla."[45]

We may never know greater details about Morelos's business or the exact content of Ybarri's "indecent" puppet show. However, the fact that both of these cases occurred within a year of Mesilla's entry into the United States suggests how rapidly and actively Euro-Americans intervened in discussions and displays about sex and gender. Jones exercised U.S. colonial authority by declaring a Mesillero puppet show not only immoral but also illegal. As we will see, enforcing gendered divisions of space became one of the most critical elements of their colonial plans.

Members of the Euro-American and Mexican American elite shared comparable assumptions about the "proper place" of men and women in society in the mid-nineteenth century. Space, in other words, had gendered connotations. Common presumptions in both the United States and Mexico idealized patriarchal households in which men held the ultimate authority and provided for their families through labor in "outer/public/political" spaces. Women complemented men's roles by working and caring for children in "inner/private/domestic" spaces, where their virtue could be protected and they could act as the moral center.[46]

In 1846, though, Mexicans did not share as strict a gendered divide between public and private as Euro-Americans did, especially in sparsely populated territories like New Mexico. Mexico's laws and common practices certainly defined women's roles by always putting them in relation to men, despite women's independent access to public venues. A woman's position in Mexican society was predicated on the patriarchal assumption that she "belonged" to a family headed by a man.[47] Before the U.S. invasion in 1846, however, women in Mexico conducted business in public, retained their property after marriage, and filed suits in local courts without much concern.[48]

Men were also defined by familial relations and by their authority to judiciously manage private and civic affairs. The ability to provide food, clothing, and shelter for their dependents, as well as securing the "purity" of women in their households, structured notions of manhood.[49] While women had the right to appear in court, men had the privilege, expectation, and duty to represent their wives and daughters.[50] Men, however, did not have unchecked authority in the household. If a man became abusive, women could draw on the law for intervention.[51] Moreover, men served the civil and military demands of remote places like New Mexico, defining a role through their relationship to the state. According to the historian Steve Stern, economic class and hierarchical power relations further defined relationships between men. Elite notions of honor and dignity that defined manhood hinged on the negation of the assumed "crude excesses of the poor and barbaric."[52]

In New Mexico the demands for all able-bodied members to contribute to the household income, even among the elite, meant that the constraints on gendered space were less rigorously enforced.[53] Upper-class Mexicans might have found widows who managed their own property or poor married women selling items or earning wages in public as less than ideal, but they did not register such actions as particularly unusual or threatening prior to the U.S.-Mexican War.[54] The severity of the public/private spatial dichotomies in Mexico was therefore not part of this gender regime as it had been in the United States.

Notions of gendered space developed along different lines in the United States, whose political revolution stopped short of social revolution. Starting in the early republic, dominant Euro-American ideologies aggressively narrowed the meaning of the "public" to exclude women.[55] By 1830 the middle-class notion that men and women conducted their affairs in different physical locations had pervaded assumptions about the family, even though, in practice, the situation remained complicated by class, region, and race.[56] The idealized division placed women in the private sphere of the home, performing primarily domestic duties, while men dominated politics, business, and commerce in the public sphere.[57] These presumptions of "separate spheres" for men and women had concrete legal ramifications. For instance, when U.S. women married, they lost ownership of their property to their husbands, allegedly to preserve the women's purity and the civilized social order.

As historians have shown, though, working-class women earned wages in the public sphere throughout U.S. history, while nineteenth-century middle-class women participated in reform and engaged in open debates around political issues such as abolition, temperance, and prostitution, even during the height of the "separate spheres" ideology.[58] In short, the gender divide between public and private was honored more in the breach than in the observance in the United States. Yet the ideology of separate spheres proved a durable and useful means to help explain and justify a wide-ranging set of injustices in the nineteenth century.[59] Working-class American women (of all racial backgrounds), that is to say the majority of women in the nation, became "dirty, disruptive and disorderly" because they did not live up to the ideal.[60]

Gendered divisions of space also became a marker of civilization and whites' "superiority" over racial "savages." For nineteenth-century European and Euro-American thinkers the "lower races" did not exhibit significant difference between men and women. Blurring of gender lines through a lack of separate spheres was ample evidence that a group, like Mexicans, was racially inferior and underdeveloped.[61] The trajectories traced by racial bodies through gendered spaces figured into larger meanings of interior frontiers and differential racialization. Euro-Americans in the late nineteenth century and the early twentieth, for instance, circulated images of Asian men as feminine, passive, and weak in comparison to white men by linking racial identities to notions of gendered labor and space.[62] Images of "Chinese laundrymen," Asian domestic servants, or "Japanese flower gardeners" placed Asian men within the domestic sphere—itself resonant with existing portraits of the "Orient" as a decidedly feminized "fairyland."[63] Many Euro-Americans fantasized that Asian men willingly removed themselves from the public sphere to do labor that they considered "women's work."[64] In this way the associations among gender, labor, and space provided another means for articulating purportedly obvious racial differences. Much as Asian men were deemed deviant because they appeared in private ("women's") space, so, too, Mexican women were scorned for occupying public ("men's") space.

Race and economic class were critical to the discussions about which women could legitimately affect the public sphere. Across the United States in the late nineteenth century, white women activists used a rhetoric of motherhood or their "natural" moral sensibilities to justify all sorts of entries into the public sphere. Some middle-class suffragists suggested that allowing white women to vote would counterbalance the power of the (male) "black vote."[65] It was not just male agents of the law, therefore, who intervened in gender relations in nineteenth-century New Mexico. White women also became critical to the remaking of New Mexico as American because they could foster a clean division between public and private space.

Here, too, the Euro-American colonization of New Mexico resonates with overseas colonization projects carried out by both European and U.S. imperial powers. Anne McClintock and Amy Kaplan both discuss how nineteenth-century British and U.S. imperialism deployed notions of "domesticity"—the separation of the private and the public—to justify and explain colonial relations.[66] Domesticity, McClintock reminds us, connoted both a place, "defined by architecture and geography," and a set of social relations imagined to be the basis for civilized society.[67] The ideal home allowed women to exercise their "natural" talents and moral sensibilities by creating a clearly bounded and rigidly ordered home in which men could escape from their work in public and the strain of politics.[68] Not coincidentally, the term *domestic* also distinguished the nation from foreign countries ("domestic policy" vs. "foreign policy").[69] "To domesticate," likewise, meant "to civilize."[70] The discourse of domesticity, as a result, was cross-relational in explaining both women and men's roles in the home and the process of conquest abroad.[71] Likewise, "Americanizing" New Mexico required that it be "home" for Euro-Americans.[72] To make it that home demanded that the dominant Euro-American gendered understanding of space be enforced there as well.

Many Euro-American writers and officials figured white women as the symbolic American mothers who could transform New Mexico into a domestic place, both literally and metaphorically. In June 1848 the *Santa Fe Republican* printed an article that linked the arrival of "several American ladies" with the rehabilitation of New Mexico. Although the editor halfheartedly acknowledged "the qualities of the enchanting señoritas of New Mexico," he proclaimed that the mere presence of Euro-American women would greatly improve the community. White women, he suggested, had a singular power to connect the remote territory with the rest of the country through their civilizing influence:

There is a community of feeling—a refinement of soul, in fact an excitement of all the better and nobler feelings of our nature in the company of the lovely beings of our own country that no other association in the wide world is calculated to arouse. The refining influence that we have all in some degree felt at home . . . is about to be revived and [we] congratulate our readers that American society, with all its pleasures and ennobling effects, is about to create a new era in the condition of our territory. We feel that distance is about to be annihilated, and that, though a thousand miles away, we are still at home.[73]

For this author, the thousands of miles separating the newly occupied territory from the great population centers of the nation would be symbolically eradicated when "refined" and "lovely" Euro-American women graced its presence.

White women could combat "disorder" along the border in a number of ways. Within the domestic sphere white women's hiring of Mexican women to clean their houses became a noble sacrifice by the late nineteenth century. Employing Mexican women as servants was not just about reducing white women's own domestic work; it was almost a form of charity because it trained those same Mexican women to be good wives and mothers in American fashion. A self-described Euro-American "ranchwoman" in Las Cruces explained to eastern readers that the Mexican woman "has in her the material for an excellent domestic."[74] To make use of that raw "material," though, Euro-American women needed to train Mexican women "to pleasant household ways of orderliness, and love of those details which make a home a home." White women's beneficence in teaching domestic servants how to clean their houses to their liking, she imagined, would provide Mexicans with much needed skills and sensibilities that they could take back to their own households and communities.

Yet Euro-American women's service as U.S. imperial agents along the border was not limited to the domestic sphere. The Philadelphia monthly *Godey's Lady's Book* printed an article in April 1847 that celebrated the opening of public schools in Galveston, Texas, noting that white women had transformed the "new state of Texas." The article argued that (Euro-)American women found their "true sphere" of influence as wives and mothers. On the frontier between Mexico and the United States, *Godey's* explained to its urban readers, men were in danger of following their "passions" and succumbing to the untamed environment. To make the "frontier" safe and civilized, it was a white "woman's high mission, her

rogative and duty to counsel, to sustain, ay, to control him."[75] Com-
ably, the image of the "pioneer" woman in Arizona figured white
men as the agents of civilization.[76] In these cases the ideology of
separate spheres was mobilized to domesticate a foreign zone. If women
were imagined to bring order and morality to the home, so, too, they
could work as nation builders who could fold Texas, Arizona, and New
Mexico into the civilized American realm. Further, they could keep Euro-
American men from "going native" by checking the draw of their passions and the corrupting influences of the colonial context.

Fifty years later, the Las Cruces newspaper the *Doña Ana County
Republican* echoed these sentiments. In this case the paper highlighted a
particular white woman who literally remade the town. Celebrating the
work of Mary S. McFie, the *Republican* characterized her as a "typical
western woman." Hers and other Euro-American women's ways of thinking, the paper acknowledged, had transformed the "West." As president
of the Women's Improvement Society of Las Cruces (wis), McFie had
lobbied for "city beautifying" projects like the construction of local parks
and public services. The wis also sponsored patriotic events such as
community-wide Independence Day celebrations that "Americanized"
the Mesilla Valley. The paper hailed these efforts as taming the wild
border region.[77] Not only did McFie and her associates symbolically
reconfigure the Mesilla Valley through their alleged moral influence, but
they also elevated social relations in Las Cruces by literally restructuring
the landscape.

As this article suggests, Euro-American women's visibility was a vital
part of the overall colonizing effort in New Mexico. While civic leaders
viewed Mexican women as immoral for venturing into the public sphere,
they conversely regarded white women in public roles to be pursuing
their "natural womanly" duties as wives and mothers. The article claimed
McFie's public importance logically extended from her marriage to an
associate justice of the territorial supreme court. Describing her efforts,
McFie insisted that she and the other women in the wis only assisted
their husbands as any dutiful wife would do. "We expect to aid our
husbands to improve and beautify our town," she stated, "or probably, I
should say, do it for them."[78] Men, McFie implied, could not be depended
on to beautify Las Cruces. A later article emphasized the civilizing influence of the wis by claiming "it really has an eye to the improvement of
men and manners."[79] In this way McFie invoked local circumstances and
Mexicans' supposedly "semisavage" status to increase Euro-American
women's role in public affairs.[80] Such Euro-American women created

historical and racialized narratives that justified their involvement in public projects and politics through their expertise in counteracting "disorder" and "dirtiness" of Mexican housing, religion, morality, and food habits.

The historian Louise Michelle Newman explains that late-nineteenth-century feminism was shaped by U.S. imperialism and racialized notions of civilization and primitivism. White middle-class women, she reveals, applied the separate-spheres ideology to Native Americans, formerly enslaved African Americans, immigrants, and colonized populations in Africa, Latin America, and the Caribbean even as they subverted the confinement of patriarchal homes for themselves.[81] Fashioning themselves into agents of colonization or reformer activists permitted these white women to turn their "natural" roles as mothers and homemakers into something synonymous with political activism. These middle-class white women did acquire expanded political power and personal freedom but only at the cost of perpetuating the subordination of nonwhite Others.

White women served a comparably complicated role in the discourse around gender in New Mexico. Their appearance in this narrative reminds us that "race" is not a unitary category applied in homogenous ways to different kinds of gendered bodies; rather, gendered categories, like "woman," are themselves inflected by racial ideologies. Mexican women were thought of as wanton because they left their homes to work in public, violating the "natural" ordering of separate spheres that marked whites' superiority. In a strikingly inconsistent attitude that cannot be explained with reference to the categories of gender alone, it was because white women were considered a priori superior to Mexican women that they were licensed to bring their domestic talents to bear in both the public and private spheres. It would be no exaggeration to say that it was the presence of abjected Mexican women that, however indirectly, afforded middle-class Euro-American women an entrée into those same public spaces along the border.

The Bonds of Patriarchy: Mexican and Euro-American Cooperation

Euro-Americans did not inevitably act alone in their policing efforts. By the last decades of the nineteenth century, many members of the Mexican elite had joined with Euro-Americans to pass legislation that defined and limited gender and sexuality in the territory. Part of this legislative activity stemmed from a desire to align New Mexico with the rest of the United States. Because gender and sexual "immorality" had often been used as explanations for excluding New Mexico and its Mexican Americans from the nation, it is not surprising that those interested in asserting their commitment to American nationalism worked to change gender norms and practices. Members of the Mexican and Euro-American male elite found common cause in their desire to integrate New Mexico more thoroughly into the United States for political and economic reasons. Restricting women's access to public places became just one of many such joint efforts.

Middle-class Mexican Americans would not necessarily have viewed this move as a shift, nor would they have seen in it a substantially novel form of patriarchy. Rather, we can think of the intensified legal push to cement patriarchal authority as "discursive *bricolage*."[82] In other words, here older ideas of gender were recovered in modified forms. Mexican Americans did not necessarily see a stricter enforcement of gendered space as an importation of new American ideas; rather, they would more likely have incorporated Euro-American notions into their own existing sense of gender roles and sexuality. Such figures as D. Martinez, who chaired the territory's legislative committee on vice and immorality, used their positions to advocate a wide range of legal changes in New Mexico. For instance, he endorsed HB 86, "An Act to Define and Provide Punishment of the Crime of Open and Notorious Cohabitation and Adultery."[83] One of the legislature's other notable bills in 1889 targeted the role of women in public work. A joint contingent of Euro-American and Mexican American men introduced Council Bill 108, "An Act to Prevent Women from Entering Saloons for the Purpose of Drinking Therein." More than merely preventing women from enjoying alcoholic beverages in public, the sweeping legislation sought to preclude women from working in, or even appearing in, certain public sites.

Wage-earning women had been an issue in New Mexico since the first Euro-Americans arrived, and they drew intensified attention through this 1889 debate. Euro-Americans had continuously adduced the presence of Mexican working women, particularly in saloons or other "masculine" and "vice-ridden" spaces, as evidence of Mexican promiscuity.[84] "The position women should occupy in this world," the *Las Cruces Daily News* noted, "is the main topic of discussion just now."[85] Part of this discussion derived from the ways that Mexicans began to more rigorously police the gendered division of space themselves. The introduction and passage of Council Bill 108, therefore, served different interests for Euro-Americans' and Mexican Americans' claims to the territory. For Euro-American supporters the measure fit into a general desire to change Mexicans' gender and sexual customs. Such supporters contended that New Mexico needed the bill to make the territory fully American and open the door to statehood. Some Mexican Americans, meanwhile, utilized their support for the exclusion of women from public to show their own allegiance and integration into the U.S. nation. Many Mexican American men placed a renewed priority on defining women as belonging to the domestic realm to ensure the territory's morality. Moreover, given that such efforts were viewed by the popular discourse as a "duty of manhood," it was also a means for Mexican males to assert their own sense of themselves as "men."[86]

This is not to imply that the bill enjoyed universal support among either Mexicans or Euro-Americans. Governor Edmund G. Ross, for instance, sent an urgent letter requesting that the legislature reject Council Bill 108. Ross condemned the measure as "legislation in a vicious direction, in that it presupposes that women are something less than rational beings as compared to men, and must be hedged about with statuary enactments to keep them from degradation and vice."[87] The governor lambasted the measure as archaic and encouraged the legislature to have faith in "American civilization," which he believed had "worked a revolution in the relations of the sexes in business and public life that no legislation or statutory enactment can turn back."[88]

Proponents of the bill countered that its excluding women from public places would be vital to end vice in the territory. The legislature recorded D. M. Carr's lengthy response to Ross's letter in the official proceedings. Carr did not see the measure as simply defining women's roles. Instead, he saw it as an important measure for prescribing proper manhood and preventing prostitution:

> The Executive objects to this law because it will exclude women from honest employment. In my opinion, no honest-virtuous, good woman will thank him for his solicitude in her behalf and I am sure that no self-respecting man would desire such employment for his wife, mother, sister, or daughter. A man is verdant indeed who does not know that almost every one of the women employed as waiters, musicians and dealers of games in saloons in this territory support—in idleness a vicious, vagrant—tin horn gambler and pimp—the vilest of God's creatures, a being who subsists off the wages of the sin of a woman.[89]

Carr ended his letter with an appeal to the council's sense of masculinity. "Gentlemen," he wrote, "in behalf of decency, manhood, honor, the public weal and the love and respect all good men have for pure women, I respectfully and earnestly appeal to you to pass Council Bill No. 108."[90] Carr made the issue a question of men "defending" and "protecting" women. Moreover, he raised the ever-present fear of prostitution that had repeatedly appeared in discussions about the territory since before the U.S.-Mexican War.

Not only did defense of this measure have obvious salience for New Mexico's circumstances, but it also fit within a wider antifeminist reaction throughout the United States. Late-nineteenth-century men in government, academia, and business frequently argued that shutting women out of nondomestic work or politics was for the purpose of "defending feminine delicacy."[91] This emergent form of patriarchy denied that manhood was about the direct exercise of privilege and power. Rather, men made "noble sacrifices" to protect the honor of women from other, less scrupulous men or to "correct" certain women who would "feebly imitate" men.[92]

The historians of Puerto Rico Eileen Findlay and Laura Briggs also document that U.S. authorities would continue these imperialist strategies in the late nineteenth century and the early twentieth. Findlay and Briggs chart the complicated circuits traveled by sex and gender ideologies in making Puerto Rico a U.S. colony.[93] Briggs, in particular, argues that campaigns against prostitution became important for circumscribing the island's relationship with the mainland.[94] These campaigns created a sense of Puerto Rican women's racial difference from Euro-Americans by making them either threats who needed to be contained or "pitiable souls" who needed salvation. A separate-spheres ideology informed these efforts, Briggs reminds us, as leaders imagined that "it was the work of U.S. modernism and science to protect, not an explicit (public) colonialism, but (private) women and children."[95]

In the case of New Mexico this emphasis on manhood would be particularly powerful given that both Euro-American and Mexican men were in danger of figurative castration. These men were all the more sensitive given that their relationship to government had been limited because they lived within a federal territory. Unlike men in other parts of the nation, they could not fully participate in republican-style government. Instead, the president and Congress exercised authority over them. Despite the governor's opposition, the legislature (composed of almost equal numbers of Mexicans and Euro-Americans) passed the measure, making it into law on May 19, 1889. From then on, a woman who entered a saloon either to work or to enjoy a drink could be fined from ten to fifty dollars or imprisoned for sixty days.[96]

The bill's passage depended on cooperation between elite Mexicans and Euro-Americans. Martinez and the other supporters of the bill believed that women's identity could be understood only through their relationship to men. Likewise, Carr explained the need to frame women strictly as "wives, mothers, sisters, or daughters." This measure offered members of the Mexican elite an opportunity to redefine their own assumptions about gender, trading the exclusion of women from public employment in return for additional respectability for Mexican womanhood and the territory at large.

Previous public mixing of men and women could no longer be tolerated if real equality of the border region was to be achieved with the rest of the United States. City, county, territorial, and state police enforced this measure well into the twentieth century. New Mexico Territorial Police, for instance, arrested two Willard residents, Della Chávez and Momer Herando, on charges of "allowing women in a saloon" in February 1909.[97] C. O. Burnside faced the same charge the following year in Socorro, New Mexico.[98] These efforts would have had little effect on most women of the Mexican or Euro-American elite. Poorer women, who needed the wages earned in public, would bear the personal costs of the reorganization of the territory along gendered lines.

El Eco del Valle and Middle-Class Citizenship

Having sketched the intertwining of gender, race, nation, and space on a territory-wide level, let us look again at the Mesilla Valley. Newspaper editors there rarely seemed in agreement about the relationship between gender and race. Examination of a selection of newspapers from 1870 to 1912 suggests some of the ways that ideas about gender figured into individuals' attempts to make sense of their local circumstances. Sometimes uncovering how ideas about race informed assumptions about gender requires attention to nuance. Ultimately, the discussions of gender in these papers linked up with the development of a New Mexican identity that defined Mexicans as "natives" to that region. One of the ways that Cruceños reconciled their aspirations to be incorporated into American nationalism with their status as Mexicans was to claim a particular type of "traditional" and regionally specific gender arrangement that was distinct from either Mexico or the eastern United States.[99] To see that emergence, we need to first explore how and when notions of gender appeared in Mesilla Valley newspapers.

In an editorial printed in 1871 the *Las Cruces Borderer*'s owner, N. V. Bennett, discussed the issue of statehood, noting in the English-language section, "It is an undoubted fact that nearly every citizen of the Territory would be glad to emerge from the swaddling clothes of dependency, and appear in the full dress of political manhood."[100] At first glance the article does not seem unusual, as Bennett used a language typical of the nineteenth century, which equated politics with manhood. What is intriguing about this article is the way that Bennett opted to translate this idea into Spanish. The article was an almost exact Spanish translation, except for the omission of the reference to appearing "in the full dress of political manhood."[101] Although a minor difference, the deletion suggests that Bennett imagined Mexican manhood differently than he imagined U.S. manhood. Perhaps he did not wish to link local Mexicans' political power with manhood, because "political manhood" during this period implied a racial status as white.[102] Possibly Bennett feared that naming a lack of political power as a lack of manhood would prompt local Mexican males to demand recognition as equal men in the country with equal rights. Although it is impossible to draw definitive conclusions based on a single case, the passage raises questions about Euro-Americans' imagination of race and gender in the territorial period. It further underscores the importance of translations and the ways in which both Euro-Americans and Mexicans expressed their ideas across different languages.

This is not to say that Mexicans and Mexican Americans never discussed notions of manhood in their own papers. Articles appeared in Cruceño-owned newspapers that articulated gender expectations for Mexican men. *La Empresa*'s Spanish-language section, for instance, printed articles that offered its male readers "Máximas Útiles de Moral" (Useful Maxims of Morality).[103] These maxims usually involved the need to "control" one's desires, refraining from sex and alcohol, linking together notions of restrained manhood with ideas about citizenship. Manhood, under this thinking, became defined through public commitments to the state and responsible civic engagement. In one article, for instance, the author named a distinction between being born male and learning proper manly behavior. Taking the voice of an instructor, the author stated that a man had two "fathers," one by birth and one who taught him his morality. "Vos sois su padre por naturaleza, y yo por mis lecciones," the article stated, "vos habéis hecho un hombre, y yo he formado un ciudadano" (You are his father by nature, and I am by my lessons; you have made a man, and I have formed a citizen).[104] In this way the author put forward an imperative for Mexican men to learn the proper way to behave as republican citizens. This explicit connection to citizenship is not surprising given that Mexican men's supposedly uncivilized and unmanly behaviors were reasons that easterners gave to deny New Mexico statehood. Overall, though, Cruceño editors seemingly felt a greater imperative for policing Mexican women's roles than explicitly thinking about manhood.

The Las Cruces Spanish-language paper *El Eco del Valle* held the most substantial discussions about the meaning of gender and race in the Mesilla Valley. At the beginning of the twentieth century, *El Eco del Valle's* Cruceño editor, Isidoro Armijo, regularly featured articles about womanhood in particular.

Armijo, born in Las Cruces in 1871, came from a prominent family. His father owned a substantial parcel of land in the Mesilla Valley and had held a variety of political positions.[105] After he graduated from New Mexico A&M (today's New Mexico State University), Armijo also became an influential figure in southern New Mexico. Prior to editing *El Eco del Valle*, he spent a brief period in Puebla, Mexico, before returning to Las Cruces.[106] In 1904, halfway through *El Eco del Valle's* run, Armijo ceded control of the paper to M. F. Lerma, who continued most of Armijo's editorial policies. Examining articles on gender that Armijo and Lerma included in *El Eco del Valle* helps us understand how larger debates about race, nation, and gender figured in the shifting circumstances of the border region.

Middle-class Cruceños, especially the ones who desired statehood, were probably more sensitive to the discussions of Mexican womanhood that appeared in other parts of the United States. As I have mentioned, Euro-Americans frequently argued that all Mexicans, but particularly Mexican women, lacked a sense of sexual morality regardless of their economic class. Allusions to their "unchaste behavior" upheld racist presumptions and justified denying Mexican Americans full participation in the republic. The *New York Times* printed a letter in 1882 that explicitly argued against admitting New Mexico as a state because of its Mexican-majority population. After a lengthy diatribe the author ended by describing "the relations of the sexes in New Mexico" as definitive evidence of the unworthiness of "Greasers" for full U.S. citizenship:

It is a patent, notorious fact, blazoning itself forward with startling boldness, that in no other part of Christendom are the women of an entire community so generally without a sense of the beauties of virtue and so ready to prove their insensibility for a money consideration. Mexicans are the only people supposed to be civilized who will tell you without any apparent sense of there being something unusual in the matter that they do not know who their fathers were. A Mexican woman living first with this man and then with another as his de facto wife is not considered by her female neighbors to be committing a serious impropriety. . . . The hourly conversation and general conduct of Mexican men show plenty enough what is their opinion of the virtue of the women.[107]

For writers like this, Mexicans' supposed racial inferiority was evident in the allegedly scandalous and immodest relationships between men and women, making New Mexico unacceptable for full incorporation into the United States.

It was within this context that Armijo staged his own newspaper's presentation of gender roles. Armijo, like many Cruceños, actively promoted New Mexico's statehood, as we will see in chapter 6. It would be quite likely, therefore, that he was fully aware of the ways that eastern newspapers and politicians used Mexican women's alleged wantonness as a justification for keeping New Mexico a territory. In his own paper he consistently emphasized the need for sexual decency and showed little hesitation in setting out what he imagined as appropriate gender roles for Mexican men and women. Armijo may have written in Spanish, but he frequently adopted positions that local Euro-Americans would have likely applauded. At times he (and Lerma after him) selected and translated articles from American newspapers to present as models of appropriate gender behavior. In other instances Armijo and Lerma printed articles that held local Mexican gender roles to be superior to (Euro-) American practices.

Of course, discussions of the gender roles of Mexican men and women were not limited to the U.S. side of the border or to Mexican Americans. These articles appeared at a time when other debates about womanhood were also occurring in central Mexico. Intellectuals, politicians, newspaper publishers, and activists similarly debated women's "proper place" and men's "appropriate" behavior throughout early-twentieth-century Mexico. The Mexican essayist Ignacio Gamboa, for instance, railed against "la mujer moderna" in a 1906 essay that circulated broadly. Among other things, Gamboa claimed that feminism threatened Mexican society because it resulted in women seeking divorces and pursuing "el vicio lésbico" (the vice of lesbianism).[108] The sociologist José Hernández comparably warned that Mexican women would lose "100 percent of their charms" should feminism take hold in Mexico.[109] Closer to the border, the historical-anthropologist Ana María Alonso has documented that Chihuahua state authorities employed gender rhetoric to mobilize Mexican settlers for the Apache wars. They linked a man's honor to his military service and his ability to defend Mexican women, especially their sexual "purity," through warfare.[110]

Even male political figures who imagined themselves as progressive or as women's champions still intentionally circumscribed their roles in Mexican society. The revolution-era governor of Yucatán, Salvador Alvarado, instituted educational reforms that greatly increased the levels of coeducation in that state. Alvarado made these changes because he acknowledged that women had been unjustly excluded from public education prior to the Mexican Revolution in 1910. Yet Alvarado also assumed that a Yucatán woman's access to education was only a means to enhance her inescapable domestic destiny as wife and mother. Women's education, he argued, would prepare a woman "to be the foundation of the family as she unites with a man to make a home. To be a producer and a worker before she united with a man to make a family."[111] Single women might temporarily serve in the public as students or even workers, but they were to devote their entire energies to the home and their husbands once they married. Even when women in Mexico won victories, such as access to public education, their success was tempered by reiterations of their "natural" role within the heterosexual family.

Discussions such as these likely crisscrossed the border. Certainly, strong parallels could be drawn between the writings of Mexican-national essayists and Cruceño newspaper editors. It is reasonable to assume that educated Cruceños like Armijo and Lerma read materials by Mexican intellectuals like Gamboa or Alvarado. Circumstances on the U.S. side of the border, however, meant that the Cruceño writers would not merely parrot the debates in the Mexican press. Armijo and Lerma were more strongly invested in obtaining U.S. statehood than in joining in the currents of reform swirling around Mexican revolutionaries. Part of that statehood project involved a discourse on regional New Mexican identity, which, if it were to appeal to the U.S. nation-state, had to differ axiomatically from Mexican nationalism. As a result, rather than defend Mexican society or consider the "threat" of Mexican feminists in Mexico City, Armijo and Lerma presented their arguments (regardless of where they might have originated) as entirely local and concerned with American issues. They more readily discussed gendered ideologies as part of American nationalism than as a trend in Mexico. Indeed, they could even use Latin America as a foil for New Mexico, claiming the former had become "too feminist."

Fifty years had passed since M. Claude Jones had targeted Ybarri's "Títeres" show in an effort to police sexual expression. Seemingly, members of the Mexican elite had become more vocal about public displays of sex, particularly displays of women's sexuality. Armijo used his newspaper to crusade against "risqué" women, whom he believed demeaned the Cruceño community. In 1909 Armijo wrote a passionate plea to forbid the "hootchy-kootchy" from being performed in Las Cruces. He framed his attack on the dance as critical to the territory's morality, calling on "los padres municipales" to prevent "semejante insulto a sus esposas sus hijas y a la sociedad" (such insults to their wives, their daughters, and society).[112] His concern over removing sexually suggestive performances such as the hootchy-kootchy from the public eye reflected Armijo's expectations about gender and sexuality and the remaking of the Mesilla Valley. Middle-class Mexican men had a duty to protect Mexican women from such shocking displays.

In contrast to his discussion of fallen women, like the hootchy-kootchy dancers, Armijo selected articles on gender that glorified the domestic sphere for women. In "Los diez mandamientos del padre" *El Eco del Valle* highlighted the father as the ultimate authority in the family but also argued that the father should not use his power to interfere with his wife's role in the home. "Tendrás para tu esposa inacabable apoyo moral," the article advised, "buscando en ella consuelo sin desoír su consejo" (You will have unending moral support for your wife, seeking comfort from her, without ignoring her advice).[113] The paper further advised, "No cometas nunca la torpeza de presentar en oposición o lucha el poder paterno con el materno" (Never commit the stupidity of presenting opposition or a struggle of the paternal power against the maternal one).[114] Women had a complementary (if subordinate) role to play in relation to patriarchal authority, Armijo argued, which needed men's respect in its own right.

El Eco del Valle published a series of similar articles explicitly defining the meaning of womanhood in the years before New Mexico obtained statehood. Usually signed anonymously with a single letter, these articles dictated that Spanish-speaking women in New Mexico should conform more closely and visibly to norms of gendered privacy. The dramatic language of the editorials pinned the future of the territory, the United

States, and even civilization to Cruceñas' ability to meet a particular standard of womanhood, one more in line with the separate-spheres ideology than had been the case prior to the war.[115] Mexican women needed to concentrate on their private domestic duties so that Mexican men could assert and maintain their public authority and protect women.[116] Although women had sometimes managed their own property and businesses during the Mexican period, by the time *El Eco del Valle* printed these articles, Armijo argued that Mexican women ought not even appear in public. One such article, "Los mandamientos de la mujer casada," outlined ten duties for married women. Here the editor made the foil developing ideas about "New Women" then being promulgated in other parts of the United States and Mexico.[117] This article claimed it should be taboo for married women to leave their house unnecessarily: "Honrarás a tu estado, no saliendo de casa, a menos que la necesidad la exima," the author, "B," wrote; "procurando que en otra parte se ignoren las faltas de tus consortes y las ocurrencias desagradables que hubiere en el hogar" (Honor your state, not going out of the house, unless the need exists; going out ignores the mistakes of your companions and the disagreeable occurrences that may happen at home).[118] In place of leaving the household, *El Eco del Valle* instructed Mesilla Valley women to devote all of their energies to being a wife and mother. "No matarás el tiempo en la cama, en el tocador, en las visitas o paseo," the paper admonished, "sin hacer caso de la familia pues así matarás la fortuna de tu esposo, su amor por ti, su paciencia y el porvenir de tus hijos—a quienes amarás con suma ternura" (You will not kill time in bed, at the dressing-table, in visits or walks, without paying attention to the family, because in this way you will kill the fortune of having your husband, his love for you, his patience and the future of your children—whom you will love with supreme tenderness).[119]

Another article, "El carácter de una buena mujer," defined the "good woman" as strictly a wife and mother. This article argued that women should devote themselves entirely to their children, their house, and their (Catholic) religion, suggesting the ideal woman as "aquella que abre su boca, según dice Salomón, con dulzura y amabilidad, aquella que educa bien a sus hijos, cuida de su casa con verdadero celo e interés y desempeña igualmente todos los deberes de sociedad, de piedad y de religión" (a woman who opens her mouth, as says Solomon, with sweetness and amiability, the one who educates her children well, takes care of her house with true zeal and interest and covers equally all the duties of society, of piety and of religion).[120] In a later edition *El Eco del Valle* claimed bluntly that marriage should be a young woman's main goal: "Todas las jóvenes deben esperar casarse un día" (All young women must expect to marry one day).[121] The article thereafter advised young women to master the "art" of being a good wife. Its advice included learning how to do all basic domestic tasks and how to improve one's husband through the "honey of kindness."[122] In a similar tone another article answered the question "¿Qué es la madre?" by stating "¡Feliz la esposa que ha tenido muchos hijos y que ha sabido educarlos!" (What is a mother? Happy is the wife who has many children and has known to educate them!)[123] There was never a suggestion that women prior to the U.S. invasion had access to wage-paying work or commerce outside the home (or that many women continued such work after the invasion).

El Eco del Valle was not the only paper to carry messages such as these. An article in the Las Cruces paper *El Labrador* sketched in detail Mexicans' proper gender roles. The editorial "El hogar es escuela" argued that women needed to stay in their homes, devoting all their energies to their husband and children. If a Mexican woman strayed from these duties, she had failed to realize her true virtue. "Una madre," the article stated, "si no se sacrifica por dar a sus hijos los elementos para su dicha, formándoles una bella alma, no tiene caridad" (A mother . . . if she does not sacrifice to give her children the elements for their happiness, and molding for them a beautiful soul, does not have charity).[124]

Given how seamlessly race, gender, and space figured together, it is not surprising that Mexican Americans were not alone in emphasizing women's place in the home during this time. Members of other racial minority groups frequently advocated conforming to gendered expectations about space as one means for integrating into the U.S. nation. The historian Kevin Gaines shows how early-twentieth-century African American leaders frequently imagined the creation of stable homes and family life as panaceas for the economic and social problems facing the community. Martha Jones shows that African American leaders who advocated for women's education most often framed it as a means to make them "respectable" wives and mothers.[125] Likewise, Martin Summers documents that some African Americans saw participating in the discourse of separate spheres as evidence of their own status as middle-class American citizens. The necessary subordination of African American women within a patriarchal domestic realm was often a key feature of all of these discussions.[126] So, too, did middle-class Cruceño men like Armijo imagine that rigidly conforming to separate spheres would be a moral and civic triumph for Mexicans even as economic demands for women's wages made such conformity impossible for most Mexican households.

Armijo and the other contributors to *El Eco del Valle* recognized that their future as a dominant class hinged on being integrated into the U.S. economy and political realm. Thus Armijo and Lerma frequently printed tracts that they represented as direct translations from eastern U.S. newspapers, granting these American newspapers a special authority for naming proper womanhood. The articles disrupted the past acceptance of the public mixing of men and women in New Mexico. One such article appeared in Las Cruces's *El Labrador* in March 1905 and later appeared in *El Eco del Valle* on November 2, 1907. Both papers claimed to cull advice from "un periódico americano" to answer the question "¿Qué haremos con nuestras hijas?" (What are we to do with our daughters?").[127] Repeating common notions linking womanhood to domestic duties, the article suggested that women focus their attentions "dirigir los quehaceres de la casa" (to be in charge of the chores at home).[128]

One of the most extreme articles on womanhood in *El Eco del Valle* appeared in 1906 and suggested a limit to Mexican women's education.[129] The article acknowledged that some education for women could make them more interesting wives and instructive mothers but warned that too much education threatened to create a life of loneliness. Being educated pushed women to intrude on male pursuits, rendering them sexually undesirable. What makes this particular article interesting, however, is the way that it distinguished Cruceña women from women in "Latin" countries. The article thus tied the issue of womanhood to a wider project of naming New Mexico (and New Mexicans) as different from "some [nameless] Latin countries," which, the article mysteriously claimed, emphasized giving women a scientific education. Perhaps Lerma reacted to the first generation of women in Mexico who earned advanced degrees. Though small in number, several had become noted doctors, scientists, pharmacists, and other professionals between 1880 and 1900.[130] Contrasting the Cruceña women with such "Latina" women helped depict a distinction between New Mexico as "American" rather than "Mexican" or "Latino." It stated:

A las doncellas de algunos países latinos, se les enseña en los buenos establecimientos la física y la anatomía, la patología etc., rudimentos de todas las ciencias habidas y por haber, en fin; pero de los cuales ninguna utilidad verdadera pueden sacar las educandas. A lo mejor, se logra obtener así una marisabidilla o enciclopedia andando, que será magnifica para confinarla en alguna biblioteca; más de la cual, todo hombre prudente tendrá buen cuidado de librarse, no escogiéndola jamás para compañera de su hogar. Este es el último resultado que se obtiene, cuando nuestras jóvenes han tenido la desgracia de no contar con sus madres hacendosas y previsoras que les enseñaran lo primero que importa saber a las mujeres.[131]

(The maidens of some Latin countries are taught in the good institutions physics, anatomy, pathology, etc., in short, rudiments of all the sciences to be had; but not one of the female pupils can take any true utility from each. At best, it is possible to become a know-it-all or a walking encyclopedia, that will be splendid to confine in some library; most of them every prudent man will take good care of getting away from, never choosing her for his companion at home. This is the ultimate result that is obtained when our young women have stretched the misfortune of not having had industrious and cautious mothers who taught them the first thing that is important for women to know.)

The article urged Cruceña women to distinguish themselves from such foolish women in Latin American countries by eschewing an education in favor of a happy heterosexual marriage.

Even when one female author utilized *El Eco del Valle* to challenge such drastic exclusions of women from higher education, she still used the same language of womanhood that appeared in Armijo's other articles. Her essay, which she left unsigned, chastised those who claimed that women did not need an education. To lend authority to her argument, she drew on the already existing discourse about womanhood, warning that women without an education could fall into "sin" and "temptation" and would fail in their roles as wives and mothers. Because women yearned to engage their minds, she claimed, they would turn to reading illegitimate novels to satisfy their intellectual curiosity. "En las novelas," the article warned, "nada se aprende y lo que consiguen con su lectura es que sus pasiones se exciten y se conviertan en parlanchinas románticas, coquetas y casquivanas" (In these novels nothing is learned and what is obtained by reading them is that their [women's] passions get excited and they become romantic, flirtatious, and featherbrained chatters).[132] The article made even more dire claims, suggesting that the novels threatened women's immortal souls because their content "deadened religious feelings."[133]

This author challenged men's presumptions that women who sought an education would either abandon or be denied a role as mother. Yet she still did not fight for women's right to be in the public sphere. Instead, she framed women's education as a means to make them more proficient in the domestic sphere ("ser buenas madres de familia") and even to save their "purity," an argument not significantly different from Governor Alvarado's thinking about women's education.[134]

Such articles appeared as the Euro-American discourse around separate spheres was coming to an end, at the start of the twentieth century.[135] The articles in *El Eco del Valle* seized on these changes to argue that Cruceñas were even more tied to the home and were better images of womanhood than "American New Women." The paper printed fantastic stories about white women throughout the United States who had tossed aside their role as wives and mothers to enter the job market and the tragedies that resulted. The paper warned, "Las mujeres americanas están en todo. Ya nadie se acuerda de la época remotísima en que empezaron a ser abogadas, doctoras en medicina agentes de seguros, veterinarias y alcaldesas" (American women are in everything. Already nobody can recall the long-ago time when they began to be lawyers, doctors of medicine, insurance agents, veterinarians, and mayors).[136] The article claimed that Euro-American women's fight for their voting rights and professional work created "cierto genero de noticias" (a certain genre of news) that appeared from New York to California. This news included fantastic stories ridiculing the New Woman and urging Mexican women to eschew their examples. An eastern American woman, the article reported, became restless in the middle of a romantic boat trip and decided to swim ashore with the boat and her fiancé in tow (!). Another story even claimed that women could face legal charges if they refused the role of wife. "En Filadelfia hay un bendito dicen que es, estudiante de la Escuela de Minas," the article claimed, "que le ha puesto pleito a una preciosa joven, demandándole cinco mil pesos de daños y prejuicios, por haberle retirado su palabra de matrimonio y no quererlo por marido" (In Philadelphia there is a blessed man, that is said to be a student of the School of Mines, who has filed a lawsuit against a beautiful young woman, demanding five thousand pesos in damages and prejudices, for having withdrawn her word of marriage from him and not wanting him for a husband).[137] The article retold another incident in New York, where a young man had sought an injunction against a girl who betrayed her womanhood by pursuing him aggressively and sending him notes:

Justin Barnes, mozo de la ciudad de Ithaca, fue a quejarse al jefe de policía de que una maestra Miss Carrie Thomas, le perseguía con cartas y ojeadas que a él le causaban tanta molestia como enojo. La joven tuvo que prometer a un juez al día siguiente que desistiría de perseguir y asustar a Justin con sus amorosas demostraciones.[138]

(Justin Barnes, a young boy from the city of Ithaca, went to complain to the chief of police about the teacher Miss Carrie Thomas. She harassed him with letters and ogles that were causing him so much inconvenience and annoyance. The young woman had to promise a judge on the following day that she would desist from chasing and scaring Justin with her loving demonstrations.)

Such stories contrasted aggressive American women with an idealized Mexican woman. American women were not content to modestly submit to men's authority. As a result they became clownish and undesirable. Mexicans could therefore claim a greater morality than Euro-Americans because they more carefully ensured that women "behaved."

It was not always Mexican men who made these distinctions, either. Throughout the borderland some Euro-American men praised Mexican women as allegedly *better* housekeepers and more domestic than American women, particularly as white feminism grew.[139] This notion, Linda Gordon reminds us, coexisted with the tropes of Mexicans as "greasers" who were inherently unclean. Whereas Euro-Americans had largely chided Mexican women for violating the public/private divide in the mid-nineteenth century, by the start of the twentieth century many were arguing that they were more "naturally" inclined to separate spheres than their Euro-American counterparts. This created a stereotyped image of Mexican women as docile, pious, and homebound while also criticizing Euro-American feminists for straying from their womanly duties to the point that a racial inferior surpassed them.

El Eco del Valle's articles on womanhood suggest the heterogeneity of ideas about gender and race along the border. At times, Armijo's and Lerma's emphasis on defining womanhood through marriage and a woman's duties in the home mirrored discussions in other parts of the United States, sometimes explicitly calling for Cruceñas to model themselves on American women. At other times Armijo rejected Euro-American practices, particularly "New Women," and suggested that Mexicans retain more civilized gender relations. The decision to print articles that depicted American women as betraying their "true" roles highlighted a different notion about gender and race. Members of the territory's Mexican American elite revised their ideas about gender and sexuality by mixing together discussions in both Mexico and the United States. They did not imagine that they were the same as Euro-Americans, but differed from women in other Latin American countries. By 1900 Spanish-language newspaper *El Nuevo Mundo* could print an enι poem dedicated "a una Neo-Mexicana."[140] While the content of t..ᴄ poem was fairly predictable (praising "New Mexican" women's "rasgados ojos" [wide eyes] or "carmínea boca" [crimson lips]), it is significant that the poet named the women in New Mexico as distinctive. Cruceñas and other Mexican women were therefore defined by the limits of their location. They were neither Mexican by nationality nor American by race or custom. Instead, their attitudes and their preservation of "true womanhood" were attributes unique to New Mexico and defined them as "neo-mexicanas."

Gender and Violence

Euro-American and Mexican American middle-class confidence that adherence to a separate-spheres ideology would resolve many of the territory's problems modulated a great number of discussions. Sensational stories about violence became opportunities to debate how well the territory upheld that ideal, particularly when such stories involved lurid sexual details. Violence, some imagined, had to have involved the illegitimate disruption of the gender order. In 1902 the *Las Cruces Progress* reported a domestic dispute that escalated into a murder-suicide. Coverage of this incident suggests how ideas about race and gender informed interpretations of even the most intimate details of Mexicans' lives during the territorial period. Editors at the *Progress* described the bloody episode involving a Mexican American woman and her husband from the town of Doña Ana: "The wife of R. Montoya refused to live with him any longer and locked him out of the house. He entered the house unknown to her and secreted himself under the bed. She came in with a woman friend of hers and began telling her troubles. Montoya then rushed out and threw his wife's friend out of the room and locked the door. He then turned to his wife and stabbed her killing her immediately. After seeing that she was dead he turned the dagger on himself."[141] Stories about such domestic disputes appeared with regularity in the territorial papers.

In this case "the wife of R. Montoya" took action like many women who face an abusive relationship: she refused to continue living with a violent spouse, seemingly with the approval of supportive women friends. The

Progress's coverage of her murder, however, provided its own interpretation about her decisions. The English-language paper never acknowledged that she might have had legitimate grievances against her husband. The paper, instead, concluded that she must have been immoral
because she left her husband. "It is supposed," the newspaper ended the
story, "that trouble grew out of the wife receiving the attention of other
men."[142] Categorically, women who abandoned their roles as dutiful
wives had to be unchaste. The paper, therefore, implicitly blamed her for
her own murder and the "tragedy" of her husband's suicide.

The *Progress* also figured the household as central to the story, presenting the struggle as one of a wife locking her husband out of the home and
colluding with her female friends within that same place. Such disor-
dered households, where patriarchal authority was literally locked out,
were presented as inevitably violent and catastrophic.[143] Like other newspapers from the time, it defined all women strictly as wives and mothers
and imagined them firmly within domestic spaces.[144] Indeed, it never
named the woman in question in any other way than as "the wife of R.
Montoya." Reporting the Montoyas' grisly end revealed the editors' presumptions about gender, but it also suggested much about their ideas on
race as well. For Euro-American readers the Montoyas' personal story
likely reaffirmed stereotypes of Mexican women as immoral and unfaith-
ful. It also fed into the equally disparaging stereotype of Mexican men as
jealous, violent, and ruled by passion—notions whose spread preceded
the U.S. Army's arrival in Mexico.

Assessing the full impact and changes of gender ideologies is difficult
with a limited base of surviving evidence. It is especially difficult to
consider how women responded to the changes occurring around them.
Our small body of evidence does suggest, though, that the increasing
pressure by both Euro-American and Mexican American elites to restrict
women's activities had real consequences. Compiled census data suggest
that female property ownership declined as did independent female
heads of households from the Mexican period to the end of the territorial
period. While many factors influenced demographic changes in the territory, census data available through the *Integrated Public Use Microdata
Series* project reflect a measurable loss of female autonomy following the
Euro-American invasion.[145] In the first census after the U.S.-Mexican
War female-headed households accounted for almost 20 percent of the
total households in New Mexico. This number appeared dramatically
larger than for the rest of the United States, where female-headed households accounted for only 9.4 percent of the total.[146] Mexican women

appeared slightly more likely than their Euro-American counterparts to be the head of a territorial household in 1850. Female-headed households accounted for 22.1 percent of Spanish-surnamed households in the territory in the 1850 census. In the same census women headed 19.2 percent of Euro-American households. By 1880, though, female-headed households accounted for 15.7 percent of Spanish-surnamed households and 13.5 percent of Euro-American households. The number would continue to drop. In 1920 female-headed households accounted for 11.6 percent of Spanish-surnamed households and 9.1 percent of Euro-American households.[147] Comparing New Mexico to the rest of the United States suggests an even more striking change. New Mexico had almost twice as many female-headed households as the rest of the United States in 1850. By 1920 New Mexico had less (9.9 percent) than the national average (11.7 percent) of female-headed households.

Evaluating newspaper stories, like the article on the Montoyas, and charting demographic changes provide small windows onto territorial-era trends. Gauging how individual Mexican women and men adopted or resisted changing gender and sexual ideologies proves much more difficult. To get at this issue, we can begin by considering a 1907 case involving Zacarias Padilla, a justice of the peace in northern New Mexico, and the New Mexico Mounted Police. Unfortunately, the few records involving Padilla leave more of those questions unresolved than answered. Sifting through the surviving details only hints at some of the ways that groups of Euro-American and Mexican American men attempted to claim their own authority over women and the territory. These records also suggest, though, the ways that Mexican women asserted their agency to control their own lives.

Euro-American racist expectations about Mexican manhood, womanhood, and sexuality likely informed the police investigation of Padilla. The chief investigator, G. F. Murray, had a clear disdain for the Mexican population and seemed only marginally interested in its welfare. His efforts to police gender and sexuality hardly seemed unusual. As we saw with M. Claude Jones in 1855 and Davis in 1857, many Euro-Americans had been invoking sexual morality to justify their intrusion into the most intimate matters in Mexicans' daily lives.

Murray, a territorial mounted-police officer, filed a report with his captain in September of 1907 indicating his intention to investigate Zacarias Padilla, the justice of the peace in San Rafael. Murray did not charge impropriety in Padilla's performance of his civic office but rather targeted Padilla's personal actions. Murray accused him of sexual misconduct with a number of Mexican women. Murray reported that Padilla "has a wife and two children . . . and he has two children from another girl . . . by the name of Vibiana Varreras."[148] Varreras, Murray wrote, was seventeen years old, with "no means of support." Murray also noted, "There is another one by the name of Nestora Sandoval[.] She is soposed [*sic*] to have had a child by the J.P. and killed it and throen [*sic*] it into the Street."[149] A few weeks later Murray reported that he had found enough evidence to arrest Padilla, who, according to Murray, had abandoned his "legal wife and two children" to abduct Lola Chávez from Albuquerque, whom he quickly deserted as well. Murray's final charges claimed that Padilla "has ruined more girls in that town of San Raffal [*sic*] than all the rest of them put together and everyone there wants to see him prosecuted."[150]

Even if we accept only a portion of Murray's account, Padilla's story reveals information about the power that members of the Mexican elite were willing to exercise in sexual matters. Padilla had violated the local laws and social expectations, but his status as the son of a prominent Mexican resident influenced the outcome of his case. Murray predicted a struggle would occur when he filed his initial report, noting that Padilla's position had prevented the women and their families from seeking his prosecution. "His father is one of the wealthy Mexicans there," Murray wrote. "They cannot do anything with him as he is the J.P. there and he does what he likes."[151] In this instance both Euro-Americans and Mexican Americans claimed the authority to monitor sexual conduct.

In the end the members of the Mexican elite who intervened on Padilla's behalf protected him from prosecution. Writing directly to the governor, R. L. Baca accused Murray of illegally arresting Padilla. Baca did not refute Murray's accusations against Padilla but insisted that Murray did not have the appropriate arrest warrant. Baca coordinated with Estanislao Chaves, another justice of the peace, to discredit Murray's police procedures.[152] At the conclusion of the episode Murray found himself the target of an investigation instigated by the governor. On one level this incident shows that members of the Mexican elite effectively resisted a Euro-American's effort to intervene in their private affairs. Wealthy Mexicans had some authority in 1907 to limit outside policing of gender and sexuality within their communities.

Yet Padilla and his associates exercised authority available only to affluent men.[153] Mexican residents of San Rafael disapproved of Padilla's actions, but his relative wealth and position enabled him to avoid legal punishment. These few documents exposed how struggles between elite men could come at the cost of nonelites, especially poorer women. Neither Murray nor Baca genuinely considered Varreras and the other women's interests. In the end those women who had sought justice found that their needs went unaddressed.

This is not to say that these Mexican women did not push back against patriarchal authority. Murray, like many Euro-Americans, perceived these women merely as victims whom Padilla had "ruined." His own case notes, however, documented that these women took active and visible actions to assert their authority within their community. Varreras, for instance, did not suffer in silence. Murray recorded that it "seems as she is very disagreeable with the J.P. wife as she casues [sic] lots of truble [sic]."[154] Varreras felt that she not only had the prerogative to make herself known to Padilla's wife but to seek police intervention. According to Murray, Varreras and her mother served as his primary informants against Padilla. Euro-American and Mexican American elites might have attempted to limit the public role of women in the territory, but many Mexican women refused to accept shabby treatment and even found advantages in the new legal system. The historian Miroslava Chávez-García documents that Mexican and Mexican American women created their own opportunities after Alta California's transfer to the United States in 1848. Women's options for using legal apparatuses against an abusive or neglectful spouse, or even obtaining a full divorce, expanded from those available during the Mexican period.[155] Chávez-García argues that availing oneself of such legal options could still carry significant costs, including a loss of social status, but a small group of California Mexican women skillfully maneuvered through the new legal system to free themselves from bad marriages and improve their lives.[156]

In New Mexico, Mexican American women, like Varreras, would likewise demand that the territory's police and courts intervene for them. In doing so, they made strategic decisions about when and how they would participate in the colonial legal structure. At times they used those imperial institutions to better their circumstances within the Mexican community. One Cruceña, Nieves Ortega, for instance, refused to tolerate her abusive husband's insults and filed charges against him in 1909. Ortega testified that Trinidad Ortega, her husband, "colérica y groseramente me asaltó ilegalmente en mi casa de habitación con palabras obscenas diciéndome que era una *puta* y vagamunda en contra de mi honor y reputación tratándose así con crueldad" (angrily, rudely, and illegally assaulted me in my home with obscene words saying to me that I was a *whore* and tramp, against my honor and reputation, treating me with cruelty).[157] Though Euro-American and Mexican American elites attempted to curtail their ability to conduct business or earn wages in public, women like Varreras and Ortega demanded that territorial institutions hear their concerns.

Mexican women were constrained by existing laws, cultural practices, and the tumultuous changes that resulted from American conquest. Statistical evidence also hints that Mexican women had a decreasing public presence during the territorial period. A lack of substantial resources concerning nineteenth-century Mexican women, however, does not mean it is impossible to see some of the ways that they asserted their agency. As the Padilla case suggests, many Mexican women resisted efforts of Mexican and Euro-American men to control their lives. Women like Varreras and Ortega asserted their own expectations and demands to be treated with respect even as shifting gender ideologies demanded their silence.

Conclusion

Tensions over gender roles figured into the conflicts between Mexicans and Euro-Americans through the nineteenth century. Initially, Mexicans and Euro-Americans differed in their understanding about the relationship between gender and the organization of space. Euro-Americans who arrived in New Mexico viewed the ways that Mexican women participated in the public sphere as emblematic of a "misuse" of local lands. After the United States annexed the area, Euro-Americans imagined that imposing their gender division of space was a critical component in their efforts to remake New Mexico as an American place. White women found that the circumstances along the border paradoxically provided them with opportunities to escape patriarchal restrictions by becoming "civilizing" agents. By contrasting themselves with the supposedly immoral Mexican population, Euro-American women created opportunities to use their "natural" talents to reform New Mexico. In this way they subverted the expectation that they remain in the domestic realm even as they looked to enforce those restrictions on Mexican women.

By 1880 many elite Mexicans also participated in a discourse that restricted women's roles much more than they had in 1850. Previous traditions had idealized women's roles within the family but did not stringently keep women out of public activities, like operating a business or appearing in court. By the end of the nineteenth century, members of the Mexican elite, like Isidoro Armijo and M. F. Lerma, circulated articles that upheld a much stricter vision of separate spheres. In many ways this renewed emphasis did not overtly challenge their existing ideas about the meaning of manhood and womanhood in the territory. Nonetheless, the idealization of separate spheres became a means to define imagined differences between Mexican American women and their contemporaries in either Mexico or other parts of the United States. In a historical reversal, as Armijo and other Mexican elites attempted to impose the strict gendered division of space, women in other areas of the nation worked to undermine and redefine the meaning of gender roles. Armijo and others circulated tales about these "New Women" in fantastic stories to urge Mexican women to eschew their examples.

Scattered incidents covered in this chapter suggest the important ways that ideologies of gender and sexuality figured into discussions about the meaning of race, nation, and region from 1848 to 1912. Discussions among members of the territory's elite refigured the particular meanings of being both raced and gendered in the nineteenth century. Mexicans and Euro-Americans understood and articulated their sense of identity and difference by drawing on these intersectional identities, sometimes to create new understandings of themselves. Many Mexican and Euro-American elites felt an imperative to rename the racial and national meaning of the border region after 1880. We turn now to the writings of prominent individuals who attempted to define the racial and national meanings of the territory through the language of a regional "New Mexican" identity.

CHAPTER 5

"It Must Never Be Forgotten This Is New and
Not Old Mexico": Local Space in Euro-American
Knowledge and Practice, 1880–1912

In 1880 territorial officials created the New Mexico Territorial Bureau of Immigration as an institutionalized effort to attract more Euro-American settlers to New Mexico.[1] This office promoted and advertised the territory's mineral wealth and agricultural potential to prospective immigrants or investors, most visibly through the publication of numerous short pamphlets that focused on a particular region or industry in the territory that awaited Euro-American development. In 1908 the bureau released one such pamphlet on Doña Ana County for nationwide distribution. This short brochure suggests striking changes in the representation of the Mesilla Valley and the issues of race, nation, and region.[2]

Like other pamphlets in the series, this one promised easy economic success for potential settlers, who would find "returns from the land are generous and sure."[3] The corporate authors touted the possibility of growing everything from beans to peaches in irrigated fields. Alfalfa, the leading crop in the Mesilla Valley, fetched up to fifteen dollars per ton, representing a potential profit of fifty dollars per acre.[4] More than mere promotion of the valley's agricultural bounty, this pamphlet justified New Mexico's place within the United States. Euro-Americans claimed that scientific engineering had transformed the region's desert into a major agricultural center for the nation. In a rhetorical flourish that was already commonplace in 1908, the pamphlet's authors fostered the idea that New Mexico had a historic destiny within the United States and civilization. Technological innovation and historical longevity intertwined in the declaration that the Mesilla Valley was the "cradle of irrigation in America." New Mexico was not an inert part of the United States: its boosters were claiming that it was in fact a progenitor of the nation.

Yet the pamphlet also shows that only Las Cruces figured centrally into

6. Las Cruces at the turn of the century. Boosters took pride in the coal power plant, steam laundry, and brick buildings. They believed these things made their town entirely "progressive." Courtesy Archives and Special Collections Department, New Mexico State University Library.

these efforts to sell the valley or New Mexico. La Mesilla, despite having been the social and economic center of Doña Ana County for most of the nineteenth century, was entirely sidelined in this discussion. Las Cruces, the pamphlet stated, had been transformed under "the magic wave of development that has swept over all New Mexico within the past five years." No longer a "sleepy 'adobe' town," Las Cruces was a "hustling little city of the most progressive type," complete with waterworks, electric power, an ice factory, two flour mills, a cannery, and a steam laundry (see Figure 6).[5] It also provided residents with three public schools that "compare favorably with those of any town of equal size in any section of the United States."[6] As we have seen, architecture had significant meaning in terms of national identity. The transition from adobe buildings to civilized conveniences like a steam laundry or electric power would have been read by many as a change from being "Mexican" to being "American."

Government officials, business leaders, and writers offered new ways to conceptualize New Mexico, particularly its nonwhite majority, as part of the larger U.S. nation between 1880 and 1912.[7] They orchestrated a vision of the territory as uniquely American, dissociating it entirely from the bordering Mexican nation. The transformation of Las Cruces from an "adobe town" to a "progressive city" was no mere marketing ploy. It served the interests of those who wished to incorporate the territory into the U.S. nation and economy.

Unlike its discursive predecessors, this pamphlet neither effaced the Mexican bodies in the valley and New Mexico nor promised that Mexicans would inevitably vanish once larger numbers of Euro-Americans arrived in the territory. Instead, it noted the presence of Mexicans in Las Cruces obliquely and without ever using the term *Mexican*. Circuitously, the pamphlet made reference to three Spanish-language newspapers printed in Las Cruces and to the significant Catholic presence—readily understood code words for Mexicans in the region.[8] Most important, though, it highlighted the availability of "farm hands" for hire at the bargain rate of seventy-five cents to a dollar per day, or eighteen dollars to twenty-five dollars per month.[9] Rather than hinder the advance of civilization, the pamphlet promised, Mexicans would actually serve as a readily available labor force in the cause of Euro-American expansion.

Inspired by such materials as the 1908 pamphlet, this chapter asks, How did Euro-Americans achieve an understanding of New Mexico as being entirely American, despite its undeniably nonwhite majority? Part of the answer to this question depended on developing a specific language of colonialism that organized the local Mexican population into something that benefited the nation through labor, "scientific" study, and even entertainment.

In the same period, alternative means for defining Mexican identity, such as the national articulation common in La Mesilla, came under attack. The same pamphlet that hailed Las Cruces as progressive relegated Mesilla to the past, as the "scene of many history-making events."[10] With the exception of the newly constructed brick San Albino's Catholic Church, the pamphlet advised, Mesilla was still "an 'adobe' town, picturesque, but not yet awakened to the new life that has found its more energetic neighbor." Thus La Mesilla and Las Cruces continued to embody contrast through the end of the territorial period in 1912. Mesilla stubbornly remained Mexican, suffering economic consequences of that decision, while Las Cruces became "progressive" by remodeling itself into a town that was regionally New Mexican but nationally American at the same time.

This chapter begins by rehearsing the counterarguments that politicians and public leaders consistently used to justify their refusal of statehood for New Mexico. Starting around 1880, Euro-American writers and officials began to argue that New Mexico and its multiracial population benefited the United States; their arguments developed in ways that would have been unimaginable in 1848. Significantly, their writings almost never implied that Mexicans as American citizens connoted racial equality with Euro-Americans. Quite the opposite, Euro-Americans posited that New Mexico had achieved a type of racial harmony because Euro-Americans had successfully asserted their colonial authority to subdue the "weaker Mexican" population. The following sections consider a variety of ways that Euro-Americans explained New Mexico's unique racial and national circumstances. Euro-American writers considered here produced texts for different purposes, but they all labored to remake New Mexico's meaning within the larger United States, arguing that the territory created racial stability under the sign of a single national identity.

I begin with prominent territorial figures before focusing more specifically on writers in the Mesilla Valley. Because a monolithic expression of New Mexico's meaning in the United States never existed, I do not attempt to trace the origins of a single discourse on race or regional identity among Euro-Americans at the end of the territorial period. Instead, I show that multiple, sometimes competing, groups wrote about the region's racial diversity and national orientation, often contradicting each another. Even the same person could write about the relationship between New Mexico's Mexicans and Euro-Americans in different ways depending on the circumstances and the language of presentation.

Rather than attempt to excavate such a unified expression of what living in territorial New Mexico meant, I consider how different Euro-Americans deployed a common language about race and nation in the region, if for different purposes. Government figures, like the territorial chief justice L. Bradford Prince, or travel writers, like Charles Lummis, or college students, like Charles Miller, wrote for diverse audiences and often without demonstrable connections to each other. Some of them, like Prince and Lummis, actually disliked each other intensely and held opposing views on many key issues. Their animus even included name calling, as Lummis referred to Prince as the "old Bullfrog."[11] Taken together, though, these men all drew on coherent (and remarkably persistent) presumptions about race, nation, and region. Euro-Americans' writings from New Mexico became defensive of the territory, especially when confronted by Euro-American easterners, who frequently questioned the fitness of these westerners for full citizenship. Many of the latter responded with a notion of a racially unified New Mexican identity that placed themselves as colonial leaders.

Euro-Americans had claimed New Mexico was a natural part of the United States since before the United States and Mexico officially went to war in 1846. Those claims to land, though, most often disavowed the incorporation of Mexicans as full citizens of the United States. What changed in the 1880s was that Euro-Americans began to write about Mexicans' roles in New Mexico as something that defined the land as a *unique* part of the United States. New Mexico's population differed from those of other U.S. border states, particularly Texas and California, even after decades of colonial administration. Despite an overall growth in population, Euro-Americans still did not attain a majority in New Mexico, unlike its neighboring states. In 1900 the Mexican population in New Mexico outnumbered Euro-Americans by almost three to one.[12] Therefore, Euro-American colonial leaders devised new ways to explain how both the land *and now* the people of New Mexico were ready for full admission to the nation, despite their racial heterogeneity. Mexicans thereby became the defeated "natives" of a land that had been thoroughly pacified by Euro-American colonizers.

The notion of a racially unified New Mexican identity emerged as a peculiar solution for those who wished to obviate deeper discussions about Mexicans and Euro-Americans' economic and social relationships along the border. Being New Mexican, Euro-Americans like Prince argued, implied coexistence in racial harmony under the benevolent protection of the United States. Mexican Americans and Euro-Americans (and sometimes Native Americans) could each claim the New Mexican identity because it took the presence of both (or all three) to create what was distinctive about the territory.[13] New Mexico, for them, meant a place that was bicultural or, on occasion, even tricultural.

Nonetheless, these Euro-Americans walked a tightrope. They conceded that Mexicans could obtain U.S. citizenship, but they also had to explain how that citizenship did not conflict with presumptions about Euro-Americans' racial superiority or colonial authority. Some Euro-Americans could even assume the seemingly contradictory positions of arguing that New Mexico's Mexicans were ready for full citizenship even as they commented on their racial inferiority to other Americans.[14] For most Euro-Americans the same racially unified New Mexican identity that made the territory ready for equal inclusion in the United States necessarily implied a territorial racial hierarchy.

The regional identity accompanied an uneven and inconsistent pro-

cess of differential racialization that distinguished the Mexicans
Mexico from *Tejanos* or *Californios*. Notably, New Mexico did n
rience the same growth in Mexican immigration as Texas and C:
did in the early twentieth century. Between 1900 and 1910 the numbei ui
Mexico-born Mexicans doubled in the United States, and it doubled
again between 1910 and 1920.[15] New Mexico, however, received only
20,000 of the estimated 480,000 immigrants who moved into the United
States. Between 1900 and 1920 the percentage of "foreign-born" individuals in New Mexico increased just slightly, from 7 percent of the population to 8 percent of the population.[16] Indeed, New Mexico's percentage of
foreign-born residents was by then well *below* the national average.

As the demographics in neighboring states shifted, many in New Mexico, both Mexican and Euro-American, sought to distance the territory's
Spanish-speaking population from the newly arriving Mexican immigrants in Texas and California. They differentiated between a "native"
Mexican individual born in New Mexico, and who therefore properly
belonged in the United States, and one who was born in Mexico and was,
therefore, "foreign." They argued that New Mexico's specific circumstances allowed its Mexican population to be American in ways that their
neighboring Tejanos and Californios could not imitate.

For the regional discourse to make sense to these thinkers, New Mexico's history, people, and even environmental conditions had to become
distinct from, and incomparable to, anything in Mexico. The invention of
this peculiarity created a historical narrative, dependent on a transhistorical imagined geography that presumed that New Mexico had all
along been destined to join the United States.[17] La Mesilla, as a center of
opposition against incorporation into the United States and of strong
national ties to Mexico, suffered a serious decline in the late nineteenth
century as this newly emerging regional identity attained hegemony.

These discussions on the region's meaning coincided with rapid economic, technological, and demographic changes in New Mexico and the
greater U.S. Southwest. During the last decades of the nineteenth century New Mexico experienced enormous financial growth, spurred on by
the arrival of the railroad and the concomitant access to new markets
that it brought.[18] Between 1880 and 1910 the value of farm products
produced in the territory increased by almost ninefold.[19] Southern New
Mexico, in particular, received many of these benefits as the federal
government invested in irrigation projects, transforming the Mesilla
Valley into one of the richest agricultural sections in the territory.[20] New
Mexico also received an unusually high level of precipitation at the

threshold of the twentieth century, which further enhanced the success of these projects.[21]

The railroad arrived in northern New Mexico in 1880 and reached Las Cruces the following year, facilitating migration and tourism by Euro-Americans. Not by happenstance, the railroad bypassed La Mesilla in favor of Las Cruces. The combination of these changes resulted in a rapid surge in Euro-American migration to New Mexico during the last decades of the nineteenth century.[22] In 1870 fewer than ten thousand Euro-Americans lived in the territory.[23] By 1910 that population had exploded to nearly one hundred thousand. Texas, Missouri, Colorado, and Illinois sent the greatest numbers of Euro-Americans into New Mexico.[24] Moreover, the territory's total population grew by almost 70 percent between 1900 and 1910, from 195,310 to 327,301.[25] New Mexico's internal political boundaries multiplied with the surging population as the territory witnessed a frenzied creation of new counties.[26]

Figuring New Mexico as a specific subject influenced local practices, particularly in southern New Mexico. More than merely engaging in abstracted discussions, the proponents of a regional New Mexican identity created economic and social consequences for those who resisted their efforts. Unlike the rest of the territory, which had only 8 percent foreign born, the majority of the Mesilla Valley's population did not claim the United States as its birth country. According to compiled figures from the 1880 census, almost 60 percent of the residents in Doña Ana County reported their birthplace as Mexico.[27] Of the twenty thousand Mexican migrants who did arrive in New Mexico after 1900, most settled south of Socorro. By 1915 the Spanish-speaking population accounted for 71 percent of Doña Ana County voters.[28] This made extracting southern New Mexico from Mexico all the more difficult.

Statehood Denied

Campaigns for statehood figured prominently in the creation of a regional New Mexican identity. Members of the Euro-American and Mexican American elite, who stood to benefit the most from statehood, needed to find new ways to respond to the argument that the territory was not American enough to become a state. Before New Mexico finally became the forty-seventh state in 1912, leaders repeatedly tried to shed the territorial status, making direct appeals to the president and Congress in 1850, 1865, 1871, 1875, 1881, 1889, 1892, 1893, 1902, and 1908.[29]

They found few allies. Outside the territory, newspaper publishers, business leaders, and politicians continued to argue between 1880 and 1910 that the preponderance of the territory's "mixed-race" population necessarily meant that New Mexico should not be a full state.[30] Typical of this claim was a piece in the *Los Angeles Times*, ironically titled "A Statehood Argument" in 1897. It mocked the plea to fully admit New Mexico into the United States because of the large Mexican presence, implicitly contrasting that territory's history with California's. The Mexican population in Alta California, after all, had been mostly driven out of the state in the mid-nineteenth century. While migration would rapidly expand Mexican communities after 1910, Alta California's 1900 census reported only 8,086 Mexican-born residents in the state.[31] Given the history of Mexican dispossession and disfranchisement, the article could tap into commonly accepted notions that Mexicans were "backward" and hostile to "progress" without much fear of a local backlash. "Native [Mexican] citizens [in New Mexico]," the paper claimed in a tongue-in-cheek tone, "protest against improved methods of irrigation."[32] As evidence, the article produced a petition, purportedly circulated by Mexicans, to outlaw the importation of technology into New Mexico. The humor of this piece relied on the presumption that Mexicans were so out of step with the rest of the United States that they would actively refuse technology that improved their daily lives.

The author of the article might not have understood, or perhaps dismissed, Mexicans' skepticism about irrigation and other "improvement" programs in New Mexico. Transforming farming through technology might have seemed an obvious and irrefutably positive act, but such projects often carried a high price for small-scale Mexican American farmers. Certainly by the 1930s, Mexican Americans overtly protested irrigation projects because dispossession usually followed shortly after their completion. Taxes and bonds issued for irrigation projects often bankrupted Mexican American landholders, leaving them susceptible to eviction or forcing them to sell part or all of their lands to meet these new costs.[33] From the distance of Los Angeles, however, the challenges to importing and financing technological changes could be used to construe Mexican Americans as irrational Luddites deserving of their colonized status.

In another example, a *New York Times* opinion piece called on President Theodore Roosevelt to withhold his support for admitting New Mexico as a state. The author implicitly argued that New Mexico's rightful role within the United States was as a colony, like other recently acquired territories with nonwhite majorities (including some that never attained statehood, like Puerto Rico). The presence of New Mexico's "Spanish" residents precluded it from being made a state. The author wrote: "A President who would confer Statehood on Spanish New Mexico would, to be consistent, bestow American Statehood upon Cuba, Porto Rico, or the Philippines. On what principle is any territory kept a Territory if New Mexico is to be admitted?"[34] Admitting New Mexico, the editorial predicted, would set an intolerable precedent for all U.S. nonwhite territories. For this author, using race to keep these lands subordinate territories was a matter of principle.

An 1883 *New York Times* article even took subtle jabs at the fiction that New Mexico's or Texas's Mexicans were of "pure Spanish blood," an increasingly common discursive attempt to distance established U.S.-Mexican populations from their "mixed-race" counterparts in Mexico. The article tied together several violent episodes along the border to suggest a "notion of the manners and customs of the Greasers."[35] Covering a shootout in New Mexico, the paper noted the assailants were "several persons with Castillian names, but without any signs of familiarity with the most celebrated product of Castile." It then turned to the story of a Texas schoolmaster with a "strictly Andalusian name" who killed an "Extremaduran" man. The *Times* emphasized that jealousy motivated the murder, noting it was "about a girl—of course about a girl, since it was not about the Spanish substitute for draw poker." This article's sarcasm discredited attempts to remake New Mexico's Mexicans as "Spanish." The *Times* conceded that Mexicans in New Mexico and Texas shared some cultural markers, such as proper names, with those on the Iberian Peninsula; however, it emphasized that violent and lustful actions exposed Mexicans' racial status as not truly "pure Spanish/white."

As eastern newspapers debated New Mexico's future, there appeared on the national stage one figure who had the political power and the public exposure to define the territory's role in the nation. Senator Albert Beveridge from Indiana, who served in Congress from 1899 to 1911, became the most prominent critic of New Mexico's statehood campaign and summed up the previous arguments for keeping it a territory. Beveridge, the chair of the Senate Committee on Territories, dismissed the proposition that New Mexico's Mexican population had become sufficiently "American." He headed an official 1901 "investigation" that culminated in a tour of New Mexico, including the Mesilla Valley. Once the investigation concluded, Beveridge and the other committee members again rejected New Mexico's petition for statehood.

Although this rejection stemmed partly from partisan motivations (Beveridge, a Republican, feared that admitting additional territories as states would unsettle the political ratio of senators in Washington), it was not merely a matter of political expediency. Beveridge used race as the official explanation for ruling against New Mexico. Indeed, even before he became the chair of the territories committee, Beveridge declared white U.S. imperialism to be "the mission of our race, trustee, under God, of the civilization of the world."[36] Certain racial groups, in Beveridge's mind, were destined to be colonized because they were not "naturally" inclined to self-government. Giving an impassioned speech to Congress justifying U.S. annexation of the Philippine Islands, Beveridge made his sentiments clear. Filipinos, he claimed, "are not of a self-governing race. They are Orientals, Malays, instructed by Spaniards in the latter's worst estate."[37]

Beveridge held similar assumptions about the colonized Mexican population he encountered when he toured New Mexico the following year. His congressional report on his visit documented with anxiety the dominance of Mexicans over the territory's population, explained with concern that Spanish was widely used in legal and governmental proceedings, and lamented that the Mexican population was woefully "ignorant" (as measured through a supposed 30 percent literacy rate in any language). Based on these arguments, President Theodore Roosevelt privately expressed his opposition to New Mexico and Arizona statehood, claiming that the report's "facts" made "a strong case against the admission of these 2 territories."[38] Newspapers across the rest of the United States picked up Beveridge's statements that capitalized on Euro-American racism and fostered disdain for the New Mexico territory. He compared New Mexico to the Philippines in an effort to position the territory as a "foreign" colony, racially removed from the rest of the United States.[39] One southern newspaper printed a letter from Beveridge directly linking his rejection of New Mexico's statehood to the large presence of Mexicans. "Its enormous 'Mexican' preponderance in population, whose solidity fifty years of American influence has not changed," the paper quoted, "is the chief reason against the admission of that Territory."[40] In the senator's home state the *Indianapolis Journal* affirmed his racist sentiments as an "unanswerable argument" against New Mexico statehood.[41]

Nonetheless, Euro-Americans within New Mexico did attempt to answer his criticisms, just as they had attempted to answer his predecessors. An editorial entitled (in good social Darwinist fashion) "The Fittest Shall Survive" appeared in the *Las Cruces Progress* in 1902. The editor made clear that he was reacting to "Easterners" who imagined Las Cruces as "only a dirty, sleepy Mexican town," an obvious reference to Beveridge's recent tour of southern New Mexico.[42] To respond to this evaluation, the editor turned to the racially ambiguous language that had become characteristic of the New Mexico press by 1902. Never directly naming Mexicans, the editorial endorsed the perception that "natives" had misused local land in the past.[43] "It can be said," the editor wrote, "without reflection upon anyone—that in the past many of the residents of the [Mesilla] valley have been contented to live as their fathers before them lived. . . . It has truly been a land of mañana. But that day and sentiment is slowly but surely passing."[44] As one might expect, the paper reported that the arrival of many "active energetic and enterprising Americans" signaled that supposed change. The article, though, did not directly call for the displacement of Mexicans, as Bennett's *Borderer* had thirty years before. It concluded with the paper's racially ambiguous motto: "Let's get together."[45]

Even as other editorials eschewed discussions of New Mexico's racial structure, some did reassert that race must figure into the territorial government's policies. One editorial, first published in a newspaper in Gallup, went on to circulate in many of the territory's papers. Though the author did not call for a displacement of Mexicans, he still argued that the "dominant race" needed to become a solid majority of the population before New Mexico could win statehood. "The way to bring about statehood," he wrote, "is to develop our Territory so that its destinies will be in the hands of a character strong and intelligent enough to guard the high privilege sought in the beneficence."[46] This editorial accepted congressional criticism and posited that only a measurable demographic shift would convince easterners. "Not that we do it in measure," it concluded, "but it must be multiplied a hundred fold before we can hope to impress the mind of the East with the justice of our claims." Interestingly, this editorial also created a vision of a unified and singular "eastern mind" that judged the territory. This divide between easterners implicitly assumed that New Mexico's Euro-Americans contrastingly belonged with the latter region.

Efforts to distinguish New Mexico appeared contemporaneously with wider trends that increased the investment in local regional identities in the late-nineteenth-century United States. These regional identities never overtly countered a sense of a unified national American identity, but they nonetheless explained divisions between groups of Euro-Americans based on nostalgic notions of the local past. Histories of the Civil

War became tied to romantic myths of the South as populated with "teel" and "valiant" whites. Those southern whites, under this thin had been "wronged" by white northerners who imposed a radical ag during Reconstruction.[47] At the same time, nineteenth-century New England boosters claimed their region as the heir of colonial history and the crucible of "American morality."[48] Idealized visions of that region's history inspired newly constructed colonial-style architecture as a defining feature of towns across the Northeast.[49] Likewise, epic visions of the "West" appeared everywhere, from Buffalo Bill Cody's Wild West show to Frederick Jackson Turner's frontier thesis.[50] Part of the invention of the "West" included notions that the region made a particularly hardy Euro-American who contrasted with more effete and urban easterners.[51] Western champions promulgated the notion that a strenuous life in the "open frontier" implicitly, or explicitly, countered the supposedly decadent, claustrophobic, and life-sapping eastern cities. For white westerners their region became imbued with mythic "pioneers" who "tamed" wilderness and uncooperative Native Americans.[52]

So, too, New Mexico became part of that larger story of "westward expansion," and many Euro-Americans within the territory expected to be valorized for taking up the hard work of settling the land. Eastern politicians and publications, however, frequently distinguished New Mexico from other "tamed" and profitable western places. Unlike the Great Plains or California, they might suggest, New Mexico's Euro-American population had failed to properly "civilize" the territory, and it remained an economic burden. Some voices within New Mexico, like the Gallup essayist, therefore continued to endorse eastern demands that Euro-Americans become the majority population in New Mexico before it could become a state. However, this argument appeared less and less frequently in the territorial press by the beginning of the twentieth century. Rather, Euro-Americans who favored immediate statehood spent a great deal more time trying to advance an impossibly contradictory vision of New Mexico and its population. Euro-Americans could not refute that the large Mexican presence made the territory unique in the United States. Yet, if New Mexico was to become a state, they had to find other ways of assuring eastern critics that the territory was not so dissimilar to other regions of the United States. One strategy was to redirect the statehood discussion away from race and toward comparisons of New Mexico with other parts of the United States. "The truth is," the *Doña Ana Republican* printed, "that in the territory, as a whole, and in the Mesilla valley in particular that life and property are as safe as they are in any part of the United States."[53] This article's implicit argument fashioned markers other than race as the salient issues for defining an American community. In this instance the editors used the assurance that the territory protected "life and property" in an attempt to turn the debate away from race. Implicitly, territorial Euro-Americans acknowledged that they could not win a discussion in which the population's racial composition defined the region. Their only option was to shift the discussion to alternative means for thinking about New Mexico's meaning in the nation.

Responding to Albert Beveridge's 1901 report, the *Las Cruces Progress* printed a similar article that purposefully construed New Mexico as *more* American than other colonies of the United States. Using the common racially ambiguous language of "we," the letter claimed a regionally united criticism of Beveridge:

> He said we are not fit. Possibly we are not fit. We don't know. We thought we did know, but in the Majestic Presence of the Mighty Senator from Indiana who is possessed of the power to decide the question after seeing one side only, and the worst side, in that presence we hesitate. Perhaps the Cubans are better able to manage their own affairs than are we in New Mexico. Perhaps the Hon. Senator from Indiana cannot afford to spend more than two or three days in investigating conditions in a section of his own country so long as there are the Philippines on the other side of this sphere to be looked after.[54]

This response to Beveridge made a particular point of claiming New Mexico as part of the senator's "own country," thus asserting a geography of the United States that included New Mexico while excluding places outside of North America. At the same time, the continued use of ambiguous language obfuscated New Mexico's racial structure. The writers of this article, instead, contrasted the territory with other places under U.S. control, like the Philippines or Cuba, which they deemed more Other or foreign. They could create an imagined difference in U.S. imperialism by defining westward expansion, which was continental and therefore "naturally" part of the United States, against a supposedly "newer" form of imperialism that was "overseas."

Comparisons of this type became one means by which Euro-Americans could conceptualize New Mexico's place within the United States. The resulting responses to easterners like Beveridge thus did not attempt to deny New Mexico's large Mexican population. Instead, they sought to defuse criticism by distinguishing New Mexico from other U.S. locales with still more numerous "foreign" (which was to say nonwhite) populations. They also implicitly used geography to help their cause. By contrasting New Mexico, which was on the continent, with islands "thousands of miles away," they made a claim to the natural fit of the territory into the nation. This comparative move was persuasive because it did not threaten U.S. notions of race or imperialism. On the contrary, some writers argued that because New Mexico had been made part of the United States, the Mexican population accepted, and even welcomed, Euro-American dominance. In short, what had developed by 1900 was an understanding of New Mexico as an entirely American region that was harmoniously governed under an ironclad racial hierarchy.

"We Realize Now the Unity of Our Whole People": Racial Harmony in Anachronistic Space

To understand the multiple ways that the regional identity appeared after 1880 as an answer to criticism of the territory, we first need to understand how ideas about race, nation, history, and civilization figured in the territorial discourse. After the Civil War Euro-Americans increasingly invoked a "New Mexican" identity to bridge what had previously seemed an impossible chasm between Mexicans and Americans. These efforts, as I noted in chapter 2, often showed an uneven approach to discussing race and nation in the first decade after the Civil War. Even Euro-American writings that supposedly defended Mexicans still contained language that presumed white superiority. One *Mesilla News* editorial expressed outrage that easterners disparaged local Mexicans' "character, their loyalty, their morals and manners."[55] Yet the editor did not seek to discredit the validity of these disparagements per se. He upheld, instead, Euro-American racial assumptions and agreed that Mexicans "have been ignorant" but meekly offered that this was "a fault ... that they are rapidly overcoming."[56] This reasoning granted Mexicans a precarious position in the territory and nation. It opened up the possibility for Mexicans to claim to be part of the United States even as it reinforced assumptions about their inferiority to Euro-Americans.

From 1880 onward many members of the Euro-American elite argued that the region's unique historical and cultural dynamics gave it a singular role within the nation despite, or even because of, its racial diversity. Making it a full state, in other words, would not alter the colonial relationships set up by Euro-Americans. LeBaron Bradford Prince became one such advocate, even authoring the act that created the Bureau of

Immigration of New Mexico. Prince, born in New York in 1840, claimed a lineage to one of the first *Mayflower* settlers of Plymouth Colony, granting him an unquestionable claim to American identity.[57] Through his early adulthood Prince dabbled in New York politics and became a known figure in the Republican Party. After declining the position three times, Prince ultimately agreed to become chief justice of the Territorial Supreme Court of New Mexico in 1879.[58] As the lead jurist he grew enamored with the territory. For the next several decades Prince was intimately involved with the territorial government, statehood campaigns, and the writing of the region's history. He ultimately served as the appointed governor of the territory from 1889 to 1892. His speeches and writings show how one of the territory's most outspoken advocates attempted to build cross-racial unity through a sense of shared place and nationalism.

To compensate for the incongruity of calling Mexicans "Americans," these writers drew on circulating ideas about race and civilization. They created a temporal racial hierarchy that they used to explain the progressive advancement of New Mexico to statehood. In the late nineteenth century the predominant social Darwinist discourse divided all humanity in terms of different levels of development. All human races, under this thinking, advanced through a linear series of stages from savagery to civilization.[59] Conveniently enough for themselves, Euro-Americans claimed that only the white races had attained full civilization. Other groups, like Africans or Native Americans, represented what whites had once been before they "evolved" thousands of years ago.

New Mexico's Euro-Americans used ideas about colonialism in a surprising way after 1880. They agreed that Mexicans and Native Americans were "less evolved" and therefore easily controlled by the more civilized (and civilizing) whites, but they turned this into an argument *for* statehood, claiming that their inferior status guaranteed that these groups would pose no threat to the United States. Moreover, the common argument continued, New Mexico's nonwhite, but docile, Mexican majority differed racially and culturally from other Mexicans because of the territory's peculiar history. As the discourse developed, many Euro-Americans began to replace the term *Mexican* with *pure-Spanish* to name the territory's Spanish-speaking population. Using the term *Spanish* was not a sudden departure in terminology; many Euro-Americans had used it interchangeably with *Mexican* since before the invasion. As we will see in chapter 6, though, by the start of the twentieth century this substitution implied a closer position to whiteness than *Mexican* could but was not racially equivalent or equal to *Anglo* (as *pure Spanish* often also meant "inbred" for these Euro-Americans).[60] New Mexico's Mexicans might not yet be fully civilized, Euro-Americans contended, but they still inhabited a higher stage of evolution than the term *Mexican* implied. New Mexico could therefore join the United States as an equal state without upsetting the nation's racial balance, despite its quasi-white Spanish majority.

Other historians have treated the creation of Spanish identity in late-nineteenth-century New Mexico.[61] I would suggest, though, that there is a danger of perceiving a monolithic understanding of whiteness that neglects the more complicated understandings of being Spanish or Mexican. I believe that U.S. race studies have become too fixated and dependent on "whiteness" as part of an easy binary for understanding racializing processes. We need to pay more attention to the differential racialization that also created distinctions within groups ostensibly labeled as white. True enough, Euro-Americans did have to solicit the cooperation of the territory's Mexican elite, but these Euro-Americans never came to recognize their middle-class Mexican American collaborators as peers. On the contrary, this new Spanish identity was a quadrangulation, itself an empty signifier, created in the discursive interstice opened up through the triple negation of "Indian," "Mexican," and "Anglo/white" identities. Counter-intuitively, "pure Spanish" also did not necessarily mean "not racially mixed." Many Euro-Americans imagined that Iberian ancestry always already implied a racial mixture of "white" and "Moor." So although participants in the regional discourse might presume that New Mexico's Spanish were not racially mixed, like mestizo Mexicans, with Indian blood, neither were they fully "white." Their racial mixing occurred in the more distant past of medieval Spain.

Reconfiguring the meaning of race and nation in the territory required more than a linguistic sleight of hand to efface the term *Mexican*. Euro-Americans who wrote about the regional identity often solved the dilemma of Mexicans' being U.S. citizens by tying them to a bounded historical narrative that ended with New Mexico's triumphal entry into the United States. This became a regionally specific rewriting of the national, and imperial, discourse of Manifest Destiny. They argued that the territory's development would inevitably remake Mexicans into Americans because they represented one stage in the territory's progressive advancement into becoming American. Mexicans qualified for inclusion in the progressive narrative to statehood because they had been the territory's caretakers in the past. They had established the colonial mechanisms that U.S. imperialism would ultimately perfect in New Mexico. Mexicans had also foreseen the arrival of the United States and willingly joined with Euro-Americans to better themselves. Without these past efforts Euro-Americans would have had a harder time steering the territory's present and future.

Prince delivered a speech commemorating the arrival of the railroad in New Mexico in 1880. The chief justice characterized New Mexico's geographic boundaries as a unique zone where "two almost distinct civilizations" united.[62] Casting the railroad as a symbol of American progress, this Euro-American pondered the meaning of its arrival in Santa Fe, now refigured as a part of U.S. prehistory, "the most ancient capital on American soil."[63] Prince spoke about the racial characteristics that he believed were specific to either Mexicans or Americans in the territory, but he gave that familiar racial characterization a positive valence. "Here is the historic race of old Spain," Prince stated, "full of the spirit of chivalry[,] of hospitality, and generosity, preserved through more than two centuries. . . . And coming now is all the enterprise and energy, the determination and perseverance, the aspiration and the ambition of the American character."[64]

Prince predicted that the "mingling" of Mexican/Spanish and (Euro-) American racial characteristics would result in a population "such as the world has never equaled before."[65] He promised that racial animosity in New Mexico would quickly disappear as the two distinct groups of Mexicans and Americans forged a joint nationalism that could only occur in New Mexico. Under this united New Mexican identity, moreover, Mexicans could finally be considered fully American: "We realize now the unity of our whole people as we have not in the past. Shall we not then, to-day, determine forever to drop the use of the terms 'American' and 'Mexican' as heretofore too much employed as words of division among those who are all equally American citizens?"[66] Prince drew from a developing discourse on New Mexican identity that remade the meaning of race, nation, and region in the last decades of the nineteenth century. The elite vision of a New Mexican identity transcended, but did not eliminate, the racial categories and united the local population under the U.S. banner. Moreover, it had no use for competing forms of Mexican identity, like the national one in La Mesilla. When he called for the dropping of unsavory terms, Prince intended only the demise of *Mexican*, especially as a counter to American nationalism.

Prince would again invoke these ideas about New Mexican identity a few years after his 1880 Santa Fe speech in his *Historical Sketches of New Mexico from the Earliest Records to the American Occupation* (1883).[67] The dedication to that volume articulated the racial meaning of the newly emerging regional New Mexican identity as "Three fold in origin and language, but now one in nationality, in purpose and in destiny."[68] As was common for Euro-Americans attempting to balance the tricultural model with their own presumptions about race, Prince arranged the three racial groups along a temporal axis, noting the contributions of each group by cementing it in a particular era. "The history of New Mexico may be divided into three epochs," he wrote, "the Aboriginal or Pueblo, the Spanish, and the American."[69] In other words Prince cast modern Pueblos and Mexicans in the role of living fossils, embodiments of New Mexico's past, while casting Euro-Americans as part of the territory's present and future:

> To the Pueblos, still representing in unchanged form the aboriginal civilization which built the cities and established the systems of government and social life which astonished the European discoverers nearly four centuries ago;

> To the Mexicans, who, in generosity, hospitality, and chivalric feeling, are worthy sons of the *Conquistadores*, who, with undaunted courage and matchless gallantry, carried the cross of Christianity and the flag of Spain to the ends of the earth;

> To the Americans, whose energy and enterprise are bringing all the appliances of modern science and invention to develop the almost limitless resources which nature has bestowed upon us.[70]

Defining modern Native and Mexican Americans through the imagined accomplishments of their ancestors became a common means for Euro-Americans to secure their vision of both racial hierarchy and cross-racial (but explicitly not race-transcendent) American nationalism. Contemporary Native and Mexican Americans might have contributed important elements to New Mexico, Euro-Americans would argue, but only whites could bestow "order and progress" on the region. Unambiguous in his proclamation of Euro-American supremacy, Prince could even end his dedication with a rousing call for the three groups to work together for the future. "To All, as New Mexicans," Prince dedicated the volume, "Now unitedly engaged in advancing the prosperity, and working for the magnificent future of the Territory."[71]

Having worked out such a vision of New Mexico, Prince took advantage of his eastern upbringing and political connections to assert New Mexico's readiness for statehood in venues across the nation. One of his most passionate writings appeared as a letter to the editor in the *New York Times*. He responded to an article entitled "Greasers as Citizens," which had dismissed New Mexico's petition for statehood based on its large Mexican population. Prince rejected the claim that New Mexico's Mexicans were a "mongrel breed."[72] First, he assured readers that the "suggestion of a mixture of 'negro' blood in the general population is specially unfortunate, as the census of 1870 showed that even at as late a date as that there were but 172 persons of African descent in the whole territory." If people of African descent did not reside in New Mexico, Prince reasoned, then the Mexican population could not have produced offspring with them. He then asserted that the Mexican and indigenous populations were so segregated that they had never intermarried either, meaning that each race remained distinct. Racial "purity" thus figured prominently in his advocacy.[73]

For Prince's logic to work, though, New Mexico had to be imagined as a distinct and isolated site. Its geography had to be static and "natural," its general character stagnant, and its borders well-nigh impenetrable. He could assert that Mexicans and Native Americans or African Americans did not intermarry only if he assumed that the population was fixed and limited within that place and therefore in possession of a "knowable" ancestry. The reimagining of New Mexico history as static and isolated defined the "native" people residing there. Acknowledging continued migration back and forth across the border would threaten his assertions. Prince could not, and did not try to, explicitly overturn the presumption that Mexicans were generally a "mixed" race. Rather, he tried to carve out a particular place for the Mexicans and Native Americans in New Mexico as uniquely "pure." Prince intended to eliminate a national Mexican identity by claiming "we are all equally American citizens."

Obviously, many Euro-Americans found this vision of a regionally specific racial identity unconvincing. One writer even accused Prince of betraying the white race for defending New Mexico's Mexican population. A Euro-American from Colorado explicitly rejected Prince's defense of the "scum of greasers" in a follow-up *New York Times* piece.[74] "To class the Mexican," he wrote, "whose skins, except in rare instances, are about as dark as those of the average Georgia 'niggers,' under the head of 'whites,' is a piece of bare-faced deceit."[75] The author further claimed that Prince was one of a few Euro-Americans in New Mexico who had become a "galvanized Greaser," meaning that he had "fallen to the estate and likeness of a Greaser in his associations, his tastes, his ideas and habits."[76] Even claims of a direct lineage to the *Mayflower* could not protect New Mexico boosters from assertions that they degraded themselves if they came to the defense of Mexicans.

Far from being a phenomenon limited to the Mexican-U.S. border, the fear of "galvanized Greasers"—or, in more general terms, of "going native"—constituted a prominent feature of the discourse on high imperialism. Ann Laura Stoler points out that in the nineteenth-century European context white settlers in the colonies attracted suspicion as possibly unfit for participation in colonial rule. Life in the colonies threatened one's status as European because the colonial cultural context could transform and contaminate the colonizer's "cultural essence, social disposition, and personhood itself."[77] Even after the ascent of social Darwinism, European and Euro-American imperialism frequently depended on Lamarckian (rather than Darwinian) understandings of environment. The French colonial *milieu* or Dutch *omgeving* became a means to describe the threat that certain places had for Europeans, whose racial essence could be altered or corrupted by the physical, psychological, climatic, and moral surroundings of the colonies.[78] A Dutch citizen who became overly familiar with the indigenous population could "unwittingly transform into something Javenese."[79] So also New Mexico threatened to compromise white settlers. In southern New Mexico the *Las Cruces Borderer* ran articles that suggested such ideas. "At present New Mexico is dragging a century behind the age," Bennett wrote in one editorial, "and even our civilization attaches to itself something of the ancient ruins standing gloomily in our midst. We seem to be waiting for an influx of life giving, enterprising element, instead of rousing the dormant energies within ourselves."[80] Bennett suggested that the minority of Euro-Americans could not overcome the "gloomy" Mexican ruins and majority population. In the minds of colonial settlers the line between colonizer and colonized thus proved a fragile one that needed constant policing.

Prince's critic deployed a similar logic. As a colony with a majority Mexican population New Mexico threatened Euro-American superiority. In case his readers missed the point, the Colorado correspondent stated explicitly of Prince that "he seems to have fully disclaimed his birthright as a civilized white man, and to have thrown himself, body and soul, into the arms of Greaserism, striving after Greaser approbation."[81]

Even with such critics, the new regional identity proved useful in yoking an uneasy combination of goals: agitating for statehood, of course, but also promoting tourism, eliding racial tensions, and even justifying the economic exploitation of nonwhite populations. Boosters did eventually win statehood in 1912 through a combination of political maneuvering and reinventing the territory and its populations. Territorial representatives exchanged their votes and political favors for adoption of a statehood resolution during the Republican Convention of 1908.[82] President Theodore Roosevelt finally endorsed statehood for New Mexico and its sister territory, Arizona, in the last year of his second term. Although Beveridge and others tried hard to thwart New Mexico's admission, the territory had become qualified for admission, despite its nonwhite majority, in the minds of many Euro-Americans.

Shortly after New Mexico gained statehood, the Bureau of Publicity of the State Land Office published a pamphlet that used the regional identity in all of these ways. Ostensibly designed to tout the mineral and agricultural resources within the state, the pamphlet made the supposed uniqueness of New Mexico its real selling point to potential Euro-American settlers. As before, this uniqueness was framed in terms of a racial hierarchy explicated in temporal terms. The pamphlet's writers emphasized a peaceful concord among New Mexico's three racial groups. They collaborated in the service of Euro-American entertainment and economic advancement. Like Prince's dedication to his book, this pamphlet ordered New Mexico's contemporary racial groups in a temporal hierarchy from "ancient" to "modern."[83] The pamphlet's writers associated contemporary Euro-Americans with "modernity," Mexicans with "colonial times," and Native Americans with the "ancient past."

The pamphlet projected a vision of local Mexicans as living remnants of Spaniards' historical accomplishments. Conveniently eliding the anti-Catholic sentiment pervasive in the United States at the time, this pamphlet appealed to New Mexico's "Christian" heritage in order to claim it as one of the oldest civilized places in the nation: "Although New Mexico is one of the youngest states in the Union, it is among the oldest in the point of Christian Civilization, having been colonized by Spaniards in 1598. But, even as early as 1540 to 1541 Coronado had explored this part of the country, bringing with him several Catholic priests, one of whom remained with the Pueblo Indians for the purpose of Christianizing them."[84] John Nieto-Phillips and others have commented on this era as being marked by "Hispanophilia." Nostalgic writings about conquistadores helped soothe newly transplanted whites who were nervous about the racial complexity of the Southwest.[85] Those writings were also tied to a wider "antimodernist" trend that eschewed materialism, technology, and other markers of industrial life. Across the United States and Europe, antimodernists sought to "recover" the supposedly more authentic practices of medieval life or other historical periods.[86] These trends took form in various ways, from ancestor worship, in groups like the Daughters of the American Revolution, to arts and crafts societies, to the development of gothic revival architecture. Hispanophilia comparably figured the Iberian colonial expansion as representing a bygone era of adventure and a simpler way of life that could be celebrated.[87] What inflected the antimodernist Hispanophilia writings of Prince and others, though, was that they never claimed a Spanish heritage for themselves.

This exuberance over Spain's colonial past trapped Mexicans in the chronological void of medieval society. Euro-Americans granted that Mexicans contributed to the founding of the state and therefore had a role in the New Mexican identity, yet they could also discount modern Mexicans by safely cordoning them off as living relics. Mexicans' ancestors might have introduced New Mexico to a form of "civilization," but they could not take charge of the territory's future.

Despite emanating a rosy glow of racial unity, these arguments still hinged on previous colonizing assumptions. Indeed, Euro-American writers and politicians assigned the most limited role to Native Americans in that supposedly collective regional New Mexican identity, if they included them at all. As we will see more clearly in the next chapter, Mexicans and Euro-Americans increasingly deemed *native* to mean those of Mexican descent, not the descendants of Pueblos, Apaches, or Diné (Navajos). The notion that Native Americans, as a race, would eventually vanish from New Mexico lingered longer than the same predication for Mexicans. A 1909 *New York Times* article reported on the Smithsonian's work in New Mexico, stating explicitly that "the American Indian is passing so rapidly that the study of his race, his habits, and his history is being pressed."[88] A 1911 *New York Times* article entitled "Chronicles of the Pueblo State" declared most of New Mexico's Native Americans "have all but disappeared."[89] Contemporary Native Americans, they claimed, were "debased by a mixture of blood" and therefore not "authentically" Indian. Intriguingly, at the moment that many Euro-Americans were asserting a racial purity for "Spanish Americans," some claimed that the Pueblos were the ones who were actually racially mixed.

At other times, though, Native Americans did appear positively in discussions about New Mexico's uniqueness. A. W. Bell, a medical doctor who wrote an article for the *Journal for the Ethnological Society of London*, asserted that the Pueblo tribes were "the only native race whose presence on the soil is not a curse to the country."[90] Such efforts were early attempts to differentiate the nonwhite indigenous groups and Mexicans in New Mexico from similarly racialized groups in other parts of the nation and Mexico. Comparably, the same pamphlet that hailed

Spain for bringing "Christian civilization" allowed an important place for Indians in the racially harmonious New Mexican identity. They could serve the region as living embodiments of New Mexico's prehistory and therefore pique the interest of both tourists and scholars: "The numerous Indian Pueblos of New Mexico are another attraction to the tourist that puzzle[s] students of ancient history, for while some of these Pueblos are so ancient that the historian can shed no light on their origin they are still peopled by descendants of those who built them, and so far as known, these descendants speak the same language, dress in similar costumes and in many cases observe the same tribal customs as their pre-historic ancestors."[91]

Pueblos' (and other Native Americans') ancient role in the New Mexican identity became a Euro-American tourist attraction, another major investment for the regional identity as we will see. Claims that contemporary Pueblos wore the same clothing, spoke the same language, and retained the "same tribal customs as their pre-historic ancestors" reduced Pueblos to performing the role of living historical objects for Euro-American voyeurism. Their presence contributed to the imagined uniqueness of the New Mexican identity, but Euro-Americans ascribed them as little authority in territorial affairs as the rock formations that dotted the landscape. Elsewhere in the pamphlet, the authors made this association clear, stating that Indians gave "the state a picturesqueness that appeals to many of the great artists of the United States and the Old World, who make their temporary abode in New Mexico for the sole purpose of painting these Indians in their native habitat."[92]

Lest potential Euro-American immigrants fear that racial harmony might result in social equality, the pamphlet assured them that triculturalism would not curtail their ability to exploit indigenous labor or pose any threat to U.S. colonial authority. Elements within the archaic Native population could even be put to practical use. "The younger Indian women, educated in vocational schools," the pamphlet informed eastern Euro-Americans, "make good nurses, stenographers and house maids, and are exceptionally kind to children."[93]

Exploitable labor, scientific study, and exotic entertainment all figured in the celebration of the temporal hierarchy that defined New Mexico's triculturalism. Anne McClintock has coined the terms *anachronistic space* and *panoptical time* to explain a common imperialist trope like the one deployed in New Mexico. Nineteenth-century colonialism depended heavily on the notion that empire building involved acquiring "empty lands" waiting to be made productive.[94] These justifications, which hinged on the imagining of "virgin" lands, faced serious contradiction when confronted by established populations, both indigenous and preceding colonizers from competing empires, who were not supposed to be spatially there in the first place.[95] Moreover, the readily visible physical traces of ancient settlements, skeletons, and artifacts further complicated imperial projects by exposing a long history of use for those same, supposedly vacant, colonized lands.

McClintock argues that a solution emerged that displaced colonized populations onto "anachronistic space." This was made possible through "panoptical time," the discursive means through which time was alchemized as space, and history was figured as geography, to be controlled, organized, and consumed at a glance.[96] Human history was mapped onto a metaphorical tree that suggested an organic process of upward growth from "archaic and primitive" to "modern and civilized." If Europeans represented the culmination of human progress on that tree, then the other races represented lesser stages of development that could be mapped onto lower boughs.[97] The colonized, in the minds of the colonizers, were not exactly their temporal contemporaries. Instead, they existed in a "permanently anterior time within the geographic space of the modern empire as anachronistic humans."[98] In his discussion of the "denial of coevalness," the tendency to place anthropological referents in a time other than the present, Johannes Fabian makes the same point for the classical practice of anthropology as an academic discipline.[99]

Traveling to lands peopled by races on the lower branches of human history, therefore, became comparable to traveling through the stages of human progress. The trope of imperial progress meant that a journey around the empire represented a journey backward and forward through time. "Geographical difference across *space*," McClintock writes, "is figured as historical difference across *time*."[100] Temporally distinguishing colonies contained their heterogeneity by rendering the colonized inescapably anachronistic and therefore unavoidably out of sync with modernity.

In the United States, New Mexico became one of a number of such spaces. Native American reservations, black ghettos, the immigrant tenements of New York, and the Chinatowns of the West Coast would eventually all be figured in a roughly parallel fashion. For promoters of tourism and regional distinctiveness, however, New Mexico offered an unparalleled bonus because it contained three stages of human development: "ancient" Native Americans, "medieval" Mexicans (or increasingly "Spanish Americans"), and "modern" Euro-Americans. This articulation proved a successful part of the strategy to attain statehood, but it lived on long after that campaign was won. With statehood came an ongoing interest in marketing the territory for tourism, and the sales pitches lingered. Even after it became a state in 1912, New Mexico in its entirety remained an anachronistic space in the imagination of many Euro-Americans.

Euro-American depictions of Mexicans and Native Americans as part of the landscape avoided questions about racial equality in a multiracial New Mexican identity. Instead, the presence of "archaic" Native Americans and Mexicans in the territory could not but give curious Euro-Americans a frisson of excitement. New Mexico could feed their eagerness to take in three stages of human history in an exotic desert environment.

The effects of this strategy endured and even reached the level of science fiction. In the modernist novel *Brave New World*, published in 1932, Aldous Huxley made New Mexico the future location of the "Savage Reservation," where practitioners of bizarre archaisms like Christianity and sexual monogamy persisted in contrast to the "World State."[101] Even in a future dystopia, New Mexico remained a land out of time, peopled by living anachronisms.[102]

Learning the Border: College Students and Knowledge of New Mexico

We gain some additional insight into how Euro-Americans in the Mesilla Valley grappled with race, nation, and region in a series of senior theses written by students at the New Mexico College of Agriculture and Mechanic Arts (New Mexico A&M, later New Mexico State University) in Las Cruces. This distinct group of sources merits consideration because the conferral of university degrees is a mechanism of power in a process that forms and creates knowledge. Turn-of-the-century A&M students participated in this process as they individually systematized and recorded their knowledge of race, nation, and region.[103] Students who produced theses about the territory participated in a process that configured New Mexico as a subject with intrinsic meaning that was identifiable and open to study. The ways that they could articulate their knowledge about New Mexico, as an object of intellectual inquiry, were limited by, and in turn helped to limit, a discourse that framed the region's racial and national meaning. The discourse, in other words, created a "frame of the imaginable" that ordered the ways that historical actors discussed the territory and its racial and national relationships. We can see how that knowledge was created by young Euro-Americans who were being carefully taught to do so. Students sought the approval of their professors, who had their own expectations about these topics. Examining these works, therefore, suggests the structures that defined the meaning of being in southern New Mexico.

Charles Miller's name has appeared occasionally in New Mexico histories because of his violent death. Mexican revolutionary forces killed Miller and sixteen other Americans when Francisco "Pancho" Villa attacked Columbus, New Mexico, on March 9, 1916.[104] Beyond mentioning his untimely demise, few of those histories considered Miller particularly important. For the purposes of this study, though, it is interesting to note that Miller had dabbled with writing histories of southern New Mexico just a decade before Villa's raid.

Miller earned his degree at New Mexico A&M in 1906. His senior thesis participated in local nation building by linking New Mexico to the U.S. Civil War and was written in response to eastern Euro-Americans who did not imagine New Mexico as part of U.S. national history. On one level Miller wanted to document New Mexico's contributions during the Civil War, describing the racially ambiguous people of New Mexico as important patriotic fighters in a critical moment of U.S. national history. "Had the people of New Mexico proved less faithful, less vigilant, or less courageous," Miller contended, "the North would have felt the loss of the entire west and . . . the country bordering upon the Gul [sic] of Mexico would be considered a foreign nation."[105] Miller believed that New Mexico was instrumental in the Union victory.

Still, he showed an ambivalence about the multiracial New Mexican identity that potentially made everybody equally American. Questions about the meaning of the local space and the presence of the Other among Euro-Americans persisted. For his part Miller defined the "people of New Mexico" as composed of two separate races: "native Mexicans" and "whites."[106] Contrary to the easy narrative of "Spanish" identity replacing "Mexican" identity in New Mexico, those two categories coexisted throughout the late nineteenth century and early twentieth. At times they were used interchangeably to mean the same thing, a population that was not fully white. Miller, like many Euro-Americans, saw Mexicans as a distinct racial group that derived from racial intermixing. "The simple native population of the present day, the Mexican," Miller wrote authoritatively, "has lived here for centuries intermarrying with the Indians of which there were great numbers in earlier times."[107] While Mexicans had an acknowledged role in local affairs, Miller distanced the "mixed" population from New Mexico's economic, military, or political successes.

Miller argued that New Mexico only started to progress with the influx of the "racially superior" Euro-Americans. "Coming to more modern times New Mexico became a territory of the United States," he wrote. "Soon it became organized, its boundaries fixed and its lands taken up by immigrants from the East."[108] As others had before him, Miller equated Mexicans with the past and Euro-Americans with the modern or the future. Under this logic Mexicans and Euro-Americans (and sometimes Native Americans) were all part of New Mexico's intercultural history. Only Euro-Americans, though, shaped New Mexico's future. For Miller Euro-Americans literally made New Mexico a place by fixing it as a clearly defined cartographical space. This, he further suggested, rescued the territory from a state of chaos and ruin.

Euro-Americans had exclusive power to mold the territory and the Mexican settlers. Miller wrote that the arrival of Euro-Americans ushered in "the Americanization of the country and the Mexican inhabitants."[109] The Civil War, according to this history, was the sole moment when Euro-Americans transformed both the land and people into the American nation. The young student imagined Euro-Americans as the key agents in building cross-racial cooperation perpetuated by their supposed superiority over New Mexico's majority population. Discussions about Mexicans' and Euro-Americans' patriotism, in particular, reinforced a racial division between these two groups despite their newfound unity in a single national identity. Miller's thesis ascribed different motives to Mexican and white nationalism that emerged out of the supposed limits of their racial bodies. Both Mexicans and Euro-Americans contributed to the Union victory in New Mexico; however, Euro-Americans and Mexican Americans did not make equally rational sacrifices for the nation. "The whites were patriotic Americans all during the Civil War," Miller contended. "The Mexican who had not accustomed himself to the change of governments, was, nevertheless, greatly embittered against the Texan, his hereditary foe. It was on this account that many Mexicans fought and not through patriotism for the United States government."[110] Miller reduced Mexicans' individual actions and patriotic accomplishments by making their motivation for fighting a "hereditary" grudge match that only made sense in the narrow confines of the territory. In his history Mexicans had been too simplistic to project themselves into a larger nation before the Civil War. "It brought to the inhabitants a knowledge of the country outside of their own locality," he wrote. "It gave the Mexican a view of the strength of the government and inspired the people with confidence."[111]

Casting racially specific motives for military service did not sacrifice the region's success and contributions to the United States but actually provided quite the opposite for Miller. Establishing distinct Mexican and Euro-American motivations allowed him to reconcile a unified New Mexican regional identity with his own assumptions about race. Miller did not displace racial difference through the collective regional New Mexican identity. Rather, he implied that the New Mexican and American victory came about from differing racial groups, each contributing to a common project of the territory in racially distinctive ways. Miller allowed Mexicans to share the Union victories but only as the brave (if also hotheaded, irrational, and shortsighted) followers of (rational, patriotic, and prescient) Euro-American leaders. Their eagerness to serve these authority figures testified to the region's readiness for statehood.

If assigning Mexicans a role as Americans troubled Miller, Native Americans' incorporation into the national identity proved even more challenging. His history first presented Native Americans as another enemy who were not "naturally" inclined to become part of a nation. This is not surprising given that Euro-Americans had the most difficulty acknowledging Native Americans as even part of the regional identity. Miller demonized Native Americans as having been vicious and irrational before the Euro-American invasion of 1846. He further castigated local Mexicans for their inability to end "one hundred and eight years" of Native American insurrection.[112] Only Euro-Americans' cultural and military supremacy created the supposed regional harmony among Indians, Mexicans, and whites that marked modern New Mexico: "The war upon the Indians gave them to understand that no more depredations would be tolerated. It complete [sic] subdued them. . . . For one hundred and eight years they had killed and burned, but the Civil War had, by the presence of troops, completely put an end to their depredation. . . . By the protection from the Indians eastern capital sought investment, and immigrants from the east seeking new homes came to New Mexico. Thus the population increased and wealth and prosperity on the basis of military protection were established."[113] Miller believed that Mexicans could be "taught" to appreciate the United States (by magnanimous Euro-Americans) but that Native Americans could be subdued only by military force. In both cases Euro-Americans stood as the lone instigators of peace and progress in New Mexico. Before Euro-Americans arrived, the territory was an ill-defined site of violent chaos. After white immigration

New Mexico became a place of cross-racial cooperation that served and defended the nation.

Other students at New Mexico A&M drafted similar appraisals of the territory. Although engaged in a variety of academic disciplines, including history, linguistics, and home economics, A&M students often imagined the territory much as Miller did. New Mexico was knowable as a distinctive geographical subject because of the different racial groups who lived in close proximity and vice versa. That distinctiveness never threatened the territory's association with the United States or the colonial authority of Euro-Americans. Even those students who praised New Mexico for its uniqueness did so under the assumption that Euro-Americans necessarily dominated the other two "lesser" races.

Thora Alice Lute Foster's 1904 senior thesis drew on notions of a temporally structured racial hierarchy. Foster highlighted the "scientific" opportunities that New Mexico offered by collecting local folk stories and customs in the Mesilla Valley.[114] While Foster claimed to celebrate the "richness" of Mexican and Native American cultures, she did not intend her project as an argument for racial equality. On the contrary, her study employed such terms as *barbaric, superstitious, ignorant,* and *primitive* when she discussed the creators of that folklore.[115] Far from unusual, Foster's use of these terms would have been standard within anthropology and other academic disciplines at the time.[116] Foster argued that New Mexico gave Euro-Americans a rare chance to view three different levels of civilization in one place. She understood the study of local folklore as "a science by which the development of civilization may be traced." She continued: "Comparative folk-lore is rising in prominence because by it we trace the effects of similar events and see the different influences upon civilization."[117]

Because Foster considered Mexicans "semi-civilized" and Native Americans "primitive," she believed that Euro-Americans could find in both groups insights into Euro-Americans' own past. Studying their cultural expressions, fully in line with New Mexico as anachronistic space, became a means to understand all humanity. Previous generations of Euro-Americans lamented that they had not transformed the territory by obliterating Mexicans' cultural signs. In this instance, though, Foster celebrated the chance to see their customs. Both Native Americans and Mexicans, she happily reported, "indulge, to the fullest, their racial love of dancing, pantomime and barbaric splendor in adornment."[118] Under the regional discourse, Foster saw the persistence of these cultural expressions as safe because it confirmed circulating discussions about race and civilization. Witnessing their "barbaric splendor" was now an advantage of having New Mexico as part of the United States.

Indeed, many Euro-Americans considered the racial hierarchy itself to be the key to New Mexico's harmonious unity. As the regional New Mexican identity developed, it hardened the racial division between Mexicans, Euro-Americans, and Native Americans. Because the regional identity depended on Mexican identity as a distinctive racial identity (rather than a national identity), the importance of excluding Native Americans from being Mexican increased. Mexican identity, as a result, meant only those of mixed descent. Even in instances when Euro-Americans could not avoid acknowledging that Indians were once part of the Mexican nation state, and therefore "Mexicans," they named the racial distinction more overtly. In 1904 another Euro-American student at New Mexico A&M used the imagery of "two Mexicos" to explain the racial distinction. "There are two Mexicos," the author noted, "Mestizo Mexico—the people of mixed Spanish and Indian blood—and Indian Mexico."[119] While this author made a vague acknowledgment of "Indian Mexicans," her work focused almost exclusively on "Mestizo Mexico" as the defining category for the nation. To make sense of the region's contemporary racial divisions, those same distinctions had to be transhistorical, transnational, and unquestionable.

In a thesis produced a year after New Mexico became a state, Carrie Padon Phelps documented what she called "the primitive Mexican home in New Mexico." In her thesis Phelps often used the terms *Mexican* and *New Mexican* as interchangeable identities. When referring to Mexicans as "New Mexicans," though, Phelps created qualifiers that suggested her belief that they were a particular *type* of New Mexican: "primitive New Mexicans."[120] In a section she titled "The Rise of the New Mexican," she wrote: "Many of the Spanish soldiers were already dual in racial characteristics, being of mixed Spanish and Moorish blood. . . . The soldiers in many instances married Indian wives. Their offspring is the Mestizo or Spanish-Indian—the Mexican of New Mexico."[121] Making her discussion about the racial origins of local Mexicans equivalent to the "rise of the New Mexican" confirmed their mutual association. Unlike Spanish-language newspapers discussed in the next chapter, which frequently interchanged "New Mexican" for "Mexican," Phelps did not consider these two identities as strictly synonymous. Mexicans in Phelps's imagination might have been the *first* "New Mexicans," but she asserted a dominant place for Euro-Americans within the regional identity.

As evidence of Mexicans' racial inferiority, the thesis pointed to an absence of "regionally created literature." "The New Mexicans, past and present, have no literature," she noted. "Books were an unknown quantily [*sic*] in the primitive home and few have crept in even at the present."[122] To illustrate her point further, she made audacious claims that New Mexico's Mexicans even lacked basic speech. Degrading the "intermixing" of Native American words with Spanish, Phelps cast local Mexicans as virtual mutes who communicated through motion. "They speak the Spanish language with an interlanding [*sic*] of Indian words," Phelps wrote. "There is a world of meaning in their expressive shrugs and gestures."[123] Phelps's casting Mexicans as "primitive New Mexicans" implied that Euro-Americans were the "modern New Mexicans." Describing the influx of Euro-Americans metaphorically, she stated that "the tidal wave of progress is sweeping irresistibly over this last frontier of the United States."[124] Mexicans, she believed, resisted the modernity that necessarily arrived with Euro-Americans. "With this simple contented people innovation works slow changes," she explained. "The Mexican clings to what seems good to him."[125]

Phelps clearly viewed her Mexican neighbors as a distinct racial group. Yet she also cast New Mexican regional identity at odds with Mexican national identity. Discussing baroque needlework produced by a Mexican woman, for instance, Phelps stated, "The beautiful intricate work known as drawnwork was rather a Mexican handicraft than New Mexican."[126] The regional New Mexican identity and Mexican racial identity were overlapping categories but not interchangeable. All of the local "native" customs, after all, could have been considered Mexican traditions because they were performed by people who were racially Mexican and had been part of Mexico. Phelps, though, claimed the authority to name cultural practices as either "authentically New Mexican" or "Mexican/foreign." Geography defined people and customs. She divorced certain Mexican practices from the territory to solidify it as an American place. In this way the national border between Mexico and the United States had an important role in defining the region and people. Customs she deemed Mexican, like drawnwork, originated *outside* of New Mexico. Likewise, the territory had its own unique set of cultural practices that could be identified as separate from the neighboring republic.

For those cultural practices that Phelps labeled "New Mexican," she shifted their racial origin from Mexican to Spanish. Local music and dancing, Phelps decided, were sufficiently New Mexican or "native." "Their pleasures were simple," Phelps wrote. "The graceful dance and love of music were inherited with their soft speech and polite manners from the Spanish ancestors."[127] Making these customs products of Spanish ancestors renamed practices that Phelps enjoyed (or wished to appropriate) to move them away from the racially mixed vision of Mexicans. For Phelps, one could easily distinguish between a cultural attribute that was nationally Mexican and one that was regionally specific.

Euro-American students, like government officials, claimed New Mexico's historical development created a racial harmony within the territory. Few, if any, of them intended that explanation to erase existing ideas about the colonial racial hierarchy. Instead, the notion of a united New Mexican identity became a source of entertainment or scientific inquiry as Mexicans and Native Americans became living historical artifacts open to study. Like others who puzzled over ways to claim New Mexico as entirely American, New Mexico A&M students created notions of a unique cross-racial allegiance that was only possible through imagining the territory as an anachronistic space. Not only did this temporal hierarchy answer questions about the territory's racial diversity and national identity, but the ability to see "ancient" and exotic Mexicans and Native Americans within the United States also became a means to sell the territory as a tourist destination. Some of the most prominent boosters for New Mexico argued that the racial diversity made it a special place for Euro-Americans to spend a holiday.

An American Destination with Brown Bodies: Charles Lummis and the Meaning of New Mexico in the 1890s

Charles Lummis became the most recognized writer of a newly popular travel literature that celebrated New Mexico at the end of the nineteenth century.[128] Lummis, a well-known journalist, recorded his romanticized journey through the Southwest in a series of articles in the *Los Angeles Times* (later published collectively as *A Tramp across the Continent*). He followed up that success with *The Land of Poco Tiempo* and *The Spanish Pioneers* in 1893. By the beginning of the twentieth century, Lummis had gained a reputation as a leading authority on New Mexico and was so well known that Senator Albert Beveridge solicited his help in ferreting out the "truth" about New Mexico's readiness for statehood after Beveridge's 1901 investigation.[129]

More than just recounting his personal experiences, Lummis explained the territory's meaning to his Euro-American audience. *The Land of Poco Tiempo* tantalizingly proposed that New Mexico was "the United States which is *not* United States," calling the territory "the anomaly of the Republic."[130] That anomalousness, Lummis informed his readers, derived from the presence of Mexicans and Indians, who outnumbered Euro-Americans. In stark contrast to the tales about New Mexico published by the first-generation of Euro-American visitors, Lummis named that nonwhite majority an alluring element about the territory. As this shift suggests, by the end of the territorial period in 1912, Euro-Americans could conceive of the region as a liminal place that both "was and was not" the United States. This made it an exciting, rather than threatening, place.

Naming New Mexico as an object for Euro-American voyeuristic and erotic enjoyment celebrated an exoticism that Lummis ascribed to non-white bodies. " 'Picturesque' is a tame word for it," Lummis wrote. "It is a picture, a romance, a dream, all in one."[131] Although Lummis granted that New Mexico's "every landscape is characteristic, and even beautiful," it was not the land and rock formations that intrigued the writer or defined the geography. He dismissed these by stating they lacked a "natural picturesqueness."[132] The presence of Euro-Americans was even more uninteresting. "With them I have here nothing to do," he wrote. "They are potential, but not picturesque."[133] Only the presence of Indian and Mexican bodies piqued Lummis's imagination. "Besides [the Euro-Americans]," Lummis informed his readers, "and around them are the real autocthones [*sic*], a quaint ethnologic trio."[134] For Lummis Pueblo communities proved the most exciting: "And the Pueblos—they are picturesque anywhere and always. . . . Their numerous sacred dances are by far the most picturesque sights in America. . . . They are a more interesting ethnologic study than the tribes of inner Africa, and less known of by their white countrymen."[135] Lummis, like his foe L. Bradford Prince, imagined contemporary Native Americans and Mexicans as living links to an ancient past. His writings reassured racially nervous white readers by describing New Mexico's indigenous and Mexican populations as virtually immobilized and nonthreatening compared to the "Superior Race."[136]

Mexicans, Lummis stated, were "inbred and isolation-shrunken descendants of the Castilian world-finders; living almost as much against the house as in it; ignorant as slaves and more courteous than kings."[137] The territory's diverse populations represented three stages of human development at play in the territory. Mexicans and Native Americans became less disturbing as they symbolized what Euro-Americans had been before they "evolved." In another section Lummis made this notion explicit when he stated that an Apache man was "merely what our ancestors were a millennium ago."[138] Part of indigenous men's appeal actually derived from Lummis's belief that they represented perfection as "primitive man."[139] Describing a competitive event among Native Americans in Isleta Pueblo, Lummis wrote of New Mexico's aboriginal men in lovingly homoerotic detail, declaring them a "score of bronze Apollos."[140] He paid particular attention to their bodies, "stark but for the dark blue *taparabo* at the loins, lithe, muscular, alert." If he or his readers had looked like one of the athletes, he suggested, "civilization would give us our livelihood for the privilege of gazing, as it does now to men less endowed."[141] New Mexico became a place for whites' titillation, allowing privileged visitors to escape from civilization and to come in contact with nearly naked primitive men without actually leaving the safety of the United States. Even Lummis's reiteration of the word *picturesque* discursively froze the indigenous populations in time, as if in a photograph. Individual members of the territory's populations became objects to be viewed and enjoyed, elevating the region to a national treasure.

Mexicans figured almost as prominently as Pueblos, Navajos, and Apaches in Lummis's casting of the territory as a site for voyeuristic tourism. Mexican bodies, however, did not quite hold the same level of erotic appeal for Lummis, who found that they were "fast losing their pictorial possibilities."[142] Lummis disapproved of the change in Mexican cultural practices that had transpired since New Mexico's incorporation into the United States, but he displaced the responsibility for those changes, blaming the "Hebrew clo'man [*sic*]" who brought "atrocities" like a "combined umbrella and overcoat" that replaced Mexicans' traditional "home-woven poncho."[143] Here Lummis engaged in multiple racial fantasies all in one shot. He cast suspicion on Jewish tailors, who were supposedly degrading the "authentic" and, of course, "picturesque" Mexican forms of clothing in the territory with inauthentic hybrid clothing. Even when Mexicans attempted to adopt symbols of American culture like Euro-American clothing styles, Lummis contended that they still failed because they apprenticed with racially suspect Jews. This cross-cultural mixing, in Lummis's mind, corrupted the local Mexican population from its "natural" habits. It would have been far preferable for the Mexicans to remain timelessly unchanged rather than attempting an impossible racial and cultural transformation to modernity.

Modifying their costume might have ruined Mexicans' aesthetic appeal for his gazing eye, but Lummis still framed the lives of modern Mexicans as a living window onto Spain's colonial past.[144] This framing accomplished two tasks. First, it distinguished New Mexico's Mexicans from Mexicans living along other parts of the border. New Mexico was unique because its colonists had allegedly been isolated from the racial intermixing that transpired in the rest of Mexico. Lummis saw quite the opposite in the territory's Mexican population, describing it as "inbred." In this way New Mexico's Mexicans could be "racially pure," lacking indigenous blood, but also racially inferior to Euro-Americans because they were weak and inbred. Second, the drawing of a distinction between New Mexico's Mexicans and other Mexicans did not lessen their racial difference from Euro-Americans or make them fully white. In his travels, Lummis reported, he had placed a high priority on recording and photographing some of the most intimate and "shocking" details in local Mexicans' daily lives. All of those records became evidence of their "semi-civilized" status.

In particular, the secretive Penitente religious fraternity captured Lummis's imagination. In the early nineteenth century, as I noted in chapter 3, the Catholic Church withdrew the Franciscan friars from New Mexico. Other priests were slow to appear in their place. As a result of the dearth of a formal priesthood in New Mexico, lay Catholics in Mexican and Pueblo settlements adopted spiritual leaders and rituals to meet their immediate needs. Pueblos took advantage of the friars' disappearance by openly combining previously scorned indigenous rituals with Catholic beliefs. To fill the religious void, lay Mexican men formed the Penitente brotherhood to provide spiritual and social aid to their communities.[145] By the time the United States invaded Mexico, the Penitentes had become a critical part of many northern New Mexico communities (and some in what would become southern Colorado).

Many accounts of the early national period continue to sensationalize the emergence of Penitente brotherhoods, whose extreme views have tantalized both contemporary observers and modern historians. Much of the literature on the Penitentes expresses shock and disdain over their literal enactment of Catholic repentance through the extreme mortification of their bodies. This use of physical penance as a means for spiritual atonement attracted Euro-American criticism and became evidence of Mexicans' racial inferiority. The Catholic hierarchy, both in Mexico and the United States, sought their permanent dissolution.

Lummis had quite a different view of the Penitentes, however, when he wrote *The Land of Poco Tiempo* thirty years later. For him the Penitentes' rituals made for an exciting and forbidden scene.[146] He described the illicit thrill of spying on a Mexican Penitente procession:

Every Friday night in Lent the belated wayfarer among the interior ranges is liable to be startled by the hideous too-ootle-te-too of an unearthly whistle which wails over and over its haunting refrain. . . .

If the hearer have the courage of his curiosity, and will *explore* the sound, his eyes will share the astonishment and consternation of his ears.

It is well, however to cultivate secretiveness. Woe to him if in seeing he shall be seen! A sharp-edged knife or flint shall be over-curious of his back, and across its bloody autograph a hundred fearful lashes shall lift their purpling wales—in barbarous hint to him henceforth to keep a curb between the teeth of inquisitiveness.[147]

When the local population objected to his voyeuristic presence, Lummis took it as an adrenalin-raising challenge to see the Other in a ritual closed to most Euro-Americans.[148] Coming to New Mexico to witness such a spectacle was made all the more enticing because of the region's peculiar position as "the United States which is *not* United States."[149] Incorporating the Other *into* the United States made the tourist experience novel for Lummis. When discussing the appeal of watching the Penitentes, Lummis remarked how astonishing he thought it was that these events "took place within the limits of the United States. A procession in which voters of this Republic shredded their naked backs with savage whips."[150]

The historian Ramón Gutiérrez argues that Lummis's writings took Euro-Americans on "an Orientalist adventure" along the border.[151] Drawing from the substantial literature first spurred by Edward Said, Gutiérrez points out that Lummis used established assumptions about the "orient" as a means to articulate New Mexico's role in the United States. Lummis gave Euro-Americans a means to claim New Mexico and its exoticness as their possession despite being a minority of the territory's population.[152] Indeed, Lummis frequently made explicit comparisons between New Mexico and the ill-defined "Orient" or "Africa," spaces critical to the ways that Euro-Americans imagined the colonized Other. In one passage Lummis named New Mexico "the heart of Africa beating against the ribs of the Rockies."[153] It is hardly a coincidence that Lummis wrote in an era of the opening of new modes of difference for consumption as exotic fantasies and as social critiques—seen in another guise as the aesthetic, commercial, and tourist movement of Japonism.[154]

For this study, what is important about Lummis's "Orientalizing" of New Mexico is the way it remade the meaning of race, region, and nation. Analogies to Africa and Asia were not intended to frighten his Euro-American readers, as they might have fifty years earlier. Instead, he wrote about racial difference in the territory as an opportunity for Euro-Americans to enjoy the Other as a tourist commodity, thus making the Other safe.[155] For Euro-Americans like Lummis, being able to watch, comment on, and photograph the imagined infinite racial and cultural difference in New Mexico was exciting. Said pointed to the importance that white travelers placed on being able to observe the Other as critical to Western imperialism. Europeans, he argued, remained detached and never involved but always watching the Orient "since its almost (but never quite) offensive behavior issues out of a reservoir of infinite peculiarity." Viewing the Other, Said argued, offered Europeans a "bizarre jouissance."[156] Lummis's desire to view, but never participate in, the Penitente ceremonies or Isleta races suggests this same type of thinking. The eastern journalist was always tantalizingly close to the Other but never actually shared in their activities.

New Mexico gave Euro-Americans a chance to travel to their own version of colonized Africa. As Anne McClintock points out, "Africa" became the "colonial paradigm of anachronistic space."[157] Such comparisons were not just about positioning colonized peoples in the Eastern and Western hemispheres. Equating New Mexico with Africa or the Orient implicitly equated the larger United States with European colonial powers, assuring Euro-Americans of their own position in a global racial hierarchy.[158] Not only could Lummis have fancied himself an American version of Henry Morton Stanley or David Livingstone, but he could also have imagined that Euro-Americans were as capable of taking up the "white man's burden" as were the British.

Lummis inspired other Euro-Americans to recount similar tales about their travels through New Mexico. Lilian Whiting published a romanticized vision of her trip through the U.S. Southwest entitled *The Land of Enchantment* in 1906. Whiting, an occasional correspondent for the *New York Times*, described New Mexico with particular enthusiasm: "New Mexico is the scene of surprises. Traditionally supposed to be a country that is as remote as possible from the accepted canons of polite society . . . it reveals itself instead as a region whose temperature is most delightful, whose coloring of sky and atmosphere is often indescribably beautiful, and whose inhabitants include their fair proportion of those who represent the best culture and intelligence of our country."[159] Whiting's assessment of New Mexico included many of the elements that increasingly typified Euro-American writings about the territory between 1880 and 1912. *The Land of Enchantment* claimed that Euro-Americans could find thrills visiting a place that had a nonwhite majority, comparing New

Mexico to other locales that Euro-Americans exoticized. In one section she claimed that "New Mexico reminds one of Algiers" because it had "the same Oriental suggestion of intense coloring."[160] Rather than seeing that "intense coloring" as something to fear, Whiting recommended that her Euro-American readership visit the territory to savor the mixed population's vividness.[161]

Euro-Americans' interest in construing New Mexico as an American Orient seemingly did not go unnoticed by entrepreneurial Mexican Americans. Cruceño hotelier Martin Amador highlighted those links in an effort to make his lodging more appealing. Lummis used the Orient as a metaphor to explain New Mexico's colonial relationship to the United States, but Amador made that metaphor tangible by decorating his Las Cruces lobby with life-size statues of nude "Arab" boys wearing only turbans, exotic Buddhas on pedestals, Native American pottery, and leopard-skin rugs (see Figure 7). All of these items transformed the Amador Hotel into an Orientalist fantasy. His Euro-American guests could thereby partake of Las Cruces as a place that was "not quite the U.S." while playing out concurrent fantasies about the Near East. They could even be comforted that they had not traveled to another nation for their Orientalist adventure. A scale replica of the Statue of Liberty stood in the midst of the naked Arab boys to remind them of their safety within the nation. The other distinctions between staying in New Mexico or the Near East became blurred.

Over time, Orientalist discussions even prompted begrudging Euro-American acknowledgments of Mexican cultural symbols. At the end of the nineteenth century, after decades of denigrating local architecture, Euro-Americans less frequently criticized these styles. Previously, newspaper editors had openly called for the demolition of adobe buildings as critical to making the territory American. By 1889, however, the editor of the *Las Cruces Daily News* conceded that "the adobe home and business block are sacred institutions here as well as elsewhere in New Mexico and the Daily News appreciates them to their full worth."[162] Like other aspects of the new regional identity, this initial "appreciation" of adobe buildings did not displace Euro-American assumptions that their own architecture was vastly superior. The editor quickly followed up his comments about adobe buildings with the assurance that he still believed that only Euro-American styles represented "progress." "Be it known," he wrote, "this paper hails with delight the erection of so many stone and brick structures now going on throughout the Valley. This is progress."[163] Still, the paper now recognized that the adobe buildings made up one

7. Guests at Martin Amador's Las Cruces hotel could go on an Oriental adventure while feeling secure that they had never left the United States. Courtesy Archives and Special Collections Department, New Mexico State University Library.

part of New Mexico's unique geography. As boosters for the territory increasingly deployed the territory's racial uniqueness to attract tourists, they expected the geography and landscape to reflect that uniqueness. Euro-Americans thereafter less often called for the demolition of buildings or other cultural signs that marked the geography as Mexican.[164]

By the time New Mexico became a state, its previously scorned Pueblo and Mexican architecture had become celebrated markers of the region's special status in the United States. The *New York Times* ran a detailed article on the University of New Mexico's new buildings that had been built as a "reproduction of the ancient Indian pueblo, peculiar to the primitive tribes of New Mexico."[165] The presence of such architectural styles no longer signaled Euro-Americans' failure to change the territory into an American place, despite the paper noting that the university structures were "of a form and distinction not to be found in university buildings elsewhere in the United States." Rather, they now symbolized the statehood movement itself. As the article's author noted, "Statehood has stimulated popular interest in the affairs of the university." Linking the adoption of unique ancient architectural styles and New Mexico's statehood echoed the tricultural strategy of regional boosters. Mexican and Pueblo cultural styles defined the local geography even as it also named them part of the territory's ancient past.

Similar romantic travel narratives and architectural revivals appeared elsewhere in the United States but in ways suited to the economic and social circumstances of each individual state. Like their counterparts in New Mexico, early-twentieth-century boosters for Alta California also idealized the state's Spanish-colonial past as a means for articulating a special place for that region within the nation. There the trend found expression in an invented stucco and red-tile architecture that still resonates throughout California to this day.[166] Likewise, Texas witnessed a renewed interest in its Spanish-Mexican history. The famed Alamo (San Antonio de Valero) and other surviving Spanish missions were integrated into a triumphal narrative culminating in the state's entry into the United States.[167] Rather than obstruct American nationalism or the history of the nation-state, Phoebe Kropp argues, the creation of these regional identities became important means through which individuals could relate to the United States as a collective whole after the Civil War.[168] Popular memories and commemorations of local history fit within a teleological narrative of progress concluding with the absorption of individual regions into the nation.

Euro-Americans who employed this same strategy in New Mexico, however, faced significantly different circumstances from their counterparts in Texas or Alta California. As full states, not colonially administered territories, those latter places actually were more integrated into the United States. They also had a clear white majority in the population since the nineteenth century. It was less complicated, then, for California Euro-Americans to celebrate the region's safely dead Spanish past because they found it easy to imagine that few of those original Spanish settlers still lived there.[169] Indeed, they strictly distinguished Mexicans, almost always imagined as recent arrivals in California, from the Spaniards, whom they supposed to have vanished shortly after creating the celebrated chain of mission churches. Unlike New Mexico, where Spanish American became an available identity that implied an inherited colonial legacy in the region, *Spanish* in California referred only to an era in regional history rather than to a group of people with historical claims to that state.[170]

Early-twentieth-century formulations of Texas history excluded Mexicans in a more dramatic way. Those narratives not only relegated Mexicans to the region's past, but they also made Mexicans strictly villains whose defeat was a prerequisite for the triumphant flourishing of Euro-American liberty.[171] Most Euro-American Texans took pride in their state as a "conquered land." The region's rebellion against Mexico, as David Weber notes, came to embody "a triumph of Protestantism over Catholicism, of democracy over despotism, of a superior white race over a degenerate people of mixed blood, of the future over the past, of good over evil."[172] In 1919 one Euro-American legislature identified three touchstones that defined Texas history: (1) the Alamo, "where Texas proved to the world that liberty was to be praised more dearly than life"; (2) the San Jacinto battleground, where Texans defeated the tyrannical Mexican army; and (3) "a living monument so far as Mexican banditry is concerned . . . and it is nothing other than the brave, gallant, dashing and courageous Ranger organization!"[173] These sacred cows, like the larger narrative of Texas history, minimized the economic, political, and social differences within the Euro-American Texan community by creating a unified opposition to the "cruel," but defeated, Mexican population.[174]

Euro-Americans in New Mexico shared common assumptions and some strategies with their contemporaries in California and Texas, like the romanticizing of Spain's colonial settlements; but the historical narratives that made sense in those other regions could not so easily be reconciled with New Mexico's present. Indeed, many eastern Euro-Americans justified the continuation of territorial status for New Mexico because its Mexicans had not yet been removed, as in California, nor "defeated," as in Texas. Euro-Americans in New Mexico, looking to use regional history as an entry into American nationalism, had to resort to a new pattern of differential racialization. Local Mexicans had to be different from Mexicans anywhere else along the border.

Euro-American writers like Lummis and Whiting struck a popular chord. They adapted already existing ideas about race, nation, and colonialism to remake New Mexico by turning the foreignness of the territory's populations into a strength. Rather than languish outside of the United States, New Mexico could secure its entry into the national imaginary as a site of voyeuristic entertainment in which Euro-Americans could enact and enjoy their authority over the people living there. Being New Mexican became a novelty for Euro-Americans, who enjoyed interacting with the Other without sacrificing dominance. Lummis and like-minded Euro-Americans imagined being near Mexicans and Pueblo Indians created a sense of uniqueness and adventure.

Racial Hierarchy and Colonial Labor

Even Euro-Americans who did not find Mexicans exotic, as had Lummis and Whiting, could still articulate a place for New Mexico's Mexicans within the United States. In many instances Euro-Americans did not bother with elaborate arguments about temporal hierarchies or civilization to justify the Mexican presence. Instead, they simply claimed the Mexican and indigenous populations as assets for U.S. economic expansion. These writers noted that New Mexico's Mexicans provided cheap labor for mining, farming, and tending livestock and concluded on that basis that Mexicans had value to the region and nation. The real prize of New Mexico's unique cross-racial unity, they argued, lay in domesticating Mexicans, making them into docile workers free of rebellious impulses.

Edith M. Nicholl recorded such a vision of New Mexico in 1898. Writing on her experiences as a rancher in Las Cruces, Nicholl made no effort to conceal her racist contempt for Cruceños. Her discussion about the meaning of the territory, though, resonates with the way that other early-twentieth-century Euro-Americans configured the presence of Mexicans north of the border. As we saw in chapter 1, the first English-language personal narratives about New Mexico, like the one by James Pattie, equated the presence of Mexican bodies with making the local space Mexican in the mid-nineteenth century.[175] Early Euro-American writers imagined that the displacement of Mexicans from New Mexico would be critical to transforming the territory into an American place. Almost fifty years later, Nicholl articulated a different sense of New Mexico. She did not call for the supplanting of Mexican bodies with Euro-Americans to make New Mexico American; rather, she argued that because the territory already *was* American, the large presence of Mexicans could not threaten Euro-Americans. Nicholl reversed previous conventions by arguing that geography disciplined bodies rather than that bodies defined the geography. Because New Mexico became an American territory, the Mexican majority was made docile and subservient to Euro-American interests.[176]

Nicholl claimed that the presence of even a few members of the "superior race" could easily control New Mexico's "mongrel race." In her memoir she distinguished clearly between Old Mexico, where Mexicans ruled themselves, and New Mexico, where whites ruled them:

For it must never be forgotten that this is New and not Old Mexico, and that whilst the Mexican predominates in the population, enjoying such influence as mere superiority of numbers can bestow, unsupported by intelligence, the American is the dominating element. A nice distinction, perhaps, but an important one, for all that. To assign, therefore, to the Mexican citizen of the United States such a part as he plays in Old Mexico would be to give a false and unreal description of life in the Territory. . . . The Mexican element is, then, of necessity only a circumstance, and to assign to the native more than his due share of conspicuity [*sic*] or influence would be to present a picture untrue to life as it is with us.[177]

Edith Nicholl and Charles Lummis both addressed, each in a different way, eastern Euro-American fears that New Mexico was too foreign. Nicholl, like Lummis, reassured her racially insecure eastern Euro-American readers that New Mexico's nonwhite majority did not undermine its status as American. Almost directly refuting Lummis, though, she made no claims about the Mexican population being exciting or thrilling, explicitly stating that "the picturesque may be virtually considered *non est*."[178] She saw them merely as part of the territory's peculiar circumstance, which nonetheless did not distract from the "dominating American element" that maintained the territory as part of the United States.

Nicholl's memoir further linked the territory to the larger nation by noting that it was common to have a racial Other in the majority who worked for a minority of Euro-Americans. In an attempt to locate New Mexico's racial mix as quintessentially American, Nicholl wrote, "The Mexican laborer is like the Negro."[179] Other Euro-Americans drew specific comparisons between local Mexicans and southern African Americans as well. A student at New Mexico's College of Agriculture and Mechanic Arts structured her senior thesis around a similar analogy to the U.S. South. Agnes Williams saw few problems with the territory's unfair labor relations or the Euro-American quest for Mexican land grants. Williams explained away economic and social injustice by claiming it was really Mexicans' preference to have Euro-Americans in charge. Although she compared local debt peonage as the equivalent to slavery in the South, she dismissed the practice by stating, "It is true that some Mexicans prefer to work for others as peons."[180] Her thesis, though, revealed a touch of defensiveness as it argued Mexicans "are never deprived of their liberties or rights as American citizens. This is the only way in which the word peon is used in the Valley."[181] Linking New Mexico to the South addressed Euro-American fears about New Mexico's racial structure by reminding them that having a nonwhite majority was common throughout the United States. Having Mexicans as American citizens, they argued, was only as unusual as having African Americans as citizens. Citizenship did not mean equality.

For her part Nicholl organized a racial hierarchy for hired labor, even explaining that it was important to "avoid [white] American female help," because they did not work hard enough and "associate[d] with you as your equal—or, better still, your superior."[182] It was far better to select a racial Other as a worker, as they seemingly "knew their place." She specifically suggested hiring a "Chinaman," or "if his wages are beyond the capacities of your purse . . . provide yourself with a Mexican woman, and do the fine cooking with your own hands."[183]

Nicholl or Williams might have found such arguments persuasive, but other Euro-Americans patently dismissed such comparisons. One writer for the *New York Times* argued that both African Americans and Mexican Americans were racially inferior to whites. Yet he went further to argue that "in his present condition the Mexican is far less fitted to be intrusted [*sic*] with political power than was the negro when emerging from slavery."[184] In a twist peculiar for the nineteenth century this Euro-American argued that the experience of slavery had actually made African Americans more able citizens, at least when compared with the Mexican population. Unlike the circumstances of slavery, he argued, "the Mexican has no similar pressure to guide his steps."[185] In Euro-American racial imaginings it made sense to compare Mexicans with African Americans. Both groups were less advanced because they were in a stage of civilizational infantilism. They each needed Euro-American tutelage before they could join the nation as full citizens. Whether Mexicans were more or less advanced than African Americans, however, was not clear.

For those in New Mexico such comparisons nonetheless suggested that incorporation of a nonwhite population into the United States had a precedent. Such writings also reveal the ways that these Euro-Americans imagined other U.S. regions. The South, for instance, was also coded as a space marked by a racial Other. They effaced the problems of southern violence—both physical, in the case of lynchings, and psychological, in the systematic deployment of terror as a means by which Euro-Americans controlled African Americans—to create a mythical image of the southern region as free of strife.[186] They then deployed this fictitious image to legitimate an equally romanticized image of New Mexico. They claimed that, just as whites were able to dominate numerically superior

African Americans in the southern states, so they could dominate Mexicans in New Mexico—a situation that would apparently please everyone.

Ideas about racial difference gave Euro-Americans a peculiar solution to reconciling New Mexico with the rest of the United States. Though many Euro-Americans did not celebrate Mexicans' majority in the territory as Lummis did, they still explained away this circumstance and less often called for Mexicans' removal. New Mexico might have been a special case in the United States because of the majority Mexican population, but it did not mean that it was irreconcilable with the rest of the nation. These types of reconfigurations between race, region, and nation would be common in Euro-American writings. Yet, Mesilleros threatened the tidy picture of this regional identity.

How Do You Solve a Problem Like Mesilla?
Limits of the Regional Identity

Presenting New Mexico as entirely American was a key element for Euro-Americans who adopted the New Mexican identity. Imagining the territory and people as nationally American, however, was more difficult for Euro-Americans living closer to the actual border with Mexico. La Mesilla, in particular, vexed boosters who sought to assert that the territory was united in their devotion to the United States.

During the 1870s the language of daily life often became a key marker in the debate over U.S. civilization in the Mesilla Valley. Use of Spanish or English signified a murky jumble of ideas about race and nation. Whether it was a symbol of cultural change or racial triumph, Euro-Americans used the spread of English as a sign that they had transformed the territory and openly celebrated any circumstance of "English Only." One newspaper attempted to capitalize on a growing resentment against Spanish in 1878. The title banner heralded it as "Being the Only Newspaper in the Rio Grande Valley published entirely in the English Language."[187] In another instance Albert Jennings Fountain, a Euro-American newspaper owner in the town of Mesilla, ran an article that directly celebrated the link between language and civilization. Fountain triumphantly reported that the use of English was on the rise across the globe. English would prevail over other (racialized) languages, Fountain stated, because the language had "simplicity, conciseness and strength."[188] In a town where Spanish speakers greatly outnumbered Anglophones, Fountain's hardy proclamation that the English language was "progressive, aggressive, dominant, and unyielding" against "the barriers of heathen-ism" must have appealed to many Euro-Americans.[189]

More than Cruceños, Mesilleros' refusal to speak English disturbed many Euro-Americans along the border and received frequent comment in newspapers. Because they imagined Mexican identity to be based on performance, Mesilleros continued the exclusive use of Spanish as a key marker of their town's Mexican association. They likewise thwarted at-tempts to introduce English. Their numeric dominance in Mesilla al-lowed for the institutionalized use of Spanish for most town functions.[190] Mesilla's exclusive attachment to Spanish did not fit with the emerging bicultural regional identity where Mexicans bowed to the dominant will of Euro-Americans.

The Euro-American editor of *Newman's Semi-Weekly* condemned Mes-illeros across several issues of his publication. Perhaps the most disconcert-ing element for the editor was Mesilleros' control over county courts, which inverted colonial authority. The editor fretfully wrote that Mesilleros conducted trials in Spanish, even with Euro-American defendants. Point-ing to a recent conviction, the Las Cruces editor proclaimed that a Euro-American man lost his right "to an impartial trial" because Mesilleros had translated his case into Spanish for the jury.[191] According to his logic American legal institutions and American towns could have only one lin-guistic marker: English.[192] Oddly, the author did not feel the court's deci-sion to convict the man to be wrong. He candidly acknowledged that he believed the defendant was thoroughly guilty. Still, he contended that "that part of the trial which we saw was a mockery upon justice" because the Mesilla courts conducted their proceedings in Spanish.[193]

In 1881 another Las Cruces newspaper editor similarly attempted to escalate tensions within the valley. Mesilla's continuation as a "Mexican town," he proclaimed, infringed on the rights of white Americans. Like most other Euro-Americans, this editor understood Mexican identity as a racialized state of being. Mesilla, technically in the United States, did not satisfy their expectations for an American town. "Is it proper," he posed to readers, "that the American population of this county should be represented by only four names in the list of petty jurors and not a single one in that of grand jurors?"[194] Under the law, of course, Mesilleros were American citizens and operated the courts under United States guide-lines. For the Las Cruces editor, though, the Mexicans who composed the jury pool were not truly Americans.

Euro-Americans' obsession with remaking southern New Mexico as American increased their ire at Mesilla's resistance and Mexican majority. They saw Mesilleros as standing in the way of the territory's full integration into the United States, either through becoming a state or attracting eastern investment. Some newspaper editors occasionally acknowledged this hostility between Americans and Mesilleros. The Euro-American editor of the *Mesilla News*, for instance, stated, "We believe that there is a large majority of all classes of citizens—excepting Mexicans—who are decidedly in favor of admission to the union."[195] In other words, the majority of the minority population, Euro-Americans, favored statehood, but the majority of the majority population, Mesilleros, rejected it.

Euro-Americans therefore characterized Mesilla as "wild" and "uncivilized" because of the townspeople's refusal to incorporate themselves into the territory or nation. Not surprisingly, Euro-Americans repeatedly, and optimistically, claimed an end to Mesilla's rogue status at different moments but always prematurely. In 1876 Governor Samuel B. Axtell arrived in Mesilla to celebrate the installation of the town's telegraph lines. The governor and other Euro-Americans believed this technology would finally end Mesilla's resistance to U.S. imperialism. As the first to send a telegram from the town, he transmitted an English-language message that read, "There is no more wild west. La Mesilla is united with Washington, D.C., today."[196] While many Mesilleros refused to acknowledge any deep association with the rest of the United States, Axtell hoped that the symbolic and technological linking of the town to the central government would reorient Mesilleros to American nationalism, ending their "wildness."

As new ideas about the "harmony of the races" grew in Euro-American writings, Mesilleros continued to claim a national Mexican identity and demanded that Mesilla reflect that identity. In the 1870s even the Spanish-language papers owned by Euro-Americans carried articles that celebrated Mexican nationalism in Mesilla. In 1878, for instance, Mesilla's Spanish-language newspaper printed the poem "A mi patria." Significantly, the poet claimed Mexico as his "patria," not the United States. One verse spoke of the author's honor in claiming a Mexican identity and his patriotic love:

El patrio amor que enardece a este pueblo, mi hermano,
Amor que no muere, y crece
En todo aquel que merece
El nombre Mejicano.

(The native love that inflames this people, my brother,
Love that does not die, and increases

In all that deserve
The name Mexican.)[197]

Though Euro-American newspapers celebrated the remaking of the valley as "American," the Spanish-language section of the *Mesilla News* still acknowledged local expressions of Mexican nationalism.

Because the regional identity depended on distinguishing New Mexico from Mexico, however, Mesilla's history proved an uncomfortable problem for Euro-Americans. Most decided to ignore Mesilla. Another early-twentieth-century Euro-American student at New Mexico A&M, however, took a different strategy for explaining Mesilleros' relationship to the region. Maude McFie's senior thesis distanced Mesilleros from Cruceños and Mexicans in the rest of New Mexico. Mesilla's founders, according to McFie, originated in northern Mexico rather than New Mexico. "It was founded shortly after the treaty of Guadalupe Hidalgo in 1848," McFie wrote, "when Mexico threw her gates open to receive back her people who had gone up into United States territory and settled."[198] While Mexicans in New Mexico had moved *south* to found Mesilla, she implicitly labeled Mesilleros as foreign to both the United States and New Mexico. In this odd view of the past McFie positioned New Mexico as perpetually "United States territory." She preferred to create an image of Mesilleros as outsiders who had traveled north from Mexico, across the border, into the United States and then had returned to their true nation. The rest of New Mexico's Mexicans had always been in the territory, but Mesilleros crisscrossed the border numerous times. By casting Mesilleros as "Mexicans from Mexico" she and her informants created a distinction between Mesilleros and Cruceños (and others) as "native New-Mexican" Mexicans.[199]

McFie further downplayed historical tensions between Mesilleros and the invading Euro-Americans. Instead, she retold the events of 1854 around rousing images of Mesillero patriotism for the United States that echoed other narratives around the regional identity. The moment that Euro-Americans raised the U.S. flag in the "midst of a vast crowd" at the center of Mesilla on July 4, 1854, marked the end of any Mexican nationalism. Based on accounts she collected from Cruceños, McFie concluded: "The people [of Mesilla] were told plainly they were now American citizens; the stars and stripes then floated from one of the great cotton wood trees, and with a shout from the crowd, the ceremony ended. Of course there was complaint, and some bitterness at the change, but the Mexican population soon adjusted themselves to the new regime and have proved

good, law-abiding citizens."[200] This vision of a domesticated past reflected the increasing desires of both elite Mexican Americans and Euro-
Americans to ignore Mesilla's history of dissent. The core of McFie's
narrative relied on interviews with "Don" Barbaro Lucero and Adolf Lea,
whom she felt obliged to mention were "both from Las Cruces."[201]

Lucero's racial position as a Mexican gave McFie's account a particular
type of authenticity. Though she seemingly could not find a Mesillero
informant, Lucero's participation legitimated her claims that the "bitterness" of local Mexicans had disappeared. McFie, though, did not fully
trust that her readers would accept the word of a single Mexican. She
offered additional assurance: "His statement . . . has been corroborated
by Messrs. S. G. Bean, Adolph Lea, Horace Stephenson and others."[202]
The common agreement on Lucero's testimony emerged from a collective desire to reimagine Mesilla both in the past and at the time of McFie's
thesis. Effacing Mesilleros' militancy and retention of a Mexican national
identity became a means for both Mexican and Euro-American elites to
discount Mesillero resistance as always already divorced from the New
Mexican identity.[203]

Most Euro-Americans did not reconsider that Mexicans existed as an
entirely separate racial group even as they endorsed a bicultural New
Mexico. Moreover, the boundary between Mexico and the United States
that was created in 1854 took on a transhistorical character. Many Euro-
Americans argued that not only was contemporary New Mexico separated from Mexico, but it had *always* been distinct from the neighboring
nation. As McFie's dependence on Lucero suggests, this vision of the
region was not just the invention of Euro-Americans. We will see in
chapter 6 how Cruceños and other Mexican Americans in the territory
inserted their own assumptions into the regional discourse. These assumptions often put them at odds with Mesilleros as much as with their
Euro-American neighbors.

Conclusion

Euro-Americans became increasingly interested in securing New Mexico's statehood for their own political and economic interests between
1880 and 1912. To convince Congress—and perhaps themselves—that
New Mexico was really and truly American, territorial leaders spun a
string of writings and created potent new symbols to connote their sense

of a unified regional identity. They obfuscated tensions between racial groups and formed a bridge reaching from the local to the national. Addressing easterners who had overwhelming economic and political superiority, regional business leaders and government officials worked to fix New Mexico and its people as strictly American nationals. Rather than denying the territory's racial diversity, they pushed against the notion that a national U.S. identity included only Euro-Americans. New Mexico, as a geographic entity, existed under a special, almost utopian, set of racial dynamics because it fell under the protection of the United States. They tentatively acknowledged that Mexican and Native Americans each had a role in the region but deployed a panoply of discursive strategies to keep these racial groups subordinated. Most Euro-Americans insisted that the regional identity did not undermine Euro-American racial superiority even as it granted Mexicans U.S. citizenship.

Published sources and senior theses suggest some of the ways that Euro-Americans articulated the meaning of race and nation through a regional New Mexican identity. These documents show how the writers retained their ideas about a colonial racial hierarchy to structure their ideas about a bicultural and even tricultural regional identity. Hiram Hadley, the president of Las Cruces's New Mexico College of Agriculture and Mechanic Arts, explicitly remarked on New Mexico's multiracial future in 1897. In a speech to a high school graduating class, Hadley argued that New Mexico's racial diversity made the territory special within the United States. In an increasingly common contrivance, Hadley predicted that the interactions between Mexicans and Euro-Americans would result in a territory populated by remarkably loyal citizens. He stated, "This work is progressing, and the little school is the most important factor. In it, side by side, in the classroom and on the playground, our youth of different languages and different nationalities are assimilating their ideas and their thoughts. Is it too much to expect that [the] grand result will be American citizens devoted to New Mexico and loyal to the flag of our common country? This should be the ideal which every true friend of New Mexico should keep constantly before him."[204] Like other Euro-Americans, Hadley did not envision the Mexican/Euro-American relationship as equitable. He imagined Euro-Americans as a superior race who brought modern civilization to New Mexico.[205] Still, Hadley's vision of a regional New Mexico unity provided a role for Mexicans as U.S. citizens that had not existed in the first decades after the U.S. conquest. Colonial institutions such as schools allowed Mexicans to apprentice in the hard work of becoming fully American. A regionally specific New Mexican identity mediated Euro-Americans' concerns about the territory's nonwhite majority.

As we will see in the next chapter, Mexican Americans also attempted to assert their position in the territory and nation by using a New Mexican identity. This regional identity was necessarily loaded with contradictions and uncertainties that created uneasiness for both Euro-Americans and Mexican Americans. Although the regional identity was used in English-language and Spanish-language texts and newspapers, the meaning of that identity was not always clear. Mexican American government officials and owners of Spanish-language newspapers frequently used the identity for their own purposes. The next chapter evaluates some strategies that Mexican Americans used to reconcile the regional identity with the racial hierarchy imposed by Euro-Americans. These struggles would have specific consequences for the Mesilla Valley in the last decades of the territorial period.

CHAPTER 6

"New Mexico for New Mexicans!":
Race and the Redefinition of Regional Identity
for Mexicans, 1880–1912

At the threshold of the twentieth century Senator Albert Beveridge of Indiana delivered the most outspoken opposition to making New Mexico a state. When named chairman of the Senate Committee on Territories in 1901, Beveridge expressed his disinclinations toward both New Mexico and Arizona for reasons partisan and racial. "My present tendency," he recorded, "is in favor of the admission of Oklahoma and the Indian Territory as a single State and the rejection of the applications of New Mexico and Arizona."[1] A Republican, Beveridge privately disliked the idea of admitting new states that could add additional Democratic senators. Although New Mexico had previously voted Republican, Beveridge suspected that it harbored Democratic sympathizers.[2] Publicly, Beveridge did not discuss these issues, instead taking the less contentious line (!) that he opposed statehood because Mexicans inherently lacked the abilities necessary to be full U.S. citizens.

When an omnibus statehood bill included New Mexico in 1901, Beveridge countered by launching an investigation into the territory's "readiness" to shed its territorial status. He took a committee, composed of Senators Henry E. Burnham of New Hampshire, William P. Dillingham of Vermont, and Henry Heitfield of Idaho, on a tour of New Mexico and Arizona. During this trip Beveridge encountered a racial terminology unfamiliar to him. Prominent Mexicans tenaciously asserted that they were "native New Mexicans," a claim that perplexed the senators. These Mexicans drew on an emerging vision of the territory as having distinct characteristics that differentiated it (and them) from the rest of the United States or Mexico.

The Cruceño business leader Isidoro Armijo used such terms when he testified in favor of statehood before the visiting congressional committee. When Beveridge asked Armijo about "the proportions of the different races" in the Mesilla Valley, Armijo responded that the "majority [were] native."[3] Beveridge challenged that answer, asking, "By that [do] you mean Mexican?" Armijo baulked at being identified as Mexican and further defined the meaning of being native. He stated, "I mean American citizens, not Mexicans; born in the United States . . . of Spanish extraction. I am of Spanish extraction myself, but I was born in the United States and I am an American." For Armijo status as native implied a racial category different from Anglo, which he willingly accepted, but he resisted the label *Mexican*, seemingly because that term implied foreign status.

The senator discounted such an assertion and upheld his own vision of racial divisions that defined the border region. He responded to Armijo, "But you understand down here, and the committee know that themselves, that the words 'Mexican' and 'American' down here are used as they are not used anywhere else in the United States. We are just getting at the racial blood; that is all."[4] After he had concluded his tour, Beveridge dismissed the term *native* as simply another name for "Mexican." The committee chair circulated a memo explicitly discounting the proposition that "native New Mexicans" were racially or culturally different from Mexicans anywhere else in the world. "The Mexicans or natives as they are called out there," the memo stated, "live largely in settlements to themselves . . . and where this is the case the Mexican language is spoke [*sic*] almost entirely and Mexican customs, habits, practices, and mode of living prevails [*sic*], and is, I am informed, the same as when the territory was acquired from the Republic of Mexico in 1848."[5]

While Beveridge held that Mexicans in New Mexico had the same customs and "racial blood" as those in Mexico, most Mexican and Euro-American supporters of statehood who testified before his committee subscribed to a regionally specific language that inflected broader notions of race and nation. As I have established, members of the Euro-American territorial elite deployed a tricultural New Mexican identity after 1880. Prominent Mexican Americans joined in this regional discourse with equal enthusiasm.[6] Together, they created an image of New Mexicans that incorporated and transcended the imported Euro-American racial categories of "Mexican, Indian, and Anglo."[7] Eventually, prominent Euro-Americans and Mexican Americans promised, participation in "triculturalism" would eliminate racism in the territory as it fully incorporated the region into the United States.[8] The ambiguity about the precise meaning of *triculturalism* allowed the New Mexico discourse to be used by different groups for their own purposes.

As this chapter will show, members of the territory's Mexican elite attempted to synthesize their own notions of race and nation into a "native New Mexican" identity between 1880 and 1912. Compared with previous generations, the Mexicans of this period had greater opportunities to express their opinions about race, nation, and region in the public realm. By the last decades of the nineteenth century, Mexicans held major political positions in the territory, including the office of the governor. Likewise, Mexican business leaders also challenged the existing Euro-American dominance over New Mexico's printed discourse by creating their own bilingual and Spanish-language newspapers.[9] Most territorial newspapers since the adoption of the Treaty of Guadalupe Hidalgo had been bilingual but were still owned and edited by Euro-Americans until the end of the nineteenth century. In the generation after conquest, New Mexico's Mexican elite increasingly published their own papers.[10] After 1870 the number of Spanish-language newspapers available throughout New Mexico increased dramatically, with a total of seventeen new newspapers by the late 1880s and forty-four Spanish-language newspapers in the 1890s.[11] Indeed, the Mexican population of New Mexico produced more Spanish-language materials than its counterparts anywhere else along the nineteenth-century border.[12]

Like many Euro-American newspapers, most of these Mexican-owned newspapers configured New Mexican identity as bridging the gap between Mexicans' racial status and the national American identity. Their discussions of this regional identity, though, differed in some crucial ways from discussions by Euro-Americans. Mexican Americans claimed a level of authenticity in being native New Mexican that they argued Euro-Americans could not match. By the late nineteenth century many Spanish-language newspapers and political leaders defined Mexicans' racial identity through the territory's geographic limits. Both Armijo and Beveridge considered that the majority of the territory's population was divided into two distinct racial categories, Americans and Mexicans, as a matter of "blood." Beveridge saw most of New Mexico's population as immutably Mexican, regardless of their citizenship status. Armijo, however, distanced the territory's population from the moniker of "Mexican" through a separate identity as native. Only those Mexicans in New Mexico could assert such a claim because of the territory's assumed isolation from the rest of Mexico.

It might not be self-evident that the abstract creation of a regional New Mexican identity should have affected the Mesilla Valley, far removed from New Mexico's political and social centers. In fact, the ways that individuals articulated the meanings of race, nation, and region had profound implications for Cruceños and Mesilleros. As this chapter documents, those who disavowed the emerging vision of New Mexico faced tremendous social pressure with real consequences for local economic and political life. La Mesilla and Las Cruces traded places in the economic and social order of the region. From 1850 to 1870 the town of Mesilla had been the cultural and economic center of southern New Mexico, but by 1912 Las Cruces had overtaken its neighbor in population and volume of trade. The final section of this chapter considers how the development of a New Mexican regional identity influenced the means by which individuals made sense of economic and social changes in the Mesilla Valley that occurred from 1880 to 1912.

Americanos de raza Mexicana o de sangre Española: Members of the Mexican American Elite and the Regional New Mexican Identity, 1880–1900

By the 1880s Mexican and Euro-Americans often claimed a unity of purpose based on their commitment both to New Mexico and to the U.S. nation. The regional identity became a means for elite Mexican Americans and Euro-Americans to advocate for shared economic or political interests, particularly in the quest for statehood. In one such instance Colonel José Francisco Chaves introduced and secured the adoption of a joint resolution in the territorial legislature in 1889, after the territory's hopes for statehood had again become mired in partisan and racial conflicts. New Mexico had been included in House and Senate omnibus bills for statehood, along with South Dakota, Washington, and Montana.[13] After debating the omnibus bill, the House Committee on Territories returned a majority and minority report. Although the majority and minority reports agreed on statehood for South Dakota, Washington, and Montana, the minority report expressly rejected statehood for New Mexico. In the debate over the bill W. W. H. Davis's *El Gringo* and other such accounts were entered as evidence that the territory's Mexican population was "illiterate, superstitious, and morally decadent."[14] Even supporters of New Mexico's place in the 1888 omnibus bill feared that the territory was still "too foreign," effectively killing its chances in the larger House.[15] Newspapers in the eastern and midwestern states, representing the vested interests of those regions, reiterated stock objections whenever New Mexico sought statehood.[16] The *Chicago Tribune*, for instance, printed an article in February 1889 that disparaged New Mexico's "mongrel" population, stating that alone justified denying statehood. For the *Tribune* editors, they were "not Americans but 'Greasers,' persons ignorant of our laws, manners, customs, language, and institutions."[17]

Rebutting such assessments became a paramount priority for officials in New Mexico. In the same month as the *Chicago Tribune*'s scathing attack, New Mexico's territorial legislature, composed of both Euro-Americans and Mexican Americans, approved Chaves's resolution. The measure overtly criticized the U.S. Congress for allowing eastern Euro-American "ignorance" to unfairly penalize the "people of New Mexico."[18] Chaves argued that New Mexicans had already proved their fervent American nationalism beyond any other territory. In keeping with the newly emerged discourse on New Mexican identity, though, the resolution conspicuously refused to describe the territory's majority population in established racial terms. Drafters of the resolution consciously obscured the Mexican racial identity in favor of a regional New Mexican identity. Accordingly, the resolution relied on such phrases as "Spanish-speaking citizens" and "native people of New Mexico." The legislators must have hoped that renaming the local population in relational terms to the territory would replace their perceived "foreignness" with a vision of the native people of New Mexico as devoted Americans.

Chaves and his fellow legislators dedicated lengthy sections of the resolution to a catalog of historical events highlighting patriotic contributions by native New Mexicans. During the Civil War, the resolution proclaimed, New Mexicans "heroically spent their blood and freely gave their treasure in upholding the national flag—in this devotion sacrificing more men and more money than all the territories combined then existing."[19] This mode of recounting history elided the emphasis on race in defining full U.S. citizenship, suggesting in its place that Mexicans' actions and devotion to the Union made them worthy and full citizens. The resolution further directed attention to the fact that the majority of New Mexico's natives had been *born* in the United States because the territory had already been part of the nation for more than forty years: "The present territory of New Mexico contains as large a proportion of citizens born and bred under the American flag as any other territory or any northern state of the union."[20] Fully cognizant of the era's Anglo-Saxon panic over the influx of immigrants from eastern and southern Europe, Chaves implicitly claimed that local Mexicans were therefore *more* American than the immigrants who dominated some eastern states.[21] The resolution passed with widespread support from both Mexican American and Euro-American leaders, an indication that there was an increasingly accepted means for mobilizing racially ambiguous language and a regional New Mexican identity. For members of each group this identity accounted for both their relationship to each other and the territory's rightful place within the United States.

At times Euro-Americans and Mexican Americans could even use each other's statements as mutually reinforcing evidence of the regional identity's validity. In one instance a Cruceño-owned newspaper, *El Labrador*, quoted a Euro-American territorial supreme court associate justice who responded to derogatory statements about New Mexico's Mexicans as "greasers." The justice declared that he would rather work with New Mexico's Mexicans than with U.S. citizens in other parts of the country. "No se hizo esperar mi respuesta," he stated, "y esta fué que más me gustaría tener un pleito sometido a un jurado de los mismos americanos de raza mexicana o de sangre española que de cualquiera otro jurado que se pudiera encontrar en Omaha" (My response was immediate, and it was that I would rather have a court case submitted to a jury of Americans of Mexican race or Spanish blood than to any jury that one can find in Omaha).[22] This associate justice upheld the suitability of New Mexico's Mexicans as jurors on account of their family ties, their ability to be "buenos hijos, buenos esposos y buenos padres." Moreover, he claimed that Mexicans were not intimidated by wealth or an attorney's eloquence.

As in the legislature's resolution, the judge's statement attempted to shift the criteria for full U.S. citizenship away from racial concerns. Instead, he proposed that actions, such as being good fathers or ignoring the privileges of wealth, sufficed to make Mexicans commendable republican citizens. The statement concluded with an explicit plea for the statehood movement: "Nuestra población hispano-americana es una razón para admitir a los Territorio en la Unión y no para obstínate en excluirlos de ellos" (Our Hispano-American population is a reason to admit the Territory of New Mexico into the Union and not to continue to exclude them).[23] This vision of Mexicans reversed assumptions that presumed that their racial identity contrasted with an American identity. Instead, the editor offered a hyphenated "hispano-american" identity and claimed that they were actually better Americans than those in Omaha. In such writings the distinctions between the "Mexican race" and those of "Spanish blood" were moot.

Such discussions differed significantly from, and even became a foil for, the parallel discussion about statehood in neighboring Arizona. That territory's political and social trajectories had diverged sharply from those of New Mexico; nonetheless, Arizona struggled to attain statehood as well. In 1863, shortly after the Union army expelled the Confederacy from La Mesilla, the remaining Euro-Americans lobbied Congress to divide New Mexico, a territory half the size of Europe, into two parts. To achieve this division, Arizona's Euro-Americans had argued that the territory could never flourish if they were forced to remain under the authority of the racially inferior Mexican majority in New Mexico.[24] Arizona, with its much smaller population, became a Euro-American majority territory by 1870.[25]

Through the nineteenth century, Euro-American mining interests came to dominate Arizona, subjecting Mexican and Mexican American laborers to harshly segregated circumstances and depressed wages.[26] Despite these rough changes, Mexican Americans retained significant authority within Tucson and other parts of southern Arizona.[27] Most Euro-Americans, however, promoted Arizona as strictly an Anglo territory that happened to have foreign Mexican laborers. In sharp contrast to the narrative of racial harmony proposed in New Mexico, boosters of Arizona statehood developed a historical narrative centering on the domination or expulsion of other groups by white "pioneers," a narrative not too dissimilar from its counterparts in Texas.[28]

Nonetheless, Albert Beveridge had also rejected statehood for Arizona owing to its low population density and the unchecked power of mining interests in 1901. He and other senators proposed that if both Arizona and New Mexico agreed to be rejoined, they could be admitted as a single state.[29] Reducing New Mexico to an appendage of Arizona, Beveridge noted, would have diluted the political authority of Mexicans in that region, but the sudden incorporation of a large Mexican population would have also diluted the political authority of the Euro-American majority in Arizona, a possibility that they flatly rejected. New Mexico's petitions for statehood promised racial harmony between Mexicans and Euro-Americans. Euro-Americans in Arizona, in contrast, predicted a "race feud" between those same two groups should the two territories be (re)integrated.[30]

For their part Mexican Americans in New Mexico also rejected a merger with Arizona. Within New Mexico elite Mexican Americans found that they could exploit ambiguities in the regional discourse to assert their own authority in territorial affairs. They knew very well that their Mexican American peers in Tucson, much less in direful places like Texas, were rapidly losing their economic and political power. Members of the Mexican elite in Tucson wrote explicitly in their own Spanish-language papers about feeling under siege in nineteenth-century Arizona.[31] Members of New Mexico's Mexican American elite claimed a special role in the region as "native New Mexicans" that they imagined would stave off their own loss of power. This native status, they argued, granted them authority within the territory, pushing at the racial hierarchy that Euro-Americans assumed.

One José Escobar wrote in the *Las Cruces Nuevo Mundo*, "Si América es para los americanos, digamos nosotros: Nuevo México para los neo-mexicanos, sin que esto signifique que se excluya del todo al buen elemento anglo-sajon que ha invertido aquí sus capitales y que de hecho está tan derechoso como los hijos legítimos de esta sección del país el manojo y emolumentos de las oficinas públicas" (If America is for Americans, then let us say: New Mexico for New Mexicans, without having this mean the exclusion of the good Anglo-Saxon element that has invested its capital here and, in fact, is as much entitled to hold and benefit from public office as are its true sons from this part of the country).[32] Escobar thus acknowledged that Euro-Americans had a place in New Mexico as a bicultural region. In this case, though, he implied Euro-Americans were less connected to the territory than its "hijos legítimos," the Mexicans. Thus, while *New Mexican* could serve as a cross-racial term, it could also take on an exclusive sense to indicate Mexicans only, as in Escobar's call for "Nuevo México para los neo-mexicanos." New Mexico could be a sanctuary in the midst of states and territories ever hostile to Mexican Americans.

At stake for these Mexicans was more than just a rhetoric about geography or statehood. They sought to ensure their own access to economic and political positions and the preservation of cultural elements that they deemed critical. As different Mexican Americans elaborated on the meaning of a bicultural New Mexico, they crafted sophisticated arguments in an attempt to reconcile their own cultural practices with those of American elites as a whole.

Going Native: Mexican Claims to the Region

Mary Louise Pratt argues that "autoethnographic expression is a widespread phenomenon of the contact zone" in imperial contexts. She suggests that examining such expressions is therefore "important in unraveling the histories of imperial subjugation and resistance."[33] By "autoethnographic expression" Pratt means the instances in which colonized subjects represent themselves through the colonizer's own terms.[34] This involves both partial collaboration with, and appropriation of, the parlance of the conqueror. The colonized's self-representations take on the projected representations by the colonial powers. They tend to be bilingual (or multilingual), dialogic, and shot through with the colonized's own positions. The intended readerships, moreover, are heterogeneous as the works address both the colonized and the colonizers.

The writings of New Mexico's elite Mexican Americans at the end of the nineteenth century offer excellent examples of such autoethnographic expressions. Mexican American business leaders, politicians, and scholars frequently adopted imperialist vocabulary and presumptions within their writings about New Mexico and collaborated in making its colonial status appear inevitable, natural, and beneficial. Yet those same Mexican Americans also infused those representations with counterunderstandings of race, nation, and region as they worked to restore their own authority on the border.

Settling their assumptions about race, region, and nation challenged Mexican Americans at the end of the nineteenth century.[35] Participating in the regional discourse required them to accept Mexican identity as a distinctive racial classification according to the dominant Euro-American system. Mexicans in New Mexico, in other words, imagined their relationship with each other as racially based by 1880. Prominent Mexican Americans claimed (and Euro-Americans could on occasion recognize), however, that they had a special racial status as *native* New Mexicans. Thus, geography could be invoked in the building of a new quasi-racial category. Now that New Mexico had become a distinct place with a unique history, its native residents, presumed to be knowable through a shared heredity in that place, also became distinctive and nameable. To be clear, *native* did not mean racially "Indian"; actually, it meant quite the opposite. However, claims of native identity also went beyond simple claims to whiteness or Spanish identity, though that was often an implicit assumption of nativeness. Rather, these claims conveyed more authority for natives in the region than Euro-Americans because they had a stronger connection to New Mexico as descendants of the "first" colonizers.

Where Euro-Americans wrote about a racially unified New Mexican identity that was dependent on a racial hierarchy, Mexican Americans reconfigured the territory's supposed racial unity as an equitably shared commitment to the region and nation. Cruceño newspaper editors, like most of their Mexican counterparts elsewhere in the territory, adapted the regional New Mexican identity to counter their subordinate position. They created their own set of interior frontiers that named the territory as uniquely theirs and not "Euro-American." In one edition of *El Labrador*, Cruceño José Gonzales railed against "personas forasteras" who "en apariencia representan estar llenas de bondad para aquellos con quienes tienen contacto, pero que al investigar su verdadero estado moral se les halla un corazón tan degradante y una mente tan falta de razón" (foreign persons who appear to be full of kindness for those whom they come in contact with, but upon investigation their real sense of morality is found in a degraded heart and a mind lacking reason).[36] By formulating discussion of the nation vis-à-vis the region, Euro-Americans became the suspicious foreigners and Mexicans the legitimate settlers.

At times the native regional identity could even supplant Mexican racial identity. By 1910 Isidoro Armijo had become the editor of Las Cruces's *El Eco del Valle*. As we saw from his testimony before Beveridge's committee, Armijo defended native New Mexicans as nationally American and simultaneously *not* Mexican. This did not mean that Armijo believed that natives had always found equal treatment under the U.S. flag. Outside of testifying for statehood, Armijo expressed concern that the other Spanish-language newspapers too easily occluded deeper discussions about the meaning of race in the territory. Armijo was mindful that the bicultural regional identity obscured ongoing tensions between Mexicans and Euro-Americans even as he used that same identity to advocate for Mexicans' citizenship rights. The Cruceño editor proposed that the territory needed explicit discussions about racism along the border, including in New Mexico. He complained that "los periódicos españoles de Nuevo México han permanecido silenciosos por tratarse de cuestiones de raza que ellos no desean levantar" (the Spanish newspapers of New Mexico have remained silent about handling questions of race that they do not want to raise).[37]

Contrary to some scholars' assumptions that the emergence of a Spanish identity in New Mexico involved a total disavowal of other Mexicans in the U.S., Armijo clearly felt an allegiance to the Tejanos living in that neighboring state.[38] The regional discussion on race and nation proved more complicated, and New Mexicans' relationship with (other) Mexicans was uncertain. Members of the Mexican American elite, however, kept themselves apprised of the racial injustices that appeared along the border. They also imagined that Mexicans in New Mexico shared in a common struggle with Mexicans in other parts of the U.S. This sense of shared purpose coexisted with efforts to also name New Mexicans as different from those other Mexicans. Armijo directed his readers' attention to the discriminatory practices that prevented Mexican and Euro-American children from attending the same public schools on the U.S. side of the border. Armijo, like many Mexicans in New Mexico, considered Texas the worst place in all the United States. He also seemed to imagine that New Mexicans had an obligation to defend Texas Mexicans facing abuse and discrimination.

Even as he suggested a common cause among Mexicans and Mexican Americans across the border, however, the editor used markedly different language when discussing Mexicans in New Mexico and Mexicans in Texas. When Armijo discussed Texas, he expressed a profound bond with the "mixed" origins of the Mexican people: "El porvenir de nuestra gente por el solo hecho de que en nuestras venas corre la sangre de abnegados y sublimes héroes como Cuauhtémoc y Moctezuma, sangre noble española y azteca, es triste, es melancólico" (The future of our people is made by the fact that in our veins runs the blood of self-sacrificing and sublime heroes such as Cuauhtémoc and Moctezuma, noble Spanish and Aztec blood, it is sad, it is melancholy).[39] As the Cruceño shifted his discussion to New Mexico, he ceased all mention of Montezuma or of the "noble Aztecs." Rather, he referred to its population as "Hispano-Americans." Racism, Armijo bemoaned, occurred in both Texas and New Mexico, but New Mexico's "Hispano-Americans" were natives to their territory. This status implied a special priority that Armijo did not acknowledge for Mexicans in Texas, possibly because he saw them as immigrants and therefore foreign. Thus, even as he suggested that native New Mexicans and Texas Mexicans should unite over a shared struggle against racism, Armijo distinguished between the two groups based on region and national identity. As this discussion shows, the claim to being New Mexican carried a price of potentially attenuating solidarity with their counterparts elsewhere in the United States.

Editors like Armijo recognized that discrimination against Mexicans elsewhere along the border exposed their own tenuous relationship to U.S. citizenship. States like Texas, whose social and legal orders reified the Mexican/American dichotomy, undermined native New Mexicans' aspirations for national incorporation. Armijo and his allies therefore had to navigate between Scylla and Charybdis. On one side they knew that efforts to disenfranchise Mexicans in any other part of the United States could easily set disastrous legal and social precedents for them as well. At the same time, they also had to distance themselves from other Mexicans on cultural, national, and even racial terms through the invocation of New Mexico's supposed geographic uniqueness. The disidentification with other Mexicans cannot be dismissed as only an opportunistic ploy. Rather, Armijo critiqued racist exclusions of *all* Mexicans from public services while also claiming natives' greater claim to U.S. citizenship.

Armijo ended his editorial with a hypothetical scenario. What would happen, he asked, if Cruceños acted like (Euro-American) Texans? What if they excluded "nonnatives" from the town's public schools? Armijo intentionally sketched a fantastical scenario and claimed that Cruceños would never pursue it. Still, he imagined that Cruceños, as natives, had the same authority in New Mexico as Euro-Americans had in Texas:

> Las escuelas públicas son públicas, no son especiales. ¿Como les parecería a los señores que no son nativos que se excluyeran de las escuelas de Las Cruces a los niños americanos? No, no sería propio ni justo. Pero la regla que no aplica para ambos igual también sale sobrando.[40]

> (The public schools are public, they are not special. How would it seem to the gentlemen who are not native if the Las Cruces schools excluded American children? No, it would not be proper nor fair. But the rule that does not apply for both equally is worthless.)

In this passage Armijo made an indirect analogy between Mexican nationals who migrated into Texas and Euro-Americans who migrated into New Mexico. For Armijo both groups were "foreign" to those places. Euro-American Texans could therefore learn from native New Mexicans' gracious welcome of their newly arrived white neighbors.

For Cruceño editors like Armijo, native status became the most powerful argument for ending racist policies throughout the territory. It was a double insult, they argued, for native New Mexicans to attend segregated schools because they were both U.S. citizens and the heirs of the "first settlers" in the region. In this way they resurrected claims to being colonial authorities themselves, in the process implicitly barring Indians from ever being "first settlers," "Mexicans," or even "natives." This hardening of Mexican identity suggests a new sense of permanent and static racial and national identities not in evidence in Mexico under the colonial caste system. Indians were now rendered inassimilable—an obstacle that Mexicans had overcome in the region before it could be ready for entry into the United States.

The Las Cruces–based *El Labrador* reprinted a similar editorial about education in 1903. In this instance the editor expressed his outrage that some New Mexico towns with a Euro-American majority (including Cerrillos, Roswell, Carlsbad, Raton, and Silver City) had instituted a segregated school system. Compared to the centuries-long history of Mexicans' residency in New Mexico, the editor claimed, Euro-Americans were nothing but newly arrived "foreigners":

> Con eso se quiere ni más ni menos que marcar con el sello de la esclavitud y la inferioridad a los nativos del país, sentando por regla y principio que los niños de descendencia española oriundos de los primeros pobladores que conquistaron y poblaron este territorio no tienen iguales derechos que los hijos de recién venidos que de pocos años a este parte se han resentado [*sic*] en Nuevo Mexico.[41]

> (With that, they want nothing less than to mark the natives of this country with the stamp of inferiority and slavery, established by rule and principle that the Spanish children, who are descendants of the first settlers who conquered and populated this territory, do not have the same rights as the children of those newly arrived who established themselves only a few years before now in New Mexico.)

Mexican American editorials like these created a notion of being native that was a complicated mixture of colonialism, race, and regional identity. This writer and his peers usurped indigenous populations' rights to the region by declaring that Mexicans had an exclusive hereditary claim to the territory as "los primeros pobladores."

More radical stances took the notion of native status even further. Camilo Padilla, a member of the educated elite, hardly applauded the arrival of Euro-Americans as the harbingers of "progress" as L. Bradford Prince did. In an 1892 article for *El Mosquito*, Padilla wrote:

> El suelo neo-mexicano, el cual está rociado y comprado con la sangre de nuestros padres, debería ser para nosotros tan sagrado como es el patrio suelo para el buen patriota y ciudadano. . . . Así es que cuando se vé á un nuevo-mexicano vender un terreno á un extranjero, aquello parece profano, porque el vendedor demuestra lo poco que aprecia aquella herencia legada por sus antepasados.[42]

(The New Mexican ground, which has been sprinkled and bought with the blood of our parents, should be as sacred to us as is the nation for the good patriot and citizen. . . . Therefore, when one sees a New Mexican sell a piece of land to a foreigner, it seems a sacrilege, because the seller demonstrates how little he appreciates the inheritance bequeathed to him by his ancestors.)

When Euro-Americans wrote about the bicultural regional identity, they presented their race as bringing civilization to New Mexico and crafting racial harmony. Mexicans inverted this trope to present Euro-Americans as straggling settlers who appeared uninvited, but welcome nonetheless, in an already civilized territory. These writings suggested that some Mexican Americans did not want to be treated as equals with Euro-Americans in the territory; rather, they wanted to be treated with much more respect than Euro-Americans.

The term *native*, though, could be slippery. It did not always have a clear correlation to Mexicans alone, and some Euro-Americans bent the structures of the emerging identity by claiming it for themselves. Pat Garrett, who became famous for shooting Billy the Kid in 1881, declared his intention to run for mayor of Las Cruces in 1896. Garrett, despite his birth in Alabama, considered himself "un nativo."[43] Apparently Garrett's opponents played on the New Mexico regional identity to discredit his election bid. Drawing on the enmity between Mexicans and Euro-Americans in their neighboring state, Garrett's enemies named him a "Texan." The former sheriff addressed this label, noting, "Vds. sin duda en los venideros treinta días oirán no muy poco de la presunción de un 'Tejano' de hiel de venir aquí para gobernar los asuntos de su condado" (Without doubt you will hear in the next thirty days more than a lot about the presumption and gall of a 'Texan' coming here to govern the matters of this county).[44] Garrett's response muddied the "native" identity. "Señores," he stated, "Estoy listo para comparar registros con cualquier que cree que no soy nativo de esto hermoso país" (Gentlemen, I am ready to compare records with any who believes that I am not a native of this beautiful country).[45] Garrett did not use the regional native identity as a racial identity, unlike Mexican elites. Instead, he claimed it as a matter of contribution to the territory through actions. Garrett's idea of being a native New Mexican hinted at the older idea of Mexican nationalism that was based on performance and civic action. This type of slippage in the meaning of *native*, though, appeared infrequently.[46] More often, it replaced the earlier race-infused term *Mexican*. That association would be personified in the tenure of Miguel A. Otero as governor of New Mexico.

"Greasers," "Ignorant Gringos," and New Mexico's First "Native" Governor, 1897–1906

Mexican elites gained their greatest opportunity to influence regional New Mexican identity with the appointment of Otero as the territory's chief executive in 1897.[47] One of the consequences of New Mexico's territorial status was that its governors were appointed, in true colonial fashion, by the U.S. president and confirmed by Congress rather than elected by popular vote. During his administration President William McKinley often touted his commitment to "home rule for the territories."[48] McKinley's selection of Otero probably seemed like a comfortable means to fulfill that promise for New Mexico. Otero had ancestral links to the territory that preceded U.S. interests, but his eastern education and experiences with the federal government likely reassured those in Washington, D.C., who doubted a Mexican could govern.[49]

The approval of the president of the United States and Congress for Otero's position and public persona therefore afforded him, and wealthy Mexican Americans, a new authority in discussions about race, region, and nation. The governor consistently pointed to his steadfast U.S. nationalism as representing the inclinations of all native New Mexicans. Simultaneously, Otero and other members of the Mexican American elite worked to circumscribe competing visions of race and nation, particularly lingering elements of Mexican nationalism.

Shortly before his inauguration, Otero delivered a speech in which he named the importance of being the first "native" governor since the Treaty of Guadalupe Hidalgo. Although this speech was laden with racial implications, in it, he dissociated himself and the territory's population from the racial term *Mexican* through the new category of *native New Mexican*. Although this identity contained a racial sense as "not Anglo," it distanced the Mexican elite from Euro-American presumptions of their "foreignness."[50] Otero attempted to remake the territory's national significance:

> I am proud to return to my home and friends . . . as the Governor of our great territory—the first native born Governor of New Mexico. This marks a new epoch in our history. It is a proclamation from the President of the United States to the people of the whole world, that New Mexico has attained a condition of self control—that she has grown not only in wealth and in population, not only in natural development and physical elements of civili-

zation and advancement, but also in mental power and strength in self command and in self government.[51]

In this speech Otero claimed both that he was the embodiment of all native New Mexicans and that they, in turn, were the embodiments of the territory itself. Mexicans in New Mexico, he reasoned, had the attributes that Euro-Americans had once imagined themselves to monopolize: mental and physical strength, self-control, and, of course, civilization. In his presentation Mexicans had emerged from a colonized status to claim their place as full citizens in the nation.

Otero's inaugural address used a similar language as he framed the historical importance of his administration. Speaking before a vast crowd, he stated, "I am proud of the fact that I am a New Mexican. . . . I am proud that at last it has been recognized that in one of us may be embodied the principles of true American citizenship."[52] Avoiding the discussion of his status as Mexican, he named the significance of his appointment as proving "native patriotism." Those in the audience would have understood that his appointment had both racial and regional significance. It is not surprising, then, that Otero consistently claimed that his "greatest political ambition is to have New Mexico placed among the sisterhood of states worthy of being given every political privilege to which statehood will entitle it."[53] When he wrote his three-volume autobiography years later, he subtitled the second volume *Death Knell of a Territory and Birth of a State, 1882–1897*. Otero equated the titular "birth" as a state with his own appointment as governor in 1897 (New Mexico would not actually become a state until 1912). By his logic the territory was guaranteed statehood when he, a native, became the chief executive.

Influential Mexican Americans also applauded Otero's inauguration as a key step in proving natives' investment in American nationalism. One Mexican attorney, E. V. Chávez, extended his congratulations to the governor in the summer of 1897. Chávez, like other elite Mexican men, imagined Otero as a representative of his own racial and regional identities, referring to himself and Otero as "Spanish Americans." Chávez thus cast that racial identity as a unique part of the regional New Mexican identity: "It has been my earnest desire ever since I became a man that one of the great political parties of this nation should recognize in a proper manner that element of American citizens of our fair Territory generally designated as 'natives'; this has now been done by the appointment of a true Son of our soil to the highest office . . . in New Mexico."[54]

Chávez's language linked together patriarchal assumptions about citizenship and the region. It was when he became a man, he noted, that he saw the need for full citizenship. Further, Otero, as a "true *son*" of the territory, anticipated the full integration of native New Mexicans into the United States and their eventual release from their position as feminized colonial subjects.

Prominent members of the Euro-American elite also commented on Otero's role in the territorial government as racially significant. Offering sympathetic, though paternalistic, advice to Otero after his reappointment in 1901, a Euro-American from Washington, D.C., wrote to Otero about his duties as a native New Mexican. A. C. Campbell's letter, dispatched from nearly two thousand miles away, revealed how widespread the understanding of regional New Mexican identity had become. "You are looked upon as a leader of an advanced movement among the Native race in New Mexico," he wrote. "The hardest thing to combat is [the perception] that the 'Mexicans,' as the native race is termed, is not in harmony with American ideals."[55] The language used in this letter revealed changes in the way some eastern Euro-Americans imagined the people of New Mexico. Campbell privileged Otero's status as part of the "native race in New Mexico" as the authentic racial identity, implicitly hinting that reference to "Mexicans" was a less accurate term.[56] This preference suggested that native racial identity derived meaning from the local geography that was dissociated from the nation-state of Mexico.

Despite his universal endorsement as native, the new governor's personal history could have complicated his claims of being a typical New Mexican. Otero descended from one of the wealthiest families associated with the territory. Although his racial status as Mexican was unquestioned at the time, he had been born to a Mexican father and a Euro-American mother. In the first decades after the U.S.-Mexican War, some Euro-Americans predicted that intermarriage between Mexicans and Americans would result in the incorporation of those offspring as fully American. This did not come to fruition, nor did the United States develop a racial category for a racially mixed individual of Mexican and Euro-American descent. Rather, thinking about Mexicans as a racial group employed similar logic as those dictating African American racial identity, but it was never taken to such legal extremes in the case of Mexicans. *Mexican* became the default category for any person with any Mexican ancestry.

Aside from his maternal genealogy, Otero's claims to nativeness were further complicated by the fact that he had not spent much time in the territory. As the reference in his inaugural speech to "returning to my home and friends" suggests, he spent most of his life outside of New Mexico, making even more problematic his claims of being the first native governor.[57] Regardless of those counterfactors, newspapers and other public writings named him the quintessential native New Mexican.

Even before his inauguration on June 14, 1897, Otero and his supporters had consciously encouraged the use of *New Mexican* to construct the public image of the new governor. Newspapers like the *Santa Fe New Mexican* substantiated Otero's claims by printing stories that linked his family to administrators during Spain's imperial rule.[58] Invocation of New Mexico's colonial past became a common means by which elite Mexicans could upgrade their racial and social status. Mexicans like Otero traced their origins to racially "pure" Spanish conquistadores who first brought civilization and Christianity to the territory. At the same time, prominent Mexican Americans rarely mentioned New Mexico's history under Mexico's jurisprudence or acknowledged claims to Mexican identity as a national (as opposed to racial) identity.[59]

A year after his inauguration, Otero's office released an official biographical sketch with a vision of his family history that can only be described as fantastical, linking him to conquistadors like Hernán Cortéz. This 1897 biography even claimed that one of his ancestors was a "prominent and leading citizen" in Santa Fe since 1605, meaning that his forefather would have been critical to the town five years before its founding.[60] Reimagining personal and territorial history in these ways accomplished three objectives. First, it connected New Mexico's natives to a romanticized mission of colonizing the territory. As we have seen, notions of colonizers bringing civilization had important racial and social implications during this period. Along the same lines, the regional identity's links to the colonial past also implied a type of whiteness through the appeal to pure Spanish/European blood. Finally, it also granted native New Mexicans a claim to govern the territory because of their historical lineages. Native New Mexicans considered their ancestors' presence in the territory hundreds of years before the founding of the United States as sufficient rebuttal to Euro-Americans' claim to the same territory.

If native identity was built on colonial ideologies, Otero's vision excluded the indigenous population as equally native New Mexican or American. For the Mexican elite it was their relationship to the rest of the nation, not indigenous peoples, that constituted the most salient issue in the regional identity. A speech delivered by Otero to commemorate the

Rough Riders in 1899, for instance, adamantly configured local Mexicans as Americans while excepting indigenous people from full participation in the nation. The speech lambasted racist congressional objections against making New Mexico a state but expressed the governor's own racist beliefs about American Indians.

Otero balked at easterners, whom he saw as "forgetful of the fact that nine-tenths at least of the class [Mexicans] thus so unjustly and un-blushingly decreed, are born citizens of the United States and are . . . entitled by birth to all the rights and privileges of such citizenship."[61] Only the Mexican population in the territory, however, deserved congressional salvation according to the speech. Compared to those natives, the indigenous populations were "savages" and undeserving. He particularly complained about accusations that Mexicans were "illiterate." The governor declared that the United States Congress had done nothing to help native New Mexicans build schools "while millions almost have been spent in supporting indolence the brutal savages of the Territory and in futile efforts to Civilize and educate them." He drew a firm line between Mexicans, who he admitted needed education but were Americans nonetheless, and "brutal savages" who could never attain civilized status because of their race.[62]

In a similar vein romantic tales from Spain's past figured in the governor's commitment to obtaining statehood for New Mexico. As the most prominent spokesperson for the territory, Otero boldly asserted the superiority of New Mexico's colonial history over other areas in the United States. When the governor gave a speech at an official White House function, he used the opportunity to inform his Euro-American audience about New Mexico's unique place in the national history. Although the event was intended to celebrate the White House's centennial, Otero practically dismissed the Executive Mansion as a recent novelty compared to the venerable Governor's Palace in Santa Fe. After a few obligatory remarks about the glories of the Capitol, he reminded his audience that U.S. history appeared brief when contrasted to New Mexico's:

> During the century which this celebration commemorates, this beautiful city [Washington, D.C.] and the building in which we are have been the vital centers of all the marvelous growth of the nation. . . . At that time the Executive Office of the Territory I represent was venerable with age and rich with history. It is that known as the "Old Palace," and has been occupied longer than any other building in America as the seat of government. Since 1540 [sic] Santa Fe has been the capital city of the Kingdom, Province,

District, and Territory of New Mexico, and its palace which was built in 1598 [*sic*] has been occupied by the Viceroys, Captains General, and Governors.[63]

Tales about the ancient palace must have left a strong impression on his audience, even if the governor did not get the historical details exactly correct. By laying claim to the oldest seat of government in the United States, Otero highlighted Mexicans' governance over the territory as predating even the founding of the United States. As mentioned, congressional leaders frequently argued that Mexicans could not self-govern as a justification for keeping New Mexico a territory. Otero's history lesson, therefore, would have had significant resonance.

The governor imagined and accepted the existence of a racial difference between Mexicans and Anglos, but he discounted the proposition that racial difference precluded the former from full American citizenship. During an interview given near the end of his term, Otero emphasized local Mexicans' suitability for republican participation. "The 'Mexican' as you call him," Otero stated, "is a first class citizen today and is quite well posted on public affairs concerning the territory."[64] The governor highlighted the image of New Mexico's Mexicans as exceptional Americans by downplaying their interests in anything outside of the United States. The typical native New Mexican, Otero claimed, was "too busy making a living, and has to work too hard" to be invested in "foreign affairs." Otero went on to note that the native New Mexican "takes great interest in domestic politics but beyond that bothers himself very little concerning the name of the Emperor of Japan, or whom King Alfonso [of Spain] will marry."[65] Dissociating Mexicans from world affairs severed their association with eternal "foreignness." Interestingly, Otero implied that a true mark of being American was a narrow interest in domestic affairs and obliviousness to the larger world.

The governor frequently bristled against the Mexican/American dichotomy that had divided the territory since midcentury. Writing in English to a prominent Mexican in the territory, he scorned the marking of divisions between natives and Americans. "I make no distinction between what you term 'American' and 'Natives,'" he noted. "I believe we are all Americans and I very much dislike to have any distinction made in this particular."[66] Years after he had finished his service as governor, Otero would push this vision of absolute American identity even further, disdaining efforts to create a Mexican American identity. Writing to congratulate a Mexican academic on a widely printed speech, Otero opined that the American national identity should trump all "hyphenated" identities. He wrote: "Like you, I cannot gather much comfort in patriotism of the PURE TYPE through any hyphenated citizenship. What this country wants in every state of the union is the 'True Blue American,' no matter from what country his forefathers may have sprung. Your well worded, timely and able address should be translated and read in both languages in every school in the State of New Mexico."[67] Otero wanted American nationalism to eliminate the need to name racial markers. At the same time, he did not see speaking Spanish as particularly problematic to claims of being American, as he advocated translating the text for the Spanish-speaking population. For him that nonhyphenated American identity did not imply that one also needed to adopt Euro-American cultural markers.

Letters exchanged between Otero and his son, Miguel Otero III, offer clues in assessing the limits to the New Mexican identity. Otero III had enjoyed some celebrity as the young son of the governor.[68] In 1906 Governor Otero decided to send Miguel to South Bend, Indiana, to attend the University of Notre Dame, his own alma mater. From there young Miguel kept a regular correspondence with his father that detailed his shock and dismay at leaving the safety of New Mexico. Otero had configured New Mexican identity as a means by which Mexicans could be incorporated into an American national identity, but his son's letters from Notre Dame also revealed boundaries Otero had placed on American cultural elements over Mexican and New Mexican traditions. "I have been miserable because you wouldn't let people call me Mike," Miguel wrote his father. "Nobody can pernounce [sic] my name. They call me 'Otero' etc. It makes me mad."[69] More than a mere dispute between a parent and his son, this subtle communication suggests the governor's own thinking and ideas about his racial and regional identity. Otero might have praised certain Euro-American cultural practices, but he did not intend to allow his own family to abandon elements that he believed made them distinctly New Mexican. Even though the correspondence between father and son took place in English, the governor still deemed his son's desire to modify his name to "Mike" too great an infringement on his (and his family's) identity.

Miguel's other complaints about life at the Catholic university suggest the geographical specificity of racial categories. In New Mexico economic class played an important part in articulating native identity. The young Miguel's life in the governor's palace and his family's ranch seems to have shielded him from any overt racism while in the territory. In Indiana that elite status did not register in the minds of many of his Euro-

American classmates. For these peers Miguel was merely a "greaser," son of a governor or not.[70] Miguel's letters to his father expressed dismay at his fellow students' "ignorance" of the proper meaning of his own racial and class status:

> A Mexican or *"greaser"* as they call it is the last people on earth to these ignorant *"gringos"* here. They think greaser is the correct word for us. A kid at our table was blowing about them and I said, Now look here have you any idea what a greaser as you call it is? He said yes I do, they are Mexicans, I said, your [*sic*] a liar, the correct pernunciation [*sic*] for a *"greaser"* is a low class of dirty ignorant Mexican people. He said if that was so why did they call them greasers? And I said, because you don't know any better. That settled his hash and he didn't say any more. I have had several disputes about kids calling me greaser. I don't like this school very much.[71]

Miguel's notion that his fellow students were simply ignorant about the "true" meaning of the term *greaser* suggests that his elite status enabled his participation in the New Mexican identity.

The types of racial knowledge that he and his Euro-American peers had differed in many, though not all, ways. Miguel identified with being Mexican and understood that identity as a racial category. His naming of his fellow students with the equally racially charged name of *gringos* suggested that he also imagined a clear divide between his racial identity and theirs. However, the way Miguel imagined Mexican identity differed from his classmates and involved issues of economic class. Notre Dame's Euro-American students made no distinction about whom they should label "greaser." For them the term had meaning only as a name for anyone who had a Mexican body. Miguel, on the other hand, opposed his Notre Dame colleagues calling *him* "greaser" but did not object to the term per se. Miguel's willingness to redirect the racist term based on his economic status hints at the class tensions that existed within New Mexico's Mexican population.

Miguel's shock at being labeled with the racist term *greaser* also suggests that some changes had transpired under his father's administration. Only nine years earlier, Governor Otero had been forced to address the use of the term *greaser* when it appeared embedded in official government documents. During a minor scandal, which erupted when Miguel was only five years old, Otero's office had quickly reproduced an army report on New Mexico without having read the text. Much to Otero's embarrassment, the author of the report harshly criticized the Mexican population, called them greasers, and questioned their ability to serve as

U.S. citizens and jurors.[72] Otero instantly wrote a letter of apology for the report, confessing that he had not actually read it until after it had been released. In his letter Otero took the opportunity to grapple with the term *greaser*. The term had no place within New Mexico, he warned, and it threatened the racial harmony that many believed was unique to the territory. "Were [the author of the report] alive today," Otero wrote, "I have no doubt he would frankly confess the error into which so many newcomers fall—especially in the use of the word 'Greaser,' which I have never heard except in the States, or by very late comers to the Territory."[73] As is suggested by this invocation of "the States" as an area culturally distinct from New Mexico, Otero cast the racist language as something "outside" of the territory's geographic boundaries. Eventually "new comers," Otero implied, stopped using racist language once they realized the racial harmony that he purported to exist within New Mexico. In this instance Otero used the circulating language of a bicultural New Mexico in an effort to undermine the perpetuation of racist language. Given Miguel's shock at being labeled a "greaser," it seems attitudes in the territory changed enough that the term was not frequently applied to elite Mexicans—or at least not expressed to Miguel Otero III. Still, the term certainly circulated and was even used by Mexican elites like Otero's son.

Beyond his family, Miguel Otero's rhetoric and vision of New Mexico proved immensely popular at both the local and the national level. He achieved not only a second term as governor (something none of his U.S.-era predecessors had managed) but even an unthinkable third appointment to the office.[74] Much of Otero's success resulted from his embracing of the emerging New Mexican identity. As prominent Euro-Americans and Mexican Americans looked to define the racial and national meaning of "New Mexican" identity, Otero crafted an image of himself as the living embodiment of what it meant to be a native of that place.[75]

Otero's strategies would be continued by a successor who used similar arguments about natives as he pursued his own political ambition. The Mexican politician Octaviano Ambrosio Larrazolo became another important symbol of the bridging between Mexicans and the rest of the nation after New Mexico achieved statehood in 1912. Even more than Otero, Larrazolo's personal history suggested that New Mexico's population was more deeply implicated in transnational exchanges than the regional rhetoric implied. Larrazolo was born in Chihuahua in 1859, migrated to Arizona in the 1870s to study with Tucson's Bishop Salpointe, and eventually followed the cleric to Santa Fe in 1875. Larrazolo appeared as a frequent political candidate in New Mexico, winning the governorship in 1918, and ultimately becoming the first Mexican to be elected to the U.S. Senate in 1928. Despite his birth in Mexico, Larrazolo took on a native New Mexican identity just as had Otero.[76]

As the regional discourse increasingly highlighted Spain's colonial history in New Mexico, local communities became equally interested in publicly commemorating those events in ways not previously seen in New Mexico. In 1907 Larrazolo addressed one such Albuquerque commemoration celebrating the conquistador Francisco Vásquez de Coronado's expedition into New Mexico. In his speech Larrazolo named Mexicans as "the native people of New Mexico" and called on those "from other states in this Union" to spread the message about New Mexicans' heroic history and nationalist commitment throughout the United States.[77] As testimony to that nationalism, Larrazolo created a narrative that connected contemporary Mexicans with Spain's missionaries, as well with former U.S. soldiers. He urged his audience to tell other Americans "that these people have lived under the rule of kings, of emperors, of triumvirs, of military dictators, and finally under the flags of two republics, that through all the vicissitudes of their varied existence they have ever been true and faithful citizens."

Moreover, he emphasized that Mexicans had participated in and supported U.S. expansion in other contexts, noting that "some of the best and proudest blood of New Mexico was spilt in the far distant Philippines in the defense of the flag." Pointing to Mexicans' participation in the Spanish-American War had significant implications for race and gender. Proexpansionist leaders (including Albert Beveridge) had argued that the "childlike" Filipinos needed mature white American men to civilize them and prepare them for self-government.[78] Inserting Mexicans into the battle for the Philippines, therefore, connoted their manhood and nationalism as American colonizers. Larrazolo concluded by directly challenging the dominant national perception of Mexicans. "Tell them," he implored his audience, "that we are not a race of degenerate and ignorant people, but that we are fully abreast of our time." In this way Larrazolo used the same type of language as Otero and other members of the elite to create a regionally specific version of Mexican racial identity that was not at odds with American national identity. He also directly countered the imagining of New Mexico as an anachronistic space by insisting that Mexicans were "fully abreast of our time."

Despite his own birth in Chihuahua, Larrazolo inserted himself as representing the "native" community that he envisioned as both racial and regionally specific. Community leaders dissociated the territory from the Mexican republic even in instances when an individual, like Larrazolo, migrated across the borderline. Even a "foreign" birth could be ignored or forgotten under the rubric of a regional, native New Mexican identity, assuming one was of the right economic class.

Un hijo nativo: Benjamín Read's "New Mexican" History, 1890–1912

While Otero served as the most visible public symbol of the regional identity, a small circle of intellectuals also began to write prolifically on "native New Mexican" identity. Although he never captured the public's imagination as had Otero, Benjamín Read gained the respect of elite men like L. Bradford Prince and Octaviano Larrazolo by producing substantial histories that articulated a conception of being native New Mexican.

Read was born in Las Cruces on September 20, 1853, the son of a Euro-American father and a Mexican mother.[79] After his father died, around his third birthday, Read identified most with his mother's family and the larger Mexican American community.[80] His mother moved to Santa Fe, in northern New Mexico, where Archbishop Lamy took a personal interest in the Cruceño's development. Purchasing the youth's textbooks and ensuring his attendance at St. Michael's College in Santa Fe, Lamy gave Read opportunities unavailable to most Mexicans in New Mexico.[81]

While still a young man, Read held a variety of influential positions. He worked as the private secretary and translator to two territorial governors; he served as the superintendent of schools in Santa Fe; he held his own law practice; and he won election to the New Mexico legislature, eventually serving as Speaker of the House.[82] These professional accomplishments impressed his contemporaries, but it was Read's desire to write a comprehensive "Neo-Mexicano" chronicle that brought his peers' greatest praise. Read named the territory's history as exceptional within the United States and distanced it from any association with the modern Mexican nation-state. From the 1890s Read began collecting and translating a massive assortment of materials from Spanish to English (and vice versa, as he published in both languages). He eventually printed, at his own expense, several works documenting his vision of the territory's history. A crucial part of his project, he claimed, was to provide histories "por un hijo nativo de Nuevo México" to balance the biased and inaccurate stories about the territory.[83] Read explained why he wrote about New Mexico in his 1910 *Guerra México-Americana.* "Si con mis insignificantes escritos se realiza mi ideal," Read wrote, "redundando ellos en honor de verdad y honra de los hijos de Nuevo México, quedarán mis deseos ampliamente recompensados" (If with my insignificant writings my ideal is realized, returning honor to the sons of New Mexico and the honor of the truth, my wishes will remain amply compensated).[84]

Read's accounts won him the highest accolades from prominent Euro-Americans and Mexican Americans throughout the territory. In one circular advertising his *History of New Mexico,* Read received endorsements from public figures such as the French archbishop of Santa Fe, Juan B. Pitaval, Octaviano Larrazolo, and L. Bradford Prince.[85] Those who praised Read revealed that they merged ideas about racial and regional identities. They configured New Mexican identity, in other words, in terms of geography and corporeality. New Mexicans had distinctive racial characteristics shared only with those from the region. Read published many congratulatory letters sent to him from members of the educated elite in his *Illustrated History of New Mexico.* Such homage came from one Manuel Otero (probably unrelated to Governor Miguel Otero), a low-ranking public official who described Read's work as a "benefit of our race." Otero identified "our race" as "every true and loyal descendant of the Castillian race."[86] Likewise, Aurelio Espinosa, a linguist, praised Read's work as an "honor and benefit of the New Mexican people." Espinosa, too, made clear in his letter that he understood "New Mexican people" as implying a particular racial meaning. "Your work deserves a thousand eulogies," he wrote, "on account of the great and merited value and weight (unnoticed by others) which you give our race in the conquest, colonization and social organization of the Territory."[87] Only those considered racially Mexican counted as the "New Mexican people" in Espinosa's letter. Yet the New Mexican identity also made the meaning of Mexican racial identity murky.

By the turn of the century, as these accolades suggest, not a few well-to-do Mexican Americans accepted elements of the Euro-American discourse that named them a racially distinct group. They recast that racial status, however, by imagining that their bodies manifested racial traits shared only with other native New Mexicans. Being native, therefore, meant more to Read and his readers than simply one's birth location or residency in New Mexico. Native status implied an ownership and hereditary entitlement to the territory.

Yet Read's own identification as native was not necessarily clear-cut.

Like Otero, Read had one Mexican parent and one Anglo parent. Like Larrazolo, Read differed from other Mexicans whose ancestors had lived in New Mexico at the time of the Treaty of Guadalupe Hidalgo. Read's maternal grandfather, the wealthy Ignacio Cano, had migrated to New Mexico directly from Sonora, Mexico, in the mid-nineteenth century. Despite the notion that "native New Mexican" implied a historic lineage to that particular place, Read's own family tree was just one generation into residency in New Mexico. Though this genealogy threatened to make him "foreign," Read considered himself (and nobody seemed to challenge it) a native.

Indeed, Read often refused the racialized term *Mexican* as a description of himself or the people of New Mexico.[88] In his Spanish-language text *Guerra México-Americana*, Read deployed a variety of expressions to avoid referring to the people of New Mexico as "mejicanos." He used terms ranging from "Neo-Mejicanos" to "los habitantes de Nuevo México" or even "los abandonados descendientes de Oñate, Otermin y De Vargas."[89] The parade of alternative names for the local people of New Mexico stood in contrast to Read's references to neighboring states like Texas or Chihuahua. When discussing these states, Read referred simply to "mejicanos."[90] Read's intentionally convoluted language emphasized an imagined difference between New Mexico and other areas across the U.S.-Mexican border. Rather than directly challenge Euro-American racist ideas about Mexican identity, Read attempted to distinguish the regional New Mexican identity from the earlier language that had defined Mexicans as incompatible with American nationalism. Like other participants in the regional discourse, he frequently claimed that the "sons of New Mexico" descended directly from the "first Spaniards who conquered New Mexico."[91]

Otero, Larrazolo, and Read all shared a common theme in their discussions about New Mexican identity: each put forward the idea that Mexicans and Euro-Americans agreed about the markers of "civilization" that distinguished them as colonizers rather than the colonized. Asserting Spain's imperial past as a critical part of New Mexico's present was a means for making local Mexicans ongoing agents in—and not subjects of—imperialism. These men frequently reminded their audiences that Spaniards were the first to bring Christianity, "stability," "civilization," and "order" to the region and the "savage heathens" in this hemisphere.[92]

Euro-Americans' and Mexican Americans' promotion of Spanish identity was a critical part of their larger claims about New Mexico's suitability for statehood and full incorporation into the nation. Spanish identity

efore did not make sense without the accompanying discussion of
v Mexico's "uniqueness." When discussing the U.S. invasion of New
xico, Read called Euro-Americans "extranjeros" (foreigners).[93] By re-
......nding readers that it was Euro-Americans who migrated to New Mexico—not (New) Mexicans—this language inverted Euro-Americans' accusations that Mexicans were too "foreign" to be part of the United States.

The solid divide between Spanish and Mexican identities, however, did
not always appear consistently. Evidence suggests that nineteenth-
century claims to Spanishness were not universal and that they might
have been limited to the upper class. Indeed, some nonelite citizens
continued to claim a Mexican identity. A single individual could even
name the local population as Mexican, Spanish, and native within the
same discussion. In a 1904 letter to the editor of Las Cruces's *El Labrador*,
for instance, P. Pino de Huerta referred to Mexicans as both "hispano-
americanos" and "mexicanos" interchangeably.[94] Articulations of Mexicans' racial identity circulated unevenly and cannot be assumed to have
been consistent. In this way Read and like-minded Mexicans worked to
dissociate themselves from the Mexican nation-state for more complicated reasons than a mere desire for whiteness. Because this assertion of
Spanish identity had greater importance when directed to a Euro-American readership, claims to being Spanish American appeared more frequently in English-language texts, with *mexicano* lingering as a common
term in Spanish-language texts. More often, Mexicans like Read preferred ambiguous references such as "our race" or "native New Mexican."

For New Mexicans to appear as an identifiable group, then, they also
had to be distinct from Mexican nationals. Read argued that native New
Mexicans had never participated in the Mexican nation-state because of
their relative geographic "isolation." This isolation led New Mexicans to
have a universal inclination to join the United States and to feel no sense
of Mexican nationalism.[95] Commenting on the U.S. invasion of New
Mexico, Read recast the Mexicans' response as an eager embrace of U.S.
imperialism. He stated that historical events "que vinieron dando por resultado la frialdad de los habitantes del territorio hacía su madre patria, y,
en último resultado, su anexión voluntaria a la Unión Americana" (came
as a result of the inhabitants' coldness to what their mother country was
doing and ultimately resulted in their voluntary annexation to the American Union).[96] At the conclusion of his book Read wrote that "por causa de
ese aislamiento y abandono, apoderándose de ellos una indiferencia, re-
specto de su amor patrio, hasta el grado de casi anhelar la intervención del
gobierno Americano" (on account of this isolation and abandonment,

indifference seized them in regards to their love of country to the degree of almost longing for the intervention of the American government).[97]

It was not enough, of course, for Read to disavow Mexican nationalism on behalf of the territory. In many of his other works Read wrote obsessively about New Mexicans' "innate sense" of American patriotism. One of his English-language texts asserted that New Mexicans had collectively chosen to cast their lot with the invaders because they never felt any sense of Mexican nationalism. That decision, moreover, brought "the happiness and higher civilization of the inhabitants" once they joined the United States.[98] Consequently, any resistance to the invading United States Army had to have originated outside New Mexico. Read implicitly endorsed the Euro-American characterization of Mexicans in Mexico as degraded and uncivilized, but he also claimed that *New* Mexicans had been rescued from that degradation through their territory's incorporation into the United States.

For Read every major historical event provided an opportunity to expound on the U.S. nationalism of New Mexicans. In his hands the Civil War became a defining moment for the territory's patriotism. Recall that Charles Miller's thesis about the Civil War insisted that Mexicans had acted out of blind instinct and vengeance. In contrast to this prevailing narrative, Read argued in his *Popular Elementary History of New Mexico* that Mexicans had joined the war out of a lofty devotion to the Union. Native New Mexicans, Read argued, "unhesitatingly threw themselves into the field of honor."[99] The discussion of the Spanish-American War became a similar opportunity to highlight U.S. national identity. "The sons of New Mexico," Read wrote, "who went to that war were all descendants from the first Spaniards who conquered New Mexico, and it was but natural to expect that they should at least cherish in their hearts, the natural sympathy inherent in persons of the same race."[100] However, Read continued, native New Mexicans had in fact shown an unmatched devotion for the United States when they choose to expand the country's colonial possessions, even to the extent of fighting against their own race. Read thus imagined Spanish identity as racially and regionally specific but never in opposition to U.S. national identity. On the contrary, he celebrated New Mexicans' sacrifices to the United States, noting that New Mexico sent "to the field of battle more soldiers, in proportion to their population, than any State in the Union."[101] He consistently argued that American national identity proved more important to native New Mexicans than racial solidarity or any allegiance to Mexico or Spain.

Neither Euro-Americans nor Mexican Americans confused the contemporary Spanish identity with the idea that being "Spanish" was racially the same as being "Anglo." Indeed, in many Spanish-language texts there was not a clear divide between *hispanos* and *mejicanos*, but there was absolute clarity that Anglos were neither. The Cruceño Pino de la Huerta did not distinguish between Spanish and Mexican, but he was certain that Mexicans differed racially from "la raza anglo-sajona" (the Anglo-Saxon race) and also "los Judíos" (the Jews). Pino de la Huerta's use of the categories "Hispano," "Anglo-Saxon," and "Jew" reveals the patterns of differential racialization in southern New Mexico.[102] Though he drew a line between Jews and Anglo-Americans, he accused the two groups of conspiring to deprive Mexicans of their rights, playing upon anti-Semitism to justify his position:

> Ahora bien, un Judío goza de todos los privilegios de ciudadano, y ¿porqué no? Nos fijamos acaso los hispano-americanos en que los padres de estos mismos Judíos crucificaron a nuestro Redentor diez y nueve siglos pasados? No por cierto. No se acusará que nosotros hemos iniciado este espíritu de intolerancia que está en pugna con los principios fundamentales de nuestra constitución Americana.[103]

> (Now a Jew enjoys all the privileges of citizenship, and why not? Do we Spanish-Americans pay attention to the fact that the ancestors of these Jews crucified our Redeemer nine or ten centuries ago? Certainly not. We will not be accused of inciting the spirit of intolerance that conflicts with the fundamental principles of our American Constitution.)

In this instance distinctions between Spanish and Mexican were not as important to the author as distinguishing Mexicans from other racial groups. Pino de la Huerta created a racial hierarchy that placed Mexicans above Jews because of their religion. Whatever the actual status of Jewish people, the figure of "Jews" had long played an important role in determining rights and racial identity in Europe and Latin America. Recall that Spain's complicated caste system had medieval precursors that merged genealogical and religious associations. Perhaps we can read Pino de la Huerta's discussion of Jews as the twentieth-century reformulation of such notions, inflected with contemporary ideas about race and nation. For this Mexican American, religious and racial identities still intertwined and mattered in the nation. In the larger United States, many Protestant Euro-Americans also perceived "Jews" as a threat to the social order and morality.[104] If even the racially suspect ("not quite white") and religiously heterodox Jews could be full citizens, Pino de la

Huerta argued, then the exclusion of fully Christian *hispano-americanos* was especially outrageous.

Read shared a common goal with his Mexican contemporaries: to prove that a distinct racial identity did not conflict with American national identity. Rather, they claimed that their racial and national identity emerged from the specificity of their region. In imagining the history of that region, Read depicted New Mexico as culturally, racially, politically, and even spatially at odds with the Mexican republic. Like other characteristics of his writing, this element of Read's narrative anticipated many later formulaic histories. He seamlessly charted natives' development through Spain's Christian missionary work, to their disavowal of Mexican citizenship at the time of the war, culminating in their military service for the United States in the Civil and Spanish-American wars.

Despite his wide praise among an educated elite, Read's work never captured the popular imagination or even circulated beyond a small social circle. Even his triumphal obituary in the *New Mexico Historical Review* noted that his work "hardly struck a popular chord."[105] His many writings, though, provide opportunities to explore the intricate decisions that individuals made during the development of a regional New Mexican identity and the rise of a regionally specific racial identity.[106]

Strategies for Biculturalism

Mexicans like Otero and Read did not write histories or editorials about New Mexico as entertainment or only because of their intellectual curiosity. They used ideas about a bicultural regional identity as part of a strategy that would affirm Mexican Americans' full citizenship locally and nationally. Read made explicit links between native nationalism and their entitlement to fair treatment under the law in an editorial in the *Santa Fe El Nuevo Mexicano*:

> Nuestra gente ha sido tratada tan vilmente desde que el territorio fué incorporado a la nación americana, que desde entonces hemos estado nosotros y los que nos precedieron constantemente ocupados en refutar asaltos inmotivados, injustos, crueles y cobardes. La prueba de la buena ciudadanía se halla en el verdadero patriotismo. ¿Ha dado el pueblo nativo esa prueba? Que responda la historia.[107]

(Our people have been treated so vilely since this territory was incorporated into the American nation, since then we and those who preceded us have been occupied in refuting unmotivated, unjust, cruel and cowardly assaults. The proof of good citizenship is in true patriotism. Have the native people provided this proof? Let history respond.)

Another of his editorials, printed in the December 1, 1911, edition of a Wagon Mound newspaper echoed these sentiments. Critiquing "Los así llamados Americanos (the so-called Americans)," the author demanded that local Mexicans be recognized as equal citizens. He wrote, "Somos Americanos verdaderos todo el sentido de la palabra" (We are true Americans in every sense of the word).[108] Read's nationalism did not blind him to the inequities that Mexicans faced in New Mexico. For many Mexicans the territory did not yet exist as a racial utopia where all were "unitedly engaged in advancing the prosperity, and working for the magnificent future of the Territory."[109]

Prominent Mexican Americans saw the regional identity as a means to ensure the continuation of their own cultural practices, which had been under attack since Euro-Americans arrived. They argued that it was their presence that made the territory exceptional in the United States, and therefore means should be taken to preserve their cultural expressions, most critically the Spanish language. Circumstances in neighboring Arizona could only have made New Mexico's Mexicans more anxious about the issue. Both Arizona and New Mexico attained statehood at the same time in 1912. Yet at the moment that Arizona became a state, Euro-Americans there passed laws that denied the vote to any person unable to "read the Constitution of the U.S. in the English language."[110] Such measures implicitly demanded that English be the exclusive language of public institutions and marker of full citizenship. It is small wonder that New Mexico's Spanish-language newspapers printed editorials and letters from members of the Mexican elite demanding that local residents continue to use and build their Spanish skills. One author lamented that Euro-Americans' arrival had corrupted New Mexican Spanish and offered proof that it had changed considerably since 1848: "Cuando entraron los americanos," the author noted, "el español se cambió más y más, púes palabras y estilos ingleses fueron introducidos" (When the Americans entered, Spanish changed more and more, as English words and styles were introduced).[111] After offering examples of such "barbarismos" (barbarisms) in New Mexican Spanish, the author concluded:

¿Qué podemos hacer para purificar el español que hablan? En mi opinión mía la mejor cosa para hacerlo sería, que demandemos que intrucción [*sic*] en español sea dada por todos los maestras mexicanos del territorio, y que pongamos libros de los mejores autores españoles en el alance de los jóvenes.[112]

(What can we do to purify the Spanish they [young people] speak? In my own opinion, the best thing to do is that we seriously demand instruction in Spanish to be given by all the Mexican teachers in the territory and that we put books from the best Spanish authors in the hands of the youth.)

The author of this editorial expected that the territory's public schools would maintain Spanish in the territory, an idea that was quite popular among almost all Mexican Americans.

Another such article made the link between Spanish and Mexicans' sense of identity more direct. *El Eco del Valle* printed in 1909, "El idioma [español] es el símbolo de la raza," the author wrote; "el idioma es el lazo que nos une hoy a ese mundo poderoso que germinó por los esfuerzos de los antepasados, y que hoy constituye los pueblos del porvenir" (The [Spanish] language is a symbol of the race; the language is the link that connects us to that powerful world that germinated from the ancestors' efforts, and that today constitutes the people of the future).[113]

Mexicans' approaches to maintaining Spanish, though, differed. Some resisted efforts of "English-only" by claiming that everybody, regardless of race, should use multiple languages to reflect New Mexico's biculturalism. Benjamín Read lamented, "Es una verdadera lástima que, ya que el inglés y el castellano están destinado a ser, quizás por siglos, las lenguas dominantes en América, sean tan pocos los que de nuestra raza aprenden el inglés, como los de habla inglesa que hablan nuestra lengua" (It is truly sad that, while English and Spanish are destined to be, perhaps for centuries, the dominant languages in America, there are few of our race that know English, or those who speak English that speak our language).[114] Other members of the Mexican American elite took bolder positions and tested the limits of the supposed inclusiveness of the bicultural discourse.

In 1898 the Mexican American superintendent of public education, M. C. de Baca, intervened in the sensitive debate over language. For the first time in the territory's history he required that primary-school teachers have proficiency in both English and Spanish as a condition for employment, stating that law and customs mandated instruction in two languages.[115] "The teacher should have a knowledge of both languages," Baca wrote in an open letter, "in order that he might make himself understood to all his pupils and also in order that he might be able to use Spanish books adopted by the territorial board of education."[116] To give his decision the force of law, Baca interpreted the territorial legal codes in a crafty manner. He acknowledged that no specific provision required that teachers instruct Spanish, but he construed the wording of an existing statute to his advantage:

> Section 1520, of the compiled laws of 1897, provides "That it shall be the duty of the superintendent of public instruction to recommend the most approved text books, in English or English and Spanish, for the common schools of the territory after the same have been adopted by the territorial board of education, etc.," in view of the fact that the said territorial board of education adopted text books in Spanish and in English it becomes the duty of teachers to use said books in the public schools and therefore, the teaching of the Spanish language is compulsory.[117]

Baca and the territorial school board's adoption of both English-language and Spanish-language books, he argued, required that students and teachers needed to know both to participate in the territory. For Baca, New Mexico's biculturalism required more than a tacit acknowledgment of Mexicans' presence. He expected that the territory would provide institutional support to Mexican customs and that Euro-Americans would adopt some of those cultural performances.

Most Euro-Americans hardly found Baca or his fellow Mexican Americans' efforts at enforcing Spanish within the territory amusing. Many Euro-Americans even accused local Mexicans of willfully refusing to learn English. Some postulated that Mexicans feigned a lack of competency with the language to frustrate their employers. The Las Cruces rancher Edith Nicholl stated: "The native woman has an inveterate objection to learning English. She often understands it, as can be proved somewhat disagreeably on occasion; but she will deny such an accusation with her latest breath. A shriek of 'No sabe! no sabe!' [*sic*] and a frantic waving of hands, greets the mild but firm insistence that she understands the language of her country."[118] We might read a complicated set of strategies at play between Nicholl and her Mexican servants. Their adamant claims that they would not learn English not only suggests their desire to retain Spanish but also that they were probably avoiding tasks that they found unreasonable. By pretending an inability to understand the request made of them, they could decline without being forced into making an outright refusal that might cost them their job.

From Nicholl's perspective, however, the refusal to learn English stood as a testament against Mexicans' commitment to the United States. This discussion of her Mexican housekeeper noted that the language of "her country," the United States, was English, and that she should therefore learn it. In another section Nicholl expressed her frustration that Spanish remained the dominate language in the territory. She predicted that less-seasoned newcomers to New Mexico would "break out in a tirade against a Constitution which permits such lapses from commonsense in its code of citizenship, etc."[119] She also suggested that many American employers found only frustration when they insisted that their Mexican American employees learn "the language of their own country—the American [*sic*]."[120] Clearly, Mexicans and Euro-Americans were sharply divided over the future role of Spanish in the bicultural region.

Within a few years Euro-Americans had taken control of the school superintendent position from Baca and redoubled their efforts to claim the territory as an English-speaking place regardless of what they also claimed about bicultural harmony. One of Superintendent Baca's Euro-American successors took the dominance of English as his personal goal. Hiram Hadley (who also served as the president of New Mexico A&M college, in Las Cruces) bemoaned the resistance that he faced from Mexicans throughout the territory. Hadley ranted in a personal letter: "I am most anxious about the counties in which the native [Mexican] people largely dominate. I think I know what is best for them, but there is a certain amount of race prejudice to overcome, and whilst they insist on having native teachers who are poorly qualified and *will* use the Spanish language in the schools, those counties who employ English-speaking teachers well qualified are getting far ahead of those who do not."[121] Hadley's letter suggested that most Euro-Americans did not yield their control over which cultural markers would survive in New Mexico. In paternalistic fashion Hadley ignored the obvious Mexican American desire to retain Spanish by insisting that he knew "what is best for them."[122] He measured students' success by their mastery of English rather than their retention of Spanish, which he saw as "being behind."

Beyond manifesting these ethnocentric assumptions, though, Hadley's letter also exposed the fragility of Euro-Americans' position in the newly emerging New Mexican identity. Baca had already proved that Mexicans could use Euro-American institutions, such as public schools, to fulfill their own expectations for New Mexico, at least in the short term. Some Euro-Americans feared an upending of the racial hierarchy that would undermine their imagined place as the "dominant race" in the region. Hadley himself described the backlash against Euro-American control as "race prejudice." Even as Hadley and his fellow Euro-Americans wielded their power against Mexican Americans, many believed they had some-

how become victims of unfair "native prejudice." This nervousness be-
lied Euro-Americans' certainty of their colonial hold over New Mexico.
Euro-Americans' inability to enforce the use of English was taken se-
riously, especially given that some Euro-Americans, like L. Bradford
Prince, faced accusations of "betraying their race" when they tolerated
Mexican cultural habits, much less adopted them.

The flexibility of the regional New Mexican identity allowed Mexicans
and Euro-Americans to argue for their different agendas. That flexibility,
however, also caused consternation for both groups. The meaning of a
bicultural territory stayed uncertain; however, proponents of the regional identity castigated those who threatened the unifying rubric of the
regional New Mexican discourse.

My People All Belong to the Mexican Race: Regional and Racial Identities in the Mesilla Valley, 1880–1912

After 1880, individuals who argued for New Mexico's geographic uniqueness most often had a common desire to mark the region and people as
nationally American. Leading Cruceños, as we have seen, readily adopted
the regional discourse in their newspapers and statehood activism. The
town of La Mesilla, however, and even much of southern New Mexico,
continued as an unpopular reminder that not all of the Mexicans wanted
to be recognized as Americans or even as New Mexicans. According to
the 1880 census, 59.3 percent of Doña Ana County adults above the age
of sixteen reported their birthplace as Mexico. This percentage stood in
stark contrast to the rest of the territory, where only 3.1 percent reported
their birthplace as Mexico.[123] From 1880 to 1920, demographic trends in
Doña Ana County differed from those in the rest of New Mexico because
of Mexican migration. In 1920 Spanish-surnamed individuals accounted
for 44.2 percent of the total population in southern New Mexico but only
34.4 percent in the rest of the territory.[124] These numbers could imply
that new immigrants found the Mesilla Valley an attractive destination
and that transnational migration occurred with considerable frequency.
It could also suggest that residents in Doña Ana retained a link to the
Mexican nation longer than did other parts of New Mexico.

It should be obvious, though, that agents for the Mexican government
had little interest in Mesilleros or their brand of nationalism, at least
while they resided in Mesilla. Back-and-forth migration and trade kept
the national border fluid in southern New Mexico; however, Mexico's

policies during the Porfiriato (1876–1911) painstakingly avoided any actions that might have antagonized leaders in U.S. government or businesses. Occasionally, the Mexican government launched small initiatives to draw Mexicans and Mexican Americans south of the border. They appealed to a sense of Mexican nationalism to persuade these settlers to build colonies and fight nomadic indigenous groups.[125] These efforts were dwarfed, however, by President Porfirio Díaz's massive program to integrate Mexico's economy with that of the United States. Díaz imagined that foreign investment, especially from the United States, would modernize Mexico. Shortly after coming to power in 1876, Díaz prioritized asserting political authority over the northern border states.[126] His own military officials coordinated with the U.S. military and police. Moreover, northern Mexico witnessed a massive boom in railroad construction during the Porfiriato, mostly through U.S. investment.[127] By the time of the Mexican Revolution, in 1910, over a third of all of Mexico's exports passed through northern ports (compared with just 2 percent in 1878).[128] If Mexican officials had any awareness of Mesilleros, they were not likely to encourage their nationalist sentiments, which could jeopardize the diplomatic and economic relationship between the two nations. From their perspective Mesilleros had been U.S. citizens since 1854 and were therefore not their concern.

Mesilleros were thus left to develop their own sense of Mexican identity independent of the Mexican government. Nonetheless, they often linked their town to events in Mexican national history. Mid-twentieth-century oral legends, for instance, claimed that the Mexican revolutionary hero Francisco (Pancho) Villa had visited Mesilla for several days in 1915.[129] Whether true or not, Mesilleros' memories of Villa's visit integrated their town into the story of the Mexican Revolution. This stood in contrast to Mexican Americans in other parts of the state, who vigorously and loudly condemned Villa and the revolution's violence, especially after the attack on Columbus.[130] Indeed, more than 115 Mexican Americans from New Mexico volunteered as part of Companies E and F of the U.S. Punitive Expedition sent to apprehend Villa.[131]

Like Mexicans everywhere in New Mexico, Mesilleros created a series of Spanish-language newspapers at the end of the nineteenth century. These Mexican-owned papers did not follow their contemporary papers in other parts of the territory, including Las Cruces, which defined Mexicans as natives of New Mexico. Instead, Mesillero editors frequently defended the territory as an explicitly Mexican territory. Where other Mexican-owned papers argued for both English and Spanish in the territory (reflecting a bicultural sensibility), Mesilleros advocated the exclusive use of Spanish. The editor of Mesilla's *El Democrata*, for instance, overtly refused to publish an English-language version of his paper, and he printed a terse statement (in English!) that rejected such a demand in 1878:

> According to the last census, there were in New Mexico 91,874 inhabitants. Of these 87,086 were born either in the Territory or in Mexico, and it is safe to say that everyone so born who has any education whatever reads the Spanish language. Of the 4,788 who were natives of *other* countries, at least one half have acquired a knowledge of the language, leaving only 2,391 men, women and children in the Territory who do not understand Spanish. . . . We believe the proportions have not changed materially since the census was taken and so consider that space can be much more profitably occupied omitting all English entirely.[132]

The editor rejected identifying New Mexico as part of the United States or even to mention Americans. Instead, he referred to those born in the "Territory or in Mexico" and those born in "other" countries. For the editor, those born in New Mexico or Mexico were the same and spoke the same language. Only those born outside the region would not understand Spanish. This Mesillero editor linked the exclusive use of Spanish to Mexicans' authority over the region. By writing his statement in English, the editor showed that he had the bilingual skills to run an English paper, but he actively refused to do so. Keeping English out would mean the maintenance of the territory as a Mexican place.[133]

When Euro-Americans visited the Mesilla Valley, they often complained specifically about Mexicans' dominance in La Mesilla and its monolingual population. A student in Las Cruces's New Mexico College of Agriculture and Mechanic Arts, for instance, noted that Mesilleros still controlled the town in 1918. "Last nite [*sic*] we camped in Mesilla, N.M.," he wrote to his mother. "There wasn't a white man or woman in the town, all Mexicans. . . . Most of them could not talk English."[134] For this Las Cruces Euro-American, Mesilla appeared unusual because of the almost exclusive use of Spanish along with the absence of whites. Las Cruces, the city of his college, and other New Mexico towns contrasted with Mesilla and no longer seemed as foreign.

By 1891, though, even Mesilleros' articulations of Mexican identity included racial implications. Pedro García served as the first editor of Mesilla's *El Defensor del Pueblo.* He reacted to the discursive trend that distanced New Mexico and its population from Mexico and other Mexicans. *El Defensor del Pueblo* asserted that all Mexicans needed to unite to fight Euro-American imperialism along the border. In its early editions the paper assumed the motto "Justicia e igualdad ante la ley" (Justice and equality before the law). An 1891 editorial proclaimed that being Mexican meant "un deber que tenemos por obligación de defender nuestra sangre" (a duty that we have for the obligation of defending our blood).[135] As had been common in Mesilla since its founding, the editor promoted a strong sense of Mexican identity and made claims to the territory. The Mesilla paper, though, differed from previous Mesilleros' articulations of Mexican identity as it incorporated elements from Euro-American discourse. Specifically, El Defensor del Pueblo's call for Mexican unity was both national and racial as it drew on a notion of shared blood. Even in Mesilla, Euro-American ideas about Mexican identity as racial were starting to gain ground.

El Defensor del Pueblo still differed from its counterparts in other parts of New Mexico, however. It did not attempt to shift the regional discourse of biculturalism to its advantage. On the contrary, it dismissed the notion of a bicultural unity in New Mexico entirely. El Defensor del Pueblo responded to influential leaders like L. Bradford Prince, who argued that Euro-Americans brought progress to New Mexico as their supposed contribution to the territory.[136] Running counter to the dominant narrative on New Mexico, the Mesillero paper stated that Euro-Americans, "con la sonrisa hipócrita de la maldad en la boca, vinieron y dijeron: yo soy tu hermano y deseo vivir entre vosotros para que progresemos" (with a hypocritical and evil smile on their mouth, they came and said: I am your brother and I want to live among you in order for us to progress).[137] The article called the story of a racially united New Mexico a lie.

Mesilleros retained dominance of their town; their refusal to adapt to the regional New Mexico identity displeased prominent Mexican Americans and Euro-Americans elsewhere. Elite groups worked to dismantle Mesilla's role as a site of opposition after 1880. Las Cruces, as a result, gained economic and political preference by being construed as more authentically New Mexican or American. We saw this in the Bureau of Immigration pamphlet discussed at the start of chapter 5 and again when a Santa Fe newspaper owner visited southern New Mexico in 1904 and declared Las Cruces "la floreciente y progresista ciudad" (the flourishing and progressive city) of the Mesilla Valley.[138] Mesilla did not receive any mention at all. By the turn of the century, Mexican and Euro-American business leaders considered Las Cruces the economic and cultural center of southern New Mexico and preferred to simply ignore Mesilla.

La Mesilla and Las Cruces differed not only ideologically but economically as well. In 1885 New Mexico conducted a territorial census, occurring in the midst of the shifting of power and population from Mesilla to Las Cruces.[139] While these incomplete manuscript census records present difficulties of interpretation, they do suggest the emergence of class differences between the two towns. By far, commercial farming was the most common occupation for either Mesilleros or Cruceños, but Las Cruces had experienced more professionalization than its neighbor. In 1885 more than 12 percent of Cruceño male heads of households reported their occupation as a skilled profession. In Mesilla, however, only about 4 percent of Mesillero male heads of households reported earning a living through skilled labor or commerce. If we consider the combined households of both Euro-Americans and Mexicans, then the economic gap between the towns appears even greater. Around 27 percent of *all* male heads of households in Las Cruces reported their primary income from a professional occupation. In Mesilla, however, only 7 percent of the population reported similar occupations. Mesilla, in the midst of population decline, was also rapidly becoming a working-class town, while professionals seem to have been attracted to Las Cruces.

Though scanty, evidence suggests that Mesilleros also became increasingly dependent on Las Cruces as the driving trading center of southern New Mexico, something their town once claimed. Subtle hints of these changes are to be found in the minute details of daily life, like an unknown twelve-year-old Mesillero's diary. In one entry he recorded his hopes for a little rifle as a birthday present in 1881: "Esta mañana mi papá fue a Las Cruces a comprarme un regalo" (This morning Papa went to Las Cruces to buy me a gift).[140] While we do not know if his specific wish was fulfilled, it seems that his father had to make a trip to Las Cruces for any special shopping. By 1928 the *Rio Grande Republican* noted that La Mesilla lacked even basic commercial services like "a bank, a lumber yard and a hardware store."[141] The rapid loss of population resulted in urban blight. Significant adobe buildings sat abandoned in the town's once bustling center (see Figure 8).

Cruceño newspaper owners and business leaders capitalized on the remaking of race, nation, and region while also castigating their neighboring town. Vying for control of the valley, Las Cruces's English- and Spanish-language newspapers both cast Mesilla as a threatening and dangerous town unworthy of American investment. These newspapers focused on violence and disorder that they claimed was endemic in Mesilleros. In one edition of the *Las Cruces Daily News*, for instance, the

8. La Mesilla's rapid economic decline resulted in a sudden loss of population and urban blight. Once-massive adobe buildings sat empty and crumbling at the town's center at the beginning of the twentieth century. Courtesy Archives and Special Collections Department, New Mexico State University Library.

editors depicted their rival as riddled with brawls. A one-liner from 1889 reported, "Our reporter thinks . . . that 12 or 15 Mesilla people were in court again today for indulging in another free fight."[142] Calling attention to another incident involving a local gang, the Las Cruces newspaper dismissed economic class divisions within Mesilla as a distinguishing factor of citizenship. Even upper-class Mesillero families, the paper claimed, were just as involved in the town's disorder: "Reportes bien alarmantes hemos recibido del pueblo de La Mesilla, en donde según dicen principalmente en las noches, se cometen infinidad de escándalos y abusos, llegando a la barbaridad de los perturbadores del orden publico, hasta ensuciar las puertas de inmundicias de casas de familias honradas y decentes" (We have received very alarming reports from the town of Mesilla, according to what they say, principally at night, there are committed infinite scandals and abuses, the barbarity of disturbers of the public order have reached the point that they have sullied the houses of honorable and decent families).[143] In yet another instance the *Doña Ana County Republican* reported that in Mesilla "a free fight occurred Tuesday evening on the streets among an intoxicated gang. None of the 'quiero mas vino' were badly hurt. There were no officers near."[144] National newspapers occasionally printed similar articles on Mesilla as well. The *Los Angeles Times* drew a direct connection between the town of Mesilla and civil unrest in Mexico in 1892. Reporting on a band of "rebels" who had taken control of several towns in Chihuahua, the article claimed that the leader had come from the town of Mesilla. Even more dramatically, they stated that he was "the same man who participated in the Mesilla riots in 1871."[145] In this article Mesilla even exported its danger to other nations.

At the same time, newspapers circulated stories about Las Cruces as the "new" center of prosperity and progress. They used a language of New Mexican identity that configured Euro-Americans and Cruceños as united in a common U.S. nationalism and commitment to the economic success of the territory. Recording local celebrations on the Fourth of July in 1907, for instance, the *Las Cruces Citizen* emphasized that the celebration included both Euro-Americans and Mexican Americans. The paper recounted the events sponsored by the Women's Improvement Society: "Hon. R. L. Young delivered the English address, highly commending the ladies for their patriotism and the noble work they have done for our town, and Hon. Isidoro Armijo, a native of Las Cruces, who possesses a big American heart and who is always ready to serve and say many good words for his country, delivered an oration in Spanish. The park was soon alive with patriotism which was kept up to midnight without anything to mar the beauties and pleasures of the occasion."[146] The image of Mexicans and Euro-Americans celebrating their shared patriotism for the United States fit within the larger vision of New Mexico as bicultural. Cruceños had a role in the United States and the region through Armijo's "big American heart" and Spanish-language speech.

If such festivities showed that Las Cruces was more "American" than was Mesilla, Cruceño business leaders claimed, then it should be rewarded as the site of government and economic power in southern New Mexico. Edward Said reminds us that determining geography and the significance of place was always a critical component of European and Euro-American imperialism. Imperialist geographies, Said elaborates, create a "hierarchy of spaces" based on presumed value for the metropolitan center and economy.[147] Certainly we have seen how New Mexico as a whole figured as a "lesser place" within the U.S. hierarchy of spaces, but we can also see how this same exercise of imperial power worked out locally within "lesser spaces." Las Cruces had greater worth than Mesilla because Cruceño and Euro-American business leaders worked to make it nationally "American" compared with the unredeemed "Mexican" neighboring town.

A Spanish-language editorial called for Las Cruces to replace Mesilla as the county seat in 1882. The author argued that Las Cruces had "asociaciones de progreso e industria que sus primeros hombres le presente con su ayuda y cooperación, para elevarse la altura de un pueblo culto y progresista" (the associations of progress and industry that the finest men present with help and cooperation, that elevate the status of an educated and progressive people).[148] The editorial declared that Las Cruces had already replaced Mesilla as the economic and social center of the Mesilla Valley. Moreover, the author positioned Las Cruces as a town aligned with the rest of New Mexico and the United States, unlike its neighbor. "Las Cruces, es el transito general de los pueblos, tanto al Sur como al Norte del N.M.," the article stated; "como también para las demás ciudades comerciales de la Unión" (Las Cruces is the transit point for people from southern as well as northern New Mexico; it is also like other commercial cities in the Union).[149] This piece made a direct assertion about the sameness of Las Cruces to other places in New Mexico and the United States. Euro-Americans and Mexican Americans in Las Cruces ultimately did strip Mesilla of its status as the county seat in 1882.[150] To hasten the move as quickly as possible, Martin Amador, the Cruceño businessman whose Indian depredation case opened this book, offered use of his hotel as the new county offices until a proper building could be readied in Las Cruces.[151]

Not all Mexicans (or even Cruceños), however, embraced the vision of a distinct native New Mexican identity. Indeed, some repeated stereotypes about Mexicans when those stereotypes suited their own political agenda. The same Martin Amador appeared before Albert Beveridge and the Committee on Territories along with Isidoro Armijo. Amador had explicitly defended Mexicans' right to full U.S. citizenship when engaged in the case over his own lost property. He also supported making Las Cruces the political and economic center of southern New Mexico. When the congressional committee arrived in New Mexico, however, Amador did not appear as enthusiastic about Mexican Americans in New Mexico. His motives for opposing statehood are not entirely clear. Perhaps, given that he had become a remarkably successful businessman during the territorial period, he believed that maintaining the status quo was in his best interest. Some Mexicans in New Mexico also opposed statehood because they imagined it would increase the Euro-American population, further reducing Mexicans' political and economic well-being.[152] Whatever the case, Amador adamantly rejected making New Mexico a state. Unlike Armijo, he made no distinction between natives and Mexicans. Instead, he asserted, "My people all belong to the Mexican race." Amador then dismissed the Mexican majority's readiness to be full citizens. This Cruceño businessman took an unpopular position by affirming the assumptions by Beveridge and other committee members about Mexicans. He agreed that local Mexicans were uneducated and unable to exercise the responsibilities that statehood would bring: "I think our people is not able now to support statehood, because most of the people here is ignorant; and I do not think we are ready to support statehood yet for about ten years, until our children grow up. We got good schools now, and we send our children to school, and they are doing well; but the old residents are mostly Mexicans, you know. You take them in the election time, and you take them what you call the emblem; they go by that and they do not know who they vote for."[153] The contrast between Armijo's and Amador's testimony suggests the critical ways that native New Mexican identity figured in the statehood movement. Armijo redirected claims of New Mexico's "foreignness" by drawing on new identities for New Mexico's Mexicans as "native" and "Spanish." Uninterested in statehood, Amador retained the racial language of "Mexicans" and the foreignness that such a vocabulary implied to Beveridge and the other committee members. He did not anticipate, however, that most of his Cruceño neighbors would take the testimony personally.

Amador's resistance to the statehood movement cost him. Cruceños remembered the details of his statements long after Beveridge left New Mexico. Refugio Ruiz de Amador, Martin Amador's wife, informed the senator of her husband's death some months after the committee had returned to Washington, D.C. Amador's refusal to cooperate with the statehood movement (and the concurrent regional discourse) had made him a social pariah in Las Cruces. "I doubt not but what the disease that carried him off," she wrote, "was brought on by the constant worry and mental strain caused by those who declared themselves his bitter enemies, *for the truthful testimony rendered unsolicited* by him to the Commission of which you were a most prominent member."[154] As this incident suggests, those who resisted or refuted the fundamental components of the regional New Mexican discourse faced harsh consequences. In Amador's case his fellow Cruceños declared him an enemy to be ostracized.

Amador's isolation mirrored the increasing economic isolation of La

Mesilla. His embrace of a Mexican racial identity may not have been congruent with Mesilleros' vision of themselves as nationally Mexican. Mesilla's fortunes likewise changed, however, as the New Mexican identity became more prominent. Mesilla, by refusing full incorporation into the United States, contested the American nationalism that was becoming an explicit requirement in being "New Mexican." Individuals or groups who opposed this new vision faced tremendous pressure and even serious retaliation. Likewise, those who participated in the emerging discourse earned economic and social rewards.

Cruceños effectively remade their town as the acknowledged locus of power in the Mesilla Valley.[155] By 1889 the Las Cruces Daily News could reprint a story from the Santa Fe New Mexican that called the town "the center" of the Mesilla Valley.[156] When Governor Miguel Otero presented his annual reports on the status of the territory in 1903, he named Las Cruces the only major settlement in southern New Mexico, ignoring Mesilla completely. He further labeled Las Cruces as strictly an "American" town. Otero offered the town's founding in 1848 "by the American officers from the post then existing at Fort Selden" as evidence of its "authentic American" status.[157] In another section of his report he downplayed the history of the Mesilla Valley before the arrival of the railroad, the point at which Las Cruces became dominant and Mesilla was sidelined.

Otero's family actually had strong connections to southern New Mexico, and he likely knew of the valley's history. After he retired from politics, the ex-governor wrote a biography of southern New Mexico's Billy the Kid, who faced trial in La Mesilla.[158] When he composed his official reports to the secretary of the interior, though, Otero omitted any reference to the Mesilla of his day or the Mesilla during the period when it was the central hub of southern New Mexico. Rather than attempt to reconcile Mesilla with the New Mexican identity, he simply ignored the valley's history between the colonial period and 1881. He reported: "The Mesilla Valley was first settled by the Spaniards about two hundred years ago; but the advent of the people from the States, which was contemporaneous with the completion here of the Atchison, Topeka and Santa Fe Railway in 1881, marked the date of orchard planting and agricultural and general material development, and the beautiful valley has become very appropriately known as the 'Garden Spot of New Mexico.'"[159] According to Otero's report, nothing of note happened in the Mesilla Valley between the arrival of the Spaniards in the early seventeenth century and the completion of the railroad at the end of the nineteenth century.

Numerous recent historians have taken a critical interest in historical memory and the social and political uses of history. Creating narratives about the past, like Otero's on the Mesilla Valley, almost inevitably involves efforts to understand one's present. Michel-Rolph Trouillot's pathbreaking study of Haiti has shown the complicated processes by which only some stories became part of a corpus that defined a standard and accepted narrative about the nation's past.[160] Similarly, the historian of modern Germany Alon Confino reminds us that national memory often constructs a sense of common destiny, concealing social and political frictions within that society.[161] Reflecting on the applicability of Confino's argument to the present case, we can think of the nationalist narratives on New Mexico as fulfilling a need to repress discussions of how little Mexicans had been incorporated into the United States. Such narratives overcame real friction by enabling Mexicans to feel connected to the larger nation through a localized history. Likewise, they served the reverse of integrating the local border region and its populations into a larger narrative about the nation. Mesilleros could not be part of that story because they overtly refused such incorporation. To think of this another way, the French historian Henry Rousso tells us that "memory is a structuring of forgetfulness."[162] Forgetting Mesilleros' militant Mexican national identity became the most common means for Mexican and Euro-American elites to discount their resistance. If members of those elite groups had to acknowledge Mesilla, then they rendered Mesilleros as always already divorced from native New Mexicans, separate and distinct.[163]

Benjamín Read's histories similarly effaced historical dissent within the Mesilla Valley. Born in Las Cruces, Read was surely familiar with the historical dynamic of the two major towns in southern New Mexico. Yet in his many histories of New Mexico, Read commented only briefly on the Mesilla dispute. When he did mention it, he actively dissociated Mesilla's history from the wider history of the region. Because Read imagined the New Mexican identity as inseparably linked to American nationalism, for instance, he could not acknowledge that any "New Mexicans" had viewed the invading U.S. Army with hostility during the U.S.-Mexican War. Even more threatening for Read was the possibility that New Mexicans might have been nationalist (in terms of nation-state) Mexicans who had actively refused an American identity. The historical circumstances and motives of the settlers that led to the founding of Mesilla, therefore, threatened to undermine Read's argument and vision of New Mexico.

Read's solution, like Otero's, was simply to ignore the founding of Mesilla and never to mention the "New Mexicans" who chose to leave the United States after 1848. Commenting specifically on the Mesilla Valley, Read discounted Ramón Ortiz's success in recruiting New Mexicans to move following the Treaty of Guadalupe Hidalgo.[164] In his *Illustrated History of New Mexico*, for example, Read mentioned the Mexican plan to "repatriate all the sons of New Mexico" south of the borderline.[165] He claimed, however, that Ortiz could not find anyone willing to leave New Mexico. Never acknowledging the founding of Mesilla, Read cut short this discussion by stating that Ortiz returned to Mexico "without having obtained any results whatsoever."[166] Likewise, in his *Guerra México-Americana*, Read only briefly acknowledged the dispute that eventually incorporated Mesilla into the United States in 1854. Like his *Illustrated History*, Read refused to acknowledge that the town of Mesilla or any New Mexican had ever resisted the United States:

> Por ese tratado quedó la posesión del gobierno Americano de las provincias de Nuevo México y California confirmada. Más el estado Chihuahua siguió por algún tiempo reclamado la parte Sur Oeste de Nuevo México, pero por fin se arregló esa cuestión con la compra que hizo el gobierno Americano en 1853 al gobierno Mejicano del territorio en disputa.[167]

> (For that agreement, the American government took possession of the provinces of New Mexico and California. But the state of Chihuahua continued for some time claiming part of southwestern New Mexico, but at last this question was settled when the American government did purchase from the Mexican government the disputed territory.)

Read reconfigured the Mesilla contravention to match his vision of New Mexico's timeless American nationalism. Rather than configuring the battle between Mesilleros and Cruceños as a conflict that set New Mexicans against one another, Read placed the blame for the dispute on the Mexican state of Chihuahua. Doing so safeguarded his idea that New Mexicans differed from Mexicans, particularly in their national allegiances. Any dissent against the United States must a priori have originated outside the geographic boundaries of New Mexico and, therefore, outside "America."

In this way members of the Mexican elite worked to suppress the articulation of competing ideas about Mexican identity that retained a link to Mexican nationalism. Late-nineteenth-century Mexican American business leaders resented Euro-American attempts to label them as inferior, but they also saw their economic and social interests as dependent on their repositioning themselves as a distinctive type of American. Cruceños therefore cast Mexicans who refused to accept the Euro-American definitions of their identity, like the Mesilleros, outside the authentic New Mexican identity. Supporters of statehood did not tolerate anything that threatened their ability to secure a place for Mexican Americans in the national sphere.

By the 1930s an English-language newspaper discussed the loss of Mesilla's economic and political position in southern New Mexico as ancient history. Mesilla, the author avowed, had not achieved the "stream of progressive existence enjoyed by communities and growing towns all over southern New Mexico."[168] She suggested that Mesilla could still become like its prosperous neighbors unless "the people of Mesilla reject the opportunity." In this subtle way she reminded readers that Mesilla's economic decline resulted from Mesilleros' refusal to participate in the regional New Mexican identity. For her, Mesilleros had created their own economic misery because of their historical opposition to the changing notions of national identity.

Conclusion

When New Mexico first became part of the United States, most Euro-Americans clearly presumed that the territory's inhabitants existed as racially "Mexican." They explicitly equated New Mexico's Mexicans with Mexicans in any other part of Mexico.[169] By the early twentieth century, though, it was no longer clear if *native* New Mexicans were as interchangeable with (other) Mexicans. In 1910 a *New York Times* article reported the lynching of a man named Rodriguez in Rock Springs, Texas.[170] At issue was whether the victim was a "native of New Mexico" or a "Mexican." If the man had been Mexican, the *Times* reported, then there would be greater diplomatic problems between the United States and its neighboring republic. In this instance the racial meaning of these two identities grew ambiguous as national identity became more important. Being a native New Mexican connoted being a U.S. citizen, even if in practice it was difficult to distinguish native New Mexicans from Mexican nationals. Although being labeled "native" often connoted a particular racial status, this article implicitly subsumed that racial status under a national American identity.

Within the regional discourse Euro-Americans did not deny that Mex-

icans and Native Americans constituted the majority of New Mex
population. They argued, though, that the historical peculiarities o
region made it uniquely American and therefore that it was irrelevant
that Euro-Americans were a minority. Most Euro-Americans argued
that New Mexico existed as a site of bicultural or tricultural harmony
because their racial superiority brought order to the region.

For Mexican Americans the regional identity became a means through
which they could assert a role in the region and nation. Such assertions
would continue long after New Mexico achieved statehood. Cruz Alvarez,
a prominent Mexican American in the Mesilla Valley, wrote a romantic
tribute to New Mexico in 1945. His words echoed the nineteenth-century
vision of a distinctly regional and tricultural New Mexico. Alvarez discussed the state's contributions to World War II as symbolizing the entire
history of the region. He wrote: "By their heroism in the battles of the
European and Mediterranean countries, the Pacific and Indian Ocean
areas and the frozen Aleutians, [New Mexicans] displayed the valor, courage and sagacity of the American Eagle, the Spanish Lion and the Indian
Thunderbird; out where the grandchildren of Shakespeare and Cervantes
—proud each one of their ancestry, language, culture and history—smile
and work hand in hand their destiny under the Stars and Stripes . . . that, my
friends, is the New Mexico of today!"[171] In this account Euro-Americans,
Native Americans, and Mexican Americans all contributed equally to New
Mexico and the nation. Racial discord had no place in the rosy imagining of
three groups united to fight for the United States. Alvarez's statement
suggests how profoundly hegemonic the regional New Mexican identity
had become by the middle of the twentieth century. For Mexicans who
wished to discuss nationalism and racial identities, the tricultural identity
had become the language of choice.

To understand how so many Mexicans adopted the regional identity, one
needs to consider the ways that race, nation, and region were interwoven in
the last part of the nineteenth century. Euro-Americans considered their
own political and economic ambitions thwarted because Congress used
the territory's nonwhite majority as an excuse to deny statehood. They
turned to explaining the region's meaning to strengthen their own position in the nation. New Mexican identity, construed as multiracial *and*
"uniquely American," represented significant ideological shifts in the
meaning of geography, nation, and racialized bodies. Intellectuals, government leaders, and other public figures came to imagine that their own
identity was distinct from other Mexicans and was intimately connected
to the weaving of the territory into the larger U.S. nation.

Mexicans reversed the linkages with history, race, and region. Where Euro-Americans saw the trajectory of the regional history as making contemporary Mexicans living anachronisms, as part of the territory's "past," Mexicans argued that the territory's history gave them special priority over the territory's present and future as "natives." Native identity, which was reinvented specifically to distinguish Mexicans from Indians and Euro-Americans, implied that Mexicans had a hereditary claim to New Mexico as the first colonizers. Mexicans mobilized a similar language as Euro-Americans about civilization and progress, but their narratives claimed that it was Mexicans who first brought order and progress to the region, thus preparing for its triumphant, inevitable admittance into the United States. As the first to bring civilization to New Mexico, Mexicans argued, they had a special role in the territory and the nation as a whole. These Mexicans were not at all foreigners to the United States. It was the Euro-Americans who were the actual interlopers in that American place.

This native identity also implied that New Mexico's geographic boundaries created a distinctive type of Mexican. A narrative developed around New Mexico that isolated the territory from the rest of Mexico. Many elite Mexicans in New Mexico used this narrative in an attempt to traverse the racial barrier that kept other Mexicans, like Tejanos, from full citizenship. Part of this strategy appeared through claims of a "pure Spanish" identity. Stories about the "uniqueness" of New Mexico necessarily presumed that individuals in New Mexico always lacked a Mexican national identity and therefore did not overtly resist Euro-American imperialism. Historical evidence to the contrary suggests that we need to consider how these presumptions became so widely accepted. New Mexico stands out in the historical record for the large number of Mexicans who claimed their right to maintain their Mexican citizenship after annexation.[172] La Mesilla, moreover, was a physical manifestation of overt Mexican resistance to Euro-American imperialism. Popular (and even scholarly) histories of New Mexico, however, have almost erased these stories from the local history and the history of the border. Many researchers have thereby neglected the complexity of claiming Mexican, New Mexican, or American identity. Histories have uncritically reiterated a late-nineteenth-century myth that New Mexican elites never considered themselves part of the Mexican nation and only considered themselves pure Spanish. This narrative ignores the many individuals in New Mexico who actively claimed a Mexican national identity and takes at face value a mythology developed as part of an invented regional history.

We can think of the regional New Mexican discourse by adapting the concept of "cultural hegemony."[173] Hegemony used in this way does not encompass only political or economic forms of rule but also the process through which dominance is maintained as ruling groups interact with those who contest subordination. Giving their consent to regional and U.S. authorities involved a "contradictory consciousness," a mixing of approbation and resistance, for Mexican Americans.[174] New Mexico's Mexican population had its own conceptions of the region and the relationship between race and nation that were reformed as members of the Mexican elite borrowed from Euro-American discourses to claim their place in the state. The emergent regional discourse on "New Mexico" reinscribed racial and national boundaries and discouraged alternative conceptions. As with all forms of hegemony, ruling elites, whether Mexican or Euro-American, could never attain total consent. Despite overt efforts to erase their dissent, Mesilleros refused to participate in the remaking of the territory or their sense of Mexican identity.

EPILOGUE

"Neath the Star Spangled Banner": Multiculturalism and the Taxonomic State

New Mexico finally shed its official colonial-territorial status to become the forty-seventh state in 1912, making it the second-to-last of the contiguous states to be admitted (before Arizona later the same year). By then, appeals to a unified sense of region had apparently reconciled conflicting notions of race and nation. This historic solution occasioned the first instance in which a territory was incorporated into the Union with a majority of voters who were not Euro-American. Considering how rigidly race structured notions of nationalism and belonging in the United States, it is perhaps not astonishing that it had taken almost seventy years to achieve this resolution of the New Mexico "problem." After 1912 the new state would provide other firsts for Mexican Americans in the United States: the first elected Mexican American governor (Ezequiel Cabeza de Baca in 1917); the first Mexican American elected to serve in the U.S. Senate (Octaviano Ambrosio Larrazolo) in 1928; and the first Mexican American senator elected to serve multiple terms (Dennis Chávez) from 1935 to 1962.[1] The apparent settlement of divergent notions of race and nation through appeals to region was itself less than stable, however, and remains fraught with unresolved internal contradictions to this day. With statehood (male) Mexican Americans did indeed attain greater access to locally defined political positions, but statehood by no means transformed the region into the promised utopia of interracial harmony. Nor could statehood really mean an end to U.S. imperialism in New Mexico, even if the "natives" could now be seen as marginally white-Spanish. Before scrutinizing these ideological fault lines, however, it will be useful to review the central narrative of this book, which has examined in some detail how a particular discourse around region emerged to reconcile racial and national conflict along the nineteenth-century border.

Before Mexico and the United States went to war in 1846, leaders in each nation were already struggling to reconcile Enlightenment ideals of universal citizenship with conflicting racial presumptions. Those presumptions, likewise informed by Enlightenment philosophies, dictated that certain groups lacked sufficient capacity to participate as full citizens in self-governance. Early-nineteenth-century thinking about Mexican national identity attenuated these problems by prioritizing a stylized repertoire of cultural practices that transcended, but never fully displaced, racial categories as loci of identity. In other words, the practices and policies that came to define nineteenth-century national belonging stressed *acting* like a Mexican. Older colonial notions about race and performance were reinterpreted to uphold existing racial and social divisions even as Mexico City forbade the specific use of racial categories as qualifications for equal citizenship. In northern Mexico, including New Mexico, state officials distinguished between indigenous groups whom they considered "civilized," which was to say "Mexican," and those whom they considered "savage."[2] Almost regardless of their racial status, individuals with sufficient means could demonstrate the requisite mastery of reason to qualify for full citizenship through their adoption of certain cultural acts, like speaking Spanish, converting to Catholicism, and participating in the state economy. When New Mexico was part of the fledgling Mexican republic, therefore, Mexican identity encompassed a wide range of racial groups, though it did not embrace them all in the same way or to the same extent. La Mesilla, as a product of that nationalism, could therefore (and did) include without contradiction a range of racial groups as Mexican, including, for instance, a Pueblo man who led the Mesilla Guard against *indios bárbaros*.

Euro-Americans had similarly grappled with questions about race and citizenship, but they had arrived at very different resolutions. Race figured explicitly in legal definitions of citizenship at the state and federal levels. During the Jacksonian era the possibility of using cultural performance as a means to access the rights of full citizenship became increasingly limited, as race more and more harshly circumscribed the possibilities of American identity. Moreover, Euro-Americans projected their own assumptions about race and national identity onto their neighboring republic, presuming that a national Mexican identity implied a mestizo, or mixed, racial ancestry, just as Americanness presumed a

identity. As early as the 1820s, Josiah Gregg, W. W. H. Davis, and
r Euro-Americans who wrote about their travels into northern Mex-
described local communities as constituting an identifiable racial
group created by the "amalgamation of Indians and Europeans."

In the decades from the opening of the Santa Fe Trail in 1821 to the
end of the U.S. Civil War, Euro-Americans hardened the racial dichotomy that defined Americans as white and Mexicans as mestizo. Many
Euro-Americans began to argue that Mexicans' national identity was in
fact a racial identity, one that would make them incompatible with full
integration into the United States. This insistence produced a dilemma
for American expansion: in spite of the imperative in Manifest Destiny to
acquire more and more land for the United States, the fact of New
Mexico's majority Mexican population meant that, unlike Alta California
or Texas, it could be administered only as a U.S. colony ("territory")
because it was considered too foreign for membership as a full state.

In their efforts to claim American national identity, Cruceños and
other Mexican Americans within the territory began to conceive of their
relationship to each other as more racial than national. They also began
to experiment with ways of naming themselves that would render them
distinct from either Mexican nationals or Euro-Americans, while at the
same time allowing them to be nationally American. Such a strategy
of differentiating New Mexicans from Mexicans elsewhere developed
slowly and irregularly. At the time of the U.S.-Mexican War, leading
Euro-American authorities stated explicitly that the people in New Mexico did not differ racially or culturally from people living in any other part
of Mexico. In 1848 the U.S. Senate recorded, with no apparent objection,
the memoir of a Euro-American who journeyed through New Mexico
that testified to the "sameness" of New Mexico's population to other
Mexicans. "The manners and customs of the New Mexicans proper," he
wrote definitively, "are very similar to those over all Mexico, described so
often by travelers to that country."[3] Race created the link between New
Mexico and the rest of the Mexican nation, he explained: "The principal
ingredient in the Mexican race is Indian blood which is visible in their
features, complexion, and disposition."[4] For this author Mexican identity's exclusively racial character transcended region and became synonymous with national identity and influenced cultural practices.

Nevertheless, by the end of the nineteenth century the expectation that
Mexicans in New Mexico were the same as Mexicans elsewhere no longer
appeared certain to many Euro-Americans in the region. Between 1880
and 1912 there arose a new discourse that configured the meanings of

race and nation through the imaginings of place. Concomitant with economic and demographic changes in the territory, Mexicans and Euro-Americans increasingly wrote about New Mexican identity as both multiracial *and* "uniquely American." Intellectuals, government leaders, and other public figures attempted to articulate a knowledge of New Mexico by weaving the local space into the larger nation and minimizing racial tensions within the territory. Euro-Americans and Mexican Americans frequently used similar language to explain the meaning of the regional New Mexican identity. They described New Mexico as being defined by the three distinctive racial groups that united in a common American nationalism. Racial meaning for both Euro-Americans and Mexican Americans, therefore, was subsumed under a patriotic "American–New Mexican" identity.

The regional New Mexican discourse proved persuasive because it could serve both Euro-American and Mexican American political programs without exposing the contradictions between parts of those programs. The discourse that coalesced around New Mexican regional identity created a sense of the territory as a unique place within the United States, with the promise of taming the heterogeneity of its racial mix through American nationalism and a bicultural or tricultural harmony. This regional identity contained internal contradictions from its very inception. These contradictions have much to suggest not only about historical New Mexico and imperialism but also about the state of the "multicultural" United States today.

The Iconography of Unity through Subordination

Inconsistencies between the rosy rhetoric of multicultural harmony and the lasting subordination of the Mexican population manifested in the very design of the New Mexico seal and coat of arms as adopted in 1887 (Figure 9). The original territorial seal, in place since 1851, had starkly represented U.S. dominion over the territory through its solitary American eagle clutching an olive branch and arrows in its talons. After 1887 New Mexico's official seal carried the image of both an American bald eagle and a Mexican eagle holding a snake in its mouth and standing on a cactus. Foreshadowing the later official adoption of the Hawaiian state flag, which incorporated both the Union Jack intact and an echo of the U.S. Stars and Stripes, the imagery of the New Mexican icon came to reflect the area's place in overlapping colonial histories. When New

9. Seal of the state of New Mexico.

Mexico became a state, a commission consisting of both Mexican and Euro-American elites successfully advocated converting this territorial seal into the official state seal in 1913. New Mexico's official iconography, therefore, depicted a kind of unity between Mexicans and Americans. At the same time, it also declared unambiguously that Mexicans would be subsumed under the greater American nationalism by depicting the Mexican eagle as almost half the size of the American eagle. When the legislature adopted the image, it also explicitly named the relationship between the two eagles as one based on protection, stating the Mexican eagle was "shielded by the American eagle."[5] The state seal acknowledged New Mexico's status as literally a liminal space.

While the state's official iconography crudely, but powerfully, connoted a unified sense of purpose among both Mexicans and Americans, this project has shown a more complicated and contradictory variety of ideas about race and nation that circulated along the nineteenth-century border. Shifting borders in the nineteenth century left the possibilities for the racial and national meaning of Mexican and American identity in flux. Differing strategies developed as Mexican individuals attempted to make sense of their circumstances and their position in the meta-ideologies of race and nation. By focusing on the local context of southern New Mexico, we have seen how they grappled with their lives along the border in ways that have often been invisible to historians of the region, particularly those who are only interested in Spanish identity or questions that presume whiteness as the issue of greatest import.

Caution is warranted when we encounter facile narratives about Spanish identity, particularly if such discussions rely on an implicit assumption that scholars (whether in the interwar years or in the twenty-first century) have privileged access to knowledge about the "truth" of historical subjects' "real" racial identities. Recent historical accounts of New Mexico often end with wry comments about "mixed-race" people's delusional claims to "pure Spanish blood."[6] Even Chicano/a studies scholars who explore how socially constructed ideas about race have informed the creation of Spanish identity cannot seem to help from claiming that Mexicans, by definition, really are a mixed race. This line of thinking asserts inadvertently that there is an intrinsic essence to Mexican identity that depends upon having ancestors who were Indian, European, African, and Native American.[7] This reinforces notions that culturally created racial categories are "naturally" based on heredity. It also camouflages the processes through which the United States and other imperial powers homogenized the diversity of Latin American populations through their own understanding of race. Indeed, some are so obsessed with ascertaining the "racial truth" about New Mexico's and Colorado's Spanish-speaking populations that they have conducted DNA studies on these communities. Scientific authorities have definitively declared that such a community "more closely resembles an Amerindian population . . . than it does a European population."[8]

Rather than effect a deconstruction of racial categories or expose assumptions about "whiteness," this approach actually legitimates colonial categories and freezes colonial assumptions into place. Interpretations of DNA once again locate race as inescapably tied to one's body. We must wonder, why is it so important to know? In spite of the claims of the scholarship on "Spanishness," the emergence of Spanish identity was not, in fact, a discernible phase in a unidirectional historical trajectory, marking the end of Mexican identity in New Mexico. Instead, these two identities constantly overlapped and interweaved, particularly in the instances in which the same historical actor used both (or neither) to articulate identity. In this regard it is also critical to recognize that language context, English or Spanish, often informed the choice of which of those identities was deployed. Notions of being "Mexican" continued to circulate, especially in Spanish-language publications, at the same time as Spanish American identity.

Mexicans as Racial Outsiders
and Perpetual Foreigners

We can understand the relentless nineteenth-century debates about Mexicans' suitability for inclusion in the U.S. nation as being a product of what Ann Laura Stoler has designated a "taxonomic state."[9] Creating meaning for New Mexico as a distinctive place furthered the category making by sorting the region's heterogeneity into identifiable populations that could then be placed into a hierarchy. The three broad racial categories of "(Euro-)American," "Mexican (American)," and "Indian" flattened out variations between and within each of those groups to make each one distinct. Differential racialization between Indians and Mexicans became a priority in that first decade of occupation. As a consequence of the introduction of "knowable differences" as stressed in this new taxonomic framework, national, familial, and personal links between Mexicans and Indians were forgotten. Likewise, the divisions among various groups of Mexicans that derived from their own assumptions about nationalism were passed over or actively silenced.

The supposed incompatibility of American Indian and Mexican identities continues to inform the latter in the United States to this day. Mexico remains a "mixed-race" nation in the minds of most Americans, who rarely acknowledge its racial diversity or even its indigenous past and present. The ethnographer Renya Ramirez, for instance, notes that indigenous individuals who migrated from Mexico to Alta California were not viewed as "authentically Native American" because they no longer lived on their ancestral homelands (which are outside of U.S. boundaries) and because the U.S. federal government did not "recognize" them as a "tribe."[10] The exclusion of indigenous Mexican groups from the category of "Native American" suggests the durability of the nineteenth-century U.S. presumption that Mexico was a racially monolithic nation composed only of persons of "mixed race." Because dominant U.S. attitudes conflate a Mexican national identity with a Mexican racial identity, all migrants must be racially "the same." The creation of "Mexican" as both a racial and national category involved, as we have seen, more than just the United States and its expansionist desires. Rather, U.S. leaders and writers participated in a global discourse that used racial ideologies to name Mexico and the rest of Latin America as "backward" and therefore in need of white colonial intervention.[11]

Securing *Mexican* as a distinctive racial category would be critical to later figurations of that category as always "foreign" to the United States. This could be done in a way that preserved the presumption that Mexico, its populations, and its history were somehow always distinct from the United States. Even the U.S.-Mexican War, which violently exposed the social, political, and economic interconnections between the two nations (and obviously altered the trajectory of each), is mostly ignored or reinvented as a precursor to the U.S. Civil War. Making the first war a retroactive product of the second safely secures it as strictly an "American" event.

As some scholars have suggested, Mexicans thereby appear in the United States as an "alien presence rather than as part of 'American' history."[12] Through various periods of the twentieth century, in other words, popular and political discussions most often made Mexicans and Mexican Americans unwelcome intruders who lacked any historical or cultural connections to (other) Americans.[13] State-sponsored programs of mass deportations could then be justified in the 1930s, 1950s, 1980s, and 2000s because those individuals did not "belong" in the nation. This making of Mexicans as racially and nationally foreign legitimates their present exclusion from basic civil rights, but it also allows the United States to avoid confronting its own imperial past. Perceiving Mexicans and Mexican Americans as perpetual "new arrivals" means that the United States does not have to consider what it meant to be on the receiving end of its nineteenth-century imperial ambitions. Remembering that many Mexicans paid a heavy price for the U.S.-Mexican War (on both sides of the border) draws into question enduring myths that U.S. westward expansion was noble, antiauthoritarian, or even legal.

New Mexico's Mexican-majority population always threatened that historical amnesia. The meaning of that space and population, therefore, had to be remade before it could be considered part of the unified nation. If the imagining of the U.S. nation involved the exclusion of "Mexican foreigners," then "New Mexicans" had to be disambiguated from that category. If American westward expansion was thought necessary to make those lands productive, then "New Mexicans" had to be welcoming hosts of U.S. imperialism. The region and the people living there had to be made part of the nation in ways that totally divorced it from the neighboring republic or the negative consequences of colonial occupation.

As this study has suggested, Mexicans and Mexican Americans were not just passive victims in this process. Some, like the Mesilleros, overtly rejected that imperialism. Others collaborated with remaking the meaning of the region as they sought their own incorporation as Americans. The bi- and tricultural discourse was not strictly an invention of Euro-American colonizers who imposed it unilaterally on the region's docile populations. Instead, it developed out of a longer history of imperialism in New Mexico whose origins actually predated the arrival of Euro-Americans. Mexican imperialism in the region did not subside instantly, even after Mexico's army and bureaucrats had retreated southward. Indeed, interculturalism developed in New Mexico because U.S. colonial authority there was too unstable or fragile to cope in more assertive ways when racial, national, and economic tensions threatened to erupt or create allegiances counter to the goals of the state.

Simply put, New Mexico's political and economic institutions could not function without the active accommodation of the Mexican population. Therefore, for the ideology of bi- and triculturalism to spread and win acceptance across racial and class lines, it had to secure the participation and endorsement of those Mexicans who wished to uphold U.S. hegemony for their own purposes.[14] Most Mexicans eventually accepted the new racial and national taxonomies in part because they wished to uphold differences that *they* imagined distinguished them from Euro-Americans and Native Americans, even as they sought economic and political incorporation into the U.S. nation as Americans. In some instances Mexicans deployed the New Mexican discourse in ways that more aggressively challenged the colonial status quo, refuted Euro-American racism, and pushed for their full citizenship.

The move toward triculturalism actively obscured the enduring transnational connections among New Mexico's populations by making American nationalism the only option for political identity. This naturalized the international border between Mexico and the United States as timeless and inviolate. Dividing "New" and "Old" Mexico was necessary to fix the former, and the people within its borders, to the goals of U.S. imperialism.[15] The nascent New Mexican identity reinforced Euro-American racial hierarchies and required unquestioned devotion to the United States. While its development implied a final resolution of the debates about racial and national identities, the status of the Mexican American community was actually left unsettled for decades to come. "The matter was never resolved," one Mexican reflected in 1977. "Some say we are Spanish, others that we are Indians, and others that we are Mexicans."[16]

Fantasies of Racial Harmony Live On

Notions of intercultural harmony persisted in New Mexico during the twentieth century. In 1955 Lora Vale Oldman, director of the New Mexico State Jefferson Davis Highway Project, authored a salute for the state flag for a ceremony in Las Cruces. The flag, itself "harmonious," blended representations of two of the state's major "racial" populations, overlaying the Zia Pueblo's icon for the sun on Spain's national colors of red and yellow. "I salute the flag of the State of New Mexico," Oldman's simple pledge went, "the Zia symbol of loyalty and united cultures."[17] By the mid-twentieth century the notion that being New Mexican meant cross-racial unity had become so ingrained that citizens of the state were expected to salute it (even at an event honoring the president of the Confederacy).

La Mesilla's distinctive history, however, would continue to rankle as an unpleasant inconsistency in that vision and would therefore remain subject to revisionist rewriting. One Ruth Thurman Myra wrote an operetta entitled "Bells of Old Mesilla" for her master's thesis at the University of Colorado in 1954. Myra set her work shortly after the signing of the Mesilla/Gadsden Treaty and promised that it would "contribute a measure of real understanding between Anglo-American and Spanish-American, through the plot which draws upon a situation of Anglo acceptance of Spanish hospitality."[18] Myra grounded her fantasy on assumptions about regional New Mexican identity. The operetta elided all discussion of La Mesilla's origin or Mesilleros' hostility toward incorporation into the United States. Instead, Myra presented a spectacle of New Mexico as a menagerie populated by "the children of the American Eagle, the Spanish Lion, and the Indian Thunderbird proud of their ancestry, history, language, and culture" who "work out their destiny hand in hand neath the Star Spangled Banner." American nationalism, Myra contended through her jaunty libretto, had united three discrete racial populations in Mesilla. Without evincing any sense of irony she noted that her American-nationalist operetta's first performance would take place during a celebration of Mexican Independence in Mesilla.

Myra's stage production underscores the continuing divide between those who wanted to believe in a unified regional New Mexican identity and the Mesilleros. Though the town clearly intended to celebrate a Mexican national holiday, Myra couched her fantasy within a vision of a united tricultural region benevolently administered by the United States.

Myra conveniently ignored the significance of the fact that another national celebration was taking place on U.S. grounds by U.S. citizens.

Though Myra's musical rendition of New Mexico's history may seem too overtly ideological to be taken seriously, many historians of the U.S.-Mexican border have continued to produce similar narratives. They unwittingly promote rationales designed in the late nineteenth century for U.S. national identity as the only viable option for Mexicans in the region. As a corollary historians have ignored a substantial body of evidence of contemporaneous and competing Mexican identities because it did not fit with their presumptions about U.S. imperialism, the emergence of Spanish identity, or their assumptions about intercultural harmony.

Nor do these issues have implications only for New Mexico. During the 1990s such scholars and cultural critics as Gayatri Spivak, Lisa Lowe, Ann DuCille, and others focused on the role of "multiculturalism" in late-twentieth-century cultural politics. To place the historic development of biculturalism and triculturalism in New Mexico against a broader American trajectory, we can use this scholarship and perhaps, in turn, reinvigorate those debates.[19]

Lowe argues that late-twentieth-century multiculturalism, a supposed celebration of difference that implied equal institutional representation, emerged as a reaction to the 1960s civil rights movements. As a result of these movements, grassroots activism within and between various segregated groups forced into the spotlight the social and economic inequalities in the United States that revealed the melting pot metaphor as a fantasy.[20] Contrasting these cross-racial coalitions working to transform society, Lowe argues that multiculturalism substituted the aestheticization and commodification of racialized cultural elements for economic and political equality. In her analysis "multiculturalism" was a reactionary narrative that claimed American culture as democratically incorporating and representing every constituency equally. This narrative, Lowe reminds us, should not be taken at face value. Rather than fulfill the democratic promise of political equality and active appreciation for cultural pluralism, multiculturalism actually obfuscated the important differences and contradictions within and among racial and ethnic minority groups. It masked exclusions that restricted racial minorities' areas of physical residence and their access to public services.[21]

While Lowe and others have characterized this type of multiculturalism as a unique product of late-twentieth-century neoliberalism, the present study has shown that predecessors to it emerged in much earlier forms of nineteenth-century U.S. empire building. Like its descendent in late-twentieth-century multiculturalism, New Mexico's older bicultural-ism and triculturalism also substituted a form of "universal pluralism" for empirical social, economic, and political equality. Biculturalism and tri-culturalism, like multiculturalism, did not depend on self-evident as-sumptions about the relationship between race and nation. Rather, they actually constituted and narrowed the possibilities of particular racial categories for nationalist purposes.

More often, New Mexico's development in the twentieth century did not refute or end U.S. imperialism in the region, nor has statehood mitigated its effects. New Mexico has become a destination to which many Americans, despite contributing nothing to the region during their working lifetime, feel at liberty to retire and whose meager resources they feel free to consume. Since U.S. domestic tourism began to grow in the first decade of the twentieth century, Santa Fe and Taos have emerged as heavily publicized spots for tourists interested in "exotic" getaways that require no passport. New Mexico lives on in the national imaginary as the "U.S. which is not the U.S.," a spiritual and cultural playground for priv-ileged Euro-Americans. Despite the recent development and promotion of "eco-tourism" or "sustainable travel" in New Mexico, on the whole tourism and its concomitant frame of thinking brings only minimal benefit to Mexicans, Native Americans, and poor whites.[22] Though on a much smaller scale than Santa Fe, even La Mesilla's plaza has been reoriented to serve vacationers rather than the town's actual residents. By 2008, with the exception of San Albino's Catholic Church, Mesilla's plaza was dominated by high-end specialty markets, including a Nambé outlet, and tourist traps capitalizing on Billy the Kid and other (Euro-American) "Wild West" icons. Less than one block from the plaza lived the actual residents of the town, often in grinding poverty.

Ongoing colonialism has thus kept New Mexico's nonwhite majority population in positions of economic and social inequality. Stephen Cas-tles's notion of "substantial citizenship" helps us understand this turn of events. While Mexican Americans had attained technical citizenship, as a group, they had not achieved substantial citizenship, meaning an equal chance for participation in society through politics, work, and social programs.[23] According to estimates from the 2007 American Commu-nity Survey Project of the U.S. Census Bureau, New Mexico had the third-highest percentage of its population living below the poverty line (18.1 percent) of the fifty states.[24] The percentage of the state's popula-tion living in poverty was also much higher than the other border states: Alta California (12.4), Arizona (14.2), and Texas (16.3). New Mexico had the lowest median income among the border states ($41,452), compared to Alta California ($59,948), Arizona ($49,889), and Texas ($47,548). The median income of "Hispanic" (the U.S. Census's official term) households in New Mexico was even lower ($34,854), especially when compared to their "non-Hispanic white" neighbors in New Mexico, who earned almost nine thousand dollars more on average ($43,696).[25] The median income of American Indian households in New Mexico was only slightly lower than Hispanic households ($32,020). Hispanic households in New Mexico also had a lower median income than their Hispanic counterparts in the other border states: Alta California ($46,212), Arizona ($39,346), and Texas ($35,709). The median income for American Indian households in New Mexico was marginally higher than the same households in Arizona ($30,228) but substantially lower than Alta California ($43,712) and Texas ($40,725).[26] As much scholarly ink as has been spilled over the origins and veracity of Spanish identity, it has mattered little in the daily lives of Hispanic and Spanish residents of the state. Nor have visions of multicultural harmony substantially improved the conditions of the majority populations in the state of New Mexico.

Native People, Native Lands

As a closing consideration, it is worth highlighting how important New Mexico, as a geographically defined space, became to discussions of race and nation. As a means of identification *New Mexican* and *nuevomexicano* appeared infrequently before the late nineteenth century. By the time of statehood in 1912, these terms had become a primary means for explaining racial and regional relationships. By setting up region as a term trumping appeals to race, the new discourse sparked a series of rival claims to an authentic regional identity, which soon figured in the language of "nativeness." Mexicans frequently claimed that as native New Mexicans they possessed a distinctive type of racial Mexican identity. Claiming native status became a means by which Mexican elites could challenge the Euro-American racial hierarchy and retain their authority over New Mexico. These figures distanced themselves from the negative connotations of being "Mexican/foreign" to identify themselves as completely "American," and to claim an innate dominion over the region. Eventually the notions of nativeness would transcend class to become open to almost all Mexicans in the territory, even some who had migrated across the international borderline.

While we can understand these claims as part of the particular circumstances of New Mexico, they have larger implications for any case in which one group begins to use imaginings of geography and ancestry as a means to claim a native identity. Claims by one group to nativeness are often dependent on imperialism and an understanding of a place as knowably "ours." In the United States such claims are frequently mediated by existing notions of race, nation, and region, often in ways that obscure the differential access to "native" identity and appear totally natural. We can, for instance, raise questions about Puerto Rico. Is one a "native Puerto Rican" based on one's birth on the island? One's racial identity? *Puerto Rican*, like *New Mexican*, becomes entangled with racial and national implications that have never quite been established.

Popular twentieth-century usage of "native Texan," in contrast, more often implied an individual of Euro-American ancestry than an individual with either indigenous or Mexican ancestry. In one such usage in 1986 Susan Chadwick wrote an article defining the meaning of being a "native Texan" for *Texas Monthly*. Although her article was written tongue-in-cheek, Chadwick nonetheless revealed a presumption that to be "native" meant also to be "Anglo" in the Lone Star State. "In the early days of Anglo Texas, becoming a Texan took only a few months," Chadwick wrote. "Actual native Texans were a minority in the state until 1880."[27] For Chadwick the generations of indigenous and Mexican settlers who lived in Texas prior to 1880 did not qualify as sufficiently native (or, seemingly, as Texans at all). For her, "actual native Texans" could only be part of "Anglo Texas." That type of native identity hinged on an understanding of colonialism that privileged only one population's claims to the state. For Chadwick native Texas history did not start until Anglos had been born in sufficient numbers in the nineteenth century.

More than just regional state identities, though, the analysis of space and identity or belonging as developed in *Border Dilemmas* implies that even "Native American" identity should be scrutinized more closely. Decades of activism by indigenous communities and their allies meant that by the late twentieth century *Native American* had begun to replace *Indian* in U.S. discourse as part of an effort to highlight various indigenous groups' ancestral claims to local lands. Yet who "qualified" as Native American was not as self-evident or obvious as it might appear. Existing notions of U.S. nationalism, geography, and race circumscribed Native American identity in particular ways that maintained the authority of the state and the status quo. Renya Ramirez reminds us that geography and imaginings of space have often been critical to the meanings of Native

American identity in the United States. Classical anthropology, ethnographers, agents for the local and federal government, and other authorities contributed to dominant discourses that limited Indian communities and cultures to discrete territories within the nation.[28] Indigenous persons who departed from those spaces were imagined to have been cut off from a certain element of their native identity. Ramirez offers a starting corrective for these notions by employing the idea of the "hub" to highlight how many Native Americans maintain their cultural connections in ways that endure even after they leave particular places.

Native New Mexican, Puerto Rican, Native Texan, and *Native American* are all historical identities that different groups have used to assert their political, economic, and social priority over particular spaces. Yet all of these claims to native identity could only be understood through other existing assumptions about local place and who "belonged" to a territory. Indeed, we should even reexamine classic texts on the border that used imaginings of space to declare a uniqueness to particular populations. Américo Paredes argued that the space known as the Rio Grande Valley created a distinctive group of people, whom he referred to as "borderers."[29] A quarter of a century later Gloria Anzaldúa imagined that the international divide between the United States and Mexico created a "third country" and a unique "culture."[30] In both instances Paredes and Anzaldúa used the location known as the "border" to name a group of people as both "unique" (they only shared traits with other "borderers") and particular (something that could be found only at that particular location). Such renderings allowed for a triangulation of identity that simultaneously disavowed a strictly Mexican or American identity for that population. Yet it also naturalized those identities as having "cores" that could be found in other spaces. It enforced national identities as coherent elsewhere by suggesting that it was only in border spaces that they became altered.

These same impulses could be seen a century earlier in New Mexico, though with slightly different logic. The specific development of the regional discourse in New Mexico permitted prominent Mexicans and Euro-Americans to articulate their own distinct positions in the process of naming the racial and national meaning of the region, but it also gave them the power to exclude others. The processes of defining "native New Mexican" identity limited the possibilities of racial and national meanings and erased dissent against U.S. authority. Proponents of the regional discourse sometimes discounted certain places or histories by excluding them from being "authentically New Mexican." La Mesilla, considered an oppositional community and irreconcilable with the emerging New Mexican identity, suffered economically as the regional discourse brushed aside its earlier and ongoing status as a nationalist Mexican town. Las Cruces, a community founded as an American town, seemed a better place for those who subscribed to the New Mexican identity. Although Mesilla had dominated southern New Mexico for several decades, beginning around 1880, Las Cruces quickly drained its population and economic revenues.

The history of southern New Mexico opens questions about articulating racial, national, and regional identities. Future works will explore more elaborately how these notions crossed national borders, intersecting with larger discussions about Mexico's national identity. These particular circumstances highlight the greater importance of turning our attention to the local and to the importance of space in the articulation of meta-ideologies of race and nation. Actually being in a particular place—the difference of being in Las Cruces or La Mesilla—impacted individuals' lives materially and ideologically. Local space was never value-neutral. Declaring space as part of either "Mexico" or "the United States" was an act of power that organized social, political, and economic relationships along the U.S.-Mexican border. Many struggles between Euro-Americans and Mexican Americans in the nineteenth century resulted from differing attempts to control the meaning of the border region that also structured local relationships. The regional discourse around New Mexico ultimately reinscribed the centrality of colonialist racial hierarchies and U.S. hegemony.

NOTES

Introduction

1. Callahan, "Mexican Border Troubles," 109.
2. Biographical outline, Amador Family Papers, MS 4. For a discussion of the Terrazas family see Wasserman, *Capitalists, Caciques, and Revolution.*
3. The Indian Appropriation Act of 1885 reorganized and clarified the rules for investigating Indian "indemnity." Claimants had to prove the value of their property; that they had not been negligent in guarding it; and that Native Americans had indeed taken it. Field investigations of such claims began in 1889, and Congress granted the U.S. Court of Claims jurisdiction over these cases in 1891. See Callahan, "Mexican Border Troubles," 108n28.
4. Depositions taken before Herbert B. Holt, a Commissioner of the Court of Claims throughout the United States on the fourteenth day of May, A.D. 1898. Amador Family Papers, MS 4, Martin Amador—Legal Documents, 1870–1920, Box 27, Folder 3.
5. Gonzáles, *Mexicanos*, 102.
6. Griswold del Castillo, *The Treaty of Guadalupe Hidalgo*, 65–72.
7. Deposition of Pedro Melenudo before Herbert B. Holt, a Commissioner of the Court of Claims throughout the United States on the fourteenth day of May, A.D. 1898. Amador Family Papers, MS 4, Martin Amador—Legal Documents, 1870–1920, Box 27, Folder 3.
8. For another discussion of race and "bodily comportment" in New Mexico see Mitchell, *Coyote Nation*, 5–6.
9. Deposition of Melenudo (see note 7 above).
10. Ibid.
11. Deposition of Martin Amador before Herbert B. Holt, a Commissioner of the Court of Claims throughout the United States on the fourteenth day of May, A.D. 1898. Amador Family Papers, MS 4, Martin Amador—Legal Documents, 1870–1920, Box 27, Folder 3.
12. Deposition of Melenudo (see note 7 above).
13. Ibid.
14. Deposition of Clemente Montoya before Herbert B. Holt, a Commissioner of the Court of Claims throughout the United States on the fourteenth day of May, A.D. 1898. Amador Family Papers, MS 4, Martin Amador—Legal Documents, 1870–1920, Box 27, Folder 3.
15. Ibid.
16. Ibid.

17. That insinuation, moreover, suggested how much maleness figured as a reference to citizenship along the border. Women were not included in Montoya's self-description, only himself and his sons.

18. Deposition of Montoya (see note 14 above).

19. I depend heavily on notions of nationalism first articulated by Benedict Anderson in his *Imagined Communities*.

20. By *identity* I mean the ways in which historical actors understood and articulated their image of themselves. For other examples of this use see Rosaldo, *Culture and Truth*; Scott, *Gender and the Politics of History*; and Higginbotham, "African American Women's History and the Metalanguage of Race."

21. Interview with María Gonzales Carriere, in Nichols and Banegas, *Our Heritage—Our People*, 82–96, 88–89.

22. Frietze, *History of La Mesilla and Her Mesilleros*, 181.

23. By "U.S. imperialism" I do not mean a single ideology or an absolute dominance that has been constant through time. Rather, I refer to the "multiple histories of continental and overseas expansion, conquest, conflict, and resistance" (Kaplan, "'Left Alone with America,'" 4). See also Kaplan, *The Anarchy of Empire in the Making of U.S. Culture*; and Streeby, *American Sensations*.

24. This notion of isolation is not totally a retroactive invention. Pedro Bautista Pino traveled to Spain in 1812 as a representative of New Mexico. In a bid to increase imperial investment in his territory Pino painted a dire portrait of New Mexico that many historians have taken at face value. See Weber, *Foreigners in Their Native Land*, 39–42; and González Navarro, *Los extranjeros*, 296.

25. See, e.g., Gutiérrez, *When Jesus Came, the Corn Mothers Went Away*, 337; González Navarro, *Los extranjeros*, 199 (for his interpretations of New Mexico, Alta California, and other northern territories González depends quite heavily on U.S.-based historians like David Weber); Meyer, *Speaking for Themselves*, 6.

26. Although in different ways, elements of this narrative can be seen in Gutiérrez, *When Jesus Came, the Corn Mothers Went Away*; Montgomery, *The Spanish Redemption*; Nieto-Phillips, *The Language of Blood*; Simmons, *New Mexico*; Beck, *New Mexico*; Fergusson, *New Mexico*; and Lara, "(Re)Visiting the Land of Enchantment."

27. See Almaguer, *Racial Fault Lines*; Foley, *The White Scourge*; González, *Refusing the Favor*; Gutiérrez, *When Jesus Came, the Corn Mothers Went Away*; Haas, *Conquests and Historical Identities in California, 1769–1936*; Sánchez, *Becoming Mexican American*; and Pitti, *The Devil in Silicon Valley*.

28. See, e.g., Gibson, *The Life and Death of Colonel Albert Jennings Fountain*; Fulton and Mulin, *History of the Lincoln County War*; and Jacobson, *Such Men as Billy the Kid*.

29. Weber, *The Mexican Frontier, 1821–1846*; Weber, *Myth and the History of the Hispanic Southwest*; Weber, "The Spanish-Mexican Rim"; Deutsch, *No Separate Refuge*; González, *Refusing the Favor*; Nieto-Phillips, *The Language of Blood*; Gutiérrez, *When Jesus Came, the Corn Mothers Went Away*; Wilson, *The Myth of Santa Fe*; Frank, *From Settler to Citizen*; Montgomery, *The Spanish Redemption*; and Gómez, *Manifest Destinies*.

30. About two thousand Mexicans in New Mexico declared their preference to

remain in New Mexico as Mexican citizens. The lack of evidence for this same phenomenon in California or Texas might be attributed to any number of historical circumstances: intimidation, harassment, or simply poor record keeping. See Griswold del Castillo, *The Treaty of Guadalupe Hidalgo*, 65–66.

31. Pulido, *Black, Brown, Yellow, and Left*, 4.

32. Ibid.

33. See Montgomery, *The Spanish Redemption*.

34. See Roediger, *The Wages of Whiteness*; Roediger, *Towards the Abolition of Whiteness*; Jacobson, *Whiteness of a Different Color*; Foley, *The White Scourge*; and Arredondo, "Navigating Ethno-Racial Currents: Mexicans in Chicago, 1919–1939."

35. Jacobson, *Whiteness of a Different Color*, 5.

36. McWilliams, *North from Mexico*, 35–47.

37. Ibid., 43.

38. Zunser, "A New Mexican Village," 141.

39. At a time when race has become a category of analysis in U.S. history, "whiteness studies" threatens to displace focus from understanding the greater complexity of racial ideologies. There is a danger that the current direction in race studies privileges whiteness at the expense of the Other.

40. Scholars in cultural studies use "articulation" to understand components of social formation. Articulation suggests both expressing and representing, as well as a linking of representations, in this case race and nation, to form a sense of unity. See Parker and Willis, *Cultural Studies*, 9; and Hall, *Stuart Hall*, 115.

41. Sánchez, *Becoming Mexican American*, 12.

42. For different ways that cultural-studies methodologies have been put to use see Haraway, *Primate Visions*; Stoler, *Carnal Knowledge and Imperial Power*; and Carib, *Cartographic Mexico*.

43. See Massey, "Politics and Space/Time"; Brady, *Extinct Lands, Temporal Geographies*; and McDowell, "Spatializing Feminism."

44. Quoted in Crampton and Elden, *Space, Knowledge and Power*, 9.

45. Deloria, "Revolution, Region, and Culture in Multicultural History," 364.

46. Deutsch, *Women and the City*, 5–6.

47. Massey, "Politics and Space/Time," 80; see also McDowell, "Spatializing Feminism."

48. See Massey, "Politics and Space/Time."

49. For discussions about theorizing "borders" see Rajaram and Grundy-Warr, *Borderscapes*, ix.

50. For other applications of *space* see Duncan, *Body Space*; Howard, *Men Like That*; and Mumford, *Interzones*.

51. Owen, *Las Cruces, New Mexico, 1849–1999*, 2; Baldwin, "A Short History of the Mesilla Valley," 314.

52. U.S. Congress, House, *Reports of Explorations and Surveys*, 6.

53. Baldwin, "A Short History of the Mesilla Valley," 315. According to popular legend, Las Cruces (the crosses) derived its name from the burial site of some forty travelers who died in a conflict with Apaches in 1830. See the *Las Cruces Democrat*, Sept. 27, 1899.

54. These mountains have also been known as the Sierra del Olvido (Mountains of Oblivion or Forgotten Mountains) and Los Organos (Owen, *Las Cruces, New Mexico, 1849–1999*, 1).

55. Milton, *The Mesilla Civil Colony Grant*, 4.

56. Baldwin, "A Short History of the Mesilla Valley," 317. García's heirs eventually sold his grant to Hugh Stephenson in 1851, confirmed by Congress in 1868. See Milton, *The Mesilla Civil Colony Grant*, 5.

57. Weber, *The Mexican Frontier, 1821–1846*, 182; Baldwin, "A Short History of the Mesilla Valley," 316. Heath's son attempted to confirm the grant once the United States took control of the area, but his petition was rejected.

58. Baldwin, "A Short History of the Mesilla Valley," 316.

59. Owen, *Las Cruces, New Mexico, 1849–1999*, 20–21.

60. Montgomery, *The Spanish Redemption*, 8.

61. For a detailed and nuanced discussion of marriage and race in colonial New Mexico see Gutiérrez, *When Jesus Came, the Corn Mothers Went Away*, 271–97. Gutiérrez documents that the rates of racially exogamous marriages rose substantially in the late eighteenth century. From 1760 to 1790 approximately 20 percent of marriages in New Mexico were between people of different races. See, in Gutiérrez, Table 9.10 (288).

62. See González, *Refusing the Favor*, xx.

63. See Foucault, *The Archaeology of Knowledge*, 182–83.

64. Meyer, *Speaking for Themselves*, 8.

Chapter One. Preoccupied America

1. Simmons, *New Mexico*, 126.

2. Mitchell, *Coyote Nation*, 4.

3. Simmons, *New Mexico*, 127–28.

4. McNierney, *Taos, 1847*, 1.

5. Baldwin, "A Short History of the Mesilla Valley," 316.

6. Twitchell, *The Leading Facts of New Mexican History*, 311.

7. See Waldstreicher, *In the Midst of Perpetual Fetes*; Jacobson, *Whiteness of a Different Color*; Joseph, *Everyday Forms of State Formation*; Guardino, *Peasants, Politics, and the Formation of Mexico's National State: Guerrero, 1800–1857*.

8. Anderson, *Imagined Communities*.

9. For a discussion of Mexican liberalism and race see Lomnitz-Adler, *Exits from the Labyrinth*, 274–77.

10. While I tend to think his notions of indigenous civilization are too static and rigid, Guillermo Bonfil Batalla argues that the history of postconquest Mexico can be understood as a constant confrontation between Western and indigenous "ways of life." See Bonfil Batalla, *México profundo*, xv.

11. Lomnitz-Adler, *Exits from the Labyrinth*, 276.

12. Spain had ceded Puerto Rico to the United States at the end of the Spanish-American War in 1898 (along with Guam and the Philippine Islands); therefore, the

case centered on whether the island was trading as a "foreign nation" or should be protected under the uniform taxation clause in the U.S. Constitution.

13. Kaplan, *Anarchy of Empire*, 2.

14. Ibid., 1–12.

15. The justices did not achieve a consensus about *why* that should have been the case. Instead, they submitted five different opinions, none of which received a majority endorsement. The one with the most support explained that "whilst in an international sense Porto [*sic*] Rico was not a foreign country, since it was subject to the sovereignty of and was owned by the United States, it was foreign to the United States in a domestic sense" (*Downes v. Bidwell*, 182 U.S. 244, 341–42 [1901]; quoted in Kaplan, *Anarchy of Empire*, 2).

16. *Cherokee Nation v. Georgia*, 30 U.S. (5 Pet.) 1, 16 (1831); quoted in Frickey, "Marshalling Past and Present," 392.

17. For a discussion about fears of "eternal contaminations" and nationalism see Anderson, *Imagined Communities*, 136.

18. Stoler, *Carnal Knowledge and Imperial Power*, 83.

19. Pratt, *Imperial Eyes*, 150–51; Stoler, *Carnal Knowledge and Imperial Power*, 83–84.

20. Mehta, "Liberal Strategies of Exclusion," 67–68.

21. Racist exclusion from the nation was not based simply on visually identifiable somatic features. In other words it was not merely that people "looked different." Rather, such visual differences were understood to signal invisible essences (intelligence, morality, and cultural practices) that made certain groups incompatible with the nation because they lacked the same level of reason held by "whites" (Stoler, *Carnal Knowledge and Imperial Power*, 84).

22. See Stoler, *Carnal Knowledge and Imperial Power*, 80.

23. Ibid., 81.

24. Not all Euro-Americans viewed Mexico negatively or endorsed U.S. imperialism. See Mayer, *Mexico as It Was and as It Is*.

25. Waldstreicher, *In the Midst of Perpetual Fetes*, 3.

26. Ibid., 327.

27. See Ohline, "Republicanism and Slavery"; and Kerber, "The Paradox of Women's Citizenship in the Early Republic."

28. Northern and southern delegates agreed that three-fifths of the slave population of a state would be added to the number of free citizens to determine the size of the state's delegation for the House of Representatives. In no way did they want the counting of slaves for representation to imply an equality with full citizens. George Mason, a white Virginia planter who kept more than three hundred people in bondage, argued that a percentage of slaves should count for representation, but he could not agree to any measure that would "regard them as equal to freemen and could not vote for them as such" (Ohline, "Republicanism and Slavery," 578).

29. Gender also played an important part in defining both "citizenship" and "American" identity. The Northwest Ordinance of 1787 explicitly used gender as a marker when it stated that only "free male inhabitants, of full age" would be considered when determining representation. White women could claim that they were

citizens and Americans, but they lacked many of the rights that white men claimed. For many, as much as the terms of citizenship implied "white," they also implied "male" unless otherwise specified. See Lewis, " 'Of Every Age Sex & Condition,' " 364.

30. See Cott, "Marriage and Women's Citizenship in the United States, 1830–1934," 1444; and Jacobson, *Whiteness of a Different Color*, 7.

31. Much of this power derived from the vague wording in the Constitution that promised "citizens of each State shall be entitled to all privileges and immunities of citizens in the several States" (U.S. Const., art. 4, sec. 2.1).

32. Jacobson, *Whiteness of a Different Color*, 25.

33. Ibid., 302–8.

34. For further reading on the definitions of race and citizenship in the United States see Jacobson, *Whiteness of a Different Color*; Cott, "Marriage and Women's Citizenship in the United States, 1830–1934," 1440–74; Lewis, " 'Of Every Age Sex & Condition' "; Kerber, "The Meanings of Citizenship"; Kaczorowski, "To Begin the Nation Anew"; Roediger, "The Pursuit of Whiteness"; and McLoughlin, "Experiment in Cherokee Citizenship, 1817–1829."

35. Laura Gómez, alternatively, makes a distinction between federal and state citizenship. Federal citizenship, she argues, included individuals who resided in territories. The government did not guarantee political rights until the area became a state. See Gómez, *Manifest Destinies*, 43–44.

36. Butler, "From Interiority to Gender Performatives," 366.

37. I use *performance* as the term is theorized in Judith Butler's work on gender and identity. See, e.g., Butler, "From Interiority to Gender Performatives"; and Butler, *Gender Trouble*, 24–25.

38. Butler, "From Interiority to Gender Performatives," 362–63.

39. A discussion of "blood" eventually emerged that reinvested notions of race within particular bodies. The state of Virginia took this thinking to the greatest extreme when it adopted the infamous "one-drop" law in 1930. See Bardaglio, " 'Shameful Matches.' "

40. Cott, "Marriage and Women's Citizenship in the United States, 1830–1934," 1445; Ehrlich, "The Origins of the Dred Scott Case"; see also Jacobson, *Whiteness of a Different Color*, 308–23.

41. McLoughlin, "Experiment in Cherokee Citizenship, 1817–1829," 4.

42. Young, *Redskins, Ruffleshirts, and Rednecks*, 4.

43. Dowd, *A Spirited Resistance*, 116–17.

44. Constitution of Michigan of 1850, Art. VII, Sec. 1, available on the website of the Michigan legislature, http://www.legislature.mi.gov/ (accessed March 8, 2010).

45. See Plane and Button, "The Massachusetts Indian Enfranchisement Act," 590.

46. Ibid., 591.

47. Dowd, *A Spirited Resistance*, 118.

48. Government agents deployed a doublespeak that promised to treat Cherokee individuals as "legitimate landowners and American citizens" but also stated that they required "special protection of the law." Among other things, these "protections" resulted in the inability of the new citizens to dispose of their property as

they saw fit. Euro-American officials justified this measure by arguing that Native Americans were equivalent to "minors" based on cultural practices, like English-language proficiency. See McLoughlin, "Experiment in Cherokee Citizenship, 1817–1829," 6.

49. Ibid., 9.

50. Troup to Calhoun, Feb. 23, 1824; quoted in ibid.

51. Ibid., 9n17.

52. Ibid., 23.

53. Ibid., 25.

54. Mehta, "Liberal Strategies of Exclusion," 75.

55. Phelps, "Representation without Taxation," 135.

56. For a classic text on Spain's imperial occupation of Pueblo lands see John, *Storms Brewed in Other Men's Worlds*.

57. Lomnitz-Adler, *Exits from the Labyrinth*, 286.

58. In the imperial contests over North America this had occurred in only a few other places, such as Mexico City, Louisiana, Florida, and French Canada. See Nugent, *Habits of Empire*, 69–71, 111.

59. See Hernández, "El México perdido," 29–30.

60. Vincent, "The Blacks Who Freed Mexico," 258.

61. Gonzalo Aguirre Beltrán notes that after the revolution most historical and sociological studies focused on indigenous populations (and their relationship with whites) as defining the Mexican nation. The role of Afro-Mexicans was largely ignored. See Aguirre Beltrán, *La población negra de México*, 9. For a more contemporary discussion of this see Lewis, "Blacks, Black Indians, Afromexicans."

62. The historian Ramón Gutiérrez urges scholars engaged in studies of imperialism to pay attention to the "differential condition of embodiment for women and men among both colonizers and colonized" (Gutiérrez, "What's Love Got to Do with It?" 867).

63. For other discussions of Mexican nationalism see Joseph, *Everyday Forms of State Formation*; Lomnitz-Adler, "Barbarians at the Gate?"; Rubin, "Decentering the Regime"; Mallon, "The Promise and Dilemma of Subaltern Studies"; Alonso, "The Politics of Space, Time, and Substance"; and Knight, "Peasants into Patriots."

64. In other instances some popular historians unconsciously drawing on the twentieth-century New Mexico discourse of "multiculturalism" (which I will discuss at greater length later), posit that racism did not occur in New Mexico at all, ever. See, e.g., Simmons, *New Mexico*, 118. Although the idea that New Mexico was unchanged by Mexican independence is currently prominent, some historians have argued that the nineteenth century brought the final collapse of the *casta* system in New Mexico. See Bustamante, " 'The Matter Was Never Resolved,' " 163.

65. See Reséndez, *Changing National Identities at the Frontier*, esp. 60.

66. Raúl Ramos explores how notions of nationalism similarly played out in nineteenth-century Texas. See, e.g., Ramos, *Beyond the Alamo*, 7–8.

67. Kessell, *Remote beyond Compare*, ix.

68. Guardino, *Peasants, Politics, and the Formation of Mexico's National State*, 86.

69. Gutiérrez, *When Jesus Came, the Corn Mothers Went Away*; Montgomery, "The Trap of Race and Memory"; Nieto-Phillips, *The Language of Blood*.

70. Gutiérrez, *When Jesus Came, the Corn Mothers Went Away*, 199.

71. Lomnitz-Adler, *Exits from the Labyrinth*, 263–64; Martínez, *Genealogical Fictions*, 1. See also Seed, "Social Dimensions of Race"; and Aguirre Beltrán, *La población negra de México*.

72. Martínez López, "The Spanish Concept of *Limpieza de Sangre* and the Emergence of the 'Race/Caste' System in the Viceroyalty of New Spain," 19.

73. Nieto-Phillips, *The Language of Blood*, 25–37; for more elaborate discussions see Lomnitz-Adler, *Exits from the Labyrinth*, 271–74; and Aguirre Beltrán, *La población negra de México*, 153–79.

74. Martínez López, "The Spanish Concept of *Limpieza de Sangre*," 18.

75. Aguirre Beltrán reminds us that Spain's officials also made distinctions *within* the core lineages of "español," "negro," and "indio." Individuals who were identified as "negro" and whose skin was deemed extremely dark, for instance, were referred to as "negros retintos." Conversely, those labeled "negro" whose skin was seen as "matiz menos" were labeled "negros amulatados." Aguirre Beltrán, *La población negra de México*, 166, 267–71.

76. Mexican officials and intellectuals would continually grapple with the racial diversity of the nation. In the post-Revolution era indigenous identity would be praised as defining the nation. Yet this left unanswered the role of Afro-Mexicans. The anthropologist Guillermo Bonfil Batalla, as the director of the Office of Popular Culture, developed projects under the rubric of "Our Third Root" that purported to celebrate "African contributions to Mexican multiculturalism" in the 1980s. This project, though, continued to fashion blackness as either an exception or as difference within Mexico. See Lewis, "Blacks, Black Indians, and Afromexicans," 901–2.

77. Martínez López, "The Spanish Concept of *Limpieza de Sangre*," 19.

78. Lomnitz-Adler, *Exit from the Labyrinth*, 273–74.

79. Ibid., 31.

80. Place of birth also created a divide between *peninsulares* and *criollos*. Given that the latter had been born in the Americas, they were regarded as weaker than those born on the Iberian Peninsula.

81. Martínez López, "The Spanish Concept of *Limpieza de Sangre*," 66–67.

82. Spicer, *The American Indians*, 122–25.

83. Pueblos united in one of the most successful pan-tribal revolts against white authorities in 1680. Known as the "Great Pueblo Revolt," the united Pueblo communities kept Spain at bay for more than a decade and inspired comparable revolts across the northern frontier. See Kessell, *Kiva, Cross, and Crown*; Gutiérrez, *When Jesus Came, the Corn Mothers Went Away*; and Dozier, *The Pueblo Indians of North America*.

84. Spicer, *The American Indians*, 122.

85. The complexity and depth of the interrelationships among all of these competing groups is too immense to delve into here. For a start see Brooks, *Captives & Cousins*.

86. See Weber, *Bárbaros*.

87. Martínez López, "The Spanish Concept of *Limpieza de Sangre*," 71.

88. New Mexico's genízaro population emerged from Apache, Navajo, Ute, and Comanche men and women whom Spaniards captured and pressed into domestic service. See Mitchell, *Coyote Nation*, 9.

89. See Weber, *The Spanish Frontier in North America*, 307–8.

90. Lomnitz-Adler, *Exits from the Labyrinth*, 272–73.

91. Gutiérrez, *When Jesus Came, the Corn Mothers Went Away*, 202–5.

92. Weber, *The Spanish Frontier in North America*, 327.

93. Gutiérrez, *When Jesus Came, the Corn Mothers Went Away*, 203.

94. Ibid., 205.

95. Aguirre Beltrán, *La población negra de México*, 154.

96. Antonio Salazar of Zacatecas increased his casta status as his calidad increased. Salazar served as the master mason at the mission of San José at San Antonio. Between 1789 and 1794 Salazar advanced up the casta hierarchy and was defined in scattered documents with three different ethnic identities: first indio, then mestizo, and finally español. As Salazar's status as a mason grew, his racial category improved comparably. Census officials listed all military personnel in early nineteenth-century Texas, whatever their parentage, as "españoles" (see Weber, *The Spanish Frontier in North America*, 327–28).

97. Tejanos developed a complicated set of classifications for understanding their relationship to various indigenous groups beyond a binary of *bárbaros* and *civilizados*. Juan Antonio Padilla, for instance, documented differences between bárbaro tribes based on their friendly or hostile relationship to Mexican settlers in 1819. See Ramos, "Finding the Balance," 41.

98. Even before independence the Spanish Cortes established an important precedent when it declared the "social and civil equality of Spaniards, Indians and mestizos" in 1813. Prominent policy makers hoped that diminishing racial categories would promote more egalitarian economic and social practices. This move represented an optimistic ploy to unify New Spain after centuries of racial divisions that had defined colonial economic and social relationships for centuries (Weber, *The Mexican Frontier, 1821–1846*, 47).

99. Nieto-Phillips, *The Language of Blood*, 37.

100. Ibid.

101. Lomnitz-Adler, *Exits from the Labyrinth*, 275.

102. Reséndez, *Changing National Identities at the Frontier*, 84.

103. See, e.g., Ramos, *Beyond the Alamo*, 1–3.

104. Reséndez, *Changing National Identities at the Frontier*, 84.

105. See King, "The Colored Castes and American Representation in the Cortes of Cadiz."

106. Plan de Iguala, art. 12; see also Weber, *The Mexican Frontier, 1821–1846*, 47.

107. Weber, *The Mexican Frontier, 1821–1846*, 47.

108. See, e.g., Vigil, "Opina sobre armas, municiones, comercio, norteamericanos, y indios bárbaros" (June 18, 1846), 15.

109. Lomnitz-Adler, *Exits from the Labyrinth*, 276.

110. Translated in Loyola, "The American Occupation of New Mexico, 1821–1852," 260.

111. See Nieto-Phillips, *The Language of Blood*, 37–39.

112. Ibid., 24.

113. For considerations on indio identity and politics in Latin America see Guillermo Bonfil Batalla, *Identidad y pluralismo cultural en América Latina*.

114. Hall and Weber, "Mexican Liberals and the Pueblo Indians, 1821–1829," 8.

115. Minutes of the Diputación, March 2, 1825, Mexican Archives of New Mexico, reel 42, frame 261; translated in Hall and Weber, "Mexican Liberals and the Pueblo Indians, 1821–1829," 15. It is important to note that this document emerged during proceedings that sought to dispossess Pueblo Indians of their land.

116. Alcalde Rafael Aguilar et al. to the diputación, Pecos, March 12, 1826, Spanish Archives of New Mexico, no. 1370; quoted in Hall and Weber, "Mexican Liberals and the Pueblo Indians, 1821–1829," 17.

117. Reséndez, *Changing National Identities at the Frontier*, 187–88.

118. Historia de Montezuma, Mexico City, May 25, 1846, Bandelier Transcripts; quoted in Reséndez, *Changing National Identities at the Frontier*, 258.

119. Lomnitz-Adler, *Exits from the Labyrinth*, 300.

120. Hall and Weber, "Mexican Liberals and the Pueblo Indians, 1821–1829," 8; Nieto-Phillips, "No Other Blood," 36.

121. One California delegate to the Mexican Congress questioned whether Mexico's Constitution could grant citizenship to "errant" tribes. "Can the Indian," he pondered in a personal letter, "be considered truly free while he does not understand his rights as a citizen?" (Manuel Castañares to Mariano Guadalupe Vallejo, Mexico, Oct. 22, 1845; quoted in Weber, *The Mexican Frontier, 1821–1846*, 103).

122. When Texans greedily eyed New Mexico in 1841, they attempted to use the same language of the Mexican discourse to create support within New Mexico for their invasion. Trying to distance Texas from the Euro-American discourse, they circulated a letter from Secretary of State Abner S. Libscomb that claimed that Texas, like Mexico, did not define citizenship through race. Libscomb argued that Texas based its citizenship on one's performance and actions. Using a language similar to the "gente de razón," he claimed that Texans distinguished between "civilized" and "barbarian" Indians. He further promised that the Pueblos would be treated as equals in the Texas republic. Pueblos appeared unconvinced. See Libscomb to Dryden, Rowland, and Workman, April 14, 1841; quoted in Loyola, "The American Occupation of New Mexico, 1821–1852," 252.

123. Weber, *The Mexican Frontier, 1821–1846*, 103.

124. Antonio José Martínez, *Esposición que el presbítero Antonio José Martínez, cura de Taos de Nuevo México, dirje al Gobierno del Exmo. Sor. General Antonio López de Santa Anna. Proponiendo la civilisación de las naciones bárbaras que son al contorno del Departamento de Nuevo México* (Taos, J. M. B., 1843); facsimile in Weber, *Northern Mexico on the Eve of the United States Invasion*, "Imprint Number 5."

125. *Archivo de gobernación (México), comercio expediente*, 44; quoted in Loyola, "The American Occupation of New Mexico, 1821–1852," 53–54.

126. Ibid.

127. See, e.g., *Message of the President of the United States, with the Correspondence therewith Communicated, Between the Secretary of War and Other Officers of the Government, on the Subject of the Mexican War*, 30th Cong., 1st sess., 1848, Ex. Doc. 60, 303–4.

128. Gutiérrez, "Migration, Emergent Ethnicity, and the 'Third Space,'" 485.

129. Meyer and Sherman, *The Course of Mexican History*, 327–28.

130. Weber, *The Mexican Frontier, 1821–1846*, 33–37.

131. Lecompte, *Rebellion in Río Arriba, 1837*, 13.

132. Weber, *The Mexican Frontier, 1821–1846*, 262.

133. A few even accused Euro-Americans, such as the Taos merchant Charles Bent, of secretly fostering the revolt as a way to give New Mexico to the United States. See Lieutenant Colonel Cayetano Justiniani to Minister of War and Navy, Chihuahua, Sept. 12, 1837; translated in Lecompte, *Rebellion in Río Arriba, 1837*, 110. See also Juan Felipe Ortiz to Manuel Armijo, Mexico City, Dec. 19, 1837; quoted in Reséndez, *Changing National Identities at the Frontier*, 173.

134. Weber, *The Mexican Frontier, 1821–1846*, 262.

135. "An Account of the Chimayó Rebellion, 1837," in Lecompte, *Rebellion in Río Arriba, 1837*, 94.

136. Lecompte, *Rebellion in Río Arriba, 1837*, 19–20.

137. Reséndez, *Changing National Identities at the Frontier*, 182.

138. Twelve leaders called for an armed revolt against the governor on August 3 (Lecompte, *Rebellion in Río Arriba, 1837*, 19–20).

139. They also imagined their efforts as divinely sanctioned. One circular stated that the rebels had "unsheathed the sword to defend the law and inflict the just punishment ordered by the Omnipotent." Circular to San Francisco del Rancho de Taos, Río Chiquito, Pueblo de Taos, Arroyo Seco, Plaza de San Antonio de Montes y Ranchitos; Santa Cruz de la Cañada, Aug. 3, 1837, Donaciano Vigil Papers; quoted in Reséndez, *Changing National Identities at the Frontier*, 177.

140. See Spivak, *In Other Worlds*, 206–7.

141. Unaware of the growing animus against him, Pérez dutifully promoted Santa Anna's Departmental Plan. He claimed that the new government increased the status of territories like New Mexico to be the peers of states. In reality, though, the plan reduced states to less than the equivalent of territories under the 1824 Constitution. The Centralists' plan replaced state legislatures with a five-member council. Mexico City would also appoint state governors directly rather than allowing for elections. These changes, though, would not significantly alter New Mexico's relationship to the central state. Mexico City had always appointed New Mexico's governor. See Reséndez, *Changing National Identities at the Frontier*, 175.

142. Lecompte, *Rebellion in Río Arriba, 1837*, 36–37.

143. Ibid., 41.

144. "Draft of Proceedings of a Meeting of Sept. 2, 1837," Mexican Archives of New Mexico, reel 23, frame 637–40; printed in Lecompte, *Rebellion in Río Arriba, 1837*, 45–46.

145. Lecompte, *Rebellion in Río Arriba, 1837*, 56.

146. Reséndez, *Changing National Identities at the Frontier*, 186–87.

147. Plan of Tomé, Sept. 8, 1837; quoted in Lecompte, *Rebellion in Río Arriba, 1837*, 52.

148. Lecompte, *Rebellion in Río Arriba, 1837*, 58.

149. Paredes, "The Mexican Image in American Travel Literature, 1831–1869."

150. Davis, *El Gringo, or, New Mexico and Her People*, 84.

151. Ibid.

152. Ideas about "Mexican" identity being both a racial and national identity were not unique to the United States. French investors and writers also conveyed a similar vision. See Barker, "The Factor of 'Race' in the French Experience in Mexico, 1821–1861."

153. González, *Refusing the Favor*, 47.

154. Gregg, *Commerce of the Prairies*, 153.

155. Ibid.

156. Hall, *Race and Class in Post-Colonial Society*, 170–72.

157. See, e.g., Pike, "Narrative of a Journey in the Prairie"; and Paredes, "The Mexican Image in American Travel Literature, 1831–1869," 7.

158. Hulbert, *Southwest on the Turquoise Trail*, 76.

159. Pattie, *The Personal Narrative of James O. Pattie, of Kentucky*, 54–55.

160. See also Bryant, *What I Saw in California*; Kendall, *Narrative of the Texan Santa Fé Expedition*; James, *Three Years among the Indians and Mexicans*; Gilliam, *Travels over the Tablelands and Cordilleras of Mexico during the Years 1843 and 1844*; Bartlett, *Personal Narrative of Explorations*; Davis, *El Gringo, or, New Mexico and Her People*; and Browne, *Adventures in the Apache Country*.

161. Pattie, *The Personal Narrative of James O. Pattie, of Kentucky*, 168.

162. Thomas J. Farnham, *Life, Adventures, and Travels in California*; quoted in Paredes, "The Mexican Image in American Travel Literature, 1831–1869," 21.

163. Pratt, *Imperial Eyes*, 150.

164. The "natives" of these nations, according to these writers, suffered from an innate inability to become what Europeans and Euro-Americans already were. Gaspar Mollien wrote of Colombia: "The greater proportion of the lands lie fallow; they would, however, produce considerable crops, if the inhabitants were less indifferent. No encouragement can rouse them from their indolent habits and usual routine" (Mollien, *Travels in the Republic of Colombia in the Years 1822–1823*, 57; quoted in Pratt, *Imperial Eyes*, 151).

165. Wislizenus, *Memoir*, 84.

166. Ibid., 85.

167. *El Sol* (Mexico City), April 15, 1826; discussed in Brack, "Mexican Opinion, American Racism, and the War of 1846," 169.

168. *Chihuahua La Luna*, June 29, 1839; quoted in Brack, "Mexican Opinion, American Racism, and the War of 1846," 171.

169. Translated in Loyola, "The American Occupation of New Mexico, 1821–1852," 257–58.

170. Ibid.

171. "Marcelino Castañeda, gobernador del Estado de Durango, a sus habitantes," 1846, Diocese of Durango Archives, microfilm, reel 304.

172. Ibid.

173. Mangusso, "A Study of the Citizenship Provisions of the Treaty of Guadalupe Hidalgo," 19.

174. Juan Bautista Vigil y Alarid, Santa Fe, New Mexico, Aug. 19, 1846; translated in Weber, *Foreigners in Their Native Land*, 128–29.

175. Ibid.

176. Vigil y Alarid would later return to Santa Fe in 1855 (see Sisneros, "Los emigrantes Nuevomexicanos," 6–7).

177. Report of the Citizens of New Mexico to the President of Mexico, Sept. 26, 1846; printed in Weber, *Strangers in Their Native Land*, 124.

178. Brooks, *Captives & Cousins*, 231.

179. Herrera, "New Mexico Resistance to U.S. Occupation," 30.

180. Quoted in Goodrich, "Revolt at Mora," 49.

181. Lawrence Waldo to David Waldo, Jan. 13, 1847; quoted in Brooks, *Captives & Cousins*, 283.

182. For a larger discussion of how Guadalupe figured in nineteenth-century representations of Mexico see Lafaye, *Quetzalcóatl and Guadalupe*.

183. Reséndez, *Changing National Identities at the Frontier*, 254.

184. Charles Bent to James Buchanan, Dec. 26, 1846; printed in McNierney, *Taos, 1847*, 7.

185. Ibid.

186. Goodrich, "Revolt at Mora," 50.

187. Previous plans to oust the United States had circulated among prominent ricos like Diego Archuleta and Dimasio Salazar, who believed that they had been politically marginalized by the U.S. government. See Brooks, *Captives & Cousins*, 282.

188. Brooks, *Captives & Cousins*, 283–84.

189. Dick Wootton's account, in McNierney, *Taos, 1847*, 12.

190. Brooks, *Captives & Cousins*, 284–86.

191. Jim Beckwourth's account, in McNierney, *Taos, 1847*, 22.

192. The abolitionist paper the *Washington National Era* printed an uncommon defense of Mexicans in Taos. "The [New Mexico] territory is held by force," the editor wrote, "under martial law; and the inhabitants have just as much right at any moment to rise upon their invaders, and expel them from the country at the point of the sword, as our fathers had to concert plans for expelling the British from New York and Philadelphia during the revolutionary war" (*Washington National Era*, March 25, 1847).

193. Brooks, *Captives & Cousins*, 285.

194. W. L. Marcy, Secretary of War, to the President, James Polk, July 19, 1848, Ex. Doc. No. 70, House Records, 30th Cong., 1st sess., 1848.

195. Col. Sterling Price to Secretary of War William L. Marcy, Feb. 26, 1847; quoted in Herrera, "New Mexico Resistance to U.S. Occupation," 24.

196. Brooks, *Captives & Cousins*, 286.

197. Mexicans, of course, did not continue to view themselves as allies of Comanche, Navajo, or Apache groups. Mexicans in New Mexico participated with

Euro-Americans in numerous raids against nomadic indigenous groups as early as 1851. See ibid., 292.

198. Ibid., 285–86.

199. *Santa Fe Republican*, March 8, 1848; quoted in Brooks, *Captives & Cousins*, 288.

200. Herrera, "New Mexico Resistance to U.S. Occupation," 33.

201. There is also some evidence that Shawnee and Delaware individuals also participated in Taos. See Brooks, *Captives & Cousins*, 287.

202. Reséndez, *Changing National Identities at the Frontier*, 256.

203. Ibid., 258.

204. Ibid. Stories about Euro-Americans abusing individual Indians also circulated. One incident involved members of the Missouri Volunteers, who forced a Pueblo Indian to keep pace with a horse-drawn ambulance by tying him to the back. The Euro-American soldiers whipped him as he struggled to keep from falling. See Brooks, *Captives & Cousins*, 291–92.

205. Brooks, *Captives & Cousins*, 291–92.

206. Plains Native Americans would continue to play Mexico against the United States for several years. On a diplomatic mission to Mexico City the Comanche captain Pahayuca proposed driving out Euro-Americans from New Mexico by forming a "league among the wild tribes" (Brooks, *Captives & Cousins*, 291).

207. Dick Wootton's account, in McNierney, *Taos, 1847*, 11.

208. Jim Beckwourth's account, in McNierney, *Taos, 1847*, 23.

209. Dick Wootton's account, in McNierney, *Taos, 1847*, 11.

210. Ibid., 12.

211. Ibid., 60.

212. Brooks, *Captives & Cousins*, 281–82.

213. Proclamation by Donaciano Vigil, Jan. 22, 1847; printed in McNierney, *Taos, 1847*, 42.

214. Ibid.

215. *Congressional Globe*, 30th Cong., 1st sess., 1848, 98–99; quoted in Weber, *Foreigners in Their Native Land*, 135.

216. Ibid. See also Suseri, *Seeds of Discord*, 99.

217. *Congressional Globe*, 29th Cong., 2nd sess., Feb. 12, 1847, 2:369; quoted in Suseri, *Seeds of Discord*, 94.

218. Although Stevens supported suffrage rights for free African Americans, he believed the racial composition of Mexicans barred them from the same privilege. Like Stevens, many Euro-Americans cited the "ignorance" of the local Mexican population to rationalize keeping New Mexico as a territory, not a state. Based on statistical sampling data from the 1850 census, though, one finds that there was not a tremendous gap between the literacy rates among local Mexicans and Euro-Americans. According to these data, 11 percent of those with a Spanish surname were considered literate (able to read and write in one language) in 1850. Euro-Americans in New Mexico reported a literacy rate of only 19.5 percent in 1850. The 1850 census also suggests that Mexican Americans formed most of a meager population enrolled in school. Obviously reserved for a small elite, 3.5 percent of Spanish-

surnamed children younger than fifteen years old were enrolled in school, compared to less than 1 percent of Euro-American children. In some counties Mexican Americans proved slightly more literate than their Euro-American neighbors. Records from Santa Ana County, for instance, suggest that 11 percent of Mexicans reported being literate, whereas only 7.7 percent of Euro-Americans were literate. Not surprisingly, a wider disparity appears in literacy rates through the first decades of Euro-American imperialism. Euro-Americans and Mexican Americans clearly had unequal access to education. The percentage of Spanish-surnamed children enrolled in school had risen only to 7.7 percent by 1880. The number of Euro-American children, though, increased to 13.8 percent. Literacy rates for both Mexican and Euro-Americans increased; however, the gap in literacy rates between Mexican Americans and Euro-Americans also increased dramatically through the territorial period. In 1880 Mexican American literacy rates increased to 23.3 percent, but Euro-American literacy increased to 50 percent. By 1920, 90 percent of Euro-Americans had attained literacy, but only 68.8 percent of Mexican Americans were classified as literate (Ruggles et al., *Integrated Public Use Microdata Series*). Special appreciation to Marie T. Mora for compiling and interpreting these data.

219. McWilliams, *North from Mexico*, 121.

220. For an overview of the treaty see Zorrilla, *Historia de las relaciones entre Mexico y los Estados Unidos de América, 1800–1858*, 213–35.

221. "The Treaty of Guadalupe Hidalgo as Ratified by the United States and Mexican Governments, 1848"; repr. in Griswold del Castillo, *The Treaty of Guadalupe Hidalgo*, Appendix A.

222. Translated in Loyola, "The American Occupation of New Mexico, 1821–1852," 257–58.

223. James Brooks has meticulously documented how widespread slavery was among both Native American and Mexican groups living in New Mexico even after Mexico officially outlawed slavery in 1829. The treaty maintained the fiction that Mexico had eliminated bondage within its borders, with the exception of supposedly "savage" tribes who traded Mexican citizens (ignoring the reverse, where Indians continued to be held in bondage). See Brooks, *Captives & Cousins*, 329.

224. "The Treaty of Guadalupe Hidalgo" (Griswold del Castillo, *The Treaty of Guadalupe Hidalgo*, 190–91).

225. Reportedly, Mexican negotiators had desired an exclusion of African slavery from all the ceded territories, but they were overruled. See the *Rochester (NY) North Star*, Sept. 1, 1848.

226. For a discussion of slavery in treaty negotiations see the *Washington National Era*, Aug. 13, 1848.

227. Text excerpted from Miller, *Treaties and Other International Acts of the United States of America*, as reprinted in Griswold del Castillo, *The Treaty of Guadalupe Hidalgo*, 179.

228. Some senators, such as Sam Houston and Jefferson Davis, wanted to reject the treaty because they thought that it did not grant the United States enough territory. See Zorrilla, *Historia de las relaciones entre Mexico y los Estados Unidos de América, 1800–1858*, 230–31.

229. Article IX, "Treaty of Guadalupe Hidalgo" (Griswold del Castillo, *The Treaty of Guadalupe Hidalgo*, 190).

230. See, e.g., Deposition of Pedro Dehulade, Nov. 25, 1856, Records of the United States Territorial and New Mexico District Court for Doña Ana County, New Mexico State Records Center and Archives, Santa Fe, Box 7.

231. Mangusso, "A Study of the Citizenship Provisions of the Treaty of Guadalupe Hidalgo," 68–69.

232. Couts, *Hepah, California!* 59.

233. Ibid. (emphasis in original).

234. Ibid. (emphasis in original). According to Dobyns, Couts's reference to "Chinese shoes" did not refer literally to shoes imported from China. Rather, he used this description for a particular regional shoe design.

235. *Las Cruces Borderer*, April 10, 1872.

236. Article VIII, "Treaty of Guadalupe Hidalgo" (Griswold del Castillo, *The Treaty of Guadalupe Hidalgo*, 189–90).

237. Larson, *New Mexico's Quest for Statehood, 1846–1912*, 82.

238. Speculation exists that Calhoun's official position served as a ruse for a secret mission arranged by the president. Little evidence has surfaced to support these claims. See Larson, *New Mexico's Quest for Statehood, 1846–1912*, 27–29.

239. Mangusso, "A Study of the Citizenship Provisions of the Treaty of Guadalupe Hidalgo," 81.

240. Griswold del Castillo, *The Treaty of Guadalupe Hidalgo*, 71.

241. Ibid.

242. Larson, *New Mexico's Quest for Statehood, 1846–1912*, 28.

243. Prominent Mexicans voiced their opposition to Calhoun's tactics. Former governor Donaciano Vigil despised "the miserable Colonel Calhoun," who he believed had "united with the vile clergy of the Territory." In a private letter Vigil bitterly wrote about Calhoun's administration. "The great principle of freedom," he stated, "has been so quenched out that it is enjoyed only nominally" (Donaciano Vigil to Antonio Jose Otero, 1852; quoted in Lamar, *The Far Southwest, 1848–1912*, 86).

244. Mangusso, "A Study of the Citizenship Provisions of the Treaty of Guadalupe Hidalgo," 86.

245. Griswold del Castillo, *The Treaty of Guadalupe Hidalgo*, 71.

246. Ibid., 71–72.

247. John Greiner, Acting Superintendent of Indian Affairs in New Mexico, to Hon. Luke Lea, Commissioner Indian Affairs, April 30, 1852, in Abel, *The Official Correspondence of James S. Calhoun*, 529–31 (italics in original).

248. *New York Times*, Jan. 11, 1853.

249. One Euro-American lawyer attempted to use Native Americans' uncertain status as part of a complicated legal strategy involving the infamous "Billy the Kid" in 1881. Because "the Kid" had committed a crime on the Mescalero Apache Reservation, the federal government claimed jurisdiction over the criminal proceedings. The defense attorney, Albert Fountain, argued that the Treaty of Guadalupe Hidalgo mandated that the Mescalero Apaches were "full" citizens of the United States. The

Apaches, Fountain noted, were Mexican citizens at the time of the treaty and, therefore, converted to U.S. citizens like the rest of the Mexican population. If the Apaches were full American citizens, then the federal laws over Indian reservations did not apply and Billy the Kid should have faced trial in the county court in Mesilla. See *Newman's Semi-Weekly*, April 6, 1881.

250. Griswold del Castillo, *The Treaty of Guadalupe Hidalgo*, 72.

251. Ibid.

252. "Memorial of the Legislative Assembly of the Territory of New Mexico to the Hon. Senate and House of Representatives of the United States in Congress Assembled, March 10, 1858," Territorial Papers of the United States House of Representatives Relating to New Mexico Territory, 1846–61, microform edition.

253. "Memorial to the Senate and House of Representatives of the United States of America in Congress Assembled, n.d. (1860?)," Territorial Papers of the United States House of Representatives Relating to New Mexico Territory, 1846–61, microform edition.

254. Ibid.

255. "Memorial of the Legislative Assembly of the Territory of New Mexico to the Hon. Senate and House of Representatives of the United States in Congress Assembled, March 10, 1858," Territorial Papers of the United States House of Representatives Relating to New Mexico Territory, 1846–61, microform edition.

256. See, e.g., Almaguer, *Racial Fault Lines*; and Foley, *The White Scourge*.

Chapter Two. "Yankilandia" and "Prairie-Dog Villages"

1. Guadalupe Miranda to the Mayor of El Paso, Mexico, 1853; printed in Griggs, *History of Mesilla Valley, or, The Gadsden Purchase*, 85.

2. Mexican officials on the border and in the capital were particularly concerned about contraband evading customs taxes in the postwar period. Some even wondered if repatriates were responsible for the lucrative smuggling operations. See Hernández, "El México perdido," 140; and Zorrilla, *Historia de las relaciones*, 247–50.

3. Twitchell, *The Leading Facts of New Mexican History*, 311.

4. The Rio Grande was/is shallow and mostly unnavigable in New Mexico. Contemporary descriptions from c. 1848 noted that it ranged from fifty to three hundred yards wide and was shallow enough "to be forded almost anywhere" (Connelley, *Doniphan's Expedition and the Conquest of New Mexico and California*, 229).

5. González de la Vara, "El traslado de familias de Nuevo México," 16; see also a letter from E. F. White claiming jurisdiction for those towns on behalf of the United States in 1848 in the microfilm edition of the Archives of the Ayuntamiento de Ciudad Juárez, roll 61.

6. For additional discussion of discrimination against Mexicans in California see González Navarro, *Los extranjeros*, 397.

7. Almaguer, *Racial Fault Lines*, 130.

8. Zorrilla, *Historia de las relaciones*, 261.

9. Johnson, *Revolution in Texas*, 10.

10. Werne, *The Imaginary Line*, 187.

11. Acuña, *Corridors of Migration*, 33.

12. Mora-Torres, *The Making of the Mexican Border*, 12.

13. Truett, *Fugitive Landscapes*, 37.

14. Illegal trade and border crossings apparently happened with some regularity in Mesilla. See, e.g., another incident involving wood in 1852 in Zorrilla, *Historia de las relaciones*, 247.

15. For a discussion of the relationship between architecture and social structure see Ferguson, "Dowa Yalanne," 33–35.

16. Reséndez, *Changing National Identities at the Frontier*, 226–35.

17. See Binley, "New Mexico and Texan Santa Expedition"; McClure, "The Texan–Santa Fe Expedition of 1841"; and Weber, *The Mexican Frontier, 1821–1846*, 266–67.

18. Espinosa and Espinosa, "The Texans," 308.

19. Take as one of many examples the Oct. 23, 1880, edition of the *Mesilla News*, which referred to Texans as "the traditional enemies of the people of New Mexico."

20. Texas initially claimed jurisdiction over the Mesilla Valley. Invading Texans therefore claimed "head rights" to Mesilla Valley lands through legal measures that provided 640 acres to those who had fought against Mexico. See Bartlett, *Personal Narrative of Explorations*, 148; Puckett, "Ramon Ortiz," 287–88. For a contemporary note about Mexicans' distrust of Texans in New Mexico see the *Washington National Era*, March 15, 1849.

21. Werne, "Guadalupe Hidalgo and the Mesilla Controversy," 157.

22. Abolitionist and African American newspapers at the time of the war also feared that New Mexico would permit race-based slavery. See, e.g., the *Washington National Era*, Jan. 28, 1847; and the *Rochester (NY) Frederick Douglass Paper*, Sept. 25, 1851.

23. Loyola, "The American Occupation of New Mexico, 1821–1852," 257–58.

24. These fears of slavery totally ignored (or maybe emerged from) the fact that Mexicans continued to enslave indigenous people. See Brooks, *Captives & Cousins*.

25. Ramón Ortiz to Angel Trias, June 9, 1849; printed in Agustin de Escudero, *Noticias históricas y estadisticas de la antigua provincia del Nuevo-México*, 94. See also Carroll and Haggard, *Three New Mexico Chronicles*, 145.

26. As James Brooks has shown, Mexican settlers in New Mexico frequently enslaved indigenous people without much debate. African and African American slavery, however, was rare in New Mexico. The 1850 census identified only twenty-two people of African descent in New Mexico, all of whom were free. By 1860 there were sixty-four African Americans held in bondage, mostly by Euro-American army officers in Santa Fe. See Brooks, *Captives & Cousins*, 309–10.

27. Herrera became president on June 3, 1848 (see Zorrilla, *Historia de las relaciones*, 237).

28. "That the Mexican Families Who Are in the United States May Emigrate to Their Native Country," Code of Colonization, p. 407, no. 126, Decree of August 19, 1848; repr. in Milton, *The Mesilla Civil Colony Grant*, "Exhibit 'A,' " 40.

29. Ibid.

30. Ibid.

31. Bancroft, *History of Arizona and New Mexico*, 472–73; Twitchell, *The Leading Facts of New Mexican History*, 290–91; Stoes, "Early History of Doña Ana County," 95. See also Griswold del Castillo, *The Treaty of Guadalupe Hidalgo*, 64–65. Coahuila's settlements received less attention, and Mexico seems to have reneged on a number of promises made to these settlers (as would be the case for future repatriations as well).

32. Almonte, *Proyectos de leyes sobre colonización*, 6 (my translation).

33. Ibid., 12.

34. Mangusso, "A Study of the Citizenship Provisions of the Treaty of Guadalupe Hidalgo," 50–66.

35. Those in Alta California would be relocated to Baja California or Sonora; Mexicans from New Mexico would be relocated to Chihuahua; and Mexicans in Texas (between the Nueces and the Rio Grande) would be relocated to Tamaulipas, Coahuila, or Nuevo León. For a more detailed discussion of the efforts outside of New Mexico see Hernández, "El México perdido."

36. Quoted in González de la Vara, "El traslado de familias de Nuevo México," 11.

37. Ibid.

38. For his duties Ortiz received a flat payment of two thousand dollars plus an additional dollar for every man who relocated below the new borderline. "That the Mexican Families Who Are in the United States May Emigrate to Their Native Country," Article XX (Milton, *The Mesilla Civil Colony Grant*, 47).

39. Ramón Ortiz to Governor Trias of Chihuahua, June 9, 1849, as discussed in Bancroft, *History of Arizona and New Mexico*, 472–73; see also Mangusso, "A Study of the Citizenship Provisions of the Treaty of Guadalupe Hidalgo," 50–66.

40. Ramón Ortiz to Angel Trias, June 9, 1849; printed in Agustin de Escudero, *Noticias históricas y estadisticas de la antigua provincia del Nuevo-México*, 95.

41. Ibid., 95.

42. Spell, "The Anglo-Saxon Press in Mexico, 1846–1848," 29–30.

43. *Santa Fe Republican*, May 26, 1849; quoted in González de la Vara, "El traslado de familias de Nuevo México," 15. See also González de la Vara, "The Return to Mexico," 48.

44. González de la Vara, "El traslado de familias de Nuevo México," 12.

45. Ramón Ortiz to Angel Trias, June 9, 1849; repr. in Agustin de Escudero, *Noticias históricas y estadisticas de la antigua provincia del Nuevo-México*, 95; see also Carroll and Haggard, *Three New Mexico Chronicles*, 146; and Zorrilla, *Historia de las relaciones*, 260.

46. Ramón Ortiz to Donaciano Vigil, May 5, 1849; repr. in Agustin de Escudero, *Noticias históricas y estadisticas de la antigua provincia del Nuevo-México*, 98.

47. Zorrilla, *Historia de las relaciones*, 260.

48. Puckett, "Ramon Ortiz," 287. Ortiz estimated that he could arrange for sixteen thousand colonists to relocate from New Mexico (see Ortiz to Trias, June 9, 1849; repr. in Agustin de Escudero, *Noticias históricas y estadisticas de la antigua*

provincia del Nuevo-México, 96; see also Carroll and Haggard, *Three New Mexico Chronicles*, 148). Others have suggested that he recruited only twelve hundred (Mangusso, "A Study of the Citizenship Provisions of the Treaty of Guadalupe Hidalgo," 60); and others say two thousand (Hernández, "El México perdido," 227).

49. Mitchell, *Coyote Nation*, 13. There were about fifteen hundred Euro-Americans in New Mexico in 1850, half of whom were military officers or soldiers (ibid., 14).

50. Guardino, *Peasants, Politics, and the Formation of Mexico's National State*, 86.

51. Ibid.

52. Alonso, *Thread of Blood*, 98.

53. Carib, *Cartographic Mexico*, 8.

54. Ibid., 5.

55. Ibid., 20.

56. "Regulaciones de colonización expedidas por el supremo gobierno de Chihuahua el 22 de Mayo de 1851," article 2; repr. in Milton, *The Mesilla Civil Colony Grant*, 50.

57. A Spanish vara is equal to 32.9927 inches. See Frietze, *History of La Mesilla and Her Mesilleros*, 25. Even in measuring geography Mexicans and Americans differed.

58. "Regulaciones de colonización," Article X (in Milton, *The Mesilla Civil Colony Grant*, 52).

59. Frietze, *History of La Mesilla and Her Mesilleros*, 26.

60. "Regulaciones de colonización," Article VII (in Milton, *The Mesilla Civil Colony Grant*, 51).

61. The Constitution of 1824 permitted only Catholicism in Mexico.

62. The same document dictated that the town government consist of an elected justice of the peace, six-member council, a solicitor, and a *mayordomo* (administrator).

63. "Regulaciones de colonización," Article I (in Milton, *The Mesilla Civil Colony Grant*, 50).

64. See Vaughan, "Primary Education and Literacy in Nineteenth-Century Mexico."

65. González de la Vara, "El traslado de familias de Nuevo México," 19.

66. See Ramírez Caloca, "Ascensión."

67. The founding of repatriate communities was also divisive in Chihuahua. Many chihuahuenses saw the settlers from New Mexico being given preferential treatment over migrants from other parts of Mexico. Many wondered why a Mesillero should be granted twice the amount of land if he was born in Doña Ana than if he was born in Durango. See Hernández, "El México perdido," 186.

68. Hernández's "El México perdido," for instance, almost entirely discounts notions of nationalism in its discussion of repatriate communities along the northern frontier, instead claiming settlement was a matter of "realpolitik."

69. Bartlett, *Personal Narrative of Explorations*, 214–15. See also Bartlett's response to Lane's proclamation in the *New York Times*, April 27, 1853.

70. U.S. Congress, Senate, *Report of the Secretary of the Interior*, 148.

71. Some Euro-Americans, however, did establish households or businesses in Mesilla or the surrounding area. These included Louis William Geck, a Polish immigrant who had fought in the U.S. Army during the war. Henry Cuniffe and Sam Bean, both of whom had accompanied Doniphan's Expedition, also claimed lands in Mesilla. See Taylor, *A Place as Wild as the West Ever Was*, 30.

72. González de la Vara, "The Return to Mexico," 53.

73. Owen, *Las Cruces, New Mexico, 1849–1999*, 28.

74. Wislizenus, *Memoir*, 20.

75. Ormsby, *The Butterfield Overland Mail*, 80.

76. Ibid.

77. Owen, *Las Cruces, New Mexico, 1849–1999*, 30.

78. Wilson, *The Myth of Santa Fe*, 52–67.

79. Salas, *In the Shadow of the Eagles*, 137.

80. Ibid., 136–37.

81. Ibid., 136.

82. *New York Times*, Jan. 11, 1853.

83. *New York Times*, Nov. 6, 1852.

84. Report, Maj. Steen to the Adj. Gen. U.S.A., July 12, 1853; repr. in Taos, "A Review of the Boundary Question," 26.

85. Taylor, *A Place as Wild as the West Ever Was*, 41.

86. Ibid., 45–46, 53–54.

87. Ibid., 49.

88. Ibid., 58.

89. Letter to James Calhoun, Aug. 25, 1851; repr. in Abel, *The Official Correspondence of James S. Calhoun*, 405.

90. Baldwin, "A Short History of the Mesilla Valley," 317–18. The 1847 map, published in New York, mistakenly placed El Paso thirty degrees north of its actual position.

91. Ibid., 318.

92. *New York Times*, April 30, 1853; June 4, 1853; June 20, 1853; July 1, 1853.

93. Garber, *The Gadsden Treaty*, 17–25; Twitchell, *The Leading Facts of New Mexican History*, 311.

94. Werne, "Guadalupe Hidalgo and the Mesilla Controversy," 160–64.

95. *Santa Fe Weekly Gazette*, May 7, 1853; U.S. Congress, House, *Reports of Explorations and Surveys*, 6; Garber, *The Gadsden Treaty*, 71.

96. Baldwin, "A Short History of the Mesilla Valley," 318; Larson, *New Mexico's Quest for Statehood, 1846–1912*, 81.

97. Larson, *New Mexico's Quest for Statehood, 1846–1912*, 80–82.

98. Taos, "A Review of the Boundary Question," 25.

99. *New York Times*, May 19, 1853. Translation: "A Brief Exposition on the Province of New Mexico Made by Its Deputy to the Cortes, Pedro Baptista Pino, 1812."

100. Garland to the Adjutant-General's Office, Aug. 3, 1853; quoted in Rippy, "The Negotiation of the Gadsden Treaty," 25.

101. Taylor, *A Place as Wild as the West Ever Was*, 35.

102. *New York Times*, April 30, 1853. Many newspapers took issue with the U.S. attempt to annex more Mexican land. The *Rochester (NY) Frederick Douglass Paper*, May 27, 1853, for instance, printed a scathing article against Lane and outlined the history behind Mesilla.

103. *New York Times*, May 5, 1853.

104. *New York Times*, May 4, 1853. The *Times* also noted on May 20, 1853, that Mesilla lacked agricultural value because of New Mexico's aridity.

105. *New York Times*, June 8, 1853.

106. *New York Times*, March 27, 1854.

107. Werne, "Guadalupe Hidalgo and the Mesilla Controversy," 176; Griswold del Castillo, *The Treaty of Guadalupe Hidalgo*, 59–60.

108. González Navarro, *Los extranjeros*, 392.

109. Zorrilla, *Historia de las relaciones*, 339.

110. Lilly, "Tale of Two Cities," 17.

111. *New York Times*, Feb. 2, 1854.

112. Davis, *El Gringo, or, New Mexico and Her People*, 217.

113. Ibid., 218.

114. Ibid., 217.

115. Baldwin, "A Short History of the Mesilla Valley," 318.

116. Ibid., 318–19; Owen, *Las Cruces, New Mexico, 1849–1999*, 36.

117. Owen, *Las Cruces, New Mexico, 1849–1999*, 33.

118. Loyola, "The American Occupation of New Mexico, 1821–1852," 270.

119. Eaton, "Frontier Life in Southern Arizona, 1858–1861," 174.

120. Ibid.

121. *Chicago Tribune*, March 22, 1860.

122. *Chicago Tribune*, March 27, 1860.

123. The judge in question might have been Anastacio Barela.

124. *Chicago Tribune*, March 22, 1860.

125. *Chicago Tribune*, March 27, 1860.

126. Ibid.

127. Ibid.

128. See, e.g., A. M. Jackson to Orlando Davis, Feb. 17, 1861; J. L. Collins, Superintendent of Indian Affairs, to President, June 22, 1861; M. Steck to James L. Collins, July 15, 1861; all in Wilson, *When the Texans Came*.

129. Garber, *The Gadsden Treaty*, 81–82.

130. A. M. Jackson to Orlando Davis, Feb. 17, 1861; repr. in Wilson, *When the Texans Came*, 18–19.

131. *Mesilla Times*, Oct. 18, 1860.

132. Thompson, *Confederate General of the West*, 228–29; Hall, *Sibley's New Mexico Campaign*, 6–7; Owen, *Las Cruces, New Mexico, 1849–1999*, 38–47; Simmons, *New Mexico*, 142–49.

133. These settlers clustered together in a row of houses built three blocks east of Mesilla's plaza by D. W. Hughes, Bredett C. Murray, and Robert Kelley. See Taylor, *A Place as Wild as the West Ever Was*, 85. Sam Jones created the pro-South

newspaper the *Mesilla Times* after spending time fighting for slavery in "Bleeding Kansas." See the *Austin (TX) State Gazette*, March 30, 1861.

134. *Mesilla Times*, July 27, 1861.

135. Proclamation of Brig. Gen. H. H. Sibley, Army of the Confederate States, to the People of New Mexico, Dec. 20, 1861; repr. in Cowles, *The War of the Rebellion*, 89–90.

136. Ibid. See also Thompson, *Confederate General of the West*, 238.

137. Baylor became the governor of Arizona as part of this arrangement. Twitchell, *The Leading Facts of New Mexican History*, 361–85.

138. *New York Times*, July 21, 1861.

139. *Los Angeles Semi-Weekly Southern News*, Sept. 6, 1861.

140. Swift and Corning, *Three Roads to Chihuahua*, 192.

141. Frietze, *History of La Mesilla and Her Mesilleros*, 49.

142. Taylor, *A Place as Wild as the West Ever Was*, 93.

143. Tom P. Ochiltree to General, El Paso Headquarters, Army of New Mexico, Dec. 16, 1861; printed in Wilson, *When the Texans Came*, 153.

144. The Confederate government alienated Mexicans during its tenure in other ways as well. Although the United States had begrudgingly permitted the local courts and government offices to operate in Spanish, all legal proceedings in Confederate "Arizona" were in English only. See Larson, *New Mexico's Quest for Statehood, 1846–1912*, 86.

145. Ibid., 85.

146. Henry Connelly to General E. R. S. Canby, June 15, 1862; repr. in Wilson, *When the Texans Came*, 285–86.

147. Wilson, *When the Texans Came*, 13.

148. Ibid.

149. The Confederate military commissioned a Mexican as captain in November 1861 to fight against Native Americans in New Mexico. See the *Houston Tri-Weekly Telegraph*, Nov. 1, 1861. See also the *New Orleans Daily Picayune*, Oct. 19, 1861. The Congress of the Confederate States passed a law in 1861 "declaring the extermination of all hostile Indians" in New Mexico and Arizona. John Baylor issued orders to the Mesilla headquarters to "use all means to persuade the Apaches or any tribe to come in for the purpose of making peace, and when you get them together kill all the grown Indians and take the children prisoners and sell them to defray the expense of killing the Indians." To accomplish the murderous act, Baylor suggested to "use the Mexicans, if they can be trusted" (John R. Baylor to H. H. Sibley, Mesilla, March 20, 1862; repr. in Griggs, *History of Mesilla Valley, or, The Gadsden Purchase*, 75).

150. W. R. Shoemaker to Canby, Aug. 15, 1861; quoted in Hall, *Sibley's New Mexico Campaign*, 60.

151. Canby to Assistant Adjutant General, Aug. 17, 1861; quoted in Miller, "Hispanos and the Civil War in New Mexico," 106. See also Canby to Adjutant General, Dec. 8, 1861; quoted in Hall, *Sibley's New Mexico Campaign*, 64. Captain Gurden Chapin similarly resented the presence of Mexicans in the military and wrote to his general: "No dependence whatever can be placed on the natives; they

are worse than worthless" (Chapin to Halleck, Feb. 28, 1862; quoted in Miller, "Hispanos and the Civil War in New Mexico," 113).

152. "Address of the Legislative Assembly of New Mexico," Jan. 29, 1862; repr. in Moore, *The Rebellion Record*, vol. 3, Doc. 25, 170; Miller, "Hispanos and the Civil War in New Mexico," 120n25.

153. Proclamation by Henry Connelly, governor of New Mexico, Sept. 9, 1861.

154. Ibid.

155. Miller, "Hispanos and the Civil War in New Mexico," 109.

156. Ibid.

157. *New York Times*, Oct. 26, 1861.

158. Rafael Chacon, Compiled Service Records, Civil War, New Mexico Volunteers, Records of the Adjutant General's Office; quoted in Miller, "Hispanos and the Civil War in New Mexico," 108.

159. Wislizenus, *Memoir*, 33.

160. *Mesilla Times*, July 13, 1861.

161. *Mesilla Times*, Jan. 15, 1861.

162. Taylor, *A Place as Wild as the West Ever Was*, 93.

163. Baldwin, "A Short History of the Mesilla Valley," 323.

164. This appeal to region was a double-edged sword for Mexican Americans. One famed historian used the same language to belittle Mexicans' contributions to Union battles two decades later. Hubert Bancroft asserted in 1889 that Mexicans' patriotism for the United States had been overstated. "While this sentiment of loyalty [to the United States] was undoubtedly real," he wrote, "reflecting credit on the New Mexicans, yet its fervor should not be exaggerated, apathy in national questions being a characteristic of the people." Bancroft offered an alternative explanation for Mexicans' service, suggesting that it "resulted largely from the fact that the confederate invasion came from Texas, the old hatred of the Texans being the strongest popular feeling of the natives, far outweighing their devotion to either the south or north" (Bancroft, *History of Arizona and New Mexico*, 684).

165. During the Civil War Euro-Americans did find some unlikely reasons to grant certain local Mexicans status as American citizens. They recognized Mesilla Valley Mexicans as citizens in order to charge them with treason and take possession of their land. Rafael Armijo, a significant Mesillero landowner, faced such accusations in 1863. Euro-Americans accused Armijo of giving aid to the invading Confederate army in the Mesilla Valley. Prosecutors claimed that aid took the form of "buying and selling, giving, trading, and trafficking to [those] . . . engaged in armed rebellion as aforesaid, money food clothing, services, transportation, arms, ammunition, goods, wares, and merchandise." *United States vs. Stouses*, Records of the United States Territorial and New Mexico District Court for Doña Ana County, New Mexico State Records Center and Archives, Santa Fe. New Mexico courts processed numerous cases involving treason during this period. See also Tittman, "The Exploitation of Treason."

166. Baldwin, "A Short History of the Mesilla Valley," 319–20.

167. Taylor, *A Place as Wild as the West Ever Was*, 128.

168. For discussion on land tenure conflicts in Texas see Alonzo, *Tejano Legacy*, 161–81.

169. Nugent, *Habits of Empire*, 231.

170. Nieto-Phillips, "No Other Blood," 72–76; Lamar, *The Far Southwest, 1848–1912*, 136–73.

171. Owen, *Las Cruces, New Mexico, 1849–1999*, 52.

172. For contemporary newspaper coverage of *W. L. Rynerson vs. Desiderio Ortego* see the *Mesilla News*, Jan. 2, 1875. See also the *Las Cruces Democrat*, Sept. 6, 1899; and Milton, *The Mesilla Civil Colony Grant*.

173. Owens, *Las Cruces, New Mexico, 1849–1999*, 155.

174. Lamar, *The Far Southwest, 1848–1912*, 155–60.

175. Gibson, *The Life and Death of Colonel Albert Jennings Fountain*, 96; Stratton, *The Territorial Press of New Mexico, 1834–1912*, 5.

176. *Las Cruces Borderer*, March 16, 1871.

177. *Las Cruces Borderer*, April 6, 1871.

178. See, e.g., Morton, *Crania Americana*; and Horseman, "Scientific Racism and the American Indian in Mid-Nineteenth Century."

179. *Las Cruces Borderer*, March 20, 1871.

180. Stratton, *The Territorial Press of New Mexico, 1834–1912*, 21–22; Meyer, *Speaking for Themselves*, 8.

181. *Las Cruces Borderer*, July 13, 1871.

182. *Las Cruces Borderer*, March 16, 1871.

183. *Las Cruces Frontierzo*, April 29, 1875 (caps in original).

184. *Las Cruces Borderer*, Sept. 21, 1872.

185. *Las Cruces Borderer*, Aug. 2, 1871.

186. See, e.g., *Dona Ana County Republican*, Dec. 16, 1897.

187. Unlike most Euro-American settlers, Bennett bucked the statehood movement in the 1870s. His opposition came, in part, because he believed that it would increase the number of Republicans in the federal House and Senate. To counter Republican statehood efforts in 1871, Bennett tried to instill his readers with the fear that admission as a state would mean the demise of a regional "New Mexican" identity. In one article Bennett claimed that Republican leaders planned to merge the New Mexico territory with neighboring states and territories. Bennett argued that living in New Mexico created a distinctive sense of identity that voters needed to defend against the "Republican plan." See the *Las Cruces Borderer*, Aug. 2, 1871.

188. Eastern newspapers frequently wrote disparagingly about the territory and its inclusion in the Union. See the *Cincinnati Commercial*, Feb. 26, 1875; quoted in Larson, *New Mexico's Quest for Statehood, 1846–1912*, 124–25; and the *New York Times*, March 5, 1875.

189. One of the first acts of Governor James Calhoun in 1851 was to propose laws restricting the movement of "free Negroes" into New Mexico, which was largely supported by wealthy Mexicans. See Brooks, *Captives & Cousins*, 309; and Larson, *New Mexico's Quest for Statehood, 1846–1912*, 64.

190. Mitchell, *Coyote Nation*, 109.

191.   Ibid., 99.

192.   *Las Cruces Borderer*, Aug. 2, 1871.

193.   *Las Cruces Borderer*, July 19, 1871.

194.   *Las Cruces Borderer*, July 10, 1871. English version printed July 19, 1871.

195.   *Las Cruces Borderer*, July 19, 1871.

196.   Miller, "New Mexico during the Civil War."

197.   For descriptions of violence in Mora and Taos see Elliott, *The Mexican War Correspondence of Richard Smith Elliott*, 139–55.

198.   Miller, "Hispanos and the Civil War in New Mexico," 106.

199.   Ibid., 118n10.

200.   *Las Cruces Borderer*, Aug. 30, 1871.

201.   Larson, *New Mexico Populism*, 35–42.

202.   Otero, *My Life on the Frontier, 1882–1897*, 248–52.

203.   Rosenbaum, *Mexicano Resistance in the Southwest*, 108.

Chapter Three. *"Enemigos* de la *Iglesia Católica"*

1.   Material from this chapter appeared in Mora, "Resistance and Accommodation in a Border Parish."

2.   Doña Ana District Court Records, November 1851 Term, Territory of New Mexico, Records of the United States Territorial and New Mexico District Court for Doña Ana County, New Mexico State Records Center and Archives, Santa Fe, Box 7.

3.   See MacCormack, *Religion in the Andes*, 7.

4.   Nationalism depends on both building a collective identity and contrasting that identity with excluded "foreign" groups. Religious beliefs, therefore, have often been an important means to define the nation against multiple others (e.g., a "Protestant United States" against a "Catholic Mexico"). Anthony Marx argues that the politicization of religious faith was relevant to modern state and nation building. In the case of sixteenth-century Spain, he suggests, the expulsion of "heretics" and "Jews" helped create a sense of nation through a unified Catholic identity. See Marx, *Faith in Nation*.

5.   Nugent, *Into the West*, 198–202.

6.   Taylor, *A Place as Wild as the West Ever Was*, 128.

7.   For a discussion of memory see Rousso, *The Vichy Syndrome*, 4.

8.   For additional discussions of religion in the western United States see Szasz and Etulain, *Religion in Modern New Mexico*; Szasz, *The Protestant Clergy in the Great Plains and Mountain West, 1865–1915*; Tobias, *A History of the Jews in New Mexico*; Walker, *Protestantism in the Sangre de Cristos, 1850–1920*; Dolan and Deck, *Hispanic Catholic Culture in the U.S.*; Dolan and Hinojosa, *Mexican Americans and the Catholic Church, 1900–1965*; Matovina and Poyo, *Presente!*; and Matovina, *Tejano Religion and Ethnicity*. Although lacking in a discussion about Mexicans or Mexican Americans, McGreevy's *Parish Boundaries* considers changing ideas about parishes in the twentieth-century United States.

9. For a deeper discussion of Catholicism's role in nineteenth-century Mexico see Escalante Gonzalbo, *Ciudadanos Imaginarios*, 141–60.

10. Though Spain officially required Catholic devotion, many groups retained differing religious beliefs and practices. Indigenous groups throughout the Americas resisted the total elimination of their belief systems. Periodic religious revivals occurred, including New Mexico's dramatic Pueblo Revolt of 1680. Moreover, European religious minorities also persevered in Spain's empire. "Crypto-Jews," those who ostensibly converted to Christianity but secretly maintained their traditional faith, could be found throughout the Americas. For examples in New Mexico see Gutiérrez, *When Jesus Came, the Corn Mothers Went Away*; Kessell, *Kiva, Cross, and Crown*; and Tobias, *A History of the Jews in New Mexico*.

11. By the end of the eighteenth century, New Spain's imperial authorities had grown suspicious of missionary dominance in frontier societies like New Mexico. Reformers sought to end Franciscan control of the northern frontier by requiring that secular Catholic priests (i.e., priests who were not members of a religious order, like the Franciscans or Dominicans, and who reported directly to a bishop) replace the missionary Franciscans. An unintended period of ecclesiastical decline resulted as the transition to secular priests occurred unevenly, with a few priests reluctantly superseding the disappearing friars; see Weber, *The Mexican Frontier, 1821–1846*, 72–78. From 1780 until the U.S.-Mexican War in 1846, New Mexico nonetheless witnessed a proliferation of church building and restoration, despite the shortage of priests who could staff them. Bishop José Antonio Zubiría, for instance, issued more than thirty licenses for church structures when he visited New Mexico in 1833. See Frank, *From Settler to Citizen*, 182; see also Reyes, "Race, Agency, and Memory in a Baja California Mission," 107.

12. Escalante, *Ciudadanos imaginarios*, 148.

13. Reséndez, *Changing National Identities at the Frontier*, 76.

14. Escalante, *Ciudadanos imaginarios*, 141–42.

15. Weigle, *Brothers of Light, Brothers of Blood*, 25; Yohn, *A Contest of Faiths*, 58.

16. Reséndez, *Changing National Identities at the Frontier*, 81–82.

17. Ibid., 81.

18. Ibid., 86.

19. Given the centrality of Catholicism to Mexicans' daily lives and the anti-Catholic reputation of the United States, it is not surprising that Mexican negotiators labored to ensure that the faithful received specific protection in the aftermath of the U.S.-Mexican War. The Treaty of Guadalupe Hidalgo's original Article IX outlined guarantees for the observance of Catholic practices that the U.S. Congress later redacted. See Griswold del Castillo, *The Treaty of Guadalupe Hidalgo*.

20. Lucey, "The Catholic Church in Texas," 227–28.

21. See Dolan, *The American Catholic Experience*, 177.

22. Espín, "Popular Catholicism among Latinos," 338.

23. Dolan, *The American Catholic Experience*, 295–96.

24. Ibid., 296.

25. Orsi, *The Madonna of 115th Street*, 61–62, 83–84.

26. Yohn, *A Contest of Faiths*, 58.

27. González Navarro, *Los extranjeros*, 352.

28. Horgan, *Lamy of Santa Fe*, 226–27; Padilla, *My History, Not Yours*, 18; Chavez, *But Time and Chance*; de Aragon, *Padre Martínez and Bishop Lamy*.

29. Lamy to Vatican Sacred Congregation for the Propagation of the Faith, Santa Fe, Dec. 18, 1881; quoted in Horgan, *Lamy of Santa Fe*, 407.

30. Horgan, *Lamy of Santa Fe*, 260–62; Taylor, *History of San Albino Church on the Plaza Mesilla, New Mexico*, 4.

31. José F. Durán et al. to Ramón Ortiz, El Paso, Mexico, Diocese of Durango Archives, microfilm, reel 247 (emphasis in original). Although Durán's name was prominently first, less than 10 percent of the signatures had Spanish surnames.

32. Baca appeared for service to the Diocese of Durango on October 15, 1844. See Diocese of Durango Archives, microfilm, reel 354.

33. Chavez, *But Time and Chance*, 125.

34. Taylor, *History of San Albino Church on the Plaza Mesilla, New Mexico*, 4.

35. See *The Official Catholic Directory*.

36. Taylor, *A Place as Wild as the West Ever Was*, 169.

37. *Las Cruces Borderer*, June 8, 1871.

38. Ibid. Mexicans in New Mexico often referred to any unwanted Euro-American invader as a "Texan" regardless of that person's place of origin. Many non-Texan Euro-Americans never understood that these generalizations also applied to them.

39. *Las Cruces Borderer*, June 8, 1871.

40. Ibid.

41. Ibid.; González, *Refusing the Favor*, 52.

42. Roberto S. Goizueta, *Caminemos con Jesús*, 102.

43. *Las Cruces Borderer*, Aug. 30, 1871; Hood, "Bells of Old Mesilla," 15.

44. Marlin, *The American Catholic Voter*, 91.

45. *Santa Fe New Mexican*, July 4, 1871.

46. Much of this style of electioneering probably represented an import of rituals adapted from the eastern United States that would have been unknown during the Mexican period. Certainly territorial Euro-Americans emulated other political trends and practices from Gilded Age America, as the historian María Montoya notes. See Montoya, *Translating Property*, 109; see also Dinkin, *Campaigning in America*, 65–66. For a discussion of the emergence of nineteenth-century electioneering in the United States, see Waldstreicher, *In the Midst of Perpetual Fetes*, 177–245.

47. Dinkin, *Campaigning in America*, 65.

48. *Las Cruces Borderer*, Aug. 30, 1871; *New York Times*, Sept. 4, 1871; Hood, "Bells of Old Mesilla," 15.

49. *Las Cruces Borderer*, Aug. 30, 1871; Oct. 4, 1871.

50. Petition, Rafael Bermudes, Feb. 11, 1866, Doña Ana County Records, New Mexico State Records Center and Archives, Santa Fe.

51. Owen, *Las Cruces, New Mexico, 1849–1999*, 44.

52. See Chavez, *Très Macho—He Said*.

53. Taylor, *A Place as Wild as the West Ever Was*, 124.

54. Testimony of José de Jesus Baca, Dec. 5, 1855, in *New Mexico Contested Election*, 48.

55. Taylor, *A Place as Wild as the West Ever Was*, 125.

56. Griggs, *History of Mesilla Valley, or, The Gadsden Purchase*, 93; José Angel Hernández traces out the life of Mesilleros in Ascensión with great detail (see Hernández, "El México perdido," 251–321).

57. Griggs, *History of Mesilla Valley, or, The Gadsden Purchase*, 93.

58. For a romanticized account of this move see Ramírez Caloca, "Ascensión," 245–60.

59. Taylor, *A Place as Wild as the West Ever Was*, 167–68.

60. Lilly, "Tale of Two Cities," 17.

61. Montoya, *Translating Property*, 108–9.

62. *Mesilla News*, March 6, 1875.

63. Taylor, *A Place as Wild as the West Ever Was*, 170.

64. *Mesilla News*, March 6, 1875.

65. Granjon, *Along the Rio Grande*, 59.

66. Ibid., 56.

67. Granjon, *Along the Rio Grande*, 46; Horgan, *Lamy of Santa Fe*, 270–71.

68. Sister M. Praxedes to "John Amador" (Juan Amador), June 10, 1883, Amador Family Papers, Juan Amador Correspondence—letters received 1879–1907, Box 3, Folder 1.

69. Granjon, *Along the Rio Grande*, 46.

70. Juárez, "La Iglesia Católica y el Chicano en Sud Texas, 1836–1911," 222–23.

71. Yohn, *A Contest of Faiths*, 84.

72. Hernández, "La formación de la frontera norte y el protestantismo," 63.

73. Ibid., 64.

74. Ibid., 76.

75. Yohn, *A Contest of Faiths*, 72.

76. See http://archives.nmsu.edu/exhibits/loretto/loretto1.html (accessed Jan. 25, 2009).

77. Horgan, *Lamy of Santa Fe*, 319–20.

78. Arrest Warrant for "Pedro Lassaigne," Aug. 24, 1874, Records of the United States Territorial and New Mexico District Court for Doña Ana County, New Mexico State Records Center and Archives, Santa Fe.

79. Territory vs. Pedro Lassaigne, 3rd Judicial District Court—New Mexico County of Doña Ana, Oct. 1874 Term, New Mexico State Records Center and Archives, Santa Fe.

80. Grand Jury Report, Territory vs. Pedro Lassaigne, 3rd Judicial District Court —New Mexico County of Doña Ana, June 1874 Term, New Mexico State Records Center and Archives, Santa Fe.

81. *Newman's Semi-Weekly*, April 6, 1881.

82. Territory vs. Pedro Lassaigne, Move to Quash Indictment, 3rd Judicial District Court—New Mexico County of Doña Ana, Oct. 1874 Term, New Mexico State Records Center and Archives, Santa Fe, Box 8.

83. The *Las Cruces Loretto Chimes*, "Golden Jubilee Number," 1920, Loretto

Academy Records, Rio Grande Historical Collections, New Mexico State University, Las Cruces, 13; Owen, *Las Cruces, New Mexico, 1849–1999*, 72–77.

84.   Buchanan, *The First Hundred Years*, 15.

85.   Ibid.

86.   Gordon, *The Great Arizona Orphan Abduction*, 76–77, 106.

87.   *Las Cruces Citizen*, Saturday, Aug. 18, 1906.

88.   *Las Cruces Loretto Chimes*, "Golden Jubilee Number," 1920, 13; Owen, *Las Cruces, New Mexico, 1849–1999*, 78.

89.   Owen, *Las Cruces, New Mexico, 1849–1999*, 78. An alternative version of this story recalls that Mother Praxedes played on gender assumptions to get the rubble cleared. According to this recollection the nun gathered townswomen to clear the rubble. Local Mexican men quietly went to work when they discovered that women were going to do this heavy labor. See *Las Cruces Loretto Chimes*, "Golden Jubilee Number," 1920, 13.

90.   *El Eco del Valle* (Las Cruces), Dec. 16, 1909.

91.   Juárez, "La Iglesia Católica y el Chicano en Sud Texas, 1836–1911," 234–35.

92.   Granjon, *Along the Rio Grande*, 45.

93.   Ibid., 38.

94.   Sister Mary Vida to "Master John E. Amador," Santa Fe, NM, Aug. 13, 1880, Amador Family Papers, Juan Amador Correspondence—letters received, 1879–1907, Box 3, Folder 1.

95.   See, e.g., "Terrazas-Amador Wedding," *Las Cruces Loretto Crescent*, Dec. 1909, Rio Grande Historical Collections, New Mexico State University, Las Cruces.

96.   "Emilia" Amador de Garcia to "Querida Mamá" [Doña Martin Amador], Chicago, IL, Oct. 15, 1893, Amador Family Papers: Doña Martin Amador Correspondence —letters received, 1861–1903, Box 2, Folder 2.

97.   Taylor, *History of San Albino Church on the Plaza Mesilla, New Mexico*, 5.

98.   Ibid.

99.   Granjon, *Along the Rio Grande*, 52.

100.   *Mesilla News*, Dec. 21, 1878.

101.   Ibid.

102.   See Hood, "Bells of Old Mesilla," 15.

103.   Ibid.

104.   See, e.g., the *New York Times*, Sept. 26, 1871.

105.   For other discussions about the role of memory in building collective identities see Heineman, "The Hour of the Woman"; Hobsbawm and Ranger, *The Invention of Tradition*; Irwin-Zarecka, *Frames of Remembrance*; Lipsitz, *Time Passages*; Rousso, *The Vichy Syndrome*; Wilson, *The Myth of Santa Fe*; and Trouillot, *Silencing the Past*.

106.   *Las Cruces Sun-News*, Oct. 9, 1949.

107.   Hood, "Bells of Old Mesilla," 14 (italics in original). Stories about the town's sacrifice for Mesilla's bells circulated widely enough to garner a mention in Paul Horgan's *Great River*, 805.

108.   Manuel Valles's memory may not be accurate, since these bells seem to have

been cast at two different times. A news article reported that Rev. A. Morin installed at least one bell in 1876. See the *Mesilla News*, Sept. 2, 1876.

109. *Chicago Tribune*, Sept. 18, 1887.

110. Similar attitudes could be found when Mesilleros celebrated their parish's (St. Albino) 150th anniversary in 2002. "This is a wonderful opportunity," one woman commented on the importance of the church, "for all of us to celebrate the spiritual guidance the church has provided us that has guided our lives" (*Las Cruces Sun-News*, May 5, 2002).

111. *Las Cruces Sun-News*, Jan. 15, 1995. See also *Las Cruces Bulletin, Valley Views*, Jan. 5, 1995.

112. *El Paso Times*, Jan. 6, 1995.

113. *Las Cruces Sun-News*, Jan. 8, 1995.

114. Interview with María Gonzales Carriere, in Nichols and Banegas, *Our Heritage—Our People*, 31.

115. See, e.g., *Las Cruces Sun-News*, Sept. 24, 1967, and Oct. 2, 1996.

116. Interview with Carriere, in Nichols and Banegas, *Our Heritage—Our People*, 31.

117. Mexicans named their parish after the French saint because the building was completed on the Catholic Feast Day of St. Genevieve. Granjon, *Along the Rio Grande*, 127n25, 133n40.

118. See Hood, "Bells of Old Mesilla"; *Las Cruces Sun-News*, Oct. 9, 1949; Buchanan, *The First Hundred Years*; interview with Carriere, in Nichols and Banegas, *Our Heritage—Our People*, 31; and Harris, *Las Cruces*.

119. Owen, *Las Cruces, New Mexico, 1849–1999*, 79.

120. Interestingly, the obituary in the primarily Spanish newspaper *El Eco del Valle* (July 22, 1909) referred to Father Lassaigne using the first name "Pedro," but the primarily English *Rio Grande Republican* referred to the priest as "P. Lassaigne." Likewise, Monsignor Granjon consistently referred to his colleague as "Don Pedro" (Granjon, *Along the Rio Grande*, 36–58). It is worth wondering if Father Lassaigne eventually used "Pedro" in his social relations with both Euro-Americans and Mexicans. Clearly, by the 1960s the memory of the priest's first name showed great variability. For instance, the Sept, 24, 1967, edition of the *Las Cruces Sun-News* that recounted the history of St. Genevieve's referred to the priest as "Father Pedro Lassaigne"; however, another article appearing on Oct. 10, 1967, used the name "Pierre."

121. *Las Cruces Sun-News*, Oct. 9, 1949.

122. For an assessment of architecture and racial and regional identity in New Mexico see Wilson, *The Myth of Santa Fe*. Wilson notes that many of the attempts to "return" to Mexican-styled buildings originated from Euro-American tourism and racist presumptions.

123. Sandoval, "Intrusion and Domination," 202.

124. Ibid., 220.

125. See http://www.diocesetucson.org/staug.html (accessed Jan. 27, 2009).

126. Interview with Cruz Alvarez, in Nichols and Banegas, *Our Heritage—Our People*, 44.

127. Frietze, *History of La Mesilla and Her Mesilleros*, 19.
128. *Las Cruces Bulletin*, Jan. 5, 1995.

Chapter Four. "Las mujeres Americanas están en todo"

1. M. M. Marmaduke Journal; printed in Hulbert, *Southwest on the Turquoise Trail*, 77.
2. Pattie, *The Personal Narrative of James O. Pattie, of Kentucky*, 172–73.
3. Gregg, *Commerce of the Prairies*, 182.
4. For a discussion on these Euro-American views see González, *Refusing the Favor*, 51–57.
5. Questions remain about the number of prostitutes who did work in New Mexico. Deena González notes that in Santa Fe during this period there were at least two individuals listed as "prostitute" in the census records, but she also points out that Euro-Americans frequently conflated the distinct businesses of saloons, gambling houses, and brothels in their travel narratives. What was a legitimate business for local Mexicans, like a gaming den, was seen as a "pit of vice" by Euro-Americans. See González, *Refusing the Favor*, 57. Ann Gabbert notes, too, that in the 1890s, border cities like El Paso earned nicknames like "Sin City" because they were allegedly more lax and tolerant of prostitution owing in part to their proximity to Mexico. Gabbert, however, documents that El Paso's limited toleration of prostitution was not particularly unusual in the United States. Many similarly sized cities and communities witnessed the creation of segregated districts where "vice" was tacitly permitted. See Gabbert, "Prostitution and Moral Reform in the Borderlands, 1890–1920."
6. In another context Lisa Duggan explores how sensational newspaper coverage of "lesbian-love-murder" stories worked to depoliticize and marginalize women's roles in the public while also vilifying same-sex sexual activity. See Duggan, *Sapphic Slashers*.
7. Many examples can be found in the nineteenth-century press. See, e.g., *New York Times*, Feb. 6, 1882; Feb. 28, 1882; July 23, 1882; May 20, 1883; Aug. 2, 1883.
8. See, e.g., Gutiérrez, "What's Love Got to Do with It?" 866–69.
9. The limitations on primary sources in territorial New Mexico frustrate contemporary attempts to draw a conclusive portrait of the ways that Mexicans and Euro-Americans understood, articulated, and positioned themselves in competing gender and sexuality ideologies from 1848 to 1912. The most frustrating lack for me was a lack of sources on same-sex relationships. Hopefully future archival research will unearth more about this topic. In spite of this the limitations in the body of sources does not mean that ideologies of gender and sexuality were unimportant in the past, nor do they suggest that historians are helpless in reconstructing the historical importance of these categories. I have profited from historians such as Miroslava Chávez-García (*Negotiating Conquest*), Deena González (*Refusing the Favor*), Pablo Mitchell (*Coyote Nation*), and Emma Pérez (*The Decolonial Imaginary*). Mitchell does an excellent job exploring the relationships among gender, sexuality, and U.S.

imperialism, but his work lacks a direct engagement with Spanish-language sources from the period. This chapter will expand the analysis he started by exploring both Euro-American imperialism and the ways that Mexican American elites responded and adapted to that imperialism in their own papers.

10. Kendall, *Narrative of the Texan Santa Fé Expedition*, 2:326.

11. Quoted in Eaton, "Frontier Life in Southern Arizona, 1858–1861," 174.

12. See, e.g., Pattie, *The Personal Narrative of James O. Pattie, of Kentucky*, 168; Farnham, *Life, Adventures, and Travels in California*; and Paredes, "The Mexican Image in American Travel Literature, 1831–1869," 21.

13. See Crenshaw, "Mapping the Margins"; and Crenshaw, "Demarginalizing the Intersection of Race and Sex."

14. Crenshaw, "Demarginalizing the Intersection of Race and Sex," 139–40; Crenshaw, "Mapping the Margins," 1244n8.

15. Wislizenus, *Memoir*, 27.

16. See González, *Refusing the Favor*, 68.

17. Streeby, *American Sensations*, 104.

18. Ibid., 123.

19. Spivak, "Can the Subaltern Speak?" See also Berlant, "The Queen of America Goes to Washington City"; and Cooke, "Saving Brown Women."

20. *Mesilla News*, June 10, 1876.

21. Ibid.

22. For a comparative discussion of how Germany dealt with intermarriage and citizenship law in its colonies see Wildenthal, "Race, Gender, and Citizenship in the German Colonial Empire."

23. See Hodes, *White Women, Black Men*, 199–200.

24. Martínez, "The Spanish Concept of *Limpieza de Sangre*," 18–19.

25. Davis, *El Gringo, or, New Mexico and Her People*, 89.

26. Ibid.

27. Ibid., 97.

28. For Davis the "Spanish race" was European but not wholly "white" in his mind. This early use of "Spanish" identity in New Mexico will be important to later discussions of "pure Spanish blood" in New Mexico.

29. Tera Hunter has shown how "scientific racism" in the postbellum United States mixed together presumptions about racial bodies and cultural acts. Southern whites blamed African Americans, particularly working women, for spreading tuberculosis in the late nineteenth century and the early twentieth. Many white authorities argued that African Americans' bodies were more susceptible to the disease than white bodies. Yet they also believed that location and cultural practices mediated that susceptibility. The same whites erroneously argued that the antebellum South had not seen dangerous rates of tuberculosis because African Americans were contained on rural plantations, supposedly their "natural" environment. See Hunter, *To 'Joy My Freedom*, 188–95. For discussions about the ways that race and disease intersected in border locations see Stern, *Eugenic Nation*; Molina, *Fit to Be Citizens?*; and Deverell, *Whitewashed Adobe*, 172–206.

30. Stoler, *Race and the Education of Desire*, 102.

31. *New York Times*, Feb. 6, 1882; March 26, 1882; July 23, 1882; Aug. 2, 1883; Jan. 29, 1886.

32. *New York Times*, Jan. 29, 1886.

33. Ibid.

34. Accusations of Mexican immorality persisted into the twentieth century. See, e.g., Justice Daniel H. McMillan (fifth district), testimony before Congress, in U.S. Congress, Senate, *Hearings before the Subcommittee of the Committee on Territories on House Bill 12543*, 112–13.

35. Quoted in Foote, *Women of the New Mexico Frontier, 1846–1912*, 103.

36. *Las Cruces Daily News*, July 10, 1889.

37. Chauncey, *Gay New York*, 117.

38. Kimmel, *Manhood in America*, 68.

39. *Las Cruces Daily News*, July 10, 1889.

40. Stoler, *Race and the Education of Desire*, 102.

41. Ibid.

42. Mitchell argues this notion deeply informed the ways that white professionals, like medical doctors, framed their activities in New Mexico at the end of the territorial period. See Mitchell, *Coyote Nation*, 126–27.

43. *Rochester (NY) Frederick Douglass Paper*, April 29, 1853.

44. Doña Ana District Court Records, March 1855 Term, Territory of New Mexico, Records of the United States Territorial and New Mexico District Court for Doña Ana County, New Mexico State Records Center and Archives, Santa Fe, Box 7.

45. Doña Ana District Court Records, November 1856 Term, Territory of New Mexico, Records of the United States Territorial and New Mexico District Court for Doña Ana County, New Mexico State Records Center and Archives, Santa Fe, Box 7.

46. Mallon, "Exploring the Origins of Democratic Patriarchy in Mexico," 5; Fowler-Salamini, "Gender, Work, and Coffee in Córdoba, Veracruz, 1850–1910," 52; Tutino, "Power, Class, and Family in the Mexican Elite, 1750–1810"; Arizpe, "Mujer campesina, mujer indigena"; Yohn, *A Contest of Faiths*, 52.

47. González, *Refusing the Favor*, 22.

48. For a discussion of these differences see Lecompte, "The Independent Women of Hispanic New Mexico, 1821–1846." While Lecompte traces the differences between Euro-American and Mexicans' ideas about gender, work, and public activity, she sometimes overestimates the meaning of these differences for Mexican women. She frequently overstates the historical "independence" or "equality" of Mexican women, ignoring the ways that institutionalized relationships of inequality divided power along gendered lines, configuring and enforcing male authority. See also González, *Refusing the Favor*, 44–50.

49. Chávez-García, *Negotiating Conquest*, 26.

50. González, *Refusing the Favor*, 21.

51. Chávez-García, *Negotiating Conquest*, 26; González, *Refusing the Favor*, 35.

52. See Stern, *The Secret History of Gender*, 162.

53. Gutiérrez, *When Jesus Came, the Corn Mothers Went Away*, 215.

54. Lecompte, "The Independent Women of Hispanic New Mexico, 1821–1846," 20–21, 24.

55. Evans, *Born for Liberty*, 2–4.

56. Cott, *The Bonds of Womanhood*, 197.

57. For a classic essay on this topic see Welter, "The Cult of True Womanhood."

58. See Ginzberg, *Women and the Work of Benevolence*; and Boydston, *Home and Work*.

59. After 1890 various Euro-American women committed their lives to public activity, challenging and helping to undermine the gendered divisions of space in the Euro-American discourse. See Cott, *No Small Courage*, 364–65.

60. Lott, *Love and Theft*, 122. See also Deutsch, *Women and the City*, 58.

61. Bederman, *Manliness & Civilization*, 25.

62. Yu, *Thinking Orientals*, 131. Christine M. E. Guth argues that some individuals participated in these discourses in complicated ways. She suggests that the Japanese writer and aesthete Okakura Kakuzō appealed to the Boston art collector Isabella Stewart Gardner because his appearance in a kimono upheld the stereotype of Japan as "effeminate." At the same time, Okakura also experimented with his forms of masquerade and colonialism when he donned clothing styles from India and China. See Guth, "Charles Longfellow and Okakura Kakuzō."

63. See Hearn and Bisland, *The Writings of Lafcadio Hearn*, iv. For a discussion of the ways in which "Oriental" products were marketed to white women as part of the domestic sphere see Yoshihara, *Embracing the East*, 15–44.

64. Yu, *Thinking Orientals*, 131.

65. Gordon, *The Great Arizona Orphan Abduction*, 164.

66. McClintock, *Imperial Leather*, 34–35; Kaplan, *The Anarchy of Empire in the Making of U.S. Culture*, 24–26.

67. McClintock, *Imperial Leather*, 34.

68. Kaplan, *The Anarchy of Empire in the Making of U.S. Culture*, 25.

69. Ibid.

70. McClintock, *Imperial Leather*, 35.

71. Ann Laura Stoler demonstrates that the metaphor worked in reverse as well: children within the home were often imagined to be "savages" who needed taming during the nineteenth century. See Stoler, *Race and the Education of Desire*, 150–51.

72. For a discussion of the links between domestic images and U.S. imperialism in other nineteenth-century contexts see Wexler, *Tender Violence*.

73. *Santa Fe Republican*, June 17, 1848.

74. Nicholl, *Observations of a Ranchwoman*, 144–45.

75. "Life on the Rio Grande," *Godey's Lady's Book* 32 (April 1847); quoted in Kaplan, *The Anarchy of Empire in the Making of U.S. Culture*, 24.

76. Ibid., 165.

77. *Doña Ana County Republican*, April 21, 1898.

78. Ibid.

79. *Doña Ana County Republican*, Sept. 22, 1898.

80. Comparable arguments often justified white women missionaries traveling abroad. See Newman, *White Women's Rights*, 182.

81. Ibid.

82. Stoler, *Race and the Education of Desire*, 61.

83. Twenty-eighth Legislative Assembly, Journal, Wednesday, Jan. 30, 1889, New Mexico Territorial Archives, microfilm edition, reel 7.

84. See González, *Refusing the Favor*, 48–54.

85. *Las Cruces Daily News*, May 20, 1889.

86. Kimmel, *Manhood in America*, 67.

87. Council Journal, Feb. 13, 1889, New Mexico Territorial Archives, microfilm edition, reel 7.

88. Ibid.

89. Council Journal, Feb. 14, 1889, New Mexico Territorial Archives, microfilm edition, reel 7.

90. Ibid.

91. Kimmel, *Manhood in America*, 67.

92. Ibid.

93. See Findlay, *Imposing Decency*, 9–11; and Briggs, *Reproducing Empire*, 14–16.

94. Briggs, *Reproducing Empire*, 46.

95. Ibid., 17.

96. *Las Cruces Daily News*, April 4, 1889.

97. Arrest Book, June 21, 1907–Jan. 5, 1912, New Mexico Territorial Archives, microfilm edition, reel 93.

98. Ibid.

99. Partha Chatterjee describes the complicated explanations that Bengali elites devised to reconcile changing gender practices with their own sense of an emerging nationalism. In that instance their discourse created a divide between the "spiritual" and the "material" to help explain the adoption of certain Western practices while also claiming a "traditional" way of life. Women were imagined to be the caretakers and guardians of the spiritual and therefore had to demonstrate a rejection of being "Westernized." See Chatterjee, *The Nation and Its Fragments*, 129–31.

100. *Las Cruces Borderer*, March 23, 1871.

101. This was not the only time that Las Cruces newspaper editors manipulated the translations between their English-language and Spanish-language sections. During the tense months that led to the 1871 Mesilla riot, Republicans allegedly tried to work up anti-Catholic fervor among Euro-Americans by claiming that a newly arrived Protestant bishop (who wore a Roman collar) was really a Democrat Catholic priest sent to work on behalf of the Mexican population. This story was not published in the Spanish-language section, where a Democratic priest might have drawn support to that party. See the *Las Cruces Borderer*, Aug. 16, 1871; and Taylor, *A Place as Wild as the West Ever Was*, 156.

102. See Bederman, *Manliness & Civilization*.

103. *Las Cruces Empresa*, March 20, 1897.

104. *Las Cruces Empresa*, April 3, 1897.

105. Meyer, *Speaking for Themselves*, 213.

106. Armijo served in numerous elected positions, including probate clerk for Doña Ana County and county delegate for the New Mexico constitutional convention in 1910. In addition to *El Eco del Valle*, he had also published elsewhere in the

Spanish-speaking West: *El Progreso* in Trinidad, Colorado, and *La Flor del Valle* in Las Cruces. See Meyer, *Speaking for Themselves*, 213.

107. *New York Times*, Feb. 6, 1882.

108. See Pérez, *The Decolonial Imaginary*, 31; and Macías, *Against All Odds*, 16.

109. Macías, *Against All Odds*, 16.

110. Alonso, *Thread of Blood*, 96–97.

111. Alvarado, *La reconstrucción de México*, 120; quoted in Pérez, *The Decolonial Imaginary*, 40.

112. *El Eco del Valle* (Las Cruces), Oct. 28, 1909.

113. *El Eco del Valle* (Las Cruces), June 2, 1906.

114. Ibid.

115. Montoya, "The Dual World of Governor Miguel A. Otero," 25–28.

116. *El Eco del Valle* (Las Cruces), Sept. 29, 1906.

117. Macías, *Against All Odds*, 17–18.

118. *El Eco del Valle* (Las Cruces), Dec. 3, 1905.

119. *El Eco del Valle* (Las Cruces), Dec. 23, 1905.

120. *El Eco del Valle* (Las Cruces), June 23, 1906.

121. *El Eco del Valle* (Las Cruces), March 2, 1907.

122. Ibid.

123. *El Eco del Valle* (Las Cruces), June 4, 1908.

124. *El Labrador* (Las Cruces), June 10, 1904.

125. Gaines, *Uplifting the Race*; Jones, *All Bound Up Together*, 32–33.

126. Gaines, *Uplifting the Race*, 78–80. See also Summers, *Manliness and Its Discontents*, 118–19, 125–26.

127. *El Eco del Valle* (Las Cruces), Nov. 2, 1907.

128. Ibid.

129. *El Eco del Valle* (Las Cruces), April 28, 1906.

130. Macías, *Against All Odds*, 17.

131. *El Eco del Valle* (Las Cruces), April 28, 1906.

132. *El Eco del Valle* (Las Cruces), June 8, 1907.

133. Ibid.

134. Ibid.

135. Morantz-Sánchez, *Conduct Unbecoming a Woman*, 207.

136. *El Eco del Valle* (Las Cruces), April 2, 1908.

137. Ibid.

138. Ibid.

139. Gordon, *The Great Arizona Orphan Abduction*, 145.

140. *El Nuevo Mundo* (Albuquerque), May 31, 1900.

141. *Las Cruces Progress*, March 29, 1902.

142. Ibid.

143. See also Mitchell, *Coyote Nation*, 118–19.

144. For an interesting discussion of the battles over a comparable discourse in Japan see Uno, "The Death of the 'Good Wife, Wise Mother'?"

145. To draw comparisons with the larger United States, I depended on IPUMS (Ruggles, Sobek, et al. [1997], *Integrated Public Use Microdata Series*) rather than

the manuscript census. Scholars interested in tracing these trends among particular families, however, may find the manuscript census more useful for in-depth qualitative analysis. These figures also match Deena González's findings for nineteenth-century Santa Fe. See González, *Refusing the Favor*, 86.

146. See Ruggles, Sobek, et al. (1997), *Integrated Public Use Microdata Series*. Special appreciation to Dr. Marie T. Mora for compiling and helping me to interpret this data.

147. Ibid.

148. G. F. Murray to Capt. Fred Fornoff, New Mexico Territorial Mounted Police, Sept. 30, 1907, New Mexico Territorial Archives, microfilm edition, reel 93.

149. Ibid.

150. G. F. Murray to Capt. Fred Fornoff, New Mexico Territorial Mounted Police, Oct. 18, 1907, New Mexico Territorial Archives, microfilm edition, reel 93.

151. Ibid.

152. R. L. Baca to George Curry, governor of New Mexico, Jan. 1, 1908, New Mexico Territorial Archives, microfilm edition, reel 93.

153. Pablo Mitchell similarly argues that elite Mexican Americans in New Mexico retained an unusual level of authority over such legal cases. See Mitchell, *Coyote Nation*, 74–75.

154. Murray to Fornoff, Sept. 30, 1907 (see note 149 above).

155. Chávez-García, *Negotiating Conquest*, 91.

156. Ibid., 95.

157. Ante el Hon. M. Valdez Juez de Paz del Precinto No. 3 Condado de Doña Ana, Nuevo México, Doña Ana County Records, New Mexico Records Center, Box 5 (emphasis in original).

Chapter Five. "This Is New and Not Old Mexico"

1. New Mexico Territorial Bureau of Immigration Records, 1880–1911, History, New Mexico Territorial Archives, microfilm edition, reel 96.

2. See McBride, "Doña Ana County in New Mexico."

3. Ibid.

4. Ibid., 34. This figure of fifteen dollars per ton of alfalfa was repeated in a comparable brochure published by the Atchison, Topeka and Santa Fe Railroad Colonization Department, promising a potential annual income for the average alfalfa farm of around twelve thousand dollars. See Seagraves, "Mesilla Valley, New Mexico," 5. Governor Miguel Otero also made special note of the alfalfa production in Doña Ana County in 1903. See Report of the Governor (Miguel Otero) of the Territory of New Mexico, 1903, New Mexico Territorial Archives, microfilm edition, reel 149, 278.

5. McBride, "Doña Ana County in New Mexico," 9.

6. Ibid., 11.

7. Mary Pat Brady has explored similar issues in Arizona. See Brady, *Extinct Lands, Temporal Geographies*, 20–21.

8. McBride, "Doña Ana County in New Mexico," 12, 18.

9. Ibid., 54.

10. Ibid., 13.

11. L. Bradford Prince to Edgar Lee Hewett, Feb. 28, 1909; quoted in Nieto-Phillips, *The Language of Blood*, 149.

12. Montgomery, *The Spanish Redemption*, 7.

13. Wilson, *The Myth of Santa Fe*, 73.

14. See, e.g., Prince, *Historical Sketches of New Mexico*, 4.

15. Fuller, "Occupations of the Mexican-Born Population of Texas, New Mexico, and Arizona," 64.

16. Mitchell, *Coyote Nation*, 17.

17. Brady, *Extinct Lands, Temporal Geographies*, 20–21.

18. For a discussion of the links and differences between Euro-American expansion into the "West" and other forms of imperialism see Nugent, "Frontiers and Empires in the Late Nineteenth Century."

19. Nash, "New Mexico in the Otero Era," 7.

20. Ibid.

21. Culbert, "Distribution of Spanish-American Population in New Mexico," 176.

22. Montoya, "The Dual World of Governor Miguel A. Otero," 17n7.

23. *El Democrata*, Sept. 14, 1878.

24. Mitchell, *Coyote Nation*, 17.

25. "The Population of the United States," 856.

26. Nugent, *Into the West*, 150–51.

27. Ruggles, Sobek, et al. (1997), *Integrated Public Use Microdata Series* (accessed March 14, 2010).

28. Montgomery, *The Spanish Redemption*, 67–68.

29. For a history of the various efforts to make New Mexico a state see Larson, *New Mexico's Quest for Statehood, 1846–1912*.

30. For just a few examples from one paper see the *New York Times*, May 24, 1876; Feb. 6, 1882; Feb. 28, 1882; March 26, 1882; May 20, 1883; Oct. 5, 1907.

31. Sánchez, *Becoming Mexican American*, 19.

32. *Los Angeles Times*, Sept. 20, 1897.

33. Deutsch, *No Separate Refuge*, 184–85. For another discussion of dispossession see Chávez, *The Lost Land*, 138–39.

34. *New York Times*, Oct. 5, 1907.

35. *New York Times*, Aug. 2, 1883.

36. "In Support of an American Empire," 56th Cong., 1st sess., *Congressional Record* 33 (1899–1900): 704–12, also available at http://www.mtholyoke.edu/acad/intrel/ajb72.htm (accessed Aug. 6, 2008).

37. Ibid.

38. Theodore Roosevelt to Matthew Quay, Dec. 4, 1902; quoted in Larson, *New Mexico's Quest for Statehood, 1846–1912*, 217. Roosevelt avoided making any public statements about New Mexico statehood.

39. See Braeman, *Albert J. Beveridge*, 85.

40.   Albert Beveridge to John Temple Graces, Feb. 18, 1903; quoted in Braeman, *Albert J. Beveridge*, 85.

41.   *Indianapolis Journal*, Dec. 16, 1902; quoted in Larson, *New Mexico's Quest for Statehood, 1846–1912*, 217.

42.   *Las Cruces Progress*, June 14, 1902.

43.   Euro-Americans frequently made similar arguments about Arizona, implying that Mexicans had "abandoned" what would otherwise be a bountiful area. See Brady, *Extinct Lands, Temporal Geographies*, 21.

44.   *Las Cruces Progress*, June 14, 1902.

45.   Ibid.

46.   *Doña Ana County Republican*, Sept. 8, 1898.

47.   Blight, *Race and Reunion*, 357–58.

48.   Glassberg, *Sense of History*, 133.

49.   Ibid., 134.

50.   See Kasson, *Buffalo Bill's Wild West*, 7–8; and Turner, *The Frontier in American History*.

51.   Kasson, *Buffalo Bill's Wild West*, 15.

52.   Kropp, *California Vieja*, 9. There were other variations within these regional visions, such as the creation of the "Middle West" in the 1880s to distinguish the central plains from the Dakotas and the Southwest. See Shortridge, "The Emergence of the 'Middle West' as an American Regional Label."

53.   *Doña Ana County Republican*, June 17, 1899.

54.   *Las Cruces Progress*, Dec. 6, 1902.

55.   *Mesilla News*, March 14, 1874.

56.   Ibid.

57.   *New York Times*, Nov. 18, 1881.

58.   Larson, *New Mexico's Quest for Statehood, 1846–1912*, 143.

59.   Bederman, *Manliness & Civilization*, 25.

60.   See Montgomery, *The Spanish Redemption*, 68–69.

61.   See Mitchell, *Coyote Nation*; Montgomery, *The Spanish Redemption*; Wilson, *The Myth of Santa Fe*; and Nieto-Phillips, *The Language of Blood*.

62.   *Santa Fe Weekly New Mexican*, Feb. 14, 1880.

63.   Ibid.

64.   Ibid.

65.   Ibid. See also Nieto-Phillips, *The Language of Blood*, 164.

66.   *Santa Fe Weekly New Mexican*, Feb. 14, 1880.

67.   See also Nieto-Phillips, *The Language of Blood*, 163–64.

68.   Prince, *Historical Sketches of New Mexico*, 4.

69.   Ibid.

70.   Ibid.

71.   Ibid.

72.   *New York Times*, Feb. 6, 1882; Feb. 28, 1882.

73.   See Nieto-Phillips, *The Language of Blood*, 74–75.

74.   *New York Times*, March 26, 1882.

75.   Ibid.

76. Ibid.

77. Stoler, *Race and the Education of Desire*, 104.

78. Stoler, *Carnal Knowledge and Imperial Power*, 96–97.

79. Ibid., 98.

80. *Las Cruces Borderer*, Nov. 22, 1871.

81. *New York Times*, March 26, 1882.

82. Larson, *New Mexico's Quest for Statehood, 1846–1912*, 262.

83. Bureau of Publicity of the State Land Office, "New Mexico," 6 (Center for Southwest Research, Zimmerman Library, University of New Mexico, Albuquerque).

84. Ibid., 1.

85. See Nieto-Phillips, *The Language of Blood*, 147.

86. Lears, *No Place of Grace*, 4–5.

87. Nieto-Phillips, *The Language of Blood*, 147.

88. *New York Times*, Nov. 7, 1909.

89. *New York Times*, Oct. 29, 1911.

90. Bell, "On the Native Races of New Mexico," 222.

91. Bureau of Publicity of the State Land Office, "New Mexico," 30–31.

92. Ibid., 6.

93. Ibid.

94. McClintock, *Imperial Leather*, 30; see also Deloria, "Revolution, Region, and Culture," 364.

95. McClintock, *Imperial Leather*, 30.

96. Ibid., 37–38.

97. Ibid., 39.

98. Ibid., 30.

99. Fabian, *Time and the Other*, 31.

100. McClintock, *Imperial Leather*, 40.

101. Huxley, *Brave New World*.

102. I owe a special thanks to Micah Auerback for reminding me of this point.

103. In framing what I mean by "knowledge," I draw from Michel Foucault's *The Archaeology of Knowledge*: "Knowledge is . . . the field of coordination and subordination of statements in which concepts appear and are defined, applied and transformed. . . . Knowledge is defined by the possibilities of use and appropriation offered by discourse" (182–83).

104. Katz, *The Life and Times of Pancho Villa*, 607.

105. Miller, "New Mexico during the Civil War," 7–8.

106. Ibid.

107. Ibid., 8.

108. Ibid.

109. Ibid., 47.

110. Ibid.

111. Ibid.

112. Ibid.

113. Ibid.

114. Foster, "The Folk-lore of the Mesilla Valley," 6.

115. Ibid., 5, 6, 28.

116. Fabian, *Time and the Other*, 32.

117. Foster, "The Folk-lore of the Mesilla Valley," 6.

118. Ibid., 5.

119. Miller, "Mexican Cookery," 5–6.

120. Phelps, "The Primitive Mexican Home in New Mexico," 1, 19, 34, 35.

121. Ibid., 3.

122. Ibid., 34.

123. Ibid.

124. Ibid., 1.

125. Ibid.

126. Ibid.

127. Ibid.

128. See Nieto-Phillips, *The Language of Blood*, 145–46.

129. Albert Beveridge to Charles Lummes [*sic*], Sept. 6, 1902, Albert Jeremiah Beveridge Papers, Box 137.

130. Lummis, *The Land of Poco Tiempo*, 1 (emphasis in original). Although it neglects to consider Lummis's work as a product of U.S. imperialism and often glides over his racism, Thompson's *American Character* provides an outline of his life and works.

131. Lummis, *The Land of Poco Tiempo*, 4–5.

132. Ibid., 4.

133. Ibid., 5.

134. Ibid.

135. Ibid., 7.

136. Ibid., 14.

137. Ibid., 3.

138. Ibid., 127.

139. See Bederman, *Manliness & Civilization* for critical discussion about the ways that Euro-American men used men of color and the image of the "primitive" to build their own sense of masculinity during this period.

140. Eric Lott comments that racialized images frequently contained homo-erotic elements that suggested white male desire and repulsion from the bodies and sexualities of men of color. See Lott, *Love and Theft*, 57.

141. Lummis, *The Land of Poco Tiempo*, 89.

142. Ibid., 6.

143. Ibid.

144. Ibid., 6, 14–16.

145. See Weigle, *Brothers of Light, Brothers of Blood*.

146. Lummis, *Land of Poco Tiempo*, 19.

147. Ibid., 61–62 (emphasis in original).

148. Lummis was shot while staying in Isleta Pueblo in the summer of 1888, although he ultimately recovered. Many speculated that it was the San Mateo Penitentes who intended to kill him for violating their privacy. See Nieto-Phillips, *The Language of Blood*, 155.

149. Lummis, *The Land of Poco Tiempo*, 1.

150. Ibid., 56.

151. Gutiérrez, "Charles Fletcher Lummis and the Orientalization of New Mexico," 18.

152. Ibid., 25.

153. Lummis, *The Land of Poco Tiempo*, 3.

154. For an introduction to this movement see Guth, *Longfellow's Tattoos*; and Lambourne, *Japonism*.

155. For broader discussions about tourism's role in influencing ideas about race in New Mexico see Rothman, *The Culture of Tourism, the Tourism of Culture*; Nieto-Phillips, *The Language of Blood*; Wilson, *The Myth of Santa Fe*; and Sebastian-Coleman, "Writing the Relation."

156. Said, *Orientalism*, 103.

157. McClintock, *Imperial Leather*, 41.

158. Lummis, *The Land of Poco Tiempo*, 3.

159. Whiting, *The Land of Enchantment*, 182.

160. Ibid., 195.

161. Ibid., 182.

162. *Las Cruces Daily News*, May 22, 1889.

163. Ibid.

164. Brady, *Extinct Lands, Temporal Geographies*, 17.

165. *New York Times*, May 4, 1913.

166. Kropp, *California Vieja*, 4–5.

167. For a discussion of promoting Texas missions see Bremer, *Blessed with Tourists*. Walter Buenger argues persuasively that many Euro-Americans consciously turned to crafting a regional Texas history that focused more on the U.S.-Mexican War than on the Civil War; see Buenger, *The Path to a Modern South*, 253–60.

168. Kropp, *California Vieja*, 8.

169. Ibid., 9–10.

170. Ibid., 10.

171. Fregoso, *MeXicana Encounters*, 49–51.

172. Weber, *Myth and the History of the Hispanic Southwest*, 138; see also Johnson, *Revolution in Texas*, 172; and Buenger, "'The Story of Texas?'"

173. Quoted in Johnson, *Revolution in Texas*, 173.

174. Ibid.; Fregoso, *MeXicana Encounters*, 49.

175. Pattie, *The Personal Narrative of James O. Pattie, of Kentucky*, 168.

176. Nicholl, *Observations of a Ranchwoman*, 21.

177. Ibid.

178. Ibid., 20.

179. Ibid., 41; in a similar vein Charles Miller, a student at New Mexico A&M, directly compared New Mexico's labor practices to southern African Americans' status as slaves, writing "the system of peon labor made the people of New Mexico similar to those of the south" (Miller, "New Mexico during the Civil War," 47).

180. Williams, "Mexican Words Used by English Speaking Inhabitants of the Mesilla Valley," 10–11.

181. Ibid.

182. Ibid., 159.

183. Ibid., 172.

184. *New York Times*, Feb. 6, 1882.

185. Ibid.

186. For a discussion of how notions of race, region, and myth worked in the U.S. South see Blight, *Race and Reunion*, 216–31.

187. *Las Cruces Thirty-Four*, Dec. 25, 1878.

188. *Mesilla News*, Nov. 14, 1874.

189. Ibid.

190. Eaton, "Frontier Life in Southern Arizona, 1858–1861," 174.

191. *Las Cruces Newman's Semi-Weekly*, April 9, 1881. Senator Albert Beveridge complained about the legal system operating in Spanish and considered it a justification for denying statehood during his tenure as chair of the Senate Committee on Territories. See, e.g., Memo Relating to New Mexico, n.d., no author, Albert Beveridge Papers, Library of Congress, Box 137; Albert Beveridge to Hon. Charles Emory Smith, Dec. 4, 1902, Albert Beveridge Papers, Box 137.

192. For a discussion of Mexicans' complicated participation in the New Mexico legal system see Gómez, "Race, Colonialism, and Criminal Law."

193. *Las Cruces Newman's Semi-Weekly*, April 9, 1881.

194. Ibid.

195. *Mesilla News*, Dec. 19, 1874.

196. Owen, *Las Cruces, New Mexico, 1849–1999*, 49.

197. *Mesilla News*, Nov. 30, 1878.

198. McFie, "A History of the Mesilla Valley," 30.

199. Another student reconciled Mesilla with the regional New Mexico identity in a slightly different way. In an essay for his English class one Bill Porter contended that Mesilla's incorporation into the United States also meant that it became part of the regional New Mexico identity. Moreover, he imagined that Mesilleros benefited from the changing borderline. Discussing the signing of the Mesilla/Gadsden Treaty, Porter wrote, "Until this time, Mesilla had belonged to the whole West; but now she became New Mexico's own. The people who had little or no voice in the Mexican Government now had an opportunity to express her weight in politics" (Bill Porter, Brelands English Class [n.d.], Cruz Alavarez Papers, Rio Grande Historical Collection, New Mexico State University). See also Albert J. Fountain, "Confundís de la historia del Pintoresco Pueblo de La Mesilla," Albert Jennings Fountain Papers, 1885, Center for Southwest Research, University of New Mexico, Albuquerque.

200. McFie, "A History of the Mesilla Valley," 30.

201. Ibid., 16.

202. Ibid.

203. Mesilleros hardly gave up their militancy through the nineteenth century. The Mesilla Spanish-language newspaper *El Defensor del Pueblo*, for instance, split with other Spanish-language newspapers by overtly congratulating the controversial "White Caps." See Stratton, *The Territorial Press of New Mexico, 1834–1912*, 131.

204. Hiram Hadley, "Commencement, Raton High School," May 28, 1897, Hiram Hadley Papers, Rio Grande Historical Collections, New Mexico State University, Las Cruces.

205. Ibid.

Chapter Six. "New Mexico for New Mexicans!"

1. Albert Beveridge to Albert Shaw, Jan. 10, 1902; quoted in Braeman, *Albert J. Beveridge*, 83.

2. Albert Beveridge to Hon. Charles Emory Smith, Dec. 4, 1902, Albert Jeremiah Beveridge Papers, Box 137; see also Albert Beveridge to Fred Purdy, Feb. 28, 1903, Albert Beveridge Papers, Box 141.

3. U.S. Congress, Senate, *Hearings before the Subcommittee of the Committee on Territories on House Bill 12543*, 100.

4. Ibid.

5. Memo Relating to New Mexico, n.d., Albert Jeremiah Beveridge Papers, Box 137.

6. While they argued that they were racially not Euro-American, but nationally American, they rarely, if ever, used the term *Mexican American* to describe themselves. One factor behind this choice might have been the simultaneous increase in the use of the term *Spanish American*, but that is not a full explanation, as their Spanish-language texts used the term *mexicanos* frequently. Most often they identified themselves through the local geography, preferring *New Mexican* or *neomexicano*, which connoted a racial identity specific to the region and an American national identity.

7. Although Mexicans and Euro-Americans included Native Americans within the regional identity, the actual voices of the latter seem to have been suppressed from the public discourse, as few records of their participation in this identity exist.

8. Nieto-Phillips, "No Other Blood," 122.

9. Meléndez, *So All Is Not Lost*, 24–26; Meyer, *Speaking for Themselves*, 4.

10. Meléndez, *So All Is Not Lost*, 24; see also Meyer, *Speaking for Themselves*. Between 1880 and 1912 the Mesilla Valley witnessed the creation of numerous Spanish-language newspapers: *El Democrata*, *El Tiempo*, and *El Eco del Valle*, to name the most prominent. The Cruceño newspaper *El Defensor del Pueblo* ran with the subtitle "Justicia e Igualdad Ante la Ley," promising in the first edition that "se redecir a la defensa de los intereses de los Mejicanos residentes en los Territorios Nuevo Mexico y Arizona" (it [the paper] will reaffirm the defense of Mexican residents' interests in the territories of New Mexico and Arizona) (*El Defensor del Pueblo* [Mesilla], July 26, 1890).

11. Meyer, *Speaking of Themselves*, 8.

12. Ibid.

13. Larson, *New Mexico's Quest for Statehood, 1846–1912*, 149.

14. Ibid.

15. These fears prompted the omnibus bill's inclusion of the controversial Sec-

tion 20, which sparked dismay in the territory because it would have required that New Mexico be renamed "Montezuma" out of fear that "New Mexico" would always be confused with the Republic of Mexico. See Larson, *New Mexico's Quest for Statehood, 1846–1912*, 149.

16. Ibid., 148.

17. *Chicago Tribune*, Feb. 2, 1889; See also Larson, *New Mexico's Quest for Statehood, 1846–1912*, 148.

18. Joint Resolution Introduced by Col. Francisco Chávez, Twenty-Eighth Legislative Assembly, Dec. 31, 1888–Feb. 28, 1889, New Mexico Territorial Archives, microfilm edition, reel 7.

19. Ibid. Horatio Ladd would use almost identical language when he published *The Story of New Mexico* in 1891. New Mexico, he wrote, "contains quite as large a proportion of loyal citizens who spent their blood and treasure in defending the flag of the Union, as any other territory that has been lately admitted to the Union" (Ladd, *The Story of New Mexico*, 435).

20. Ibid.

21. See, e.g., Guglielmo, *White on Arrival*, 31–38.

22. *El Labrador* (Las Cruces), Dec. 4, 1903.

23. Ibid.

24. Brady, *Extinct Lands, Temporal Geographies*, 45.

25. Servín and Spude, "Historical Conditions of Early Mexican Labor in the United States," 44.

26. For a larger discussion of mining in Arizona and cross-border developments see Truett, *Fugitive Landscapes*; and Huginnie, "A New Hero Comes to Town."

27. Chávez, *The Lost Land*, 66.

28. Brady, *Extinct Lands, Temporal Geographies*, 20–26; Gordon, *The Great Arizona Orphan Abduction*, 159–66.

29. Gordon, *The Great Arizona Orphan Abduction*, 171.

30. Ibid., 297.

31. In 1877, for instance, the editor of the newspaper *Las Dos Repúblicas* stated, "Our duty is to maintain our post against the attack of the [Anglo] hordes from the north." He further advised that Mexicans had to reassert their political and cultural authority over Arizona, claiming, "Our customs, our faith, our language, activity, industry, education, taking part in politics, influencing the legislature, and naming the governors: these are the arms with which Latin civilization must conquer the Saxon" (translated in Chávez, *The Lost Land*, 66).

32. *El Nuevo Mundo* (Las Cruces), July 10, 1897; see also Meyer, *Speaking for Themselves*, 126.

33. Pratt, *Imperial Eyes*, 9.

34. Ibid., 7.

35. Genaro Padilla offered an important break in the ways that we have evaluated members of the Mexican American elite from the nineteenth century. Padilla traced the complicated ways that certain Mexican American elites used autobiography to express their mixed feelings of loss and resistance in their "homeland." See Padilla, *My History, Not Yours.*

36. *El Labrador* (Las Cruces), June 12, 1903.

37. *El Eco del Valle* (Las Cruces), Sept. 22, 1910.

38. See, e.g., Acuña, *Occupied America*, 79.

39. *El Eco del Valle* (Las Cruces), Sept. 22, 1910.

40. Ibid.

41. *El Labrador* (Las Cruces), Oct. 9, 1903.

42. *El Mosquito* (Mora, N.M.), Dec. 10, 1892; quoted in Meléndez, *So All Is Not Lost*, 71.

43. Price, *Mesilla Valley Pioneers, 1823–1912*, 290–91.

44. *La Empresa* (Las Cruces), Oct. 17, 1896.

45. Ibid.

46. Other examples of Euro-Americans claiming to be "natives" do exist. *El Eco del Valle* printed an obituary for a Euro-American named Jerome Martin, contending he was "un hijo nativo de Nuevo Mexico" (*El Eco del Valle* [Las Cruces], Jan. 6, 1906).

47. *La Empresa* (Las Cruces), June 12, 1897.

48. Montoya, "The Dual World of Governor Miguel A. Otero," 19.

49. Ibid.

50. Montoya, "The Dual World of Governor Miguel A. Otero," 23. Otero did not attempt to overturn Euro-American ideas about race or racial categories. He firmly upheld the notion that Euro-Americans brought progress to the territory, and he frequently called for Mexicans to "assimilate" Anglo customs.

51. Speech delivered June 12, 1897, Miguel Otero Papers, Box 4.

52. "Inaugural Address of Governor Miguel Antonio Otero," reprinted in Otero, *My Life on the Frontier, 1882–1897*, 300. See also *New York Times*, Sept. 19, 1897; Oct. 28, 1898; Dec. 12, 1899.

53. "Hon. Miguel Antonio Otero: The Thrice Appointed Governor of New Mexico," Miguel Otero Papers, Box 4.

54. E. V. Chávez to Hon. Miguel A. Otero, June 15, 1897, Miguel Otero Papers, Box 1.

55. A. C. Campbell to Miguel A. Otero, January 17, 1901, Miguel Otero Papers, Box 1.

56. Prominent Mexican Americans' efforts to name "native" status as exclusive to, and synonymous with, the existing Mexican racial identity continued to gain traction with Euro-Americans as well. By 1935 they had so successfully accomplished this goal that Euro-Americans often used *New Mexican* as a replacement for *Mexican*. For example, discussing the inhabitants of Las Vegas, Helen Zunser wrote "The 'native' or New Mexicans live in the adobe house[s] of 'old town,' the 'Americanos' in the wooded and brick houses of 'new town'" (Zunser, "A New Mexican Village," 125).

57. *New York Times*, June 3, 1897.

58. *Santa Fe New Mexican*, June 5, 1897; repr. in Otero, *My Life on the Frontier, 1882–1897*, 296.

59. The *New York Times* coverage of his inauguration declared him a governor "in whose veins runs the blood of the old Spaniards" (*New York Times*, June 15, 1897).

60. "Biographical Sketch of Hon. M. A. Otero, War Governor of New Mexico, 1898," Miguel Otero Papers, Box 4.

61. Address to Rough Riders in Presentation of Medal, Feb. 1899, Miguel Otero Papers, Box 4.

62. Ibid.

63. "Speech Made in the White House at Washington, D.C., 1900," Miguel Otero Papers, Box 4. The *New York Times* noted Otero's presence at these ceremonies but made no mention of his speech (*New York Times*, Dec. 13, 1900).

64. "Interview with Governor Otero of New Mexico," July 1, 1905, 9–10, Miguel Otero Papers, Box 4.

65. Ibid., 10.

66. M. A. Otero to Juan C. Jaramillo, Jan. 26, 1905, New Mexico Territorial Archives, microfilm edition, reel 146.

67. M. A. Otero to Hon. Felix Martinez, May 22, 1915, Miguel Otero Papers, Box 2.

68. The governor's son had also been the subject of at least three failed kidnapping schemes. See *New York Times*, July 13, 1905; Aug. 10, 1905.

69. Postcard from "Miguel" to "Gov. M. A. Otero," Oct. 23, 1906 (7:30 a.m.), Miguel Otero Papers, Box 3.

70. Miguel Otero III to M. A. Otero, Oct. 27, 1906, Miguel Otero Papers, Box 3.

71. Ibid. Regrettably, Miguel Otero's responses and advice to his son did not survive.

72. Miguel Otero to "Citizens of New Mexico," Nov. 1897, Miguel Otero Papers, Box 4.

73. Ibid.

74. See "Hon. Miguel Antonio Otero: The Thrice Appointed Governor of New Mexico," Miguel Otero Papers, Box 4.

75. Otero never directly challenged Euro-Americans' dominance over the local space and even worked to increase their role in certain instances. Appointing officials to the Mexican-dominated Rio Arriba County, for instance, Otero opted to appoint eight Euro-Americans and only a single Mexican American. See Montoya, "The Dual World of Governor Miguel A. Otero," 20.

76. Larrazolo's birth in Chihuahua did appear as a campaign issue when he ran for governor as a Republican in 1918. His Democratic opponent, Félix García, claimed that Larrazolo could not claim status as a "native New Mexican." Larrazolo's narrow victory, however, seemed to quiet most of the debate about whether he was authentically native New Mexican. See Chávez, *The Lost Land*, 102–3.

77. Larrazolo, "The Missionary Fathers."

78. Quoted in Summers, *Manliness and Its Discontents*, 3.

79. Meyer, *Speaking for Themselves*, 191.

80. A. Gabriel Meléndez argued that Read was estranged from the Anglo community because of his "mixed" ancestry. See Meléndez, *So All Is Not Lost*, 126.

81. Meyer, *Speaking for Themselves*, 192.

82. Ibid., 192–93; Meléndez, *So All Is Not Lost*, 126.

83. Read, *Guerra México-Americana*, 6; see also Read, *A Treatise on the Disputed Points of the History of New Mexico*.

84. Read, *Guerra México-Americana*, 6.

85. Meléndez, *So All Is Not Lost*, 127.

86. Manuel Otero to Benjamín Read, Jan. 11, 1912, in Read, *Illustrated History of New Mexico*, 811.

87. Aurelio Espinosa to Benjamín Read, July 15, 1911, in Read, *Illustrated History of New Mexico*, 808.

88. See "Necrology," 394.

89. Read, *Guerra México-Americana*, 183, 198.

90. For example, see ibid., 177, 194.

91. Read, *Popular Elementary History of New Mexico*, 116.

92. Pursuing a similar logic, Ann Laura Stoler discusses the importance that Delhi colonial authorities placed on a "cultural of consensus on Europeanness" to distinguish themselves from Asians. See Stoler, "Rethinking Colonial Categories," 141.

93. Read, *Guerra México-Americana*, 181–207.

94. *El Labrador* (Las Cruces), June 10, 1904.

95. As I mentioned in chapter 1, the idea that New Mexicans never developed a sense of national Mexican identity because of their supposed geographical isolation reappeared in historical narratives through the end of the twentieth century. See, e.g., Meyer, *Speaking for Themselves*; or Gutiérrez, *When Jesus Came, the Corn Mothers Went Away*.

96. Read, *Guerra México-Americana*, 183.

97. Ibid., 229.

98. Read, *Illustrated History of New Mexico*, 416.

99. Read, *Popular Elementary History of New Mexico*, 115.

100. Ibid., 116.

101. Ibid.

102. When Governor Miguel Otero delivered his annual report on the territory to the secretary of the interior in 1899, he noted that there were "only two Jewish places of worship in New Mexico" (*New York Times*, Dec. 12, 1899).

103. *El Labrador* (Las Cruces), June 10, 1904.

104. See Gilman, *The Jew's Body*, 120–22; and Zaborowska, "Americanization of a 'Queer Fellow,'" 218.

105. "Necrology," 396.

106. See Montgomery, "The Trap of Race and Memory."

107. *El Nuevo Mexicano* (Santa Fe), March 13, 1909.

108. Meyer, *Speaking for Themselves*, 108.

109. Prince, *Historical Sketches of New Mexico from the Earliest Records to the American Occupation*, 4.

110. Phelps, "Representation without Taxation," 136. Of all the U.S. border states, Arizona is the least explored by Chicano/a historians.

111. *Las Cruces Citizen*, Aug. 2, 1902.

112. Ibid.

113. *El Eco del Valle* (Las Cruces), July 22, 1909. See a similar editorial in *El Labrador* (Las Cruces), Dec. 30, 1904.

114. Quoted in Meyer, *Speaking for Themselves*, 193.

115. For a more detailed discussion about nineteenth-century debates on bilingual education in the Southwest see Blanton, *The Strange Career of Bilingual Education in Texas, 1836–1981*.

116. *Doña Ana County Republican*, July 7, 1898.

117. Ibid.

118. Nicholl, *Observations of a Ranchwoman*, 144.

119. Ibid., 23.

120. Ibid.

121. Hiram Hadley, Superintendent, Department of Education, Territory of New Mexico, Santa Fe, to Alfredo Sanchez, Washington, D.C., Aug. 23, 1906 (emphasis in original), Fabian Garcia Papers, MS 71, Box 3, folder 1, Personal Papers, Alfredo Sanchez Papers, 1894–1907, Rio Grande Historical Collections.

122. Interestingly, Hadley seems to have reversed his opinion after New Mexico attained statehood. In a 1919 letter to a friend, Hadley encouraged her to learn Spanish because he thought "it a beautiful language and then the relations, commercial and otherwise, between the people of the United States and the Spanish speaking peoples is destined to increase very rapidly, and if for no other reason, the mere dollar-and-cent consideration is sufficient to stimulate this" (Hiram Hadley to Mildred Allen, Mesilla Park, Aug. 24, 1919, Hiram Hadley Papers, Rio Grande Historical Collections, New Mexico State University, Las Cruces).

123. Ruggles, Sobek, et al. (1997), *Integrated Public Use Microdata Series*.

124. Ibid.

125. See Hernández, "El México perdido."

126. Mora-Torres, *The Making of the Mexican Border*, 57.

127. Sánchez, *Becoming Mexican American*, 22.

128. Mora-Torres, *The Making of the Mexican Border*, 9–10.

129. Frietze, *History of La Mesilla and Her Mesilleros*, 118.

130. Gonzales, " 'La Junta de Indignación,' " 176.

131. Ibid., 177.

132. *El Democrata* (Mesilla), Sept. 14, 1878.

133. Lionel Cajen Frietze claims that Mesilleros were "isolationists" who, if they did learn English, only used it "when they absolutely had to" (Frietze, *History of La Mesilla and Her Mesilleros*, 35).

134. C. D. McClellan to "Mother," Sept. 5, 1918, C. D. McClellan Letter Collection, Rio Grande Historical Collections, New Mexico State University, Las Cruces.

135. *El Defensor del Pueblo* (Mesilla), March 28, 1891.

136. Prince, *Historical Sketches of New Mexico from the Earliest Records to the American Occupation*, 4.

137. *El Defensor del Pueblo* (Mesilla), March 28, 1891.

138. *El Labrador* (Las Cruces), Jan. 15, 1904.

139. New Mexico Territorial Census, 1885, New Mexico Territorial Archives, microfilm edition, reel 40.

140. Mullin, "An Item from Old Mesilla."

141. *Rio Grande Republican*, Feb. 11, 1928; quoted in Frietze, *The History of La Mesilla and Her Mesilleros*, 114.

142. *Las Cruces Daily News*, July 16, 1889.

143. *Las Cruces Daily News*, Feb. 9, 1893.

144. *Doña Ana County Republican*, Sept. 8, 1898.

145. *Los Angeles Times*, Jan. 13, 1892.

146. *Las Cruces Citizen*, July 6, 1907.

147. Said, "Secular Interpretation, the Geographical Element, and the Methodology of Imperialism," 28, 36.

148. *Eco del Siglo* (Las Cruces), Feb. 9, 1882.

149. Ibid.

150. Owen, *Las Cruces, New Mexico, 1849–1999*, 53–54.

151. Frietze, *History of La Mesilla and Her Mesilleros*, 113.

152. Chávez, *The Lost Land*, 58–59.

153. U.S. Congress, Senate, *Hearings before the Subcommittee of the Committee on Territories on House Bill 12543*, 105.

154. Mrs. Amador to Albert Beveridge, March 15, 1903, Albert Jeremiah Beveridge Papers (emphasis in original), Box 142.

155. Not everybody was convinced that Las Cruces was thoroughly "American." In 1905 the *New York Times* ran an article titled "Most Un-American Part of the United States," which used Mexicans' dominance of Doña Ana and Las Cruces as evidence of New Mexico's "foreignness." Much to the chagrin of Cruceños and Euro-Americans, who protested the article, Las Cruces became a reason for New Mexico to remain a territory. See *New York Times*, Aug. 20, 1905; Sept. 3, 1905.

156. *Las Cruces Daily News*, July 23, 1889.

157. Report of the Governor (Miguel Otero) of the Territory of New Mexico, 1903, New Mexico Territorial Archives, reel 149, 278.

158. See Otero, *The Real Billy the Kid*.

159. Report of the Governor (Miguel Otero) of the Territory of New Mexico, 1903, New Mexico Territorial Archives, reel 149, 40.

160. Trouillot, *Silencing the Past*, 25–27.

161. Confino, *Germany as a Culture of Remembrance*, 183–84.

162. Rousso, *The Vichy Syndrome*, 4.

163. Mesilleros hardly gave up their militancy through the nineteenth century. The Mesilla Spanish-language newspaper *El Defensor del Pueblo*, for instance, split with other Spanish-language newspapers by overtly congratulating the controversial "White Caps." See Stratton, *The Territorial Press of New Mexico, 1834–1912*, 131.

164. Read, *Illustrated History of New Mexico*, 456.

165. Ibid.

166. Ibid.

167. Read, *Guerra México-Americana*, 206.

168. *Las Cruces Rio Grande Farmer*, June 23, 1932.

169. Wislizenus, *Memoir*, 84.

170. *New York Times*, Nov. 14, 1910.

171. Cruz Richards Alvarez, "In the Land of Mystic Wonders," Cruz Alvarez Papers, Rio Grande Historical Collections, New Mexico State University, Las Cruces.

172.   About two thousand Mexicans in New Mexico declared their preference to remain in New Mexico as Mexican citizens. The lack of evidence for this same phenomenon in California or Texas might be attributed to any number of historical circumstances, such as intimidation, harassment, or simply poor record keeping. See Griswold del Castillo, *The Treaty of Guadalupe Hidalgo*, 65–66.

173.   See Lears, "The Concept of Cultural Hegemony"; and Lowe, "Heterogeneity, Hybridity, Multiplicity."

174.   Lears, "The Concept of Cultural Hegemony," 569.

Epilogue

1.   The Mexican American Bill Richardson, governor of New Mexico from 2003 to 2011, also made headlines when he ran for the Democratic nomination for president in 2008 and when he was forced to decline an appointment as secretary of commerce in 2009 owing to an ethics investigation. While he is often associated with being a native New Mexican, Richardson was actually born in California to a Mexican national mother and a Euro-American father. Like Otero and Larrazolo before him, this governor's biography is not consistent with his popular image within the state.

2.   Bonfil Batalla, *México profundo*, 98.

3.   Wislizenus, *Memoir*, 26.

4.   Ibid., 27.

5.   See "The Great Seal of New Mexico," on the website of the Office of the New Mexico Secretary of State, http://www.sos.state.nm.us/ (accessed Sept. 5, 2008).

6.   See, e.g., McWilliams, *North from Mexico*, 35–47; Nieto-Phillips, *The Language of Blood*; Montgomery, *The Spanish Redemption*; and Mitchell, *Coyote Nation*.

7.   Gómez, *Manifest Destinies*, 149.

8.   Merriwether et al., "Mitochondrial versus Nuclear Admixture Estimates Demonstrate a Past History of Directional Mating," quoted in Gómez, *Manifest Destinies*, 178n42.

9.   Stoler, *Carnal Knowledge and Imperial Power*, 206.

10.   Ramirez, *Native Hubs*, 142–43.

11.   Pratt, *Imperial Eyes*, 150.

12.   Attributed to Lora Romero in Fregoso, *MeXicana Encounters*, 127.

13.   I have used Paul Gilroy's discussion of Britain's postcolonial immigration "crisis" to help frame the equivalent U.S. debate. See Gilroy, *After Empire*, 98.

14.   The same is probably true about members of the individual Pueblos, but more research is needed to determine how this played out among and between various tribal groups.

15.   Rajaram and Grundy-Warr, *Borderscapes*, xv.

16.   Interview with Doña Seferina Quintana, Pecos, 1977; quoted in Bustamante, "'That Matter Was Never Resolved,'" 163.

17.   See "New Mexico Flag Salute," on the website of the New Mexico Office of the State Historian, http://www.newmexicohistory.org/ (accessed Sept. 7, 2008).

18. Myra, "Bells of Old Mesilla," iii.

19. See Lowe, *Immigrant Acts*, 84–96; DuCille, *Skin Trade*, 8–59: Fregoso, "Reproduction and Miscegenation in the Borderlands"; and Melamed, "The Spirit of Neoliberalism." For a discussion of the possibilities and limits of the political potential of multiculturalism see Spivak, *A Critique of Postcolonial Reason*, 353–58.

20. Lowe, *Immigrant Acts*, 30.

21. Ibid., 86.

22. For a recent critique of New Mexico's triculturalism and tourism see Lara, "(Re)Visiting the Land of Enchantment."

23. Castles, "Citizenship and the Other in the Age of Migration," 306.

24. Only Mississippi and post-Katrina Louisiana surpassed New Mexico in terms of poverty (20.6 and 18.6 respectively).

25. For a discussion of *Hispanic* as a term see Oboler, *Ethnic Labels, Latino Lives*, xi–xxi, 1–16.

26. See the American Community Survey on the U.S. Census Bureau's website, http://www.census.gov/acs/www/ (accessed June 25, 2009). See, in particular, tables B19013 and B19101.

27. Chadwick, "Texas Primer: The Native Texan," 115. The television show *King of the Hill* featured an episode involving the Texas Department of Transportation providing a fictional option in license plates that identified drivers as "Native Texans." See "Yankee Hankee," *King of the Hill* (airdate Feb. 4, 2001). One can also see recent 2008 usages of "native Texans" to refer to Euro-Americans in papers like the *Dallas Morning News*, July 10, 2008; or the *Houston Chronicle*, July 14, 2008.

28. Ramirez, *Native Hubs*, 12.

29. Paredes, *With His Pistol in His Hand*, 11.

30. Anzaldúa, *Borderlands / La frontera*, 25.

BIBLIOGRAPHY

Abel, Annie Heloise, ed. *The Official Correspondence of James S. Calhoun While Indian Agent at Santa Fé and Superintendent of Indian Affairs in New Mexico.* Washington: Government Printing Office, 1915.

Acuña, Rodolfo. *Corridors of Migration: The Odyssey of Mexican Laborers, 1600–1933.* Tucson: University of Arizona Press, 2007.

———. *Occupied America: A History of Chicanos.* 5th edn. New York: Pearson Longman, 2004.

Aguirre Beltrán, Gonzalo. *La población negra de México.* 1946. Veracruz: Universidad Veracruzana, 1989.

Agustin de Escudero, José. *Noticias históricas y estadisticas de la antigua provincia del Nuevo-México.* Imprenta de Lara: Mexico City, 1849.

Albert Jeremiah Beveridge Papers. Series 2: General Correspondence, circa 1889–1931. 409 containers. Library of Congress, Manuscript Division, Washington, D.C.

Almaguer, Tomás. *Racial Fault Lines: The Historical Origins of White Supremacy in California.* Berkeley: University of California Press, 1994.

Almonte, Juan Nepomuceno. *Proyectos de leyes sobre colonización.* Ignacio Cumplido: Mexico City, 1852.

Alonso, Ana María. "The Politics of Space, Time, and Substance: State Formation, Nationalism, and Ethnicity." *Annual Review of Anthropology* 23 (1994): 379–405.

———. *Thread of Blood: Colonialism, Revolution, and Gender on Mexico's Northern Frontier.* Tucson: University of Arizona Press, 1995.

Alonzo, Armando. *Tejano Legacy: Rancheros and Settlers in South Texas, 1734–1900.* Albuquerque: University of New Mexico Press, 1998.

Alvarado, Salvador. *La reconstrucción de México: Un mensaje a los pueblos de America.* Vol. 2. México: Ediciones del Gobierno de Yucatán, 1980.

Amador Family Papers. Rio Grande Historical Collections, New Mexico State University, Las Cruces.

Anderson, Benedict. *Imagined Communities: Reflections on the Origin and Spread of Nationalism.* Rev. and extended edn. New York: Routledge, 1991.

Anzaldúa, Gloria. *Borderlands / La frontera: The New Mestiza.* 2nd edn. San Francisco: Aunt Lute Books, 1999.

Arizpe, Lourdes. "Mujer campesina, mujer indígena." *América Indígena* 35, no. 3 (July–Sept. 1975): 575–86.

Arredondo, Gabriella F. "Navigating Ethno-Racial Currents: Mexicans in Chicago, 1919–1939." *Journal of Urban History* 30, no. 3 (March 2004): 399–427.

Baldwin, P. M. "A Short History of the Mesilla Valley." *New Mexico Historical Review* 13, no. 3 (1938): 314–24.

Bancroft, Hubert H. *History of Arizona and New Mexico.* San Francisco: History Company, 1889.

Bardaglio, Peter W. "'Shameful Matches': The Regulation of Interracial Sex and Marriage in the South before 1900." In *Sex, Love, Race: Crossing Boundaries in North American History*, edited by Martha Hodes, 112–38. New York: New York University Press, 1999.

Barker, Nancy. "The Factor of 'Race' in the French Experience in Mexico, 1821–1861." *Hispanic American Historical Review* 59, no. 1 (Feb. 1979): 64–80.

Bartlett, John Russell. *Personal Narrative of Explorations in Texas, New Mexico, California, Sonora, and Chihuahua, Connected to the United States Boundary Commission, 1850–1853.* London: George Routledge, 1854.

Beck, Warren. *New Mexico: A History of Four Centuries.* Norman: University of Oklahoma Press, 1962.

Bederman, Gail. *Manliness & Civilization: A Cultural History of Gender and Race in the United States, 1880–1917.* Chicago: University of Chicago Press, 1995.

Bell, A. W. "On the Native Races of New Mexico." *Journal of the Ethnological Society of London* 1, no. 3 (1869): 222–74.

Berlant, Lauren. "The Queen of America Goes to Washington City: Harriet Jacobs, Frances Harper, Anita Hill." *American Literature* 65, no. 3 (Sept. 1993): 549–74.

Binley, William C. "New Mexico and Texan Santa Expedition." *Southwestern Historical Quarterly* 27 (Oct. 1923): 85–107.

Blanton, Carlos K. *The Strange Career of Bilingual Education in Texas, 1836–1981.* College Station: Texas A&M University Press, 2004.

Blight, David W. *Race and Reunion: The Civil War in American Memory.* Cambridge, Mass.: Belknap, 2001.

Bonfil Batalla, Guillermo. *Identidad y pluralismo cultural en América Latina.* San Juan: Universidad de Puerto Rico, 1988.

——. *México profundo: Reclaiming a Civilization.* Translated by Philip A. Dennis. Austin: University of Texas Press, 1996.

Boydston, Jeanne. *Home and Work: Housework, Wages, and the Ideology of Labor in the Early Republic.* New York: Oxford University Press, 1990.

Brack, Gene. "Mexican Opinion, American Racism, and the War of 1846." *Western Historical Quarterly* 1, no. 2 (1970): 161–74.

Brady, Mary Pat. *Extinct Lands, Temporal Geographies: Chicana Literature and the Urgency of Space.* Durham, N.C.: Duke University Press, 2002.

Braeman, John. *Albert J. Beveridge: American Nationalist.* Chicago: University of Chicago Press, 1971.

Bremer, Thomas. *Blessed with Tourists: The Borderlands of Religion and Tourism in San Antonio.* Chapel Hill: University of North Carolina Press, 2004.

Briggs, Laura. *Reproducing Empire: Race, Sex, Science, and U.S. Imperialism in Puerto Rico.* Berkeley: University of California Press, 2002.

Brooks, James F. *Captives & Cousins: Slavery, Kinship, and Community in the Southwest Borderlands.* Chapel Hill: University of North Carolina Press, 2002.

Browne, J. Ross. *Adventures in the Apache Country*. New York: Harper and Brothers, 1869.

Bryant, Edwin. *What I Saw in California: Being the Journal of a Tour, by the Emigrant and South Pass of the Rocky Mountains, across the Continent of North America, the Great Desert Basin and through California, 1846–1847*. New York: D. Appleton, 1848.

Buchanan, Rosemary. *The First Hundred Years: St. Genevieve's Parish, 1859–1959*. Las Cruces, N.M.: Bronson Printing, 1961.

Buenger, Walter. *The Path to a Modern South: Northeast Texas between Reconstruction and the Great Depression*. Austin: University of Texas Press, 2001.

———. " 'The Story of Texas?' The Texas State History Museum and Forgetting and Remembering the Past." *Southwestern Historical Quarterly* 105, no. 3 (Jan. 2002): 481–93.

Bureau of Publicity of the State Land Office. "New Mexico: Its Resources in Public Lands, Agriculture, Horticulture, Stock Raising, Coal, Copper, Gold and Other Minerals. Its Attractions for the Tourist, Homesteader, Investor, Sportsman, Health Seeker and Archaeologist." Santa Fe: State Land Office, 1916.

Bustamante, Adrian. " 'The Matter Was Never Resolved': The Casta System in Colonial New Mexico, 1693–1823." *New Mexico Historical Review* 66, no. 2 (April 1991): 143–63.

Butler, Judith. "From Interiority to Gender Performatives." In *Camp: Queer Aesthetics and the Performing Subject*, edited by Fabio Cleto, 361–68. Ann Arbor: University of Michigan Press, 1999.

———. *Gender Trouble: Feminism and the Subversion of Identity*. New York: Routledge, 1990.

Callahan, Manuel. "Mexican Border Troubles: Social War, Settler Colonialism, and the Production of Frontier Discourses." PhD diss., University of Texas, 2003.

Carib, Raymond. *Cartographic Mexico: A History of State Fixations and Fugitive Landscapes*. Durham, N.C.: Duke University Press, 2004.

Carroll, H. Bailey, and J. Villasana Haggard, trans. *Three New Mexico Chronicles: The Exposición of Don Pedro Bautista Pino, 1812; the Ojeada of Lic. Antonio Barreiro, 1832; and the Additions by Don José Agustín de Escudero, 1849*. Albuquerque: Quivira Society, 1942.

Castles, Stephen. "Citizenship and the Other in the Age of Migration." In *Nations and Nationalism*, ed. Philip Spencer and Howard Wollman, 301–16. New Brunswick, N.J.: Rutgers University Press, 2005.

Chadwick, Susan. "Texas Primer: The Native Texan." *Texas Monthly*, July 1986, 115.

Chatterjee, Partha. *The Nation and Its Fragments: Colonial and Postcolonial Histories*. Princeton: Princeton University Press, 1993.

Chauncey, George. *Gay New York: Gender, Urban Culture, and the Making of the Gay Male World, 1890–1940*. New York: Basic Books, 1994.

Chavez, Fray Angelico. *But Time and Chance: The Story of Padre Martínez of Taos, 1793–1867*. Santa Fe: Sunstone, 1981.

———. *Très Macho—He Said: Padre Gallegos of Albuquerque, New Mexico's First Congressman*. Santa Fe: Gannon, 1985.

Chávez, John. *The Lost Land: The Chicano Image of the Southwest*. Albuquerque: University of New Mexico Press, 1984.

Chávez-García, Miroslava. *Negotiating Conquest: Gender and Power in California, 1770s to 1880s*. Tucson: University of Arizona Press, 2004.

Confino, Alon. *Germany as a Culture of Remembrance: Promises of Writing History*. Chapel Hill: University of North Carolina Press, 2006.

Connelley, William Elsey. *Doniphan's Expedition and the Conquest of New Mexico and California: Includes Reprint of Col. John T. Hughes*. Topeka: by the author, 1907.

cooke, miriam. "Saving Brown Women." *Signs* 28, no. 1 (autumn 2002): 468–70.

Cooper, Frederic, and Ann Laura Stoler, eds. *Tensions of Empire: Colonial Cultures in a Bourgeois World*. Berkeley: University of California Press, 1997.

Cott, Nancy F. *The Bonds of Womanhood*. New Haven: Yale University Press, 1977.

———. "Marriage and Women's Citizenship in the United States, 1830–1934." *American Historical Review* 103, no. 5 (Dec. 1998): 1440–74.

———. *No Small Courage: A History of Women in the United States*. New York: Oxford University Press, 2000.

Couts, Cave Johnson. *Hepah, California! The Journal of Cave Johnson Couts from Monterey, Nuevo Leon, Mexico to Los Angeles, California during the Years 1848– 1849*. Edited by Henry F. Dobyns. Tucson: Arizona Pioneers Historical Society, 1961.

Cowles, Calvin Duvall, ed. *The War of the Rebellion: A Compilation of the Official Records of the Union and Confederate Armies*. Washington: Government Printing Office, 1882.

Crampton, Jeremy W., and Stuart Elden, eds. *Space, Knowledge and Power: Foucault and Geography*. Burlington, Vt.: Ashgate, 2007.

Crenshaw, Kimberle. "Demarginalizing the Intersection of Race and Sex: A Black Feminist Critique of Antidiscrimination Doctrine, Feminist Theory and Antiracist Politics." *University of Chicago Legal Forum* (1989): 139–68.

———. "Mapping the Margins: Intersectionality, Identity Politics, and Violence against Women of Color." *Stanford Law Review* 43, no. 6 (July 1991): 1241–99.

Culbert, James I. "Distribution of Spanish-American Population in New Mexico." *Economic Geography* 19, no. 2 (April 1943): 171–76.

Davis, W. W. H. *El Gringo, or, New Mexico and Her People*. Santa Fe: Rydall, 1857.

de Aragon, Ray John. *Padre Martínez and Bishop Lamy*. Las Vegas, N.M.: Pan-Am Publications, 1978.

Deloria, Philip. *Indians in Unexpected Places*. Lawrence: University Press of Kansas, 2004.

———. *Playing Indian*. New Haven: Yale University Press, 1998.

———. "Revolution, Region, and Culture in Multicultural History." *William and Mary Quarterly*, 3rd ser., 53, no. 2 (April 1996): 363–66.

Deutsch, Sarah. *No Separate Refuge: Culture, Class, and Gender on an Anglo-Hispanic Frontier in the American Southwest, 1880–1940*. New York: Oxford University Press, 1987.

———. *Women and the City: Gender, Space, and Power in Boston, 1870–1940.* New York: Oxford University Press, 2000.

Deverell, William. *Whitewashed Adobe: The Rise of Los Angeles and the Remaking of Its Mexican Past.* Berkeley: University of California Press, 2005.

Dinkin, Robert J. *Campaigning in America: A History of Election Practices.* Westport, Conn.: Greenwood Press, 1989.

Dolan, Jay. *The American Catholic Experience: A History from Colonial Times to the Present.* Notre Dame: University of Notre Dame Press, 1992.

Dolan, Jay, and Allan Figueroa Deck. *Hispanic Catholic Culture in the U.S.: Issues and Concerns.* Notre Dame: University of Notre Dame Press, 1994.

Dolan, Jay, and Gilberto M. Hinojosa. *Mexican Americans and the Catholic Church, 1900–1965.* Notre Dame: University of Notre Dame Press, 1994.

Dowd, Gregory E. *A Spirited Resistance: The North American Indian Struggle for Unity, 1745–1815.* Baltimore: Johns Hopkins University Press, 1992.

Dozier, Edward. *The Pueblo Indians of North America.* New York: Holt, Rinehart, and Winston, 1970.

DuCille, Ann. *Skin Trade.* Cambridge: Harvard University Press, 1996.

Duggan, Lisa. *Sapphic Slashers: Sex, Violence, and American Modernity.* Durham, N.C.: Duke University Press, 2000.

Duncan, Nancy, ed. *Body Space.* New York: Routledge, 1996.

Eaton, W. Clement. "Frontier Life in Southern Arizona, 1858–1861." *Southwestern Historical Quarterly* 36, no. 3 (Jan. 1933): 173–92.

Ehrlich, Walter. "The Origins of the Dred Scott Case." *Journal of Negro History* 59, no. 2 (April 1975): 132–42.

Elliott, Richard Smith. *The Mexican War Correspondence of Richard Smith Elliott.* Norman: University of Oklahoma Press, 1997.

Escalante Gonzalbo, Fernando. *Ciudadanos imaginarios: Memorial de los afanes y desventuras de la virtud y apología del vicio triunfante en la República Mexicana —tratado de moral pública.* México: El Colegio de México, Centro de Estudios Sociológicos, 1992.

Espín, Orlando O. "Popular Catholicism among Latinos." In Dolan and Deck, *Hispanic Catholic Culture in the U.S.*, 308–59.

Espinosa, Aurelio M., and J. Manuel Espinosa. "The Texans: A New Mexican Spanish Folk Play of the Middle Nineteenth Century." *New Mexico Quarterly* 13 (1943): 299–308.

Evans, Sara M. *Born for Liberty: A History of Women in America.* New York: Free Press, 1989.

Fabian, Johannes. *Time and the Other: How Anthropology Makes Its Object.* New York: Columbia University Press, 1983.

Farnham, Thomas J. *Life, Adventures, and Travels in California.* 2nd edn. New York: Van Dien and MacDonald, 1849.

Ferguson, T. J. "Dowa Yalanne: The Architecture of Zuni Resistance and Social Change during the Pueblo Revolt." In *Archaeologies of the Pueblo Revolt: Identity, Meaning, and Renewal in the Pueblo World,* edited by Robert W. Preucel, 33–44. Albuquerque: University of New Mexico Press, 2002.

Fergusson, Erna. *New Mexico: A Pageant of Three Peoples.* New York: Knopf, 1951.

Findlay, Eileen. *Imposing Decency: The Politics of Sexuality and Race in Puerto Rico.* Durham, N.C.: Duke University Press, 1999.

Foley, Neil. *The White Scourge: Mexicans, Blacks, and Poor Whites in Texas Cotton Culture.* Berkeley: University of California Press, 1997.

Foote, Cheryl J. *Women of the New Mexico Frontier, 1846–1912.* Niwot: University of Colorado Press, 1990.

Foster, Thora Alice Lute. "The Folk-lore of the Mesilla Valley: A Contribution to the Folk-lore of New Mexico." Senior thesis, New Mexico College of Agriculture and Mechanic Arts, 1904.

Foucault, Michel. *The Archaeology of Knowledge.* Translated by A. M. Sheridan Smith. London: Tavistock, 1972.

Fowler-Salamini, Heather. "Gender, Work, and Coffee in Córdoba, Veracruz, 1850–1910." In Fowler-Salamini and Vaughan, *Women of the Mexican Countryside, 1850–1990,* 51–73.

Fowler-Salamini, Heather, and Mary Kay Vaughan, eds. *Women of the Mexican Countryside, 1850–1990: Creating Spaces, Shaping Transitions.* Tucson: University of Arizona Press, 1994.

Frank, Ross. *From Settler to Citizen: New Mexican Economic Development and the Creation of Vecino Society, 1750–1820.* Berkeley: University of California Press, 2000.

Fregoso, Rosa Linda. *MeXicana Encounters: The Making of Social Identities on the Borderlands.* Berkeley: University of California Press, 2003.

——. "Reproduction and Miscegenation in the Borderlands: Mapping the Maternal Body of Tejanas." In *Chicana Feminisms: A Critical Reader,* edited by Gabriela F. Arredondo, Aida Hurtado, Norma Klahn, and Olga Najera-Ramírez, 324–53. Durham, N.C.: Duke University Press, 2003.

Frickey, Philip. "Marshalling Past and Present: Colonialism, Constitutionalism, and Interpretation in Federal Indian Law." *Harvard Law Review* 107, no. 2 (Dec. 1993): 381–440.

Frietze, Lionel Cajen. *History of La Mesilla and Her Mesilleros.* 2nd edn. El Paso: Book Publishers of El Paso, 2004.

Fuller, Roden. "Occupations of the Mexican-Born Population of Texas, New Mexico, and Arizona." *Journal of the American Statistical Association* 23, no. 161 (March 1928): 64–67.

Fulton, Maurice, and Robert Mulin, eds. *History of the Lincoln County War.* Tempe: University of Arizona Press, 1997.

Gabbert, Ann. "Prostitution and Moral Reform in the Borderlands, 1890–1920." *Journal of the History of Sexuality* 12, no. 4 (Oct. 2003): 575–604.

Gaines, Kevin. *Uplifting the Race: Black Leadership, Politics, and Culture in the Twentieth Century.* Chapel Hill: University of North Carolina Press, 1996.

Galeana, Patricia, ed. *Nuestra frontera norte.* México, D.F.: Archivo General de la Nación, 1999.

Garber, Paul Neff. *The Gadsden Treaty.* Philadelphia: University of Philadelphia Press, 1923.

Gibson, A. M. *The Life and Death of Colonel Albert Jennings Fountain*. Norman: University of Oklahoma Press, 1965.

Gilliam, Albert. *Travels over the Tablelands and Cordilleras of Mexico during the Years 1843 and 1844*. Philadelphia: J. W. Moore, 1846.

Gilman, Sander. *The Jew's Body*. New York: Routledge, 1991.

Gilroy, Paul. *After Empire: Melancholia or Convivial Culture?* New York: Routledge, 2004.

Ginzberg, Lori D. *Women and the Work of Benevolence: Morality, Politics, and Class in the Nineteenth-Century United States*. New Haven: Yale University Press, 1990.

Glassberg, David. *Sense of History: The Place of the Past in American Life*. Amherst: University of Massachusetts Press, 2001.

Goizueta, Roberto S. *Caminemos con Jesús: Toward a Hispanic/Latino Theology of Accompaniment*. Maryknoll, N.Y.: Orbis, 1995.

Gómez, Laura E. *Manifest Destinies: The Making of the Mexican American Race*. New York: New York University Press, 2007.

——. "Race, Colonialism, and Criminal Law: Mexicans and the American Criminal Justice System in Territorial New Mexico." *Law and Society Review* 34, no. 4 (2000): 1129–1202.

González, Deena J. *Refusing the Favor: Spanish Mexican Women of Santa Fé, 1820–1880*. New York: Oxford University Press, 2001.

Gonzáles, Manuel. *Mexicanos: A History of Mexicans in the United States*. Bloomington: Indiana University Press, 1999.

Gonzales, Phillip B. "'La Junta de Indignación': Hispano Repertoire of Collective Protest in New Mexico, 1884–1933." *Western Historical Quarterly* 31, no. 2 (summer 2000): 161–88.

Gonzales-Berry, Erlinda, and David Maciel, eds. *The Contested Homeland: A Chicano History of New Mexico*. Albuquerque: University of New Mexico Press, 2000.

González de la Vara, Martín. "El traslado de familias de Nuevo México al norte de Chihuahua y la conformación de una región fronteriza, 1848–1854." *Frontera Norte* 6, no. 11 (Enero–Junio 1994): 9–21.

——. "The Return to Mexico: The Relocation of New Mexican Families to Chihuahua and the Confirmation of a Frontier Region, 1848–1854." In Gonzales-Berry and Maciel, *The Contested Homeland*, 43–57.

González Navarro, Moisés. *Los extranjeros en México y los Mexicanos en el extranjero, 1821–1970*. Vol. 1. México, D.F.: El Colegio de México, 1993.

Goodrich, James W. "Revolt at Mora." *New Mexico Historical Review* 47, no. 1 (1972): 49–60.

Gordon, Linda. *The Great Arizona Orphan Abduction*. Cambridge: Harvard University Press, 2001.

Granjon, Monsignor Henry. *Along the Rio Grande: A Pastoral Visit to Southwest New Mexico in 1902*. Edited by Michael Romero Taylor. Albuquerque: University of New Mexico Press, 1986.

Gregg, Josiah. *Commerce of the Prairies: The Journal of a Santa Fe Trader during*

Eight Expeditions across the Great Western Prairies and Residence of Nearly Nine Years in Northern Mexico. Edited by Max L. Moorhead. Norman: University of Oklahoma Press, 1954. First published 1844. Page references are to the 1954 edition.

Griggs, George. *History of Mesilla Valley, or, The Gadsden Purchase: Known in Mexico as the Treaty of Mesilla.* Mesilla, N.M.: by the author, 1930.

Griswold del Castillo, Richard. *The Treaty of Guadalupe Hidalgo: A Legacy of Conflict.* Norman: University of Oklahoma Press, 1990.

Guardino, Peter F. *Peasants, Politics, and the Formation of Mexico's National State: Guerrero, 1800–1857.* Stanford, Calif.: Stanford University Press, 1996.

Guglielmo, Thomas. *White on Arrival: Italians, Race, Color, and Power in Chicago, 1890–1945.* New York: Oxford University Press, 2003.

Guth, Christine M. E. "Charles Longfellow and Okakura Kakuzō: Cultural Cross Dressing in the Colonial Context." *positions* 8, no. 3 (2000): 605–36.

———. *Longfellow's Tattoos: Tourism, Collecting, and Japan.* Seattle: University of Washington Press, 2004.

Gutiérrez, David G. "Migration, Emergent Ethnicity, and the 'Third Space': The Shifting Politics of Nationalism in Greater Mexico." *Journal of American History* 8, no. 3 (Sept. 1999): 481–517.

———. *Walls and Mirrors: Mexican Americans, Mexican Immigrants, and the Politics of Ethnicity.* Berkeley: University of California Press, 1995.

Gutiérrez, Ramón. "Charles Fletcher Lummis and the Orientalization of New Mexico." In *Nuevomexicano Cultural Legacy: Forms, Agencies, and Discourse,* edited by Francisco A. Lomelí, Víctor A. Sorell, and Genaro M. Padilla, 11–27. Albuquerque: University of New Mexico Press, 2002.

———. "What's Love Got to Do with It?" *Journal of American History* 88, no. 3 (Dec. 2001): 866–69.

———. *When Jesus Came, the Corn Mothers Went Away: Marriage, Sexuality, and Power in New Mexico, 1500–1846.* Stanford, Calif.: Stanford University Press, 1991.

Haas, Lisbeth. *Conquests and Historical Identities in California, 1769–1936.* Berkeley: University of California Press, 1995.

Hall, G. Emlen, and David J. Weber. "Mexican Liberals and the Pueblo Indians, 1821–1829." *New Mexico Historical Review* 59, no. 1 (Jan. 1984): 5–32.

Hall, Martin Hardwick. *Sibley's New Mexico Campaign.* Austin: University of Texas Press, 1960.

Hall, Stuart. *Race and Class in Post-Colonial Society: A Study of Ethnic Group Relations in English-Speaking Caribbean, Bolivia, Chile and Mexico.* Paris: United Nations Educational Scientific and Cultural Organization, 1977.

———. *Stuart Hall: Critical Dialogues in Cultural Studies.* Edited by David Morley and Kuan-Hsing Chen. New York: Routledge, 1995.

Haraway, Donna. *Primate Visions: Gender, Race, and Nature in the World of Modern Science.* New York: Routledge, 1989.

Harris, Linda G. *Las Cruces: An Illustrated History.* Las Cruces, N.M.: Arroyo Press, 1993.

Hearn, Lafcadio, and Elizabeth Bisland. *The Writings of Lafcadio Hearn*. New York: Houghton Mifflin, 1922.

Heineman, Elisabeth. "The Hour of the Woman: Memories of Germany's 'Crisis Years' and West German National Identity." *American Historical Review* 101, no. 2 (April 1996): 354–95.

Hernández, Alberto Hernández. "La formación de la frontera norte y el protestantismo." In Galeana, *Nuestra frontera norte*, 61–79.

Hernández, José Angel. "El México perdido, el México olvidado, y el México de afuera: A History of Mexican American Colonization, 1836–1892." PhD diss., University of Chicago, 2008.

Herrera, Carlos. "New Mexico Resistance to U.S. Occupation." In Gonzales-Berry and Maciel, *The Contested Homeland*, 23–42.

Higginbotham, Evelyn Brooks. "African American Women's History and the Metalanguage of Race." *Signs* 17 (1992): 251–74.

Hobsbawm, Eric, and Terence Ranger, eds. *The Invention of Tradition*. New York: Cambridge University Press, 1983.

Hodes, Martha. *White Women, Black Men: Illicit Sex in the Nineteenth-Century South*. New Haven: Yale University Press, 1997.

Hood, Margaret Page. "Bells of Old Mesilla." *New Mexico Magazine*, Dec. 1944, 14–15, 35.

Horgan, Paul. *Great River: The Rio Grande in North American History*. Hanover, N.H.: Wesleyan University Press, 1984.

———. *Lamy of Santa Fe: His Life and Times*. New York: Farrar, Straus and Giroux, 1975.

Horseman, Reginald. "Scientific Racism and the American Indian in the Mid-Nineteenth Century." *American Quarterly* 27, no. 2 (May 1975): 152–68.

Howard, John. *Men Like That: A Southern Queer History*. Chicago: University of Chicago Press, 1999.

Huginnie, A. Yvette. "A New Hero Comes to Town: The Anglo Mining Engineer and 'Mexican Labor' as Contested Terrain in Southeastern Arizona." *New Mexico Historical Review* 69, no. 4 (Oct. 1994): 323–44.

Hulbert, Archer Butler, ed. *Southwest on the Turquoise Trail: The First Diaries on the Road to Santa Fé*. Denver: Stewart Commission of Colorado College, 1933.

Hunter, Tera. *To 'Joy My Freedom: Southern Black Women's Lives and Labors after the Civil War*. Cambridge: Harvard University Press, 1997.

Huxley, Aldous. *Brave New World*. London: Chatto and Windus, 1932.

Irwin-Zarecka, Iwona. *Frames of Remembrance: The Dynamics of Collective Memory*. New Brunswick, N.J.: Transaction, 1994.

Jacobson, Joel. *Such Men as Billy the Kid: The Lincoln County War Reconsidered*. Lincoln: University of Nebraska Press, 1997.

Jacobson, Matthew Frye. *Whiteness of a Different Color: European Immigrants and the Alchemy of Race*. Cambridge: Harvard University Press, 1998.

James, Thomas. *Three Years among the Indians and Mexicans*. Waterloo, Ill.: Office of "The Eagle," 1846.

John, Elizabeth. *Storms Brewed in Other Men's Worlds: The Confrontation of In-*

dians, Spanish, and French in the Southwest, 1540–1795. 2nd edn. Norman: University of Oklahoma Press, 1996.

Johnson, Benjamin. *Revolution in Texas: How a Forgotten Rebellion and Its Bloody Suppression Turned Mexicans into Americans.* New Haven: Yale University Press, 2003.

Jones, Martha. *All Bound Up Together: The Woman Question in African American Public Culture, 1830–1900.* Chapel Hill: University of North Carolina Press, 2007.

Joseph, Gil, ed. *Everyday Forms of State Formation: Revolution and the Negotiation of Rule in Modern Mexico.* Durham, N.C.: Duke University Press, 1994.

Juárez, José Roberto. "La Iglesia Católica y el Chicano en Sud Texas, 1836–1911." *Aztlán* 4, no. 1 (fall 1974): 217–55.

Kaczorowski, Robert J. "To Begin the Nation Anew: Congress, Citizenship, and Civil Rights after the Civil War." *American Historical Review* 92, no. 1 (Feb. 1987): 45–68.

Kaplan, Amy. *The Anarchy of Empire in the Making of U.S. Culture.* Cambridge: Harvard University Press, 2002.

———. " 'Left Alone with America.' " In *Cultures of United States Imperialism,* edited by Amy Kaplan and Donald E. Pease, 3–21. Durham, N.C.: Duke University Press, 1993.

Kasson, Joy S. *Buffalo Bill's Wild West: Celebrity, Memory, and Popular History.* New York: Hill and Wang, 2000.

Katz, Friedrich. *The Life and Times of Pancho Villa.* Stanford, Calif.: Stanford University Press, 1998.

Kelley, Mary. *Learning to Stand and Speak: Women, Education, and Public Life in America's Republic.* Chapel Hill: University of North Carolina Press, 2006.

Kendall, George Wilkins. *Narrative of the Texan Santa Fé Expedition.* 2 vols. New York: Harper and Brothers, 1844.

Kerber, Linda. "The Meanings of Citizenship." *Journal of American History* 84, no. 3 (Dec. 1997): 833–54.

———. "The Paradox of Women's Citizenship in the Early Republic: The Case of *Martin v. Massachusetts." American Historical Review* 97, no. 2 (April 1992): 349–78.

Kessell, John L. *Kiva, Cross, and Crown: The Pecos Indians and New Mexico.* Washington: National Park Service, 1979.

———, ed. *Remote beyond Compare: Letters of Don Diego de Vargas and His Family from New Spain and New Mexico, 1675–1706.* Albuquerque: University of New Mexico Press, 1989.

Kimmel, Michael S. *Manhood in America: A Cultural History.* 2nd edn. New York: Oxford University Press, 2006.

King, James F. "The Colored Castes and American Representation in the Cortes of Cadiz." *Hispanic American Historical Review* 33, no. 1 (Feb. 1953): 33–64.

Knight, Alan. "Peasants into Patriots: Thoughts on the Making of the Mexican Nation." *Mexican Studies/Estudios Mexicanos* 10, no. 1 (winter 1994): 135–61.

Kropp, Phoebe S. *California Vieja: Culture and Memory in a Modern American Place.* Berkeley: University of California Press, 2006.

Ladd, Horatio. *The Story of New Mexico.* Boston: Lothrop, 1891.

Lafaye, Jacques. *Quetzalcóatl and Guadalupe: The Formation of Mexican National Consciousness, 1531–1813.* Translated by Benjamin Keen. Chicago: University of Chicago Press, 1976.

Lamar, Howard Roberts. *The Far Southwest, 1848–1912: A Territorial History.* New Haven: Yale University Press, 1966.

Lambourne, Lionel. *Japonism: Cultural Crossings between East and West.* New York: Phaidon, 2005.

Lara, Dulcinea Michelle. "(Re)Visiting the Land of Enchantment: Tourism and Race in New Mexico." PhD diss., University of California, Berkeley, 2006.

Larrazolo, O. A. "The Missionary Fathers: Address Delivered at Albuquerque." Oct. 9, 1907. Octaviano Larrazolo Papers, Center for Southwest Research, University of New Mexico, Albuquerque.

Larson, Robert W. *New Mexico Populism: A Study of Radical Protest in a Western Territory.* Boulder: Colorado Associated University Press, 1974.

———. *New Mexico's Quest for Statehood, 1846–1912.* Albuquerque: University of New Mexico Press, 1968.

Lears, T. J. Jackson. "The Concept of Cultural Hegemony: Problems and Possibilities." *American Historical Review* 90, no. 3 (June 1985): 567–93.

———. *No Place of Grace: Antimodernism and the Transformation of American Culture, 1880–1920.* Chicago: University of Chicago Press, 1994.

Lecompte, Janet. "The Independent Women of Hispanic New Mexico, 1821–1846." *Western Historical Quarterly* 12, no. 1 (Jan. 1981): 17–35.

———. *Rebellion in Río Arriba, 1837.* Albuquerque: University of New Mexico Press, 1985.

Lewis, Jan. "'Of Every Age Sex & Condition': The Representation of Women in the Constitution." *Journal of the Early Republic* 15 (fall 1995): 359–88.

Lewis, Laura. "Blacks, Black Indians, Afromexicans: The Dynamics of Race, Nation, and Identity in a Mexican Moreno Community (Guerrero)." *American Ethnologist* 27, no. 4 (Nov. 2000): 898–926.

Lilly, Marjorie. "Tale of Two Cities: La Mesilla, N.M. and Ascensión, Mexico." *Desert Winds Magazine,* fall 2003/winter 2004, 10–11, 17.

Lipsitz, George. *Time Passages: Collective Memory and American Popular Culture.* Minneapolis: University of Minnesota Press, 1990.

Lomnitz-Adler, Claudio. "Barbarians at the Gate? A Few Remarks on the 'New Cultural History of Mexico.'" *Hispanic American Historical Review* 79, no. 2 (May 1999): 367–85.

———. *Exits from the Labyrinth: Culture and Ideology in the Mexican National Space.* Berkeley: University of California Press, 1992.

Lott, Eric. *Love and Theft: Blackface Minstrelsy and the American Working Class.* New York: Oxford University Press, 1995.

Lowe, Lisa. "Heterogeneity, Hybridity, Multiplicity: Marking Asian-American Dif-

ferences." In *Theorizing Diaspora*, edited by Jana Evans Braziel and Anita Man-
nur, 132–55. Malden, Mass.: Blackwell, 2003.

——. *Immigrant Acts: On Asian American Cultural Politics*. Durham, N.C.: Duke
University Press, 1996.

Loyola, Mary. "The American Occupation of New Mexico, 1821–1852." *New Mexico Historical Review* 14, no. 3 (1939): 34–75.

Lucey, Robert E. "The Catholic Church in Texas." In *The Catholic Church, U.S.A.*,
edited by Louis J. Putz, 225–31. Chicago: Fides Publishers, 1956.

Lummis, Charles F. *The Land of Poco Tiempo*. New York: Charles Scribner's Sons,
1893.

——. *A Tramp across the Continent*. New York: C. Scribner's Sons, 1892.

MacCormack, Sabine. *Religion in the Andes: Vision and Imagination in Early Colonial Peru*. Princeton: Princeton University Press, 1991.

Macías, Anna. *Against All Odds: The Feminist Movement in Mexico to 1940*. Westport, Conn.: Greenwood Press, 1982.

Mallon, Florencia E. "Exploring the Origins of Democratic Patriarchy in Mexico:
Gender and Popular Resistance in the Puebla Highlands, 1850–1876." In Fowler-
Salamini and Vaughan, *Women of the Mexican Countryside, 1850–1990*, 3–26.

——. "The Promise and Dilemma of Subaltern Studies: Perspectives from Latin
American History (in AHR Forum)." *American Historical Review* 99, no. 5
(1994): 1491–1515.

Mangusso, Mary Childers. "A Study of the Citizenship Provisions of the Treaty of
Guadalupe Hidalgo." Master's thesis, University of New Mexico, Albuquerque,
1966.

Marlin, George J. *The American Catholic Voter: 200 Years of Political Impact*. South
Bend, Ind.: St. Augustine's Press, 2006.

Martínez, María Elena. *Genealogical Fictions: Limpieza de Sangre, Religion, and
Gender in Colonial Mexico*. Stanford, Calif.: Stanford University Press, 2008.

Martínez López, María Elena. "The Spanish Concept of *Limpieza de Sangre* and the
Emergence of the 'Race/Caste' System in the Viceroyalty of New Spain." PhD
diss., University of Chicago, 2002.

Marx, Anthony. *Faith in Nation: Exclusionary Origins of Nationalism*. New York:
Oxford University Press, 2003.

Massey, Doreen. "Politics and Space/Time." *New Left Review*, no. 196 (Nov.-Dec.
1992): 65–84.

Matovina, Timothy. *Tejano Religion and Ethnicity: San Antonio, 1821–1860*. Austin: University of Texas Press, 1995.

Matovina, Timothy, and Gerald Poyo, eds. *Presente! U.S. Latino Catholics from
Colonial Origins to the Present*. New York: Orbis, 2000.

Mayer, Brantz. *Mexico as It Was and as It Is*. Philadelphia: G. B. Ziebler, 1847.

McBride, R. E. "Doña Ana County in New Mexico: Containing the Fertile Mesilla
Valley, Cradle of Irrigation in America." Santa Fe: Bureau of Immigration of New
Mexico, 1908.

McClintock, Anne. *Imperial Leather: Race, Gender, and Sexuality in the Colonial
Contest*. New York: Routledge, 1995.

McClure, Charles R. "The Texan–Santa Fe Expedition of 1841." *New Mexico Historical Quarterly* 48 (Jan. 1973): 45–56.

McDowell, Linda. "Spatializing Feminism: Geographic Perspectives." In Duncan, *Body Space*, 28–44.

McFie, Maude E. "A History of the Mesilla Valley." Senior thesis, New Mexico College of Agriculture and Mechanic Arts, 1903.

McGreevy, John. *Parish Boundaries: The Catholic Encounter with Race in the Twentieth-Century Urban North.* Chicago: University of Chicago Press, 1998.

McLoughlin, William G. "Experiment in Cherokee Citizenship, 1817–1829." *American Quarterly* 33, no. 1 (spring 1981): 3–25.

McNierney, Michael, ed. *Taos, 1847: The Revolt in Contemporary Accounts.* Boulder, Colo.: Johnson Printing, 1980.

McWilliams, Carey. *North from Mexico: The Spanish-Speaking People of the United States.* New York: Monthly Review Press, 1948.

Mehta, Uday S. "Liberal Strategies of Exclusion." In Cooper and Stoler, *Tensions of Empire*, 59–86.

Melamed, Jodi. "The Spirit of Neoliberalism: From Racial Liberalism to Neoliberal Multiculturalism." *Social Text* 24, no. 4 (winter 2006): 1–24.

Meléndez, A. Gabriel. *So All Is Not Lost: The Poetics of Print in Nuevomexicano Communities, 1834–1958.* Albuquerque: University of New Mexico Press, 1997.

Merriwether, D. Andrew, S. Huston, S. Iyengar, R. Hamman, J. M. Norris, S. M. Shetterly, M. I. Kamboh, and R. E. Ferrell. "Mitochondrial versus Nuclear Admixture Estimates Demonstrate a Past History of Directional Mating." *American Journal of Physical Anthropology* 102 (1997): 153–59.

Meyer, Doris. *Speaking for Themselves: Neomexicano Cultural Identity and the Spanish-Language Press, 1880–1920.* Albuquerque: University of New Mexico Press, 1996.

Meyer, Michael C., and William L. Sherman. *The Course of Mexican History.* 5th edn. New York: Oxford University Press, 1995.

Miguel Otero Papers. Center for Southwest Research, University of New Mexico, Albuquerque.

Miller, Charles D. "New Mexico during the Civil War." Senior thesis, New Mexico College of Agriculture and Mechanic Arts, 1906.

Miller, Darlis A. "Hispanos and the Civil War in New Mexico: A Reconsideration." *New Mexico Historical Review* 54, no. 2 (April 1979): 105–23.

Miller, David Hunter. *Treaties and Other International Acts of the United States of America.* Vol. 5. Washington: Government Printing Office, 1937.

Miller, Pearl Cherry. "Mexican Cookery." Senior thesis, New Mexico College of Agriculture and Mechanic Arts, 1904.

Milton, Hugh M. *The Mesilla Civil Colony Grant.* Las Cruces, N.M.: Milton, 1979.

Mitchell, Pablo. *Coyote Nation: Sexuality, Race, and Conquest in Modernizing New Mexico, 1880–1920.* Chicago: University of Chicago Press, 2005.

Molina, Natalia. *Fit to Be Citizens? Public Health and Race in Los Angeles, 1879–1939.* Berkeley: University of California Press, 2006.

Mollien, Gaspar. *Travels in the Republic of Colombia in the Years 1822–1823.* London: C. Knight, 1824.

Montgomery, Charles. *The Spanish Redemption: Heritage, Power, and Loss on New Mexico's Upper Rio Grande.* Berkeley: University of California Press, 2002.

———. "The Trap of Race and Memory: The Language of Spanish Civility on the Upper Rio Grande." *American Quarterly* 52, no. 3 (Oct. 2000): 478–513.

Montoya, María E. "The Dual World of Governor Miguel A. Otero: Myth and Reality in Turn-of-the-Century New Mexico." *New Mexico Historical Review* 67, no. 1 (1992): 13–32.

———. *Translating Property: The Maxwell Land Grant and the Conflict over Land in the American West, 1840–1900.* Berkeley: University of California Press, 2002.

Moore, Frank, ed. *The Rebellion Record: A Diary of American Events, with Documents, Narratives, Illustrative Incidents, Poetry, etc.* 5 vols. New York: Putnam and Holt, 1864.

Mora, Anthony P. "Resistance and Accommodation in a Border Parish." *Western Historical Quarterly* 36, no. 3 (fall 2005): 301–26.

Morantz-Sánchez, Regina. *Conduct Unbecoming a Woman: Medicine on Trial in Turn-of-the-Century Brooklyn.* New York: Oxford University Press, 2000.

Mora-Torres, Juan. *The Making of the Mexican Border: The State, Capitalism, and Society in Nuevo León, 1848–1910.* Austin: University of Texas Press, 2001.

Morton, Samuel George. *Crania Americana, or, A Comparative View of the Skulls of the Various Aboriginal Nations of North and South America.* Philadelphia: J. Dobson, 1839.

Mullin, Robert. "An Item from Old Mesilla." El Paso: Carl Hertzog, 1971.

Mumford, Kevin. *Interzones: Black/White Sex Districts in Chicago and New York in the Early Twentieth Century.* New York: Columbia University Press, 1997.

Myra, Ruth Thurman. "Bells of Old Mesilla: An Operetta." Master's thesis, University of Colorado, 1954.

Nash, Gerald D. "New Mexico in the Otero Era: Some Historical Perspectives." *New Mexico Historical Review* 67, no. 1 (1992): 1–12.

"Necrology." *New Mexico Historical Review* 2, no. 2 (1927): 394–97.

Newman, Louise Michele. *White Women's Rights: The Racial Origins of Feminism in the United States.* New York: Oxford University Press, 1999.

Nicholl, Edith M. *Observations of a Ranchwoman.* New York: Macmillan, 1898.

Nichols, Shan Stedronsky, and Ella Banegas, eds. *Our Heritage—Our People.* Las Cruces, N.M.: Curry Printers, 1974.

Nieto-Phillips, John. *The Language of Blood: The Making of Spanish-American Identity in New Mexico, 1880s–1930s.* Albuquerque: University of New Mexico Press, 2004.

———. "'No Other Blood': History, Language, and Spanish American Ethnic Identity in New Mexico, 1880s–1920s." PhD diss., University of California, Los Angeles, 1997.

Nugent, Walter T. K. "Frontiers and Empires in the Late Nineteenth Century." *Western Historical Quarterly* 20, no. 4 (1989): 393–408.

———. *Habits of Empire: A History of American Expansion.* New York: Knopf, 2008.

———. *Into the West: The Story of Its People.* New York: Knopf, 1999.

Oboler, Suzanne. *Ethnic Labels, Latino Lives: Identity and the Politics of (Re)Presentation in the United States.* Minneapolis: University of Minnesota Press, 1995.

The Official Catholic Directory. New York: P. J. Kennedy and Sons, 1994.

Ohline, Howard A. "Republicanism and Slavery: Origins of the Three-Fifths Clause in the United States Constitution." *William and Mary Quarterly* 28, no. 4 (Oct. 1971): 563–84.

Ormsby, Waterman L. *The Butterfield Overland Mail.* San Marino, Calif.: Huntington Library, 1942.

Orsi, Robert Anthony. *The Madonna of 115th Street: Faith and Community in Italian Harlem, 1880–1950.* New Haven: Yale University Press, 1985.

Otero, Miguel A. *My Life on the Frontier, 1864–1882.* New York: Press of the Pioneers, 1935.

———. *My Life on the Frontier, 1882–1897: Death Knell of a Territory and Birth of a State.* Albuquerque: University of New Mexico Press, 1939.

———. *My Nine Years as Governor of the Territory of New Mexico, 1897–1906.* Albuquerque: University of New Mexico Press, 1940.

———. *The Real Billy the Kid: With New Light on the Lincoln County War.* New York: R. R. Wilson, 1936.

Owen, Gordon. *Las Cruces, New Mexico, 1849–1999: Multicultural Crossroads.* Las Cruces, N.M.: Red Sky, 1999.

Padilla, Genaro. *My History, Not Yours: The Formation of Mexican American Autobiography.* Madison: University of Wisconsin Press, 1993.

Paredes, Américo. *With His Pistol in His Hand: Border Ballad and Its Hero.* Austin: University of Texas Press, 2006.

Paredes, Raymond A. "The Mexican Image in American Travel Literature, 1831–1869." *New Mexico Historical Review* 52, no. 1 (Jan. 1977): 5–29.

Parker, Chris, and Paul Willis. *Cultural Studies: Theory and Practice.* New York: Sage, 2003.

Pattie, James O. *The Personal Narrative of James O. Pattie, of Kentucky.* Cincinnati: John H. Wood, 1831. Reprint, Chicago: R. R. Donnelley, 1930.

Pérez, Emma. *The Decolonial Imaginary: Writing Chicanas into History.* Bloomington: Indiana University Press, 1999.

Phelps, Carrie Padon. "The Primitive Mexican Home in New Mexico." Senior thesis, New Mexico College of Agriculture and Mechanic Arts , Las Cruces, 1913.

Phelps, Glenn A. "Representation without Taxation: Citizenship and Suffrage in Indian Country." *American Indian Quarterly* 9, no. 2 (1985): 135–48.

Pike, Albert. "Narrative of a Journey in the Prairie." In *Sketches and Poems, Written in the Western Country, Additional Stories,* edited by David J. Weber, 3–32. Albuquerque: University of New Mexico Press, 1967.

Pitti, Stephen J. *The Devil in Silicon Valley: Northern California, Race, and Mexican Americans.* Princeton: Princeton University Press, 2003.

Plane, Ann Marie, and Gregory Button. "The Massachusetts Indian Enfranchisement Act: Ethnic Contest in Historical Context, 1849–1869." *Ethnohistory* 40, no. 4 (1993): 587–618.

"The Population of the United States." *Science* 32, no. 833 (Dec. 1910): 856.

Prakash, Gyan, ed. *After Colonialism: Imperial Histories and Postcolonial Displacements.* Princeton: Princeton University Press, 1995.

Pratt, Mary Louise. *Imperial Eyes: Studies in Travel Writing and Transculturation.* New York: Routledge, 1992.

Price, Paxton. *Mesilla Valley Pioneers, 1823–1912.* Las Cruces, N.M.: Yucca Tree Press, 1995.

Prince, L. Bradford. *Historical Sketches of New Mexico from the Earliest Records to the American Occupation.* Kansas City, Kansas: Ramsey, Millett, and Hudson, 1883.

Puckett, Fidelia Miller. "Ramon Ortiz: Priest and Patriot." *New Mexico Historical Review* 25, no. 4 (1950): 265–95.

Pulido, Laura. *Black, Brown, Yellow, and Left: Radical Activism in Los Angeles.* Berkeley: University of California Press, 2006.

Rajaram, Prem Kumar, and Carl Grundy-Warr, eds. *Borderscapes: Hidden Geographies and Politics at Territory's Edge.* Minneapolis: University of Minnesota Press, 2007.

Ramirez, Renya. *Native Hubs: Culture, Community, and Belonging in Silicon Valley and Beyond.* Durham, N.C.: Duke University Press, 2007.

Ramírez Caloca, Jesús. "Ascensión." *Boletín de la Sociedad Chihuahuense de Estudios Históricos* 5, no. 6 (Aug. 1944): 245–60.

Ramos, Raúl. *Beyond the Alamo: Forging Mexican Ethnicity in San Antonio, 1821–1861.* Chapel Hill: University of North Carolina Press, 2008.

——. "Finding the Balance: Béxar in Mexican/Indian Relations." In Truett and Young, *Continental Crossroads,* 35–65.

Read, Benjamín M. *Guerra México-Americana.* Santa Fe: Compañía Impresora del Nuevo México, 1910.

——. *Illustrated History of New Mexico.* Santa Fe: New Mexican Printing, 1912.

——. *Popular Elementary History of New Mexico.* Santa Fe: New Mexican Printing, 1914.

——. *A Treatise on the Disputed Points of the History of New Mexico.* Santa Fe: New Mexico Publishing, 1919.

Reséndez, Andrés. *Changing National Identities at the Frontier: Texas and New Mexico, 1800–1850.* New York: Cambridge University Press, 2005.

Reyes, Bárbara O. "Race, Agency, and Memory in a Baja California Mission." In Truett and Young, *Continental Crossroads,* 97–120.

Rippy, J. Fred. "The Negotiation of the Gadsden Treaty." *Southwest Historical Quarterly* 27, no. 1 (July 1923): 1–26.

Roediger, David R. "The Pursuit of Whiteness: Property, Terror, and Expansion, 1790–1860." *Journal of the Early Republic* 19, no. 4 (winter 1999): 579–600.

——. *Towards the Abolition of Whiteness: Essays on Race, Politics, and Working Class History.* New York: Verso, 1994.

——. *The Wages of Whiteness: Race and the Making of the American Working Class.* New York: Verso, 1991.

Rosaldo, Renato. *Culture and Truth: The Remaking of Social Analysis.* Boston: Beacon, 1989.

Rosenbaum, Robert. *Mexicano Resistance in the Southwest: "The Sacred Right of Self-Preservation."* Austin: University of Texas Press, 1981.

Rothman, Hal, ed. *The Culture of Tourism, the Tourism of Culture: Selling the Past to the Present in the American Southwest.* Albuquerque: University of New Mexico Press, 2003.

Rousso, Henry. *The Vichy Syndrome: History and Memory in France Since 1944.* Translated by Arthur Goldhammer. Cambridge: Harvard University Press, 1991.

Rubin, Jeffrey. "Decentering the Regime: Cultural and Regional Politics in Mexico." *Latin American Research Review* 31, no. 3 (1996): 85–126.

Ruggles, Steven, Matthew Sobek, Trent Alexander, Catherine A. Fitch, Ronald Goeken, Patricia Kelly Hall, Miriam King, and Chad Ronnander. *Integrated Public Use Microdata Series: Version 4.0* [Machine-readable database]: http://usa.ipums.org/usa. Minneapolis: Minnesota Population Center, 1997/2009.

Said, Edward. *Orientalism.* New York: Pantheon, 1978.

———. "Secular Interpretation, the Geographical Element, and the Methodology of Imperialism." In Prakash, *After Colonialism*, 21–39.

Salas, Miguel Tinker. *In the Shadow of the Eagles: Sonora and the Transformation of the Border during the Porfiriato.* Berkeley: University of California Press, 1997.

Sánchez, George. *Becoming Mexican American: Ethnicity, Culture, and Identity in Chicano Los Angeles.* New York: Oxford University Press, 1995.

Sandoval, Raymond Edward. "Intrusion and Domination: A Study of the Relationship of Chicano Development to the Exercise and Distribution of Power in a Southwestern Community, 1870–1974." PhD diss., University of Washington, 1980.

Scott, Joan. *Gender and the Politics of History.* New York: Columbia University Press, 1988.

Seagraves, C. L. "Mesilla Valley, New Mexico." Chicago: Henry O. Shepard, 1913.

Sebastian-Coleman, George Lindsay. "Writing the Relation: The Anglo Response to Multicultural New Mexico." PhD diss., University of Notre Dame, 1994.

Seed, Patricia. "Social Dimensions of Race: Mexico City, 1753." *Hispanic American Historical Review* 62, no. 4 (Sept. 1982): 569–606.

Servín, Manuel P., and Robert L. Spude. "Historical Conditions of Early Mexican Labor in the United States: Arizona—A Neglected Story." *Journal of Mexican American History* 5 (1975): 43–56.

Shortridge, James R. "The Emergence of the 'Middle West' as an American Regional Label." *Annals of the Association of American Geographers* 74, no. 2 (June 1984): 209–20.

Silva, Noenoe. *Aloha Betrayed: Native Hawaiian Resistance to American Colonialism.* Durham, N.C.: Duke University Press, 2004.

Simmons, Marc. *New Mexico: A Bicentennial History.* New York: Norton, 1977.

Sisneros, Samuel. "Los emigrantes Nuevomexicanos: The 1849 Repatriation to Guadalupe and San Ignacio, Chihuahua, Mexico." Master's thesis, University of Texas at El Paso, 2001.

Spell, Lota M. "The Anglo-Saxon Press in Mexico, 1846–1848." *American Historical Review* 38, no. 1 (Oct. 1932): 20–31.

Spicer, Edward H. *The American Indians: Dimensions of Ethnicity.* Cambridge: Harvard University Press, 1982.

Spivak, Gayatri. "Can the Subaltern Speak? Speculations on Widow Sacrifice." *Wedge* 7–8 (winter-spring 1985): 120–30.

———. *A Critique of Postcolonial Reason: Toward a History of the Vanishing Present.* Cambridge: Harvard University Press, 1999.

———. *In Other Worlds: Essays in Cultural Politics.* New York: Routledge, 1987.

Stern, Alexandra Minna. *Eugenic Nation: Faults and Frontiers of Better Breeding in Modern America.* Berkeley: University of California Press, 2005.

Stern, Steve. *The Secret History of Gender: Women, Men, and Power in Late Colonial Mexico.* Chapel Hill: University of North Carolina Press, 1995.

Stoes, Katherine D. "Early History of Doña Ana County." In Griggs, *History of Mesilla Valley,* 94–104.

Stoler, Ann Laura. *Carnal Knowledge and Imperial Power: Race and the Intimate in Colonial Rule.* Berkeley: University of California Press, 2002.

———. *Race and the Education of Desire: Foucault's* History of Sexuality *and the Colonial Order of Things.* Durham, N.C.: Duke University Press, 1995.

———. "Rethinking Colonial Categories: European Communities and the Boundaries of Rule." *Comparative Studies in Society and History* 31, no. 1 (Jan. 1989): 134–61.

Stratton, Porter A. *The Territorial Press of New Mexico, 1834–1912.* Albuquerque: University of New Mexico Press, 1969.

Streeby, Shelley. *American Sensations: Class, Empire, and the Production of Popular Culture.* Berkeley: University of California Press, 2002.

Summers, Martin. *Manliness and Its Discontents: The Black Middle Class and the Transformation of Masculinity, 1900–1930.* Chapel Hill: University of North Carolina Press, 2004.

Suseri, Alvin R. *Seeds of Discord: New Mexico in the Aftermath of the American Conquest, 1846–1881.* Chicago: Nelson-Hall, 1979.

Swift, Roy L., and Leavitt Corning Jr. *Three Roads to Chihuahua: The Great Wagon Roads That Opened the Southwest, 1823–1883.* Austin, Tex.: Eakin Press, 1988.

Szasz, Ferenc. *The Protestant Clergy in the Great Plains and Mountain West, 1865–1915.* Albuquerque: University of New Mexico Press, 1988.

Szasz, Ferenc, and Richard W. Etulain, eds. *Religion in Modern New Mexico.* Albuquerque: University of New Mexico Press, 1997.

Taos, Fernandez de [pseud.]. "A Review of the Boundary Question and a Vindication of Governor Lane's Action in Asserting Jurisdiction over the Mesilla Valley." Santa Fe: Collins and Kephart Printers, 1853.

Taylor, Mary D. *History of San Albino Church on the Plaza, Mesilla, New Mexico.* Las Cruces, N.M.: n.p., 1991.

———. *A Place as Wild as the West Ever Was: Mesilla, New Mexico, 1848–1872.* Las Cruces: New Mexico State University Museum, 2004.

Thompson, Jerry. *Confederate General of the West: Henry Hopkins Sibley.* College Station: Texas A&M University Press, 1996.

Thompson, Mark. *American Character: The Curious Life of Charles Fletcher Lummis.* New York: Arcade, 2000.

Tittman, Edward D. "The Exploitation of Treason." *New Mexico Historical Review* 4, no. 1 (1929): 128–45.

Tobias, Henry Jack. *A History of the Jews in New Mexico*. Albuquerque: University of New Mexico Press, 1990.

Trouillot, Michel-Rolph. *Silencing the Past: Power and the Production of History*. Boston: Beacon, 1995.

Truett, Samuel. *Fugitive Landscapes: The Forgotten History of the U.S.-Mexico Borderlands*. New Haven: Yale University Press, 2006.

Truett, Samuel, and Elliott Young, eds. *Continental Crossroads: Remapping U.S.-Mexico Borderlands History*. Durham, N.C.: Duke University Press, 2004.

Turner, Frederick Jackson. *The Frontier in American History*. New York: Holt, 1920.

Tutino, John. "Power, Class, and Family in the Mexican Elite, 1750–1810." *The Americas* 39, no. 3 (Jan. 1983): 359–81.

Twitchell, Ralph Emerson. *The Leading Facts of New Mexican History*. Cedar Rapids, Iowa: Torch Press, 1912.

Uno, Kathleen S. "The Death of the 'Good Wife, Wise Mother'?" In *Postwar Japan as History*, edited by Andrew Gordon, 293–324. Berkeley: University of California Press, 1993.

U.S. Congress. House. *New Mexico Contested Election: Papers and Testimony in the Case of Miguel A. Otero, the Seat of José M. Gallegos, Delegate from the Territory of New Mexico*. 34th Cong., 1st sess., 1856, H. Mis. Doc. 15.

——. *Reports of Explorations and Surveys to Ascertain the Most Practicable and Economical Route for a Railroad from the Mississippi River to the Pacific Ocean*. 33rd Cong., 2nd sess., 1855. H. Doc. 91.

U.S. Congress. Senate. *Hearings before the Subcommittee of the Committee on Territories on House Bill 12543, to Enable the People of Oklahoma, Arizona, and New Mexico to Form Constitutions and State Governments and Be Admitted into the Union on an Equal Footing with the Original States*. 57th Cong., 2nd sess., Dec. 1902, S. Doc. 36.

——. *Report of the Secretary of the Interior*. 32nd Cong., 1st sess., July 1852, S. Doc. 119.

Vaughan, Mary Kay. "Primary Education and Literacy in Nineteenth-Century Mexico: Research Trends, 1968–1988." *Latin America Research Review* 25, no. 1 (1990): 31–66.

Vigil, Donaciano. *Arms, Indians, and the Mismanagement of New Mexico, 1846*. Edited by David J. Weber. El Paso: Texas Western Press, 1986.

——. "Opina sobre armas, municiones, comercio, norteamericanos, y indios bárbaros." Reprinted in Vigil, *Arms, Indians, and the Mismanagement of New Mexico, 1846*, 9–16.

Vincent, Ted. "The Blacks Who Freed Mexico." *Journal of Negro History* 79, no. 3 (summer 1994): 257–76.

Waldstreicher, David. *In the Midst of Perpetual Fetes: The Making of American Nationalism, 1776–1820*. Chapel Hill: University of North Carolina Press, 1997.

Walker, Randi Jones. *Protestantism in the Sangre de Cristos, 1850–1920*. Albuquerque: University of New Mexico Press, 1991.

Wasserman, Mark. *Capitalists, Caciques, and Revolution: The Native Elite and Foreign Enterprise in Chihuahua, Mexico, 1854–1911*. Chapel Hill: University of North Carolina Press, 1984.

Weber, David J. *Bárbaros: Spaniards and Their Savages in the Age of Enlightenment.* New Haven: Yale University Press, 2005.

——, ed. *Foreigners in Their Native Land: Historical Roots of the Mexican Americans.* Albuquerque: University of New Mexico Press, 1973.

——. *The Mexican Frontier, 1821–1846: The American Southwest under Mexico.* Albuquerque: University of New Mexico Press, 1982.

——. *Myth and the History of the Hispanic Southwest: Essays by David J. Weber.* Albuquerque: University of New Mexico Press, 1988.

——, ed. *Northern Mexico on the Eve of the United States Invasion: Rare Imprints Concerning California, Arizona, New Mexico, and Texas, 1821–1846.* New York: Arno, 1976.

——. *The Spanish Frontier in North America.* New Haven: Yale University Press, 1992.

——. "The Spanish-Mexican Rim." In *The Oxford History of the American West,* edited by Clyde A. Milner II, Carol A. O'Connor, and Martha A. Sandweiss, 45–77. New York: Oxford University Press, 1994.

Weigle, Marta. *Brothers of Light, Brothers of Blood: The Penitentes of the Southwest.* Albuquerque: University of New Mexico Press, 1976.

Welter, Barbara. "The Cult of True Womanhood." *American Quarterly* 18, no. 2 (summer 1966): 151–74.

Werne, Joseph Richard. "Guadalupe Hidalgo and the Mesilla Controversy." PhD diss., Kent State University, 1972.

——. *The Imaginary Line: A History of the United States and Mexican Boundary Survey, 1848–1857.* Fort Worth: Texas Christian University Press, 2007.

Wexler, Laura. *Tender Violence: Domestic Visions in an Age of U.S. Imperialism.* Chapel Hill: University of North Carolina Press, 2000.

Whiting, Lilian. *The Land of Enchantment: From Pike's Peak to the Pacific.* Boston: Little, Brown, 1906.

Wildenthal, Lora. "Race, Gender, and Citizenship in the German Colonial Empire." In Cooper and Stoler, *Tensions of Empire,* 263–83.

Williams, Agnes. "Mexican Words Used by English Speaking Inhabitants of the Mesilla Valley." Senior thesis, New Mexico College of Agriculture and Mechanic Arts, 1894.

Wilson, Chris. *The Myth of Santa Fe: Creating a Modern Regional Tradition.* Albuquerque: University of New Mexico Press, 1997.

Wilson, John. *When the Texans Came: Missing Records from the Civil War in the Southwest.* Albuquerque: University of New Mexico Press, 2001.

Wislizenus, A. *Memoir: A Tour of Northern Mexico, Connected with Col. Doniphan's Expedition, in 1846 and 1847.* 30th Cong., 1st sess., 1848. S. Doc. 26.

Yohn, Susan M. *A Contest of Faiths: Missionary Women and Pluralism in the American Southwest.* Ithaca: Cornell University Press, 1995.

Yoshihara, Mari. *Embracing the East: White Women and American Orientalism.* New York: Oxford University Press, 2002.

Young, Mary Elizabeth. *Redskins, Ruffleshirts, and Rednecks: Indian Allotments in Alabama and Mississippi, 1830–1860.* Norman: University of Oklahoma Press, 1961.

Yu, Henry. *Thinking Orientals: Migration, Contact, and Exoticism in Modern America*. New York: Oxford University Press, 2001.

Zaborowska, Magdalena J. "Americanization of a 'Queer Fellow': Performing Jewishness and Sexuality in Abraham Cahan's *The Rise of David Levinsky*, with a Footnote on the (Monica) Lewinsky'ed Nation." In *The Puritan Origins of American Sex: Religion, Sexuality, and National Identity in American Literature*, edited by Tracy Fessenden, Nicholas F. Radel, and Magdalena J. Zaborowska, 213–34. New York: Routledge, 2001.

Zorrilla, Luis G. *Historia de las relaciones entre Mexico y los Estados Unidos de América, 1800–1858*. Mexico, D.F.: Editorial Porrúa, 1965.

Zunser, Helen. "A New Mexican Village." *Journal of American Folklore* 48, no. 1 (1935): 125–78.

INDEX

Abalos, Refugio, 103

Africa: New Mexico compared to, 204, 207–8; social Darwinism and, 186

African Americans: antiblack racism and, 98–100, 190, 315n189, 323n29; comparisons of, to Mexicans, 11, 214–16, 239, 304n218, 333n179; differential racialization and, 10, 98–100; full citizenship and, 27–28; gender ideologies and, 149, 160; Mexican imaginings of, 69–70, 305n225; miscegenation laws and, 138–39, 239; in New Mexico, 190, 308n26; views of, on New Mexico, 308n22

Afro-Mexicans, 32–33, 37, 297n61, 298n76; Spain's colonial notions of intermarriage and, 33, 138–39, 298n75

Agustín de Iturbide, 17–18, 37

Alabama, 30, 99, 236

Alamo (San Antonio de Valero), 211–12

Albino, 33–34. *See also* Casta system

Albuquerque, New Mexico, 17; Chimayó Rebellion and, 42; Coronado celebration in, 246; Padilla case and, 168; rumor of race war in, 101

Alderete, Pablo, 90

Alfalfa, 172, 328n4

Almonte, Juan Nepomuceno, 71–72

Alvarado, Salvador, 157, 163

Alvarez, Cruz, 131–32, 271

Amador, Juan (John), 122

Amador, Martin: as booster for Las Cruces, 265; economic success and, 1, 95; federal claim and, 1–5, 22, 68, 100–101; opposition of, to statehood, 265–67; Orientalism and, 209–10

Amador de Garcia, Emilia, 122–23

Amalgamation, 44, 55, 62, 138–39, 276

Americanization: Catholic church and, 107–9, 118–22, 129; gender and, 146–49; scholarship and, 8, 198

Anachronistic space: Africa as, 208; imperialism and, 194–96; New Mexico as, 200, 203, 246. *See also* Temporal racial hierarchy

Anthropology, 195, 200, 288

Antimodernist movement, 192–93

Anzaldúa, Gloria, 288

Apaches: campaigns of, of 1860s, 94; Charles Lummis and, 204–5; Confederacy and, 313n149; as distinguished from Mexicans, 193; as distinguished from Pueblos, 38; genízaros and, 299n88; Kiowa Apaches, 51–53; Lipan Apaches, 68; Mescalero-Apaches, 1, 81–83, 306n249; Mexican American hostility toward, 63, 303n197; Mexican imperialism and, 19, 31, 38, 68, 82–83, 157; as Mexicans, 5, 59; social Darwinism and, 204–5; Spanish imperialism and, 17, 34, 293n53; Taos Rebellion and, 51–52; Treaty of Guadalupe Hidalgo and, 306n249; Tubac, Arizona, and, 59, 306n234; U.S. imperialism and, 81, 87

Architecture: denigration of adobe, 79–81, 118, 173–74, 209; domesticity and, 146; French, 119–21; gothic revival, 193; Greek Revival and Italianate, 80–81; memory and, 129–31, 183, 193; Mexican state and, 75–76; regional identity and, 183, 209–11, 312n122

Archuleta, Diego, 303n187

Arizona: as Confederate territory, 89, 313n144, 313n149; demographics of, 285–86; English language law and, 254; Gadsden/Mesilla Treaty and, 80; Mexicans in, 120, 229–30, 254, 330n43, 336n31; pioneer women and, 148; Pueblo settlements in, 34; statehood campaigns in, 25, 181, 192, 223, 229–30

Anthony Mora is an assistant professor in the Department of History,
Program in American Culture, and Latina/o Studies Program
at the University of Michigan.

Library of Congress Cataloging-in-Publication Data

Mora, Anthony P., 1974–
Border dilemmas : racial and national uncertainties in
New Mexico, 1848–1912 / Anthony Mora.
p. cm.
Includes bibliographical references and index.
ISBN 978-0-8223-4783-5 (cloth : alk. paper)
ISBN 978-0-8223-4797-2 (pbk. : alk. paper)
1. Mexican Americans—New Mexico—Mesilla.
2. Mexican Americans—New Mexico—Las Cruces.
3. Mexican-American Border Region—Ethnic relations.
4. Mexican-American Border Region—History. I. Title.
F805.M5M67   2011
305.800972'1—dc22
2010028810